WITHDRAWN

The Later Wittgenstein

To my wife, Anne,
who walked with me the financial and vocational tightrope
over the apparent abyss of research required for this study

The Later Wittgenstein
The Emergence of a New Philosophical Method

S. STEPHEN HILMY

Basil Blackwell

Copyright © S. Stephen Hilmy 1987

First published 1987

Basil Blackwell Ltd
108 Cowley Road, Oxford, OX4 1JF, UK

Basil Blackwell Inc.
432 Park Avenue South, Suite 1503
New York, NY10016, USA

All rights reserved. Except for the quotation of short passages for the purposes of criticism and review, no part of this publication may be reproduced, stored in a retrieval system, or transmitted, in any form or by any means, electronic, mechanical, photocopying, recording or otherwise, without the prior permission of the publisher.

Except in the United States of America, this book is sold subject to the condition that it shall not, by way of trade or otherwise, be lent, re-sold, hired out, or otherwise circulated without the publisher's prior consent in any form of binding or cover other than that in which it is published and without a similar condition including this condition being imposed on the subsequent purchaser.

British Library Cataloguing in Publication Data

Hilmy, S. Stephen
  The later Wittgenstein: the emergence of a new
philosophical method.
  1. Wittgenstein, Ludwig
  I. Title
  192   B3376.W564
  ISBN 0-631-15424-8

Library of Congress Cataloging in Publication Data

Hilmy, S. Stephen, 1952–
  The later Wittgenstein.
  Bibliography: p.
  Includes index.
  1. Wittgenstein, Ludwig, 1889–1951.   I. Title.
B3376.W564H53   1987   192   86-26366
ISBN 0-631-15424-8

Typeset in 11pt on 12pt Garamond
by Joshua Associates Limited, Oxford
Printed in Great Britain by T. J. Press Ltd, Padstow

Contents

Preface	vii
Acknowledgements	ix
Note on Text References and Quotations	x

1 Some Preliminary Issues ... 1

    A system of reference ... 1
    Justification of the study of Wittgenstein's 'method' ... 3
    Justification of the appeal to Wittgenstein's *Nachlaß* ... 6
    Matters of method and matters of style ... 15
    The significance of TS 213 and the puzzle of MS 116 ... 25

2 Metalogic and the Domain of Logic: the Shift to Ordinary Language ... 40

3 Language Games: the Heuristic Role of the 'Ideal' ... 67

4 Language Games: the Logical *versus* the Magical Views of Signs ... 98

5 Wittgensteinian Relativism and the Dynamic View of Language ... 138

6 Metaphysics and Wittgenstein's Struggle against the Intellectual Current of Our Times ... 190

Notes	227
Bibliography	321
Index	327

Preface

From what has survived of Ludwig Wittgenstein's philosophical writings, it appears that in 1929 at around the age of forty Wittgenstein took up writing philosophy again after a hiatus of roughly a decade. What emerges in his philosophical writing after 1929 is a 'way of thinking' (*Denkweise*), a way of doing philosophy. The present study is an exegetical treatise on Wittgenstein's approach to philosophy after 1929. What is being offered is an interpretation of salient themes in Wittgenstein's later writings, which shed light on the emergence of his later 'way of thinking'.

Among the themes examined will be some which have received virtually no attention to date in the secondary literature on Wittgenstein, and also some themes which have received considerable attention. The criterion for saliency has been neither the amount of attention lavished on a topic in the secondary literature, nor even whether a theme has been featured prominently in the 'works' of Wittgenstein which have been selected for posthumous publication by the executors of his literary estate (Wittgenstein did not publish his later thoughts during his lifetime). Rather, the themes examined have been selected on the basis of their prominence within the corpus of Wittgenstein's later writings as a whole, as constituted by the materials in his *Nachlaß* (the extensive legacy of unpublished writings he left at his death).

Interpretations of Wittgenstein's later philosophy are numerous, and also diverse in their claims. Given such diversity, some are bound to be on the mark some of the time, but, even when they are on the mark, their claims have often tended to be little better than shots in the dark with very little concrete exegetical evidence supporting them. This is not to say that there have not been any very penetrating and illuminating studies of Wittgenstein's later philosophy, but rather to say that whether or not the interpretations have hit their mark rarely can be gleaned from the evidence (or lack of it) accompanying the interpretations. Too often one is left with little by means of which to choose between one interpreter's position and another's, other than a general feeling of sympathy with the intuitions of one over the other.

The unhappy state of Wittgenstein scholarship is in large part due to the fragmented and ahistorical character of the potpourri of published remarks with which scholars have been working. The present study offers an interpretation of Wittgenstein's later approach to philosophy which will be extensively substantiated by disclosing Wittgenstein's later thinking within the concrete historical context of the flow of ideas recorded in his notebooks and typescripts between 1929 and his death in 1951.

Acknowledgements

Professor G. H. von Wright has over the years, apart from his own philosophical work, taken the initiative in his capacity as one of the executors of Wittgenstein's literary estate to make available to scholars the world over the voluminous *Nachlaß* of writings left for posterity by one of the most influential philosophers of our century. The research on the *Nachlaß* which served as the basis for this book would not have even been possible without Professor von Wright's considerable efforts to catalogue and make accessible Wittgenstein's unpublished papers. Furthermore, his receptiveness to my queries, his words of encouragement and informed, constructive criticism of my work, and the spirit of professionalism with which he responded to points of criticism regarding a few of his own constructions and hypotheses about the *Nachlaß* served as a distant beacon of scholarly contact that helped sustain me through the otherwise desolate years of my research. Even should he not agree with the views expressed, what is of any value in this book is greatly indebted to him. For what is not of any value and for what may prove to be the book's errors, the blame is wholly mine.

For their generous permission to cite material from Wittgenstein's *Nachlaß*, I thank the executors of Wittgenstein's literary estate (Professors von Wright, Anscombe and Rhees). And kind permission has been granted by Routledge and Kegan Paul for the right to reproduce a figure from C. K. Ogden and I. A. Richards, *The Meaning of Meaning: a study of the influence of language upon thought and of the science of symbolism* (London: Kegan Paul, 1923), p. 14. My gratitude is also extended to an anonymous Oxford reader for his astute and helpful comments on my work during the final stages of revision, as well as to Professors Brian McGuinness and Alice Ambrose Lazerowitz for their informative replies to specific questions. To David Gauthier and T. M. Robinson I owe the opportunity of having been able to pursue my research in the first place.

Note on Text References and Quotations

Cross-references to quotations in the text take the form 'q.' and identifying note number (for example, 'q. 429' means 'the quotation identified by n. 429'). The text also includes cross-references by chapter, page (p.), note (n.), or a combination of these, and detailed references to Wittgenstein's published 'works' (though most such references are given in the Notes). For an explanation of the abbreviations used in such references to Wittgenstein, see under 'Wittgenstein' in the Bibliography, where the abbreviations used appear in square brackets after the corresponding entries. Where a specific edition is cited, it is that identified in the Bibliography.

Within quotations in the text, double obliques mark off terms or phrases that Wittgenstein entered as possible alternate wording. Broken or wavy underlines (reproduced here simply as broken underlines) were used by Wittgenstein to indicate that he was not sure about the appropriateness of a word or phrase. A horizontal line through words indicates that they had been crossed out in the manuscript. Where italics are used in an English translation, they should be taken as an indication that Wittgenstein had used a solid underline for emphasis in the original German. For the purpose of inserting my own clarifications regarding certain words or phrases in quoted material, square brackets are used; usually for citing the original German word(s) which served as the basis for the translation, but also sometimes for citing illuminating alternate phrasing from another draft of the same passage, cross-references to related remarks, or explanatory interjections.

1
Some Preliminary Issues

A system of reference

Designating a system of reference with respect to Wittgenstein's writings is on the surface quite simple, but actually rather complex and plagued by pitfalls. It would seem straightforward that the titles of Wittgenstein's published 'books' should serve to designate the materials they contain, and that his unpublished notebooks and typescripts should be identified by the clear-cut numerical system of reference devised by Professor G. H. von Wright and published in his article "The Wittgenstein Papers".[1] This in fact is the system of reference adopted in the present study. However, it is *not* the system of reference Wittgenstein used. When Wittgenstein himself refers to his own writings, the system of reference adopted in the present study may seem to be either irrelevant or sometimes even misleading. Fortunately, Professor von Wright in his account of his reference system also gives us many of Wittgenstein's own terms and means of designating manuscripts. Thus, for example, if a passage is cited in which Wittgenstein makes a cross-reference to a page or passage in "Band XII" or "Grosses Format", by consulting the information included in von Wright's account of his numerical system of reference one can unambiguously determine that Wittgenstein was referring to what *we* shall be calling 'MS 116' or 'MS 140', respectively.

However, it is not always this clear-cut, especially with respect to the titles which have been assigned to Wittgenstein's published 'works'. A good example is the term 'Blue Book'. This title has come to designate a set of remarks which Wittgenstein dictated (in English) to his class in Cambridge during 1933–4. Wittgenstein also uses the term "Blaues Buch" (Blue Book) in his writings, but for him the term designated not what *we* know as the 'Blue Book', but rather a notebook (MS 124) of remarks completely different from the material dictated in 1933–4.[2] Consequently, if one finds Wittgenstein making numerous references to "Blaues Buch" in the midst of the drafting, revising and arranging of material which is readily recognizable as remarks included in *Philosophical Investigations* one might easily be misled into thinking that what *we* call the 'Blue Book' figured prominently in the drafting and development of the ideas in *Philosophical Investigations*.

Since what has been published of Wittgenstein's later writing has appeared posthumously, the titles have in most cases been assigned by Wittgenstein's literary executors – though usually quite justifiably. In addition to the ambiguity of the term 'Blue Book', one finds Wittgenstein referring to several different manuscripts as *Philosophische Bemerkungen* (Philosophical Remarks) or simply *Bermerkungen*, and the same is the case with the title 'Philosophical Investigations'. When misleading inconsistencies do arise between the system of reference adopted in the present volume and Wittgenstein's own references to his manuscripts, such inconsistencies will be explicitly pointed out to avoid confusion.

A further difficulty is the specificity of references. All references to the *Nachlaß* will be to the Cornell University Library microfilm version of Wittgenstein's papers (made in 1967). To identify the location of a specific passage within a manuscript either a page number or an entry date will be given. If a manuscript has not been paginated, and no entry date is apparent, the passage will be cited by giving an estimation of the page number based on the sequence of pages presented in the microfilm version of the manuscript.

With very few exceptions, Wittgenstein wrote in German. Remarks cited from the *Nachlaß* will be in translation, using, where available, previously published translations of Wittgenstein's remarks. In cases where either a significantly different translation has been used in lieu of a previously published but inadequate translation of the same remark, or the remark was originally written in English by Wittgenstein, this will be pointed out in the accompanying note.

The *Nachlaß* is in a constant process of being updated both with respect to our understanding of the chronology of the materials and with respect to its content – newly discovered material is occasionally added to the collection. Several items added to the *Nachlaß* since 1969 will come into play in the present volume. These include three handwritten manuscripts (MSS 179, 180a and 180b – all circa 1945) and a typescript (TS 239, from 1942 or 1943). The notebooks contain drafts and revisions of remarks many of which found their way into the published version of *Philosophical Investigations*. The typescript, added to the *Nachlaß* in 1978, is an annotated revision of the first half of the pre-war version of the *Investigations*.[3]

Justification of the study of Wittgenstein's 'method'

The present study examines the emergence of aspects of what might loosely be called Wittgenstein's 'method' or approach to philosophy in his later writings. The overriding concern will not be the assessment of his solutions to philosophical problems. Although the study stops short of what should be the ultimate goal of Wittgenstein research – namely, an assessment of what philosophical conclusions he has to offer – it does take a very significant and essential step in that direction; for the first and perhaps most important step in providing an adequate assessment of Wittgenstein is achieving a penetrating, veridical and *substantiated* understanding of him. Much of the voluminous literature that has been written whether against or on behalf of Wittgenstein since his death has dismally failed to take this indispensable first step in the assessment of his philosophy.

It may seem, from some of Wittgenstein's own published remarks, that neglecting the veracity of his doctrines in favour of an exegetical study of the emergence of his method or overall approach to philosophy both is inconsistent with the nature of his philosophy and runs counter to the spirit of his thinking. Such an impression would be erroneous.

Aside from Wittgenstein's disorderly and often aphoristic stylistic proclivities, a frequently cited remark, which might be taken as evidence that it is inappropriate to speak of Wittgenstein's 'method' in his later writings, is the assertion in *PI* §133 para. 4, that "There is not *a* philosophical method, though there are indeed methods, like different therapies." To the extent that this remark appears to clash with a programme of giving an account of Wittgenstein's later 'method' or approach to philosophy, it also clashes with his own statement in the preceding paragraph of *PI* §133 that "we now demonstrate a method, by examples; and the series of these examples can be broken off". *PI* §133 is testimony to Wittgenstein's odd way of doing things: the four paragraphs comprising it were originally written at different points during his life. The apparent incompatibility of his suggestion that he will "demonstrate a method" and his claim that there is "not *a* philosophical method" (but rather methods) is at least in part accounted for by the fact that the two paragraphs in question were written roughly six years apart, and that when subsequently they were conjoined no attempt was made to adjust the phrasing of the remarks so as to render them more obviously compatible.[4] However, his suggestion that he will "demonstrate a method" is clearly compatible with his claim that "There is not *a* philosophical method, though there are indeed methods", if one interprets 'method' in the former remark as referring to his overall approach to the problems of philosophy, and in the latter remark as referring to specific solutions to specific problems. Thus, Wittgenstein is both indicating that he will be demonstrating his overall approach to philosophy by means of examples (which can be broken off), and also (without inconsistency) suggesting that there is not *one* specific tactic or recipe that he will be applying to all the multifarious philosophical problems – just as a cook could suggest that he has a method or approach to cooking, but equally assert that he does not use the same (one) recipe for all the dishes that he cooks.

In the ensuing chapters the interpretation of the emergence of aspects of Wittgenstein's 'philosophical method' or approach to philosophy in his later writings, although it will deal with some of his specific tactics, neither offers nor suggests that Wittgenstein offers a specific recipe which one should follow to solve all philosophical problems.

A remark which might appear to suggest that the investigation of Wittgenstein's later approach to philosophy runs counter to the *spirit* of his thinking, is his assertion in the published Preface to *Philosophical Investigations* that "I should not like my writing to spare other people the trouble of thinking. But, if possible, to stimulate someone to thoughts of his own."[5] Quite late in his life Wittgenstein jotted down another observation which seems to have the same implications: "In intellectual matters, an undertaking [attempt] usually cannot be continued, nor should it be continued. These thoughts will fertilize the soil for a new sowing (thoughts)."[6] Such remarks might be taken to imply that Wittgenstein's ambition was not to pass on a 'way of doing philosophy', but rather merely to provoke his readers into philosophical flight of their own.

Though it probably would be correct to say that Wittgenstein did not wish his readers to feel obliged to pick up and carry out his own (Wittgenstein's) specific train of thought in any given philosophical remark on a problem, and that he did wish his readers to think out philosophical problems for themselves, it does not follow from this that he did not consider it his primary objective to convey through his writings (and teaching) an overall approach to philosophical problems. Unlike the Wittgenstein of the *Tractatus*, who claimed in his Preface to be offering "unassailable and definitive" truths and "the final solution of the problems",[7] in his later writings Wittgenstein never seemed quite content with his handling of any one philosophical problem. Instead, he returned to the same problems again and again to attack them from different angles. It is quite evident from his own notebooks that in his later writings he felt his real gift to posterity to be not 'true doctrines', but rather a way of doing philosophy. No doubt he wished to provoke one to philosophical flight of one's own, but at the same time it was his ambition to teach his readers *how* to fly.

Some Preliminary Issues

In his account of Wittgenstein's lectures during the early 1930s, G. E. Moore cites Wittgenstein's reference to a "new method" and attributes to him the following claims:

> He went on to say that, though philosophy had now been "reduced to a matter of skill", yet this skill, like other skills, is very difficult to acquire. One difficulty was that it required a "sort of thinking" to which we are not accustomed and to which we have not been trained – a sort of thinking very different from what is required in the sciences. And he said that the required skill could not be acquired merely be hearing lectures: discussion was essential. As regards his own work, he said it did not matter whether his results were true or not: what mattered was that "a method had been found".[8]

Such an emphasis on imparting a philosophical "method", even to the extent that the veracity of philosophical doctrines becomes of only secondary importance, is borne out in Wittgenstein's notebooks. In a small pocket notebook (c.1931) he jotted down the following remarks in English (probably in preparation for a lecture, and perhaps even the lecture which Moore recounts):

> What I should like to get you to do is (not to agree with me in particular opinions but) to investigate the matter in the right way. To notice the interesting kind of things (i.e., the things which will serve as keys if you use them properly).[9]
>
> I don't want to give you a definition of philosophy but I should like you to have a very lively idea as to the characters of philosophical problems. If you had, by the way, I could stop lecturing at once.[10]
>
> What I want to teach you isn't opinions but a method. In fact the method to treat as irrelevant every question of opinion.[11]
>
> I don't try to make you *believe* something you don't believe, but to make you *do* something you won't *do*.[12]

Much later (1938) Wittgenstein similarly, though somewhat awkwardly, wrote, "I'm not teaching you anything; I'm trying to persuade you to *do* something."[13] This emphasis on method or a way of *doing* philosophy, and the de-emphasis of doctrines, is especially evident in Wittgenstein's remarks about the pre-war version of *Philosophical Investigations*, part I of which was, with only a few exceptions, virtually identical to the first 189 sections of what we now know as *Philosophical Investigations*. For instance, in late 1937 in a remark which echoes the point found in the published

Preface (that he wishes to "stimulate someone to thoughts of his own"), Wittgenstein wrote concerning the pre-war version of the *Investigations*, "One could call this book a text-book. A textbook, however, not in that it provides knowledge [*Wissen*], but rather in that it stimulates thinking [*Denken*]."[14] Here, one clearly finds that Wittgenstein did not consider the value of the early version of the *Investigations* to lie in the truth of the doctrines it has to offer. Furthermore, the following year (1938), in an early draft of the Preface, Wittgenstein does state *what* he considered to be of value in his early version of the *Investigations*. After roughly what we now know as the first two paragraphs of the published Preface, concerning his several attempts to collect his remarks into a book, Wittgenstein wrote, "The last attempt at a compilation is the one with which I begin this publication of my thoughts. It is a fragment and has perhaps the merit that it conveys, relatively easily, a conception of my method."[15] His ambition, then, even in the strategy behind the drafting of *Philosophical Investigations*, was to convey a way of thinking, a method of doing philosophy, rather than disseminate philosophical truths or doctrines. This ambition is quite consistent with his stated desire to stimulate thinking in others, and the account offered here (some of which will be by way of illustration) of the emergence of the sort of thinking which Wittgenstein wished to stimulate, rather than running counter to the spirit of his philosophy, is thoroughly consonant with his stated objectives.

Therefore, the present exegetical study of the emergence of aspects of Wittgenstein's method or approach to philosophy in his later writings is justified both in the sense that one must be clear what Wittgenstein is *doing* before one can adequately assess his results (thus this study is a necessary step on the way to such an assessment), and in the sense that it is precisely his approach to philosophy, and not so much his specific philosophical conclusions or doctrines, that Wittgenstein wished to convey in the first place.

Justification of the appeal to Wittgenstein's *Nachlaß*

Researching Wittgenstein's *Nachlaß* in an attempt to clarify what he is up to has its inherent risks, not the least hazardous of which is the possibility of being misled by countless remarks that he jotted down in a frenzy of philosophical activity, but which might very well have been tossed on the rubbish heap had he undertaken a circumspect and protracted re-examination of the material.[16] This danger becomes very obvious when one notes some of Wittgenstein's own self-evaluative asides in his notebooks. In one case he complains, "I know that what I have been writing here for many weeks is poor, but I write it in the hope that better might come from it...."[17] Several weeks later in the same notebook Wittgenstein admits in a parenthetical remark, "I can't find the central grammatical mistake on which all of these problems are based."[18] It is quite obvious from such remarks that many of the notebooks are works in progress and include a significant amount of groping. It might very well be argued that one would be better off limiting one's research to finished products.

However, the problem of determining what is to be taken as a 'finished product' is a problem not only for the researcher of Wittgenstein's *Nachlaß*, but also, and even more so, for anyone working only with Wittgenstein's published 'works'. During his lifetime, Wittgenstein published only two books which might be called 'finished products': his *Tractatus Logico-Philosophicus* and a spelling-book entitled *Wörterbuch für Volksschulen*.[19] None of the 'works' which have been published posthumously could properly be called a 'finished product'. In fact, there is a very broad range of degrees of refinement, not only between 'works', but within 'works'. The range spans from first-draft pocket-notebook material such as *On Certainty* and *Remarks on Colour*, to well refined sections in part I of *Philosophical Investigations*.

The researcher who should be in the least danger of confusing crude first formulations and finished products is not the one who restricts his study to published 'works', but rather the person who researches the whole corpus of materials in the *Nachlaß*. For example, the two volumes of Wittgenstein's remarks entitled *Remarks on the Philosophy of Psychology*, published in 1980,[20] were prepared from two typescripts (TSS 229 and 232) which he dictated in 1947 and 1948. That these remarks reached the typescript stage, however, is in this case no indication that they are any more refined than first-draft material. In fact the remarks in TSS 229 and 232 were dictated virtually verbatim from MSS 130-7 – with some omissions, but no rearrangement. Moreover, throughout the manuscripts from which Wittgenstein dictated for what we now know as *Remarks on the Philosophy of Psychology*, he complained about the poor quality of these remarks. For example, on the cover page of MS 130 he wrote, "This notebook contains virtually only poor assertions [*Sätze*]. Some of them though might provide stimulus for better ones. Most are mere waste."[21] Yet roughly the first 220 remarks in *Remarks on the Philosophy of Psychology* were verbatim dictations from MS 130. Similarly, on the cover page of MS 135 Wittgenstein wrote, "In this volume no more than *one* halfway decent section comes out of each ten or twenty pages."[22] However, from the 192 pages of MS 135 Wittgenstein dictated verbatim roughly 200 sections for what we now call *Remarks on the Philosophy of Psychology*. Later, in the midst of MS 136, Wittgenstein confessed,

> It seems to me I am still a long way from understanding these things, a long way from the point of knowing what I do and what I

don't need to discuss. I still keep getting entangled in details without knowing whether I ought to be talking about such things at all; and I have the impression that I may be inspecting a large area only eventually to exclude it from consideration. But even in that case these reflections wouldn't be worthless; as long, that is, as they are not just going round in a circle.[23]

And finally, in the midst of MS 137, one finds Wittgenstein parenthetically asserting, "With all of these reflections I am very foolish [*dumm*]; but I don't know how I should get over my foolishness [*Dummheit*]."[24] The point here is not that it was a mistake to publish *Remarks on the Philosophy of Psychology*, for indeed this 'work' may very well prove to be one of the most worthwhile collections of Wittgenstein's remarks published to date. Rather, the point is that one who restricts his research to the published 'works' of Wittgenstein is not less immune to being misled by material which Wittgenstein did not consider a 'finished product'.

Remarks on the Philosophy of Psychology is by no means unique in its inclusion of material with which Wittgenstein was not fully satisfied. Take for example part II of *Philosophical Investigations*. Right after what we know as paragraph 3 on p. 204 of the *Investigations* (and amidst many passages published there) Wittgenstein originally had complained, "The relations between these concepts form a landscape which language presents us with in countless fragments; piecing them together is *too hard* for me. I can make only a very imperfect job of it."[25] We know from the published Preface to the *Investigations* that even with respect to part I of the *Investigations* (the Preface was written quite some time before the material which the literary executors have appended as part II) Wittgenstein felt, "I should have liked to produce a good book. This has not come about, but the time is past in which I could improve it."[26] Wittgenstein put it somewhat more bluntly in an earlier draft of the Preface: "That this book is not good, I know. But I believe that the time is past...."[27] It would be a simple matter to take every one of the posthumously published 'works' of Wittgenstein and show that he could not be said to be satisfied with any one of them. Even Wittgenstein's later desire to publish seems to have arisen not so much because he felt relatively satisfied with a significant block of material, but rather because he learned that his results were in circulation in watered-down and garbled form.[28]

Whatever Wittgenstein's motives for wanting to publish, however, the fact remains that he did not feel he had a 'finished product' which was worth publishing. Wittgenstein's dissatisfaction (and frustration) was manifested in his assessment that his talent was "A lot of froth – but a few *fine* thoughts"[29] and that in his writing "Only every now and again does one of the sentences that I write here make a step forward; the rest are like the snipping of the barber's scissors, which he has to keep moving so as to make a cut with them at the right moment."[30] Wittgenstein never did get to the point where he felt he had adequately sorted out the fine thoughts from the "froth". The problem of so doing, the problem of distinguishing the snip that gets something accomplished philosophically from the one which is philosophically idle, is a problem not solely for the researcher of Wittgenstein's *Nachlaß*, but also, and especially, for the scholar who, in limiting himself to Wittgenstein's posthumously published 'works', lacks the benefit of the words of caution and self-evaluation which are sprinkled throughout the original manuscripts.

One can, however, give more positive arguments in defence of a use of Wittgenstein's *Nachlaß* than the *tu quoque* rebuttal presented above. First of all, even if it were generally more hazardous from an exegetical standpoint to work with Wittgenstein's notebooks rather than with his published 'works', there is a sense in which the focus of the present study, while it does not render the study immune to the dangers, does at least put it less at risk of being misled by unrefined thoughts. Granted, in his notebooks Wittgenstein seems, as he variously put it, to "paint the same face again and again"[31] or let himself "puzzle again and again over the same things"[32] while rarely providing us with what might be unambiguously considered a 'final' handling or resolution of an issue. Yet, given that the aim here is to characterize Wittgenstein's philosophical method or general approach to philosophy, then, whether or not he was successful in his own eyes in a specific attempt to solve a problem, the way in which he attempted to tackle the problem may nevertheless be informative and provide us with a valuable insight into his overall approach to the problems of philosophy.

A further argument for the use of the *Nachlaß* can be given on what might be called 'contextualist' grounds. In spite of his ambition to be "perspicuous" in his presentation, and in spite of the fact that he wrote in a very down-to-earth and untechnical idiom, it is generally acknowledged that Wittgenstein is not among the more transparent philosophers of our century. Among the major reasons why he has come across as so impenetrably aphoristic is that, aside from his obvious stylistic inclinations in this direction, much of what has been published of his writing (especially his most circulated and influential 'work', *Philosophical Investigations*) is composed of conglomerated fragments (sometimes literally clippings) selected from material spanning a broad historical spectrum of his writings and often selected from within an original bed of remarks on the same or a related subject. The main justification for our appeal to the *Nachlaß* is that one can best cut through the dense aphoristic quality of such a work as *Philosophical Investigations* by coming to grips with its fragments in their historical context (and genesis) within Wittgenstein's own development and by viewing these fragments not only within the context of the bed of remarks in which they were first conceived, but also within whatever other contexts Wittgenstein saw fit to place them during subsequent stages of revision. The validity of this argument will be corroborated by the results achieved in the succeeding chapters.

There are two issues related to this 'contextualist' justification of the use of Wittgenstein's *Nachlaß* that warrant some attention. On the one hand it should be pointed out that the above 'contextualist' stand is only one of a number of 'contextualist' positions that could be taken, some of which would seem extreme in comparison to the one taken here. There appears to be in circulation what one might call, for want of a more suitable term, a 'radical' contextualist thesis. This latter 'radical' position deserves attention because, unlike the 'moderate' contextualist position advocated here, the radical brand, rather than providing a justification for appeal to Wittgenstein's *Nachlaß*, undermines the justification that has just been given. The 'radical' contextualist position finds expression in some of the remarks made by Rush Rhees, editor of several of Wittgenstein's posthumously published 'works', and one of the literary executors responsible for Wittgenstein's *Nachlaß*.

In his editorial note to *Philosophical Grammar*, concerning the fact that some of the passages in this 'work' also have been published in some of Wittgenstein's other 'works', Rhees states,

> It would be easy to give the reference and page number for each of these. We decided not to. This book should be compared with Wittgenstein's earlier and later writings. But this means: the method and the development of his discussion here should be compared with the *Philosophical Remarks* and again with the *Investigations*. The footnotes would be a hindrance and, as often as not, misleading. When Wittgenstein writes a paragraph here that is also in the *Remarks*, this does not mean that he is just repeating what he said there. The paragraph may have a different importance, it may belong to the discussion in a different way. (We know there is more to be said on this question.)[33]

Indeed, let us say a bit more about this question, since, if Rhees is correct in his claim that it would be a hindrance and/or misleading to note (and thus examine) other contexts in which a given remark is embedded, then the 'contextualist' justification given above for appealing to the *Nachlaß* falls apart. The closest that Rhees seems to come to giving a reason for his claim is the suggestion that, if a remark found in one context is repeated elsewhere in another context, then it is not just repeated but rather somehow is *different* in the other context. Rhees further explains (but not until the 1974 version of his note[34]) that the change involved is that a remark may have a "different importance" in another context and may "belong to the discussion in a different way". By this latter explanation he cannot simply mean that finding the same remark in a different context sheds a different light on the remark, for it is not at all clear why this should be a hindrance rather than an aid in cutting through the dense aphoristic fog which surrounds so many of Wittgenstein's remarks. Rather Rhees must be suggesting that the point being made by a remark is different, given a different manuscript source or collection of material. Only if the latter were true would tracking down and examining a remark in other manuscript contexts be a hindrance and misleading.

Rhees seems to make a similar claim elsewhere. In an editorial note appended to some of Wittgenstein's remarks published in the journal *Philosophia* he comments,

> The passage dated "26.9" and beginning, "Denke Dir zwei verschieden Pflanzenarten ..." comes in the midst of the other discussions between manuscript pages 5 and 100. It was not included in the typescript of the philosophy of mathematics material. He [Wittgenstein] included a shortened version of a part of it in a remark he wrote ten years later; and a cutting of this remark was published as §608 of *Zettel*. But it does not have the same point there.[35]

The suggestion again seems to be that finding a remark in a different context (in this case the arrangement of material known as *Zettel*) has changed the point being made.[36]

Unfortunately, there is some indication that this form of 'radical' contextualism may be contagious. Anthony Kenny, who translated *Philosophische Grammatik* into English and who professed his "greatest debt" to Rhees for his assistance, also exhibits some of the symptoms of 'radical' contextualism. Concerning a remark in *Philosophische Grammatik* which also turns up in *Zettel*, Kenny offers the following (perhaps purely diplomatic) justification of the fact that his translation of the remark is significantly different from the one which Anscombe gives in her *Zettel* translation: "The parallel passage in *Zettel* 606 is translated in a way that does not fit this context."[37] Kenny's suggestion seems to be not that viewing the remark in the context of *Philosophische Grammatik* shows more clearly what the translation should be, but rather that the different context in *Philosophische Grammatik* (as opposed to *Zettel*) simply calls for a significantly different translation. The implication is not that viewing the remark in the context of *Philosophische Grammatik* made it more clear what Wittgenstein meant, but rather that the different context changed the meaning.

If the radical contextualist thesis were true, it would create utter havoc for Wittgenstein scholarship. Were the meaning or point of a remark in *Zettel*, for example, to be so strongly dependent on its context that one should say that the point of the remark there is different from in another manuscript context, one would be driven in the rather distressing direction of having to thank not so much Wittgenstein as Peter Geach for having provided us with the point made in *Zettel* – for it is Geach who is largely responsible for the particular arrangement of material we now know as *Zettel*.[38] A similar problem could also be raised with respect to some of Wittgenstein's other posthumously published 'works',[39] although *Zettel* is somewhat unique in that there was no choice but to 'arrange' the material.

It is not being denied that the particular arrangement of remarks can throw a different light on a given remark. Indeed it can, and this is one of the dangers involved in taking too many editorial liberties with Wittgenstein's material. What *is* being denied is that it is counter-productive to track down a given remark in other manuscript contexts – and *especially* if the specific context which initially confronts us is more of an editor's making than Wittgenstein's.

As a simple illustration, take §621 of *Zettel*. The context in which this remark appears in *Zettel* is completely different from that in which it appears in MS 136 (or for that matter TS 232, which has been published as volume II of *Remarks on the Philosophy of Psychology*). Even granting that the different contexts throw a different light on the remark, one would certainly be going too far if one claimed that a different point was being made in *Zettel* from in MS 136 or *Remarks on the Philosophy of Psychology* and that it would thus be a hindrance to note and examine the specific remark as it appears in these different contexts. In fact what one finds in MS 136 is that, contrary to the arrangement which Geach has provided for us, the remark we now know as *Zettel* §621 was originally (along with *Zettel* §483) part of the "Plan for the treatment of psychological concepts" which we find in *Zettel* §472.[40] Surely, it is not that the remark makes different points in these two contexts, but, quite the contrary, that the different light shed on *Zettel* §621 by its context in MS 136 makes it a bit clearer just what Wittgenstein might have been up to in *Zettel* §621.

A second issue related to a 'contextualist' justification of an appeal to Wittgenstein's *Nachlaß* is the broader question of to what extent one should seek clarification of Wittgenstein's ideas by examining them not only within the whole corpus of his own writings, but also within the context of other writers and thinkers. It seems to have become somewhat fashionable among scholars to try to clarify Wittgenstein's aphoristic remarks by considering his work in the context of the ideas of those who may have had some influence on him.[41] Although, to some extent, the present study too will appeal to 'influences' in an attempt to shed light on

Wittgenstein's later thinking, it will not emphasize them. The reason for this is not that Wittgenstein was not subject to numerous influences. Rather, the reason lies in the nature of those influences.

There is no doubt that Wittgenstein's later thinking was influenced. Early in 1940, after having written most of the remarks constituting what we now know as part I of *Philosophical Investigations*, Wittgenstein acknowledged his indebtedness to others for the 'seeds' of his thinking:

> I believe that my originality (if that is the right word) is an originality belonging to the soil rather than to the seed. (Perhaps I have no seed of my own.) Sow a seed in my soil and it will grow differently than it would in any other soil.
> Freud's originality too was like this, I think. I have always believed – without knowing why – that the real germ of psycho-analysis came from Breuer, not Freud. Of course Breuer's seed-grain can only have been quite tiny. (*Courage* is always original.)[42]

Our reason for not emphasizing a search for these 'seeds' is that, in the terms of Wittgenstein's metaphor, in most cases the seeds could only have been quite tiny, and the phenomenal transformation of them in the soil of Wittgenstein's mind produced a mature thought and philosophy which bears so little resemblance to those original seed-grains that we should do just as well by not speaking of a causal connection at all. This would clearly not be the case with just any thinker, but is to a great extent due to the sort of thinker Wittgenstein was.

Wittgenstein was not a scholar – at least, not in the sense of one who is inclined thoroughly and systematically to research the thinking of another philosopher, philosophical movement or historical period of philosophy. One can ascertain from Wittgenstein's own occasional references in his manuscripts that he was not what might be called a 'well-read' person, and that what reading he did do was not the result of any systematic research, but rather was piecemeal and seemed to be the result of what he happened to encounter or what happened to strike his fancy at the time. A little over three years before his death, he admitted as much when he wrote, "I am really also a learned man; only my learning has not accumulated through much reading [*viel-lesen*], but rather through thinking."[43]

Wittgenstein was indeed a thinker, and perhaps in this sense, as he suggests, a learned man or scholar. Yet, because he was not a 'scholar' in the first sense, one is more likely to find a 'seed' of his thinking buried away in, for example, a remark made in an editor's afterword to an out-of-print edition of *Grimms' Fairy Tales*[44] or in an apparently secondary point which Wittgenstein happened to encounter in someone else's work, than in a major or well-recognized doctrine of another thinker (or school of thinkers) to whom he is alleged to have been exposed. Even the most humdrum of things in Wittgenstein's life could serve as a 'seed' and be transformed into a significant issue in his thinking. For example, in 1931, not long after his return to philosophy, he jotted down the following insight concerning a source for an aspect of his later approach to philosophy: "I don't know whether I have ever written this, that I learned the method of putting forward a number of examples in a grammatical reflection //beginning a linguistic reflection with a group of examples// in secondary school from a teacher named Heinrich Groag...."[45] Now, we do not wish to deprive Mr Groag of his own little piece of philosophical immortality, but it does seem somewhat adventitious that it was he whom Wittgenstein observed teaching grammar by way of examples and not some other teacher, for this practice no doubt was and is standard procedure in secondary school. Wittgenstein seems to have had the sort of mind which could, so to speak, upon encountering the most ordinary of stones in its path, leap from it to a philosophically profound level. One would have little chance of recognizing such stones were Wittgenstein not to tell us which stones they were and what role they played. And, even when these stones are pointed out to us, it is not so much to the particular qualities which they possess that we owe Wittgenstein's thought, but rather to Wittgenstein's rare ability to leap from these stones in the manner that he did. This is not, however, to contend that it is of no use to research Wittgenstein's social and intellectual milieu in an attempt to uncover the sources of his thinking. Rather it is to explain why the present study does not emphasize such a broadly 'contextualist' approach.

Wittgenstein himself, however, does indicate that, in order to understand what he is doing, one should look not so much for positive influences or contributions to his thinking, but rather see it in relation to the intellectual milieu that he is combating: "At present we are combating a trend. But this trend will die out, superseded by others, and then the way we are arguing against it will no longer be understood; people will not see why all this needed saying."[46] In the infrequent instances in the present study where an apppeal is made to the intellectual and social context of Wittgenstein's thinking, it will either be to cite examples of what Wittgenstein was combating, or, occasionally, to cite some interesting positive influences which Wittgenstein himself identifies. It is not intended, however, that the 'contextualist' argument presented above for an appeal to Wittgenstein's *Nachlaß* should be extended to justify a broader and more general appeal to Wittgenstein's social and intellectual milieu.

The defence of an appeal to Wittgenstein's *Nachlaß* in an attempt to clarify his later approach to philosophy has thus far utilized three main arguments: (1) a *tu quoque* rebuttal of the charge that an appeal to the *Nachlaß* is exegetically hazardous; (2) an explanation of why the focus of this study reduces the exegetical hazards of *Nachlaß* research; and (3) a positive 'contextualist' argument in favour of appeal to the *Nachlaß*. Furthermore, the 'contextualist' basis for the third argument has been distinguished from both a more 'radical' contextualist position which runs counter to the intentions of this study, and from a more 'general' contextualist position which would in addition emphasize an extensive appeal to Wittgenstein's social and intellectual milieu.

There still remains, however, one final reason for appealing to the *Nachlaß*. This is simply that we are appealing to it, as it were, at Wittgenstein's invitation. It is fairly evident from many of Wittgenstein's parenthetical remarks in his notebooks that he anticipated that some day scholars might be reading his notebooks. Many of his asides, words of caution and capsule assessments of a body of material seem to have been written at least potentially for an audience. In one particular aside, though, he seems explicitly to extend a sort of 'invitation' to research his *Nachlaß*. Wittgenstein extended this 'invitation' roughly six weeks before his death when he wrote, "I believe it might interest a philosopher, one who can think himself, to read my notes. For even if I have hit the mark only rarely, he would recognize what targets I had been ceaselessly aiming at."[47] This 'invitation' indirectly endorses appeal to the *Nachlaß* in an attempt to clarify the emergence of Wittgenstein's later *Denkweise*, and it does so in spite of the admittedly 'unfinished' quality of his notes.

Matters of method and matters of style

The stylistic idiosyncrasies of a philosopher can sometimes be essentially linked to his method or approach to philosophy, but this need not always be the case. Often much of an author's style is incidental to his philosophical method. A tendency in secondary literature on Wittgenstein has been to view his later style as intimately linked to his method – to view Wittgenstein as having deliberately written the *way* he did because his style was part and parcel of his philosophical methodology, because he felt that this is how philosophy should be done. However, many a misguided account has resulted from mistaking an incidental stylistic idiosyncrasy for a significant aspect of Wittgenstein's philosophical method.

Although some aspects of Wittgenstein's style are indeed intimately bound up with his philosophical method (and will be discussed in subsequent chapters), the present study will not emphasize his overall style as part and parcel of his method. This de-emphasis of the methodological relevance of Wittgenstein's overall style will be justified here by the argument that much of his style, especially the gross features which have tended to be emphasized in some of the secondary literature, is incidental to his method.

Wittgenstein's style is certainly unusual. This in itself tends to tempt one into thinking that his style must be a deliberate part of his method – why else would anyone convey his thoughts in such an opaque and disjointed manner? Even some of Wittgenstein's own remarks seem to nudge us in the direction of interpreting his overall style as methodologically essential. One frequently cited remark is from the published Preface to *Philosophical Investigations*:

> After several unsuccessful attempts to weld my results together into such a whole [a book], I realized that I should never succeed. The best that I could write would never be more than philosophical remarks; my thoughts were soon crippled if I tried to force them on in any single direction against their natural inclination. – And this was, of course, connected with the very nature of the investigation. For this compels us to travel over a wide field of thought criss-cross in every direction. – The philosophical remarks in this book are, as it were, a number of sketches of landscapes which were made in the course of these long and involved journeyings.[48]

Wittgenstein goes on to suggest that *Philosophical Investigations* is really only an "album" of such sketches.

Scholars have offered diverse interpretations of what the connection might be between Wittgenstein's unorthodox style and his philosophical method. Prominent among the interpretations are what may be referred to as the 'disorderly subject-matter view', the 'conspiracy theory' and the 'mystical option'.

Garth Hallett attempts to account for the "unorthodox style and apparent disorderliness"[49] of Wittgenstein's later writing by suggesting that the *Investigations* was written "without chapters or other clear divisions and without any systematic order" because Wittgenstein did not have a theory to propound, for "theory and unity lay in the past, in the *Tractatus* which was the *Investigations*' target".[50] Hallett goes on to explain that Wittgenstein in his later writing adopted a plan to describe language as if by way of "aerial photos", and that it would not have been possible or even appropriate to give an orderly description of language, because language is analogous to a disorderly city (such as the centre of London or Rome). Thus the discontinuity and disorderliness of Wittgenstein's later writing was in a sense forced on him by language. Hallett even goes so far as to intimate that Wittgenstein could not have arranged his ideas in "a unified, coherent manner without falsifying the content".[51]

This 'disorderly subject-matter view' rests on two points which are clearly attributable to Wittgenstein's later approach to philosophy: first, "theory ... lay in the past" – i.e., unlike in the *Tractatus*, Wittgenstein in his later writing no longer considered himself to be in the business of offering theories; and, secondly, Wittgenstein's ambition in his later writings was, instead, merely to describe language.[52] Yet it does not follow from these two points alone that the description of language need be disorderly. In addition, the 'disorderly subject-matter view' rests on three points which it would be highly questionable to attribute to Wittgenstein: (1) "unity lay in the past" – i.e., unlike in the *Tractatus*, Wittgenstein in his later writing was no longer concerned to write a unified and orderly study; (2) language is intrinsically disorderly; and (3) something disorderly cannot in principle properly be investigated in an orderly manner. With respect to point (1), it will subsequently be demonstrated that for Wittgenstein 'unity' *in one's writing* was *not* a thing of the past which he rejected; rather, a unified and orderly study remained an objective and, in fact, he did not publish his later work during his lifetime precisely because he felt he had failed to write a 'book' in the more conventional sense, failed to write a unified and orderly study.

Concerning point (2), Hallett does not provide, and would be hard pressed to provide, evidence showing that Wittgenstein in his later writings considered language to be disorderly – especially since Wittgenstein seems to claim the opposite in *PI* §98, where he suggests that language is in order as it is. The landscape of language is certainly very complex, but, though this would make it very difficult, it surely would render it neither methodologically inappropriate nor in principle impossible to give an orderly description of the linguistic terrain. One might give a '*complexity* of the subject matter' *excuse* for Wittgenstein's disorderly style, but this, even if no one else could do better, would be an admission of an author's shortcomings and not evidence that his overall style is methodologically deliberate and essential. It will be seen that Wittgenstein viewed the disorderliness of his style as a personal shortcoming, rather than as methodologically essential.

As for the third point on which Hallett's view rests, there is no evidence to suggest Wittgenstein felt that something disorderly could not in principle properly be investigated in an orderly manner. For a Wittgenstein scholar, point (3) should be quite discomforting, since there would be the implication that if an investigation or account of Wittgenstein's later work is orderly, then it is not a good one. Yet, even if Wittgenstein did subscribe to the view that something disorderly could not in principle properly be investigated in an orderly manner, it would have little bearing on the issue of the methodological significance of his style, given that he did not consider language disorderly.

The 'conspiracy theory' of Wittgenstein's style is not uncommon in the literature on Wittgenstein. A form of the theory, for instance, has been championed in a PhD thesis on Wittgenstein's later philosophical method.

The theory is roughly that Wittgenstein's method was deliberately to write in what has been called a "non-linear" manner for the therapeutic goal of getting the reader to learn to "cope" for himself philosophically. Some of the non-linear aspects taken to be essential to the therapeutic nature of Wittgenstein's method are (1) writing remarks or short paragraphs which sometimes make a sudden change from one topic to another;[53] (2) deliberate mingling and overlapping of issues;[54] (3) the lack of a notion of completeness in the handling of issues, i.e. "there is no definite point at which an issue can be said to be closed";[55] (4) the giving of hints and suggestions that frequently are not followed up;[56] and (5) writing in riddles.[57] According to this theory, Wittgenstein wrote in a "non-linear" manner because he was conspiring to get each person "to fight his own way out of a philosophical problem, to shift for himself (*PI* p. 206); and, therefore, he writes in riddles so that no one is spared the pain of thinking for himself (*PI* p. ix^e)".[58]

The 'conspiracy theory' would be a plausible one, were it not for the following two circumstances. First, most of what Wittgenstein wrote was initially written for himself – that is, was written in notebooks as a personal record of his *own* struggles with philosophical problems. What we now have in published form is for the most part brief, piecemeal glimpses of this struggle. The non-linear character of Wittgenstein's writing stems more than anything else from this fact and not from a design on his part to help others "cope" – though his writing may indeed have this effect. Secondly, when Wittgenstein tried to write for others – that is, tried to write a book – he *wanted* to proceed in a linear manner, and much of what has been cited as Wittgenstein's "non-linear" way of thinking, rather than being deliberate, was the subject of his displeasure and something he wished to overcome. It was not for want of trying that Wittgenstein did not write in a more conventional linear manner. His intellect just does not seem to have been suited to such a task. It will presently be demonstrated that Wittgenstein himself admitted this.

Another view (the 'mystical option') of the methodological importance of Wittgenstein's overall style has been put forth by Timothy Binkley in his book *Wittgenstein's Language*. The 'mystical option' is the view that Wittgenstein deliberately wrote the way he did because it was methodologically essential for achieving the goal of philosophy – namely, "vision". According to Binkley, Wittgenstein wrote "non-coalescing sketches" and remarks, rather than advancing theses, because he did not intend what he wrote to "be questioned discursively but only 'accepted' presentationally".[59] Binkley suggests that "these sketches are useful only as they are alive with more than propositional meaning,"[60] or, as he elsewhere phrases the point, Wittgenstein, "Like the poet, ... said exactly what he meant, but what he meant isn't propositional."[61] According to the tale which Binkley spins, "the aim of thinking for Wittgenstein, as for a whole tradition of pre-Cartesian philosophy, is more akin to perceiving perspicuously than judging correctly".⁶²

> Philosophy is a kind of poetry whose aim is to stimulate thought, not to elicit assent. This is why Wittgenstein sets out brief sharp sketches instead of extended arguments. He strives not for truth conceived as right judgement, but rather for peace and freedom from the torments of philosophical troubles. The achievement is a vision of how things fit together, and the way to the vision is to look again and again at items in numerous contexts and against different backgrounds. The breadth and depth of the vision of the man who has learned to see the world and be at peace are the accomplishments of this kind of investigation.⁶³

Several pages later, and apparently in an even more reckless mood, Binkley compares Wittgenstein with Augustine and claims,

> both are clearly engaged in an activity whose goal is a kind of clarity of vision in contrast to accuracy of judgement. For both seeing things in the right light and finding paths from errors to truths which were obscured are more important and more relevant to philosophy than the development of systematic theories or the statement of true propositions. The goal of philosophizing is the silence of unencumbered vision, not the sound of true claims. We therefore find in both their works stylistic motifs which support and adumbrate these interests.⁶⁴

Such a phrase as "the silence of unencumbered vision" no doubt expresses something terribly profound. It is not at all evident, however, that Wittgenstein held this as the goal of his later philosophy, and it is even less evident that he deliberately wrote in the style that he did so as to achieve such a goal. It is highly unlikely that anyone who could counsel, as Wittgenstein did, that "The people who feel no need to have perspicuity [*Durchsichtigkeit*] in their argumentation [*Argumentation*] are lost [*verloren*] for philosophy",⁶⁵ and that "The one who wants to learn philosophy from this book will *test* [*prüfen*] the propositions of this book",⁶⁶ would wish his work only to be "accepted presentationally" (whatever that might mean) and not discursively questioned. However, the best way to refute Binkley's interpretation of Wittgenstein's style (as well as the other two interpretations previously outlined) is to chronicle Wittgenstein's own struggle with and assessments of his style in his later writings.

The first point that must be established is that Wittgenstein *wished* to write a 'book' in the more conventional sense. We know this even from the published Preface to *Philosophical Investigations*, where Wittgenstein admits that it was his intention to write a book in which "the thoughts should proceed from one subject to another in a natural order and without breaks".[67] During the course of his efforts Wittgenstein did not decide that a stylistically conventional book would be undesirable, but rather came to the conclusion that he no longer had the strength satisfactorily to achieve the goal he had set for himself. Wittgenstein's decision to settle for an "album of sketches" (as he put it) had nothing at all to do with a conviction that such an album would better reflect (the disorder of) language, or that such a non-linear approach would be better at prodding others to cope for themselves philosophically, or that such an album would better help others to achieve "the silence of unencumbered vision". Wittgenstein did abandon his goal, but *not* because he felt that writing an "album of sketches" was a *more* desirable goal. One of the first glimpses one gets of Wittgenstein entertaining the idea of abandoning his goal of writing a book (in a conventional sense) is in remarks written on 12 September 1937:

> I am now writing my book, or trying to write it, and write bit by bit and without any progress; from hand to mouth. It is impossible that like this something good will come out of it. I am above all much too uneasy, much too constrained in writing. If I must write *like this*, then is it better to write no book, but rather to restrict myself here after a fashion to writing remarks which are still perhaps to be published at my death?
>
> The remarks which I write enable me to teach philosophy well, but not to write a book.
>
> I am inclined to be annoyed over my incompetence.[68]

Here we find Wittgenstein complaining about the poor results of his efforts to write a book, confessing that he felt much too uneasy and constrained in writing a book, and debating whether he should simply restrict himself to writing "remarks". Although there is a suggestion that his remarks lend themselves to teaching philosophy, there is no suggestion that this is what he had conspired to do in writing them. From the final sentences of the passage it is quite clear both that Wittgenstein was coming to the conclusion that he was unable to write a book, and that he was irritated by his inability.

Wittgenstein's confession that he felt uneasy and constrained while trying to write a book is an echo of his statement in the Preface to *Philosophical Investigations* that "my thoughts were soon crippled if I tried to force them forward, against their natural inclination, in *one* direction".[69]

Some Preliminary Issues

Forcing his thoughts "forward ... in *one* direction" is what Wittgenstein needed to do in order to write a book, i.e. a continuous and sustained philosophical treatise in which "the thoughts should proceed from one subject to another in a natural order and without breaks". On 15 September 1937, three days after writing the previously cited passage, Wittgenstein explained why he felt uneasy and constrained while trying to write a book:

> When I think for myself without wanting to write a book, then I run round about the theme; this is the only natural way of thinking for me. Being forced to think forward in a straight line is for me a torture. Should I henceforth attempt it at all??
> I waste unspeakable effort on putting into order thoughts which perhaps have absolutely no worth.[70]

This passage does not sit well with the 'conspiracy theory' of Wittgenstein's style. Even if Wittgenstein wished his writing to help other people set their thinking straight,[71] he clearly did not write in a non-linear manner because he felt this was how his book should be written in order to achieve a therapeutic goal. He wrote in a non-linear manner because this was a stylistic idiosyncrasy of his which he could not overcome to his satisfaction, however much he tried. Wittgenstein simply seems to have found it torturous "to think forward in a straight line [*in einer Reihe fortzudenken*]". His "natural way of thinking" was to "run round the theme". These are not the makings of a conspiracy.

The very next day Wittgenstein wrote one of the earliest drafts of part of the Preface to *Philosophical Investigations*:

> Preface:
> This book consists of remarks which I have written (re-written) in the course of the last eight years on subjects of philosophy. I have often tried to confer them in a satisfactory order or string them along *one* thread or train of thought. The outcome was artificial and unsatifactory and my energy proved itself much too limited to carry it out. The only presentation of which I am still capable is to connect these remarks by a network of numbers in such a way that their extremely complex relation becomes visible. May this be accepted instead of something better, – which I gladly would have produced.[72]

Obviously Wittgenstein had come to the conclusion that he no longer had the strength to overcome his natural inclination toward the somewhat disjointed flurries of remarks so characteristic of his notebooks, no longer had the strength to order his remarks so as to form a more stylistically conventional book. The suggestion that he now lacked the strength to achieve his goal of writing a book is also found in another remark made during this period. In the context of a discussion of his inability to write a book Wittgenstein complained, "Life puts images before our eyes as goals and makes us go after them, and then we lose the strength."[73] Roughly two weeks later, in a remark written in a different manuscript, he seems resigned to the task of merely offering an "album" of remarks:

> My difficulty is now to know what assortment or amount of my remarks is still *palatable*.
> Because what is unpalatable is also not useful. My judgement wavers though and I don't know where the line is to be drawn.[74]

Wittgenstein's displeasure with his stylistic shortcomings and his inability to write a more stylistically conventional book was a burden carried by him throughout his later years. Only a short time after resigning himself to offering an "album" of remarks, he wrote,

> This book is a collection of wisecracks. But the point is: they are connected, they form a system. If the task were to draw the shape of an object true to nature, then a wisecrack is like drawing merely (just) a (one) tangent to the real curve; but a thousand wisecracks (lying close to each other, closely drawn) can draw the curve.[75]

Thus, although he had already abandoned the goal of writing a unified and orderly work, he hoped that his "album" would have the effect of delineating a coherent and unified view, in spite of the apparently fragmented and disjointed presentation of the remarks. Wittgenstein, however, does not seem to have taken much consolation in this. Almost a decade later (1947), though resigned to his shortcomings, he still complained,

> Just as I cannot write verse, so too my ability to write prose extends only *so far*, and no farther. There is a quite definite limit to the prose I can write and I can no more overstep *that* than I can write a poem. *This* is the nature of my equipment; and it is the only equipment I have. It's as though someone were to say: In this game I can only attain *such and such* a degree of perfection, I can't go *beyond* it.[76]

The following year Wittgenstein disconsolately admitted, "You have to accept the faults in your own style. Almost like the blemishes in your own face."[77] The fact that he considered his overall style a personal shortcoming flies in the face of the three previously outlined interpretations of the methodological importance of Wittgenstein's style. Both the 'conspiracy theory' and the 'mystical option' are clearly predicated on the assumption that Wittgenstein's style was both deliberate and methodologically preferable to a more conventional style because, allegedly, it was better adapted to his goals ("helping others to cope for themselves" and "the silence of unencumbered vision" respectively). That Wittgenstein considered his style a personal shortcoming is a clear indication that his style was neither deliberate in any significant sense, nor a methodological preference.

But what is one to make of Wittgenstein's suggestion in the Preface to *Philosophical Investigations* that his inability to write a more stylistically conventional book was "connected with the very nature of the investigation"? Did he, as Hallett suggests, reject theory and unity and opt for mere description which was of necessity disorderly because of the disorderliness of the subject matter (language)? Wittgenstein, admittedly, rejected theory, but it is obvious from the evidence presented so far that he did not *reject* stylistic "unity": quite to the contrary, he *desired* it even though he was unable to achieve it. The evidence presented also shows that Wittgenstein viewed his inability to write a unified and orderly book as in large measure due to his own undesirable, but apparently insuperable, stylistic inclinations, his own "equipment". Furthermore, it can be demonstrated that the sense in which he considered his inability at least in part to be "connected with the nature of the investigation" was *not* that a disorderly description was necessary (and appropriate) because of the disorderliness of language. In an earlier draft (c.1938) of the Preface to *Philosophical Investigations* Wittgenstein wrote,

> It appeared to me that the best I could write would remain (always merely) philosophical remarks, that my thoughts were soon crippled when I tried, against their (natural) inclination, to make them run on inflexibly in *one* line [*in einer Linie*], for my thoughts always (after a while) had to leap over to another region and I had to wait until they on their own would turn back to the former region. And that is connected of course also [*natürlich auch*] with the nature of the subject in that it necessitates that the particular thoughts relate to each other in extremely complicated ways.[78]

In the above passage it is quite explicit that Wittgenstein considered his difficulties to be connected with the nature of the investigation in the sense that the subject required his thoughts to be related in extremely *complicated* ways. The suggestion is not, as Hallett contends, that the disorderliness of language requires a disorderly treatment, but rather that Wittgenstein's own inclination to jump about in his writing is at least in part due to the *complexity* of language. It was the complexity of language, and not an inherent disorderliness in language which made Wittgenstein feel compelled "to travel over a wide field of thought criss-cross in every direction".[79] Thus there is no indication in the Preface to *Philosophical Investigations* that Wittgenstein considered it either methodologically inappropriate or in principle impossible to give an orderly description of an admittedly *complex* linguistic terrain.

In his later years Wittgenstein still considered an "album" of remarks, however brilliant they might be, inferior to a unified and orderly book. In 1948, alluding to his philosophical remarks, Wittgenstein wrote,

> Raisins may be the best part of a cake; but a bag of raisins is not better than a cake; and someone who is in a position to give us a bag full of raisins still can't bake a cake with them, let alone do something better. I am thinking of Kraus and his aphorisms, but of myself too and my philosophical remarks.
>
> A cake – that is not as it were: thinned-out raisins.[80]

Wittgenstein's "album" of remarks (*Philosophical Investigations*) is precisely that: thinned-out raisins. Evidently though, for Wittgenstein, however much time he spent sorting out the 'fine raisins' from his notebooks (or, in terms of the metaphor cited in the previous section, sorting out the "fine thoughts" from the "froth"), what he was left with was never a cake – never a book as he wished it. Although, understandably, he felt his difficulties were exacerbated by the complexity of language, here again he seems to have considered his inability to write a book as above all a personal shortcoming and a fact of his constitution.

The nature of Wittgenstein's "equipment" (to use his own previously cited expression) seems to have been such that he was very adept at gathering raisins, but, however choice these raisins, he just was not much good at 'baking a cake'. Wittgenstein had what might be called a 'stroboscopic' intellect. His undeniable genius tended to manifest itself in flashes of insight which illumined themes again and again from various angles, rather than in a sustained and orderly development of the topics. His notebooks are in effect diaries recording his insights and chronicling his personal philosophical wanderings and struggles on a day-to-day basis. As Wittgenstein himself once admitted, "Nearly all my writings are private conversations with myself. Things that I say to myself tête-à-tête."[81] When Wittgenstein wished to write a book, he turned to these 'diaries' and tried to sort out the "fine thoughts", which he then attempted to order in such a way that they formed a coherent and unified whole.[82] After he returned to philosophy at roughly the age of forty, his energies and abilities simply do not seem to have been up to the task of producing a unified and orderly treatise in which the remarks "proceed from one subject to another in a natural order and without breaks." His overall style in his later work is due above all to these circumstances, and not to any design on his part.[83]

A few years before his death, Wittgenstein wrote a note which explicitly indicates that he had decided not to publish his later work precisely because it was in effect a personal record of his own struggles, and thus stylistically unsuited to book form:

> I have no right to offer for publication a book in which simply the difficulties which I perceived are expressed and repeated over and over again. These difficulties are indeed of interest for me who was stuck in them, but not necessarily for humanity (others). They are peculiarities of my thinking, necessitated by *my* development. They belong, so to speak, in a diary, not in a book. And even if this diary might be of interest for someone sometime, I still can not publish it. It is not my stomach troubles which are of interest, but rather the remedies – if any – I have found for them.[84]

It is the task of the present study to achieve a better appreciation of the "remedies" Wittgenstein found for his philosophical troubles, i.e. to clarify his approach to philosophical problems, and to do so we shall venture into his notebooks or 'diaries'. From the evidence presented in this section there should be no doubt that an important preliminary step for the task, a step not taken by many an interpreter of Wittgenstein, is to become sensitive to the fact that much of Wittgenstein's overall style consists of features incidental to his philosophical method – incidental features which Wittgenstein himself found undesirable. The secondary literature on Wittgenstein is already overcrowded with imaginative but misguided attempts to stress the methodological significance of Wittgenstein's overall style. The present study does not emphasize Wittgenstein's overall style as part and parcel of his philosophical method, and is not intended as another contribution to such literature.

The significance of TS 213 and the puzzle of MS 116

TS 213 is Wittgenstein's longest typescript (viii + 768 pages) and the closest he ever came to writing a stylistically conventional book. It consists of nineteen chapters divided into 140 sections and even comes complete with a table of contents.[85] Most of the remarks in TS 213 were culled from notebooks written between 1930 and 1932. Among the chapters in TS 213 is one entitled "Philosophy" in which Wittgenstein offers some general reflections on the nature of his approach. In the attempt to clarify Wittgenstein's approach to philosophy some of the remarks in that chapter will be examined, as well as remarks in other chapters of TS 213. But there is a problem surrounding this typescript: namely, to what extent can this text (and its manuscript sources) be relied on as an expression of Wittgenstein's 'later' approach to philosophy? This problem arises in the following manner. The so-called 'Blue and Brown Books', having been dictated between 1933 and 1935 (and a revision of the 'Brown Book' undertaken at the end of August 1936), postdate the main text[86] of TS 213. Rush Rhees in his Preface to *The Blue and Brown Books* has claimed that, during the period of their composition, "Philosophy was a method of investigation, for Wittgenstein, but his conception of the method was changing."[87] If, as Rhees contends, Wittgenstein's philosophical method changed between 1933 and 1936, it would seem that TS 213, the main text of which was originally written between 1930 and 1932, should *not* be relied on as an expression of Wittgenstein's 'later' approach to philosophy. This is reinforced by the sub-title given *The Blue and Brown Books* by its editors, for, if these texts were "Preliminary studies for the *Philosophical Investigations*",[88] material written prior to this period of alleged methodological transformation and preliminary study should be quite far removed (methodologically) from Wittgenstein's 'later' thinking as exemplified in *Philosophical Investigations*. The relative insigificance of TS 213 as an expression of Wittgenstein's later approach to philosophy is also indirectly suggested by the fact that it has never been published. In its place we have been offered Rush Rhees' attempt to carry out a definitive revision of TS 213 as outlined by Wittgenstein in MSS 114, 115 and 140.[89] In the present section it will be argued that, quite to the contrary, TS 213 should be taken as a reliable expression of Wittgenstein's 'later' approach to philosophy. It will be demonstrated that this typescript, far from having been left by the wayside, played a significant role in the drafting of *Philosophical Investigations*, for, when Wittgenstein gave up trying to write a stylistically conventional book and decided to settle for an "album of remarks" (as documented in the previous section), one of the first and primary texts to which he turned as a source of "remarks" was TS 213. We shall find that Wittgenstein was in fact still working with the text of TS 213 even after the 'Blue and Brown Books period'. However, to demonstrate this it will be necessary to clear up the puzzle of MS 116.

MS 116 has several distinguishing features. One is that it seems to consist of 'parts' which were written at different points during Wittgenstein's career. Unfortunately, another distinguishing feature of MS 116 is that Wittgenstein only dated the last of its apparent 'parts' (May 1945). The dating of the first 315 pages is uncertain. A third distinguishing feature, and one which may shed light on the significance of TS 213, is that the first 135 pages of MS 116 clearly consist of selections (with some revision) from TS

213. If these 135 pages were written after the 1936 *Umarbeitung* (revision) of the 'Brown Book', found in MS 115,[90] and during the time when Wittgenstein was actually drafting *Philosophical Investigations* (culminating in the 1937 or 1938 typescript, TS 220, of the pre-war version of *PI* part I), then TS 213 would be significantly linked to the *Investigations*.

In his account of MS 116 published in 1969, Professor G. H. von Wright describes its early passages as follows:

> In 116 – the largest volume in the series – three parts can be distinguished. The first (pp. 1–265) is best described as another effort of Wittgenstein's to compose a book, stating his position. (Within this first part of 116 one can distinguish two subparts of roughly equal length, the second beginning on page 135.) It begins as a revision of material in the early portions of 213 (the Big Typescript), but becomes more and more unlike 213, moving, so to speak, in the direction of the *Investigations*.[91]

With respect to the dating of the early passages of MS 116, von Wright speculated,

> The manuscript volume 116 was bought in Bergen, Norway. This is a strong indication that the earliest entries in the volume cannot have been made before some time in the summer of 1936. It is a plausible conjecture that the whole of the first part of the volume was written in 1936, and before the end of August, when Wittgenstein began writing (in 115) the revision of the *Brown Book* which he called *"Philosophische Untersuchungen"*. There are no dates, however, in the first part of 116.[92]

The view expressed in the above passages is that the first 265 pages of MS 116 were written in the summer of 1936. This view rests on two pillars: one is a bit of concrete evidence, and the other seems to be an implicit assumption about the contents of MS 116. The bit of concrete evidence is that the notebook (MS 116) was purchased in Norway. Since Wittgenstein is known to have stayed in Norway from August 1936 to mid-December 1937,[93] it is likely that the notebook was purchased during this lengthy stay and therefore the remarks in it do not predate the summer of 1936. The second pillar seems to be the implicit assumption that, owing to its affinity to TS 213, the first part of MS 116 must have been written before the end of August, when Wittgenstein started his *Umarbeitung* of the 'Brown Book' – as if TS 213 represented an earlier way of thinking different from the approach to philosophy Wittgenstein was developing in the 'Brown Book' and immediately thereafter in the pre-war version of *Philosophical Investigations*. Here a quite opposite line will be taken. Instead of assuming the philosophical anteriority and relative insignificance of TS 213 for the approach to philosophy we find in the *Investigations* and on the basis of this assumption dating the 'first part' of MS 116 to a period before the 'Brown Book' revision (and the subsequent drafting of *Philosophical Investigations*), an attempt will be made to date the 'first part' of MS 116 on independent grounds and from this come to a conclusion about the relative significance of TS 213 in the drafting of the *Investigations* and in general for Wittgenstein's later approach to philosophy.

There are two primary problems which arise as a result of the view that the first 265 pages of MS 116 were written in Norway in the summer of 1936 and prior to the end of August, when Wittgenstein wrote his *Umarbeitung* of the 'Brown Book'. First, this dating is contradicted by the fact that many of the remarks in pp. 136–265 of MS 116 are drawn from and based on remarks originally written in other manuscripts (MSS 120 and 158) between November 1937 and April 1938.[94] Thus, these pages must have been written during and/or after late 1937 to 1938. This finding, however, is not very significant for our purposes, since the pages which have a crucial bearing on TS 213 are pp. 1–135. It is still quite plausible that the first 135 pages of MS 116 (the pages obviously derived from TS 213) were written in August 1936, even though pp. 136–265 were written more than a year later.

Anthony Kenny, who translated *Philosophische Grammatik*, has raised a second primary problem with dating the first 265 pages of MS 116 to August 1936. In an article on the relationship between TS 213 and *Philosophical Grammar*, Kenny posed the following problem:

> Volume XII [MS 116] is extremely difficult to fit into the history of the revision of the Big Typescript [TS 213]. Both von Wright and Rhees believe that it is substantially later than the *Zweite Umarbeitung* [MS 140] (cf. *PG*, 211).[95] The reader who approaches Volume XII [MS 116] in this belief is astonished to find that the revision it contains is, at least at the beginning, very much closer to the original text of the Big Typescript [TS 213] than are either of the earlier revisions. This fact alone, if the accepted chronology is correct, surely casts doubt on any claim of the *Zweite Umarbeitung* [MS 140] to be *the* final revision of the typescript: it means that *after* the second revision Wittgenstein came to the conclusion that his book would do better to stick closer to the original text of the typescript.[96]

Kenny also drew the further conclusion that

> I am not competent to settle this difficult question about the chronology of Wittgenstein's manuscripts. But however it is resolved,

the existence of Volume XII [MS 116] must surely support the contention that the most prudent editorial policy would have been to print the original Big Typescript [TS 213] as it stood rather than to seek for a definitive revision of it.[97]

The problem Kenny has raised is simply this: if the view of Rhees and von Wright (that the MS 116 revision of TS 213 was written in summer 1936) is correct, then the revision (MSS 114, 115 and 140) published by Rhees as part I of *Philosophical Grammar* is not definitive.[98] Kenny's conclusion is that it would have been wiser had Rhees published TS 213 instead of seeking (and apparently failing to find) a definitive revision of it.

Let us now try to resolve the question of the chronology of MS 116, and in so doing shed light on the significance of TS 213. One by-product of resolving this question will be the finding that, although Kenny's argument is unsound, the spirit of his general conclusion is correct – that it was indeed imprudent to publish *Philosophical Grammar* instead of TS 213.

First, however, it should be pointed out that the official speculation about the date of MS 116, pp. 1–135 has been revised. In a more recent comment on MS 116 von Wright argues,

> It may seem intrinsically unlikely that Wittgenstein had written the first section of MS 116 *after* having written the beginning of the *Investigations* in the autumn of 1936. Nor is there much reason to believe that he wrote it simultaneously with either the revision of the *Brown Book* or the beginning of the *Investigations*. These facts speak in favour of the view that Wittgenstein began writing in MS 116 *before* going to live in Norway in 1936. It would follow that he must have acquired the book in Norway on some previous visit. (It is improbable that he had ordered the book or that it was sent to him from Norway.) Since he called it "Band XII" and the manuscript book in which he was writing in the beginning of 1934 was "Band XI" (MS 115), it is reasonable to assume that the earliest date of the writings in MS 116 is 1934.[99]

Despite this speculation that MS 116 may date from as early as 1934, von Wright does not rule out the possibility that the first 135 pages were written at a later date, for he goes on to indicate that

> It is not known with certainty that Wittgenstein had visited Norway in the period between his return to Cambridge in 1929 and the year 1936. For this and other reasons one must, I think, keep open the possibility that Wittgenstein's revision, in MS 116, of the beginning of the "Big Typescript" (TS 213) was, after all, made in 1936 or 1937. If

this is the truth, the writings for the first part of MS 116 would thus be *later* than the writings for the first part of the early version of the *Investigations*. It is a fact that Wittgenstein later selected forty-seven remarks (and a few "Randbemerkungen") from pages 1–135 of MS 116 to be included in the final version of Part I of his great work.[100]

In the new account of MS 116 only one of the supporting 'pillars' from the earlier view seems to have remained intact. Apparently still operative is the assumption that, owing to its content, the revision of TS 213 found in MS 116 probably was *not* written during or after work on the 'Brown Book' *Umarbeitung* and the beginning of the *Investigations*. This assumption supports the view that the first 135 pages of MS 116 were written prior to the end of August 1936 (the month Wittgenstein went to Norway). The assumption of the philosophical anteriority of the revision of TS 213 found in MS 116 is also apparent in the way the issue of the dating of pp. 1–135 of the manuscript is raised. Prior to the above-quoted passages von Wright wrote,

> In manuscripts from 1933 and 1934 Wittgenstein revised parts of the content of TS 213. His efforts were evidently aimed at the composition of a work representing his position in philosophy at that time. These efforts he abandoned – under the influence, it seems, of the new developments of his thoughts which first manifested themselves in the *Blue Book* and then were continued in the *Brown Book*. Pages 1–135 of MS 116 were perhaps a last effort to revise the earlier work. When was this revision undertaken?[101]

The question itself seems to have been conceived in such a way as to predetermine the conclusion that the first 135 pages of MS 116 must have been written before the "new developments" if not of the 'Blue Book' then surely of the 'Brown Book' and the early version of *Philosophical Investigations*.

The other pillar which supported the previous official dating (1936) of MS 116, however, has not remained intact. The concrete evidence that the notebook (MS 116) was purchased in Norway and that Wittgenstein lived in Norway from August 1936 to December 1937 has been set aside in favour of the assumption that Wittgenstein made an earlier trip to Norway that we do not know about. Now the reasoning seems to be that, since Wittgenstein numbered MSS 115 and 116 as consecutive volumes (XI and XII respectively), the early pages of MS 116 must have been written around or shortly after the entries in the preceding volume (MS 115). The problem with this reasoning is of course, as has previously been pointed out (cf. n. 90), that MS 115 is itself a conglomerate of parts. By choosing to date pp. 1–135 of MS 116 to 1934, von Wright has arbitrarily linked MS 116 to the first part (1933–4) of MS 115 and not to the second part. As we know, the second part of MS 115 is the 1936 *Umarbeitung* of the 'Brown Book'. Von Wright, then, has dated MS 116, pp. 1–135, not to the period immediately following the preceding volume (MS 115) *as a whole*, but rather to the period immediately following the *first part* of MS 115. This dating seems to rest indirectly on the assumption that the MS 116 revision of TS 213 must have been written *prior* to the 'Brown Book' *Umarbeitung* in MS 115. In effect, then, the new dating of MS 116, pp. 1–135, rests rather precariously on only *one* pillar – namely, the assumption about the philosophical anteriority of their content.

Just why one of the pillars of the earlier view was discarded is not very clear, unless it was assumed that Wittgenstein would not have had enough time to write 135 pages of revision (in MS 116) between his arrival in Norway in August 1936 and commencing the 'Brown Book' *Umarbeitung* at the end of the month. What is clear, however, is that the new dating of MS 116 seems to avoid the problem which Kenny raised. Kenny's argument assumes the 1936 dating of the first 135 pages of MS 116. But since these pages have now been redated, albeit tentatively, roughly to the period (1933–4) of the other revisions (MSS 114, 115 and 140) of TS 213, it would appear that the revision of TS 213 which we find in MS 116 has no more claim to being a subsequent and more definitive revision than that (MSS 114, 115 and 140) published as part I of *Philosophical Grammar*.

As we shall now see, the 1936 dating of MS 116, pp. 1–135, initially offered by Rhees and von Wright is in fact erroneous, and thus Kenny's argument, which assumes this dating, is unsound. However, the revised dating (1934) proposed by von Wright is not right either. Rather, von Wright's initial intuitions and the possibility which he has kept open even in his more recent speculations come closer to the truth. Wittgenstein wrote pp. 1–135 of MS 116 not two years prior to 1936, but in 1937 during his stay in Norway. Consequently, although Kenny's argument is unsound, his general conclusion is correct: MSS 114, 115 and 140 are not a definitive revision of the TS 213 material (there being in fact a much later revision) and it was unfortunate that Rhees compiled *Philosophical Grammar* for publication instead of publishing TS 213.[102]

The independent evidence we have for dating MS 116, pp. 1–135, to the period of Wittgenstein's stay in Norway from August 1936 to December 1937 is straightforward and conclusive. A careful examination of the remarks in these pages reveals that, although most of these remarks are derived from TS 213, they are interspersed with remarks originating in a different manuscript source – MS 119.[103] We know from Wittgenstein's own entry dates that MS 119 was written between 24 September and 19 November 1937. Thus, just as the dating of pp. 136–265 of MS 116 was revised because of the discovery that they draw on MS 120 (the date of which we know), so we now must revise the dating of pp. 1–135 because they clearly draw on MS 119 (the date of which we also know). Consequently, the first 135 pages of MS 116 (which contain the revision of TS 213) must date from autumn 1937 *or later*.

There is, however, further concrete evidence which allows us to fix more precisely the date of the MS 116 revision of TS 213. The evidence is twofold. The first bit of supplementary evidence brings into play yet another manuscript. In the first 135 pages of MS 116 we find Wittgenstein selecting and revising remarks from TS 213. The remarks selected (and revised) follow quite precisely the order in which they appear in TS 213; going from passages on p. 1 of TS 213 straight through to a revision of a remark on p. 196 of the same typescript. Although Wittgenstein seems then to have put aside TS 213, he subsequently (in another manuscript) returned to it and *continued* the process of selection and revision initiated in MS 116. In MS 117, pp. 127–48, Wittgenstein picked up where he had left off in MS 116; selecting and revising in their original order remarks from roughly p. 210 to p. 247 of TS 213. He even in several instances simply indicates a selection from TS 213 by giving the page and paragraph numbers.[104] Von Wright has indicated that the probable date of MS 117, pp. 127–48, is the second half of 1938. Since these pages *continue* the process of selection and revision we find in MS 116, pp. 1–135, we can conclude that that part of MS 116 was written *before* the second half of 1938. It would seem, then, that the MS 116 revision of TS 213 was carried out some time between autumn 1937 (MS 119) and the second half of 1938 (MS 117, pp. 127–48). This range, however, is somewhat tentative, because we do not know for certain the date of MS 117, pp. 127–48.

A second bit of supplementary evidence allows us to date MS 116, pp. 1–135, with both more precision and more certainty. It has already been observed that some remarks in these pages are derived from MS 119 and so pp. 1–135 of MS 116 must have been written during or after autumn 1937. However, what if in MS 119 there were explicit references to the activity carried out in the first 135 pages of MS 116 – namely, the activity of selecting and revising remarks from TS 213? Such a finding would strongly suggest that in MS 116 Wittgenstein was selecting and revising remarks from TS 213 during the *same* period as he was keeping a running 'diary' of remarks in MS 119 – occasionally drawing remarks from this 'diary' and entering them along with the selections and revisions in MS 116.[105] This in fact is what we find. It will be recalled from the previous section that around autumn 1937 Wittgenstein seems to have come to the conclusion that he was unable to write a stylistically conventional book and so would have to confine himself to an "album of remarks". In connection with the issue of *when* Wittgenstein resigned himself to offering an "album of remarks" the following passage was cited:

My difficulty is now to know what assortment or amount of my remarks is still *palatable*.

Because what is unpalatable is also not useful. My judgement wavers though and I don't know where the line is to be drawn.

This remark was written in MS 119 on 3 October 1937. But *where* did Wittgenstein now turn to sort out useful remarks for his "album"? He tells us later in MS 119, when he informs us, "I have set about looking at my old typescript and separating the wheat from the chaff, if it would be purely separated! What is useful, what isn't useful?! It is difficult to say." The next day he wrote, "While checking [*prüfen*] my old remarks, it seems to me as if I should set up the household effects in some flat whilst I move things into a rubbish heap and laboriously check them and try to clean up." These references to the activity of "checking my old remarks" and "separating the wheat from the chaff" in his old typescript clearly describe what is going on in the first 135 pages of MS 116, which thus not only draw remarks from MS 119 but must have been written during the same period. The selection and revision of remarks from TS 213 which we find in MS 116, pp. 1–135, can therefore be precisely dated to autumn 1937, during Wittgenstein's stay in Norway.[106]

It is quite obvious, then, that *after* the *Umarbeitung* of the 'Brown Book' and right in the middle of the period between late 1936, when Wittgenstein presumably began writing *Philosophical Investigations* (in the missing MS 142), and 1938, when he made the typescript (TS 220) of part I of the prewar version of the *Investigations*, Wittgenstein was still working with TS 213 and considered it a valuable source of remarks. It is also clear, though, that the selecting and revising of remarks from TS 213 which took place in 1937 and 1938 (MSS 116 and 117) did not represent an attempt to salvage TS 213 itself *as a book*. Rather, having given up his attempts to write a stylistically conventional book (examples of which would be TS 213, the 'Brown Book' *Umarbeitung* and perhaps even MS 142[107]), Wittgenstein was culling out (and touching up) remarks some of which might (and did) go into an "album of remarks" (*Philosophical Investigations*).[108] This would explain what Kenny has puzzled over: namely, why the ordering of remarks in MS 116, pp. 1–135, is much closer to the original text of TS 213 than are the earlier revisions in MSS 114, 115 and 140. Since in MS 116 Wittgenstein was just selecting out and revising *useful* remarks from TS 213, it comes as no surprise that there is virtually no rearrangement of the TS 213 material.[109]

Clearing up the puzzle of MS 116 has shown that Wittgenstein was still selecting and revising remarks from TS 213 in 1937 and, given MS 117, even into 1938. The fact that he was still actively working with TS 213 during the period in which he was drafting *Philosophical Investigations* clearly suggests that TS 213 might be taken as a relatively reliable expression of his 'later' approach to philosophy. More light, however, needs to be shed on the extent and the nature of TS 213's contribution to the *Investigations*.

Aside from a few remarks at the very beginning of the *Investigations* (e.g. §§3–4) and other sundry remarks scattered here and there in the work, the remarks (or parts of remarks) which came unaltered from TS 213 fall into two major blocks of the text we now know as *Philosophical Investigations*. One of these blocks, curiously enough, is the stretch of text between (roughly) §400 and §600. Here there are at least forty remarks (or parts of remarks) which have come (in many cases via intermediate manuscripts) *unaltered* from TS 213.[110] This is somewhat odd, because this major overlap of texts is not between TS 213 and the *pre-war* version of the *Investigations*, which reached only as far as, roughly, what we now know as §190, but rather between TS 213 and the final, *post-war* version. This significant incorporation of TS 213 material into the *post-war* version of the *Investigations* clearly suggests that TS 213 (the sources for which span the years 1930–2) was not left by the wayside, but served (whether indirectly or not) as a valuable pool of remarks for Wittgenstein's later (even post-war) thinking.

There is, however, from the point of view of the present study, a more significant block of material in *Philosophical Investigations* which is strongly indebted to TS 213 and its manuscript sources. For any attempt to shed light on Wittgenstein's philosophical method or later approach to philosophy, the prime philosophical 'real estate' in the *Investigations* is the block of remarks roughly comprising §§87–133, in which Wittgenstein offers us general reflections on his approach to philosophy. The dramatic correspondences between this material and TS 213 (with its manuscript sources) are worth presenting more explicitly, and are set out in table 1.1.

One needs only a quick glance at the content of the relevant passages in *Philosophical Investigations* to see that they are key expressions of Wittgenstein's 'later' approach to philosophy. The table obviously shows us that the vast majority of these remarks were originally written between 1930 and 1932. There can be little doubt that TS 213 not only was an important general source of remarks incorporated into Wittgenstein's later writings, but also, more specifically, served as a significant source of remarks expressing his 'new' approach to philosophy – remarks which he included unaltered in his master work.

Although this evidence gives us a better idea of the *nature* of TS 213's contribution to *Philosophical Investigations*, it does not give a full appreciation of the *extent* of this contribution. The reason for this is that this evidence only concerns *unaltered* remarks which have found their way from TS 213 into the *Investigations*. There is, however, an abundance of remarks from TS 213, far more numerous than those already considered,

Table 1.1   Correspondences between *PI* §§87–133 and TS 213

PI[111]		Source in TS 213[112] (page/chapter)		Original source	
§87	(up to 2nd dash)	p. 256		MS 112	(1931)
§88	(most of para 3)	back of pp. 255–6		TS 213	
§108	(paras 3–4)	p. 71		MS 110	(1930–1)
§111	(after dash)	p. 412		MS 110	(1930–1)
§116	(para 2)	p. 412	("Philosophy")	MS 110	(1930–1)
§118	(minus last sentence)	p. 411		MS 153b/112	(1931)
§119		p. 425		MS ?	(1930–2)
§120		p. 72		MS 110	(1930–1)
§122	(minus first sentence)	p. 417		MS ?	(1930–2)
§123		p. 421		MS 112	(1931)
§124		pp. 417–18		MS 110	(1930–1)
§126		pp. 418–19	("Philosophy")	partly MS 110	
§127		p. 415		MS ?	(1930–2)
§128		p. 419		MS 110	(1930–1)
§129		p. 419		MSS 110, 112/153b	(1930–1)
§132		back of pp. 256–7		TS 213	
§133	(para 3)	p. 431 ("Philosophy")		MS 112	(1931)

which did not make it into *Philosophical Investigations* unaltered but nevertheless passed into the *Investigations* by way of revision. To get a better idea of the proportions of this indirect contribution, it is useful to appeal to a table of data (reprinted here as table 1.2) which Professor von Wright has compiled on the manuscript sources for *Philosophical Investigations*.[113]

Table 1.2, as von Wright explains in his comments about it, represents a tally of remarks in *Philosophical Investigations* as they are distributed over their *most recent* manuscript sources. It should *not*, therefore, be interpreted as an indication of when and in which manuscripts the remarks in the *Investigations* were *originally* written. As can readily be seen, if one did not exercise caution in interpreting the table, one might gain the false impression that the 'Blue and Brown Books period' (1933–6) was when Wittgenstein's 'later' thinking really originated and that virtually nothing in the *Investigations* stems from the years 1930–2.[114] 2.The table does, however, shed some light on the extent to which TS 213 contributed indirectly to *Philosophical Investigations*. Table 1.3 is a ranking, on the basis of von Wright's figures, of the manuscripts which contributed the most remarks (including *Randbemerkungen*) to the *Investigations*.

Table 1.2 Most recent manuscript sources of remarks in *Philosophical Investigations*

MS	Year of writing	No. of *Bemerkungen* (or parts of them) selected from source	No. of *Randbemerkungen* (or parts of them) selected from source
108	1930	2	
109	1930–1	1	
110	1931	8	
112	1931	5	
153a	1931	1	
114	1933–4	38	4
115 (1)	1933–4	79	2
110	1933–4	1	
116 (1)	1934? (1937?)	47	5
115 (2)	1936	26	
152	1936	34	
157a	1937	11	
157b	1937	13	
117	1937	14	
119	1937	10	
121	1937–8	1	
162b	1939–40	4	
163	1941	3	
116 (2)	1938–44	46	
116 (3)	1944?	28	1
124	1944	16	
127	1944	1	
128	1944	3	
180a	c.1945		1
129	1944–5	201	3
130	1945?	15	
116 (4)	1945	29	
Total		637	16

Bemerkungen = remarks
Randbemerkungen = marginal notes

Some Preliminary Issues

Table 1.3 Ranking of major sources in table 1.2

MS	Number of remarks
129	204
115 (1)	81
116 (1)	52
116 (2)	46
114	42

Von Wright's data indicate that, next to the sizable contribution of MS 129, the most significant contribution to *Philosophical Investigations* came from MS 115 (1) – part of Wittgenstein's 1933–4 revision of TS 213. Next comes MS 116 (1), which we have identified as Wittgenstein's 1937 revision of TS 213 material. Fourth comes MS 116 (2), which, although not a revision of TS 213, was apparently written immediately following the revision of TS 213 undertaken in the first part of MS 116 (see n. 103). And, finally, the fifth most significant contribution to the *Investigations* came from MS 114 – another part of the 1933–4 revision of TS 213. If one also adds the remarks from Wittgenstein's MS 117 revision of TS 213 (from which at least fourteen remarks went into the *Investigations*), TS 213's indirect contribution to *Philosophical Investigations* was obviously quite extensive.[115]

The number of remarks in TS 213 which found their way into *Philosophical Investigations*, whether unaltered or revised, far exceeds the number of remarks which the *Investigations* shares with the so-called 'Blue and Brown Books'. Actually, if one does not include the 1936 *Umarbeitung* of the 'Brown Book' (new material from which constitutes much of §§151–88 of the *Investigations*[116]), what has been widely circulated in English as *The Blue and Brown Books* contributed virtually nothing to the *Investigations*. Thus, based solely on the number of remarks which the texts have in common with *Philosophical Investigations*, TS 213 has a far stronger claim to the title "Preliminary study for the *Philosophical Investigations*" than *The Blue and Brown Books* has.

But what then is one to make of the widely held view that Wittgenstein's approach to philosophy underwent a transformation during the 'Blue and Brown Books period' (1933–6)? The evidence presented above with regard to the significance of TS 213, which with its manuscript sources served (whether indirectly or not) as a major general source of remarks for Wittgenstein's "album" (*Philosophical Investigations*), suggests that the 'transformations' in Wittgenstein's thinking between 1933 and 1936 were not as sweeping or dramatic as one might think. Furthermore, since

Wittgenstein drew to a great extent (whether indirectly or not) from TS 213 (and its manuscript sources between 1930 and 1932) for his general remarks in *PI* §§87–133 about his philosophical method, what transformations did take place between 1933 and 1936 do not seem to have been to any significant extent changes in his overall approach to philosophy. This is *not* to suggest that there were *no* 'transformations' or 'new developments' between 1933 and 1936; rather, what transformations there were do not seem to have been fundamentally methodological shifts.

Thus, in place of Rhees' view that during the 'Blue and Brown Books period' "Philosophy was a method of investigation, for Wittgenstein, but his conception of the method was changing" (see n. 87), the evidence suggests the following scenario. In 1929–30 Wittgenstein, at roughly the age of forty, took up writing philosophy again after a hiatus of nearly a decade, *because* he had adopted in broad outline his 'later' approach to philosophy. Only if this were the case could his manuscripts of 1930–2 have served as such a major source of general remarks on the nature of philosophy for his later work (*Philosophical Investigations*). The period 1933–6, or for that matter 1930–2, was not so much a time of transformation in his overall approach to philosophy as a protracted period of applying his new approach to the full range of issues – an activity which, in fact, preoccupied Wittgenstein for the last twenty years of his life.[117]

Consistent with the above scenario are the second-hand reports that during the early thirties Wittgenstein claimed he had found a 'new method' or 'new way of thinking'.[118] We have already seen that such second-hand reports are supported by Wittgenstein's remarks in his own notebooks from as early as 1931.[119] An early dating for the emergence of Wittgenstein's 'new method' is further reinforced by the fact that Wittgenstein singled out his conversations with Frank Ramsey during the last two years of Ramsey's life (Ramsey died on 19 January 1930) as being greatly responsible for the shift to the new way of thinking one finds in the *Investigations*.[120]

It would be a mistake to claim that there were *no* 'new developments' in Wittgenstein's writings during the early and middle thirties, but since the evidence presented above suggests that his 'later' approach to philosophy was, at least in broad outline, in place by the early thirties, one would expect the 'new developments' or 'transformations' to be of three sorts: (1) doctrinal (i.e. shifts in Wittgenstein's accounts of specific concepts such as 'pain' and 'thinking'), (2) terminological, and (3) stylistic (some of which shifts have already been discussed). The doctrinal and terminological shifts are to be expected because, although Wittgenstein's 'later' approach to philosophy was largely in place by the early thirties, there no doubt remained during the early and middle thirties quite a bit of 'old' terminological and doctrinal baggage that he had not yet (to his satisfaction) worked his way through. Wittgenstein himself was well aware that he was carrying this sort of baggage, for during this period (c. 1932-4) he noted, "To my thinking, as with any man's, cling the shrivelled remains of my former (dead) thoughts."[121]

Wittgenstein's struggle to work his way free of the doctrinal and terminological baggage of his 'old' thinking, however, was not restricted to the early and middle 1930s. Over ten years later (1944 or later) Wittgenstein remarked, "It will be difficult to follow my presentation: because it says something new, but to which still cling the egg-shells of the old."[122] Similarly, in summer 1946 he indicated with respect to a remark he had just written, "To this remark, as to many others, cling the egg-shells of former views."[123] And, finally, even as late as autumn 1947, Wittgenstein noted, "To any thinking cling the egg-shells of its origin. One recognizes in it *what* you struggled with in growing up. Which views are those of your making: from which you have had to extricate yourself."[124]

One can admit (and Wittgenstein himself seems to have been well aware) that there are doctrinal and terminological "egg-shells" still lying about not only in the notebooks of the early thirties, but even perhaps in notebooks written in the forties. However it does not follow from this that Wittgenstein's 'later' *Denkweise*, at least in broad outline, had not yet been formulated by the early thirties.

The above demonstration of the significance of TS 213 (and its manuscript sources of 1930-2) for, in particular, Wittgenstein's 'later' notion of philosophy as formulated in *PI* §§87-133 suggests that he had indeed adopted his 'later' *Denkweise* by the early thirties. Thus, TS 213 and its manuscript sources can with some assurance be taken as representative of Wittgenstein's 'later' approach to philosophy.

However, these preliminary deliberations about the chronology of Wittgenstein's thinking, though they justify using TS 213 as a source of remarks representative of his 'later' approach, and though they shed significant light on the history of his philosophical writings, are no substitute for a concrete examination of the content of the writings themselves. Addressing this task will allow us to gain more genuine insight into the emergence of Wittgenstein's later approach to philosophy.

2
Metalogic and the Domain of Logic: the Shift to Ordinary Language

If, as suggested in the last section of chapter 1, Wittgenstein took up writing philosophy again in 1929–30 *because* he had adopted at least in broad outline a new *Denkweise*, then the task of the present and following chapters would seem to be a futile one. It would seem highly unlikely that one could with any assurance of accuracy delineate some of the themes involved in the emergence of Wittgenstein's later approach to philosophy if that approach emerged during the 'lost decade' between the *Tractatus* and the manuscripts of 1929–30. However, although there is no record of Wittgenstein's philosophical deliberations *during* the 'lost decade', there is an objective and reliable basis for reconstructing at least some of the themes that were operative in the shift to his later *Denkweise*. The objective basis is Wittgenstein's post-1929 notebooks, and in particular his own references in these notebooks to developments in his thinking and factors which influenced them.

The main strategy of the present and following chapters will not be that which is most commonly found in the secondary literature on Wittgenstein: namely, first spinning an elaborate tale about the main tenets of the *Tractatus*, and then by way of contrast offering an interpretation of *Philosophical Investigations* along with a running commentary on the similarities and differences between the two works. Although this strategy is basically a sound one, and one which even seems to have had Wittgenstein's endorsement, since he at one point (1943–4) entertained the idea of publishing the *Tractatus* and the *Investigations* together so that his new thoughts could be seen "in the right light",[125] this will not be the strategy adopted here. Instead, there will be an appeal primarily to Wittgenstein's remarks in his post-1929 notebooks that point out what he was reacting to in his turn to a new *Denkweise*. Thus, instead of approaching his later thoughts from the prior standpoint of an interpretation of the *Tractatus*, the strategy will be to let Wittgenstein tell us what views he was reacting to and why. Consequently it will be of primary interest to uncover some (though by no means all) of the views *Wittgenstein claims* he was reacting to; and of only secondary interest to establish that a view to which he was reacting was a view he encountered in the thoughts of others (whether through books or conversation), or a view he himself held during the 'lost decade' but of which we have no record, or a view that is obviously present in the *Tractatus* (though there is little that is obvious in the *Tractatus*), or perhaps even a view that he may have held before the *Tractatus*. Therefore the main points to be made in the following chapters will rest primarily on what *Wittgenstein* has to say about the emergence of his later *Denkweise*, and not on speculations about and interpretations of works which lie outside the corpus of his later writings. This is not to say that no reference will be made to such works (for instance, the *Tractatus* or the works of some of his contemporaries), but rather to say that the main points to be made will not stand or fall on the basis of such references and the interpretation of material lying outside our central corpus.

The term 'metalogic' is a recurrent one in Wittgenstein's later writings. An examination of what he meant by it sheds some light on the emergence of his later thinking.

The term itself has achieved some currency in contemporary philosophy. One finds, for example, chapters on "metalogic" in recent and fairly widely used texts on symbolic logic.[126] The word has come to be used to refer to what might be called 'second-order' reflection *about* a system of logical rules; standard examples would be attempts to offer proofs of the soundness and completeness of a particular system of logical rules.

However, virtually nothing has been written about what *Wittgenstein* may have meant by 'metalogic' and what role this idea played in the emergence of his later thinking. It is quite understandable that little has been said about Wittgenstein's use of the term, since it occurs in only a few isolated and for the most part inconspicuous remarks in his published 'works'.[127] The chances are that anyone who uses the term 'metalogic' in a discussion of Wittgenstein's later philosophy either has had some exposure to his notebooks, or has resorted to the term more or less by accident, with little grasp of its significance for Wittgenstein. As it so happens, in the secondary literature on Wittgenstein we have an example of each of these two cases – though they are equally unenlightening and insignificant.

Hans Lenk in his book *Metalogik und Sprachanalyse* uses the term 'metalogic' (somewhat conventionally) to refer to the issue of whether and by which means a "logical system of rules can be distinguished *as logical* or be proven free of doubt".[128] Although Lenk discusses Wittgenstein's later philosophy at great length, he seems totally oblivious both to the sense of the term 'metalogic' for Wittgenstein and even to the fact that Wittgenstein used it.

Rush Rhees, on the other hand, is one of the executors of Wittgenstein's literary estate, so, when in his 1958 Preface to *The Blue and Brown Books* he mentions 'metalogic' in the context of a discussion of Wittgenstein's later philosophy, it may be expected that he is familiar with the term from Wittgenstein's notebooks. However, it seems that he may not have had a chance to study carefully the content of those notebooks at the time that he wrote the Preface. Having introduced for discussion the notions of "seeing something as something" and "recognizing something as language", Rhees asks the question, "But why *have* people wanted to speak of 'meta-logic' in this connection, for instance?"[129] Rhees goes on to suggest that in the 'Brown Book' Wittgenstein does something to explain why people want to speak of 'metalogic'. However Rhees does not venture to tell us which people speak of 'metalogic', what they mean by the term, or what Wittgenstein's explanation is of why people (allegedly) use the term. Actually the term does not even occur in *The Blue and Brown Books*; nor is it used in any of Wittgenstein's other 'works' published by 1958. But it does frequently occur in manuscripts which Wittgenstein wrote during and immediately prior to the so-called 'Blue and Brown Books period'; and obviously Rhees had been perusing the *Nachlaß* and had sensed that there must be something significant about the term.

Yes, the notion of 'metalogic' is significant – one need only browse through some of the manuscripts of the early and middle thirties to sense that.[130] But, no, Wittgenstein was not so much trying to explain why "people" have wanted to speak of 'metalogic' as using the term to criticize *himself*. In a manuscript written in autumn 1937 Wittgenstein jotted down the following confession: "I was for a long time tempted to believe that '*to understand*' [*verstehen*] is a *metalogical* word."[131] So Wittgenstein *himself* was inclined to speak of metalogic. The aim of the present chapter is to uncover both in what sense he once considered certain concepts to be 'metalogical' and in what manner his abandonment of his earlier view is tied in with the emergence of his new *Denkweise*.

First, however, a few words should be said about *when* Wittgenstein considered such concepts as 'understanding' (and, as we shall soon see, others such as 'meaning [*meinen*]') metalogical. Though the previously cited confession, which implicitly repudiates the view that 'understanding' is a metalogical concept, was written near the end of 1937 and it seems from Wittgenstein's remark in *Zettel* §284 that he later still considered it a worthwhile point, explicit evidence of his rejection of the view is to be found in his manuscripts from the very early thirties. In fact, *Zettel* §284 itself stems from around 1930–1. In its final form it reads as follows: "Of course the proposition 'I must understand the order before I can act on it' makes good sense: but not a metalogical sense."

A version of this remark appears in TS 213; and thus we find that it also crops up in Rhees' attempt to carry out a revision of TS 213 as roughly outlined by Wittgenstein in MSS 114, 115 and 140.[132] However, the remark was originally drafted not long after Wittgenstein's return to philosophy, for in late 1930 or early 1931 he had jotted down the following virtually identical remark: "So what then does the sentence 'I must understand the order before I can act on it' mean? For of course this sentence (saying this) makes sense. But certainly (however) again not a metalogical one."[133] A couple of pages earlier in MS 110 Wittgenstein had even more emphatically written, "As there is no metaphysics, there is no metalogic. The word 'to understand' [*verstehen*], the expression 'to understand a sentence", is likewise not metalogical, but rather an expression like *any* other of language."[134]

Although we have yet to delve into what Wittgenstein meant by 'metalogic', it is evident from the dating of some of his remarks on the subject that the "long-time" during which he was inclined to view 'understanding' as a metalogical concept must have been prior to the 1930s; perhaps during the 'lost decade' and/or during the *Tractatus* period (though Wittgenstein did not use the word 'metalogic' in the *Tractatus*).

Initially some light can be shed on what Wittgenstein meant by 'metalogic' simply by searching out what sorts of concepts he may have at one time been inclined to consider 'metalogical' – an appellation which he found it necessary to repudiate in his later writings. From the few passages already cited, it is clear that 'understanding' (*verstehen*) was one of these concepts. Another is the concept 'to mean' (*meinen*), for in MS 114 one finds Wittgenstein explicitly asserting that "The proposition 'I mean something . . .' is not metalogical."[135] Similarly, in MS 140 he wrote, "And 'understanding' and 'meaning' [*meinen*] are not metalogical concepts."[136] Yet a third candidate is the notion of (intentionally) depicting or copying (*abbilden*), since in TS 213 in his chapter "Intention and Depiction" ("*Intention und Abbildung*") Wittgenstein just as explicitly claimed that "Copying [*Abbilden*] is not a metalogical concept."[137] One finds that when Wittgenstein repudiates metalogic it is almost invariably with reference to and in the context of a discussion of what one might call 'psychological concepts': that is, concepts which on the surface of it seem in our language to serve the function of denoting mental (psychic) processes or states. And just as invariably, along with a repudiation of the view that such concepts are metalogical, one finds Wittgenstein repudiating the view that the meaning of such concepts solely consists in or rests on psychic phenomena that they might *seem* to denote.

For example, with respect to the concept 'intentional depiction or copying', the very heading of the section in which it is claimed that copying is not metalogical asserts that "The process of intentional depiction [*absichtlichen Abbildung*], depiction with the intention to copy, is not essentially a psychological or inner process. A process of manipulating signs on paper can accomplish the same thing."[138] Furthermore, the very first remarks in the section display Wittgenstein's concerns quite clearly:

> No psychological process can symbolize better than signs on paper.
> Nor can the psychological process accomplish more than the written signs on paper.
> Again and again one is under the temptation to want to explain a symbolic process by means of a peculiar psychological process; as if the psyche [*die Psyche*] can accomplish much more in this matter than the signs.
> ... The description of the psychological [*des Psychische*] must be something which can itself be used as a symbol.[139]

One finds Wittgenstein voicing similar concerns in the context of his repudiation of the view that 'understanding' and 'meaning' are metalogical concepts. In TS 213, after his claim that "there is no metalogic. The word 'to understand', the expression 'to understand a sentence', is likewise not metalogical ...", he chides,

> One regards understanding as the essential thing [*das Eigentliche*], signs as the inessential [*des Nebensächliche*]. – But in that case, why have the signs at all? – Only in order to make ourselves understood by others? But how is that possible? (But how does that take place?) – Here the sign is considered (viewed) as a drug which is to bring about in others the same stomach-aches (states) as I have.
> To the question "What do you mean?" must come the answer: "*p*"; and not "I mean that which I mean by '*p*'."[140]

What Wittgenstein seems to be struggling against here is the view that 'understanding' and 'meaning' are psychological phenomena that constitute what is most essential to language and lie in the psyche, as it were, behind the signs. In connection with this, right after the original formulation of the first of the two paragraphs cited above, Wittgenstein had mused, "In philosophy we are deceived by an illusion. But this (an) illusion is also something, and I must at some time place it completely clearly before my eyes, before I can say that it is only an illusion."[141] The sort of illusion Wittgenstein is concerned with here is fairly explicitly stated three pages earlier in the notebook: "'Being able to' [*Das Können*] and understanding are apparently described as states like toothache, and this is the false analogy under which I labour."[142]

Wittgenstein's struggle against the view that 'understanding' and 'meaning' are fundamentally psychological phenomena which lie in the psyche behind the signs is also reflected in remarks related to his previously cited repudiation of the view that the sentence "I must understand the order before I can act on it" makes 'metalogical' sense. This latter repudiation was cited from *Zettel* (§284), but was originally drafted in 1930–1 (see n. 133). The reader may perhaps recognize the sentence in question as the central concern of *PI* §505. This topical parallel between *Zettel* §284 and *PI* §505 is no coincidence, for in fact the remarks were placed adjacent to each other in Wittgenstein's chapter "Verstehen" in TS 213 and were orignally drafted on the same notebook page in 1930–1.[143] For that matter, virtually identical versions of the surrounding remarks in *Zettel* (§§283, 285, 286 and 287) and *Philosophical Investigations* (§§503, 504, 506 and 507) are to be found along with Wittgenstein's rejection of metalogic in chapter 1 of TS 213 and with few exceptions can be traced back to 1930–1 (MSS 108–10). From this network of interrelated remarks, it is again fairly clear that Wittgenstein's rejection of metalogic, in this case his rejection of the view that 'understanding an order' is metalogical, is coupled with a rejection of the view that 'understanding' (or 'meaning') is to be taken as a psychological phenomenon lying, as it were, 'behind' language. *PI* §§503–4, for instance, as they are found coupled with the rejection of metalogic in TS 213, read,

If I give anyone an order I feel it to be *quite enough* to give him signs. And I would never say: this is only words, and I have got to get behind the words. Equally, when I have asked someone something and he gives me an answer (i.e. a sign) I am content – that was exactly what I expected – and I don't raise the objection: but that's a mere answer. It is clear that nothing else could be expected and that the answer presupposes the use of language //a language// //specific language game//. As everything that is to be said //we could say//.

But if you say: "How am I to know what he means, when I see nothing but the signs he gives?" then I say: "How is *he* to know what he means, when he has nothing but the signs either?"[144]

Several pages later in TS 213, a similar point is made in a passage which is the earliest formulation of what we now know as *Zettel* §287. Wittgenstein suggests that, in a case where one 'suddenly understands an order' (with the proper intonation, whereas it had not made sense before), "I did not now have further to grasp a *sense* [*Sinn*] (something *outside* the sentence, hence something ethereal) but the familiar sound of English words perfectly suffices me."[145] Here again, along with his rejection of metalogic, Wittgenstein seems to be rejecting the view that 'understanding an order' is the grasping of something ethereal which lies behind the signs.

Although Wittgenstein does not explicitly use the term 'metalogic' (and repudiate it by name) in the context of a discussion of every 'psychological' concept he deals with in his later writings, with respect to virtually the whole spectrum of such 'psychological' concepts one finds him repudiating the same sorts of things as we have found him repudiating in those contexts where 'metalogic' *is* explicitly mentioned. Thus, one can extrapolate from his explicit linkage of 'metalogic' with concepts such as *verstehen*, *meinen* and *abbilden* to a linkage of the issue of metalogic with his overall concern with the broad range of psychological concepts he deals with in his later writings. For example, much of what we have found him repudiating thus far in the explicit context of a discussion of metalogic is quite clearly echoed in the following sweeping statement he jotted down in July 1931:

> We labour, of course, under (over) the error that to believe, to mean, to know, to wish, to search for [*suchen*], to think, etc. are *states* and that in thinking [*Denken*], behind the symbolic processes, there must be something of a different kind which contains the sense [*Sinn*] of a sentence, as it were, in amorphous form, that is to say intuitively, like having in mind an invariant picture....[146]

One need do little more than to glance at the chapter and section headings of TS 213 to see that the "etc." in the above passage extended in the very early thirties to virtually the whole range of 'psychological' concepts with which Wittgenstein wrestled throughout the last twenty years of his life – including, that is, such other familiar concepts as 'expecting', 'interpreting', 'intending', 'imagining' and 'remembering'. And time and again one finds him repudiating (often even more clearly) the same sorts of things in these other contexts as we have found repudiating in the context of his explicit denials of metalogic. For example, in the chapter "Thought, Thinking" in TS 213, we find him raising the following issue:

> Is thinking a momentary process or perhaps an enduring state, of which words are just a clumsy reproduction [*Wiedergabe*] (so that one perhaps might say, as of the impression of a landscape, "Words could never reproduce that")? The thought is required as long as its expression: because the expression is the thought.
> I once read that a French politician had said the French language is distinguished in that in it the words follow in the order in which one really thinks.
> ... The idea that one language, in contrast to another one, can have a word order which corresponds to the order of thinking, arises from the view that thinking takes place apart from the expression of thoughts and thus is an essentially different process. According to this view one might now of course say: The essential property of the negation sign no doubt reveals itself only gradually in the use, but I

think the negation all at once. The sign 'not' is just an allusion [*Hinweis*] to the thought 'not'. It only strikes me that I think the right thing. (It is just a signal.)[147]

Where Wittgenstein stood (at that time) on the issue and what view he wished to repudiate comes out quite clearly in the surrounding remarks in TS 213. In this context one finds him explicitly asserting that

> Thought is no secret [*geheimer*] – and vague – process of which we only see intimations in language, as if the negation were a blow and the thought of it were like a nondescript [*unbestimmter*] pain brought about by this blow but completely distinct from it.[148]
>
> One doesn't have thoughts, and alongside [*daneben*] language. – It isn't like this: that one has signs for others, but for oneself one has a mute thought. As it were, a gaseous or ethereal thought in contrast to visible and audible symbols.[149]

It is quite evident that here again Wittgenstein is repudiating the same sort of view as we found him repudiating when rejecting the notion that other 'psychological' concepts such as 'understanding' and 'meaning' are metalogical.

Clearly, for Wittgenstein the rejection of metalogic was intimately linked to his concerns not only with such concepts as 'understanding' and 'meaning', but with virtually the whole gamut of 'psychological' concepts with which he was so ubiquitously preoccupied in his later writings. In fact, it will presently be shown that his rejection of metalogic was, as it were, the key that unlocked the gates to the investigation of these psychological concepts. To show this, however, it is first necessary to delve deeper into what Wittgenstein meant by 'metalogic' and expose the way in which his rejection of metalogic is linked with his shift to ordinary language.

What is it that Wittgenstein is repudiating when he rejects the view (which he apparently himself held at one time) that 'psychological' concepts such as 'meaning' and 'thought' are *metalogical*? One would be mistaken, although it is tempting to read him this way, if one took him to be denying the psychological or psychophysical – for example, to be denying that there may be a psychological or psycho-physical accompaniment to the hearing of an order when one is said to 'understand the order'; or denying that there may be psychological accompaniments to speech when one speaks and '*means* what one says'. Nor should the sort of repudiations cited from Wittgenstein's manuscripts be taken as a denial that in some cases we might ambiguously speak of an 'experience of understanding', for instance, or an 'experience of meaning'. Although Wittgenstein was generally not very tolerant of the latter expressions, at least in the thirties he was receptive to the possibility that in some cases a word such as 'understanding' might refer to "a psychological reaction while hearing a sentence" (for instance, in the case where one hears and 'understands' a familiar language, i.e. grasps that a language is familiar as opposed to hearing a foreign one).[150] What Wittgenstein *does* want to deny, however, is that the overriding function of such concepts as 'understanding' and 'meaning' in our language is to denote psychic phenomena – especially in the sorts of cases he is primarily interested in: namely, cases where one might, for example, speak of "understanding (the sense of) a sentence".[151] And, perhaps more importantly, even for the cases where one might speak, for example, of an 'experience of understanding', the meaning of such an expression (just as of any other expression in our language) is determined not by an 'experience' or psychological phenomenon of some sort, but rather by the application of the expression as a term in our language. In this manner the psychological – for example, understanding or meaning (*Meinung*) *qua* psychological phenomenon – "drops out of consideration" (see TS 213, first section heading), or, as Wittgenstein somewhat obscurely put it in his MS 114 revision of TS 213: meaning (*Meinung*) *qua* psychological phenomenon "drops out of language". [152] In the first section of TS 213 Wittgenstein explains what he means by the latter suggestions:

> Language must speak for itself.
> One can also put it this way: if one always expresses oneself in a system of language and thus what a sentence means is only explained through sentences of this system, then after all meaning [*Meinung*] falls completely out of language, thus out of consideration, and language remains the only thing we can consider.
> An exposition [*Erklärung*] *tells* what a sentence *means*.[153]

In the MS 116 revision of TS 213 the above remarks were entered immediately after the following implicit repudiation of metalogic:

> There is a temptation to believe that the meaning of the word 'understanding', of the expression 'understanding a sentence', is *metalogical*.
> 'Understanding' and 'meaning' [*meinen*] are words like all others.[154]

Wittgenstein is suggesting in the above passages that psychological phenomena fall out of consideration, but 'psychological' concepts do not. And it is quite evident by now that what he means by the term 'metalogic' is not what contemporary logicians mean by it: namely, the second-order *logical* concerns with such matters as the soundness and completeness of a system of logical rules. Rather, what he means by 'metalogic' is 'something outside or beyond logic'. But the expression 'something outside logic' (even if one wishes to deny that there is anything outside logic) can only be made sense of if one specifies the *domain* of logic. Has Wittgenstein specified the *domain* of logic? Although it may seem that in the passages cited thus far he has not specified the domain of logic, he in fact *has* specified that domain. Wittgenstein has claimed that 'understanding' and 'meaning' are not metalogical, but rather are *words like any others*.[155] Thus, there seems to be an implicit specification that the domain of logic is 'words like any others', i.e. language in a common-or-garden sense. Is there, however, any more concrete evidence indicating that in his later philosophy he had shifted his view of the domain of logic to that of a concern with ordinary language?

There is no doubt that in his later writings Wittgenstein's concerns were in some sense 'logical' ones; that is to say, for him philosophy was a form of 'logic'. For instance, in 1948, in the midst of an extensive investigation of 'psychological' concepts, one finds him remarking that

philosophy is a logical affair.

Yes, it is comforting to realize that a philosophical confusion signifies that I don't yet know my way about in the logic; for there there are only important problems and not petty ones.[156]

Later in the same notebook, and still in the midst of a discussion of psychological concepts, he more explicitly asserts, "What I'm doing here doesn't look like logic, but it nevertheless is logic,"[157] and "The recognition of philosophical problems as logical ones is already a step forward: it brings with it the right attitude and method."[158]

But Wittgenstein had always characterized his philosophical concerns as in some sense 'logical' ones. What we need is explicit evidence that definitively shows: (1) that in his later writings he considered *ordinary language* to be the proper domain of 'logic' (i.e. philosophy); (2) that this 'later' view constituted a shift in his thinking; (3) that this shift was already in place by the early thirties; and (4), most importantly, how this shift is tied in with the problem of 'metalogic'. The primary concern here is to establish *that* a shift *to* ordinary language had taken place by the early thirties, and show how this is linked to the issue of metalogic. A more detailed examination of some of the numerous conceptual and methodological transformations that accompanied this shift, as well as a discussion of what view of 'logic' Wittgenstein was shifting away *from*, will be undertaken in subsequent chapters.

There are few remarks in Wittgenstein's published 'works' that more explicitly state his emphasis on ordinary language than *PI* §§108 (paras 2–4), 120 and 124. How this emphasis on ordinary language is tied in with his notion of 'metalogic' and the shift in his view of the proper domain of 'logic' comes out quite clearly when one examines these remarks in their original bed of ideas in his manuscripts.[159] As it turns out, all three passages lead us back to the heart of Wittgenstein's repudiation of a metalogical view of psychological concepts, and all three were originally written in the early 1930s soon after his return to philosophy.

PI §124 allows us provisionally to date Wittgenstein's emphasis on ordinary language to 1930–1, and at the same time establish, at least *prima facie*, a link with the issue of metalogic. This section reads as follows:

> Philosophy may in no way interfere with the actual use of language; it can in the end only describe it.
> For it cannot give it any foundation either.
> It leaves everything as it is.
> It also leaves mathematics as it is, and no mathematical discovery can advance it. A 'leading problem of mathematical logic' is for us a problem of mathematics like any other.[160]

This remark appears (verbatim) in the "Philosophy" chapter of TS 213, but it was originally drafted in MS 110 in the midst of a repudiation of the metalogical view of the concept 'understanding'.[161] In fact, immediately after the remark Wittgenstein had entered in his notebook the following previously cited passage (see n. 134): "As there is no metaphysics, there is no metalogic. The word 'to understand', the expression 'to understand a sentence', is likewise not metalogical, but rather an expression like *any* other of language."

Although the fact that *Investigations* §124 was first drafted in 1930–1 in the midst of a repudiation of metalogic provides strong evidence that Wittgenstein had already shifted to an emphasis on ordinary language by the early thirties and that this emphasis is related to his rejection of metalogic, the mere contiguity of themes does not in itself explain *how* his emphasis on ordinary language is related to his repudiation of metalogic. Tracking down the manuscript sources of *PI* §§108 and 120 helps clarify the matter.

The whole of *PI* §120, and most of §108, are included virtually verbatim in chapter 3, §16, of TS 213, headed "Logic talks about propositions [*Sätzen*] and words in the ordinary sense, not about propositions and words in some abstract sense."[162] Let us examine *PI* §120 first. As originally drafted in 1930–1 (in MS 110) it read,

> Of course when I talk about language (words, sentences, etc.) I must speak the language of everyday. – But is there then another one? Is this language somehow too coarse, material, for what we want to

say? And can there be another one? And how strange that we should be able to do anything at all with the one we have.

It surely is clear that any language that can accomplish the same thing, must amount to the same thing. That thus our own ordinary language is no worse than any other one.

That I in explaining [*Erklären*] language (in our sense) already have to use language full-blown (not some sort of preparatory, provisional one) surely shows that I can only say (adduce) obvious things [*Äußerliches*, i.e. what is on the surface, open to view] about language.

Yes but then how can these expositions [*Ausführungen*] satisfy us? – Well, your very questions were framed in this language; they had to be expressed in this language, if there was anything to ask!

And your scruples are misunderstandings.

Your questions refer to words; so I have to talk about words.

One says: the point isn't the word, but its meaning, and one thinks of the meaning as a thing of the same kind as the word, though also different from the word. Here the word, there the meaning. The money, and the cow that you can buy with it. (But contrast: money, and its use.)[163]

First of all, what is the central concern of this rather lengthy passage? In the first paragraph the topic is stated generally as "talk about language", but in the fourth the topic is specified in terms of attempts *to explain language*. In the original German, the latter paragraph opens, "Daß ich beim Erklären der Sprache (in unseren Sinne) schon. . . ." The version in *PI* §120, though somewhat different in wording, is not as different in content as Anscombe's translation would lead us to believe. In German it runs, "Daß ich bei meinen Erklärungen, die Sprache betreffende, schon. . . ." (literally, "That I in my explanations concerning language already . . ."). In this version as in the earlier one, the 'explanations' Wittgenstein is discussing are "explanations concerning language" (Anscombe does not translate the phrase *die Sprache betreffende*). But there is something very puzzling about these lines. In the MS 110 version Wittgenstein speaks of 'explaining language (in our sense)", and in the *PI* version he speaks of "my explanations" (Anscombe also does not translate the German possessive pronoun *meinen*). There are few of us who have not at some time or other parroted the adage that Wittgenstein is not offering 'explanations', but rather just describing language.[164] Yet, if Wittgenstein does not offer explanations, why does he speak of 'explaining language (in our sense)" and "my explanations"? The apparent contradiction that arises here is no doubt what led Anscombe to be so free in her translation of the passage – for it does seem like a blatant contradiction for Wittgenstein to speak in *PI* §120 of "my explanations" when he has told us in §109 and re-emphasizes in §§124 and 126 that he is not offering 'explanations'. One cannot account for the apparent contradiction by suggesting that when Wittgenstein drafted §120 in the early thirties he still considered himself to be offering 'explanations' and that he failed to notice the anomaly when later piecing together remarks for *Philosophical Investigations*, for even in the early thirties he was claiming that his task was not to explain, but rather 'to describe', language. For instance the previously cited prescription (in *PI* §124) that "Philosophy may in no way interfere with the actual use of language; it can in the end only describe it" was originally drafted in the same notebook (MS 110, p. 188) – forty-three pages *before* the first draft of *PI* §120. Furthermore, Wittgenstein's other familiar prescription that "Philosophy simply puts everything before us and neither explains nor deduces anything" (in *PI* §126) was also drafted in the same notebook (MS 110, p. 217) – a mere fourteen pages before the original draft of *PI* §120. It is quite possible for a great thinker to contradict himself over the span of a career (lesser thinkers inadvertently do it sometimes within the same breath), but it is quite unlikely that a thinker of Wittgenstein's calibre would do so so blatantly within the space of a mere fourteen pages in MS 110 – written perhaps on the same day and certainly over no more than a few days.

One way of dealing with the apparent contradiction is to read Wittgenstein, as Hacker and Baker have, as referring in *PI* §120 to 'explanations' in the sense of "the clarificatory remarks of *PI*, not the kind of explanations which are 'on the Index' in philosophy".[165] The seeming anachronism involved in this reading of the passage is a harmless one, for, although the remark was originally written in 1930–1, the approach to philosophy found in *Philosophical Investigations* was already in place at that time and, as we have seen, many of the remarks in the *Investigations* stem from the early thirties. Furthermore, this strongly self-referential reading of the passage seems to be corroborated by the 1930–1 version (MS 110), in that by the expression "explaining language (in our sense)" Wittgenstein might very well have been referring to *his own* (new) brand of 'clarification' of language and not *philosophical* attempts to *explain* language. There is, however, a serious problem with this strongly self-referential reading of the passage. Hacker and Baker have ignored not only that *PI* §120 was drafted in 1930–1, but also that there is yet a third, intermediate version of the passage. In MS 114 (*c*.1933–4) Wittgenstein worded the remark as follows: "Daß ich in den philosophischen Erklärungen über der Sprache schon ..."[166] ("That I in philosophical explanations about language already ..."). Here the apparent self-reference has been toned down considerably, and, in spite of the grammatical subject (*ich*) of the sentence, the remark suggests itself as a comment on *philosophical* explanations (whether Wittgenstein's or anyone else's) about language, rather than as a comment on 'explanations' of language in any special Wittgensteinian sense.

There is, however, a second way of dealing with the apparent contradiction. An alternative reading would be to interpret Wittgenstein as speaking *from the standpoint* of philosophers (in general) who have attempted to offer 'explanations' of language. Such a non-self-referential reading seems to be the sort of approach Anscombe took in her translation of the passage. Thus, it is quite plausible to read such phrases as 'explaining language (in our sense)" and "my explanations concerning language" in such a way that they do not involve any explicit sef-reference on Wittgenstein's part, but rather offer a comment on the activity of philosophers in general. Yet here also there is a problem. If Wittgenstein did not intend a self-reference, there is something very odd about the genesis of the remark. It seems quite implausible that he should have gone from a somewhat self-referential and personal idiom ("explaining language (in our sense)" – MS 110) to an impersonal expression ("philosophical explanations of language" – MS 114), and yet in his final version return to an even more personal idiom ("my explanations concerning language"[167]), if he did not explicitly intend a self-reference.

In *PI* §120 Wittgenstein both was referring generally to philosophical attempts to explain language *and* intended there to be an explicit self-reference as well. The explanations of language to which he is referring are those that he himself and we philosophers generally are constantly tempted to give – explanations which he himself gave at an earlier (pre-1930) point in his career. Anscombe in her eagerness to eliminate the apparent contradiction has, in her translation, eliminated the important self-referential character of the remark. On the other hand, Baker and Hacker, in their eagerness, have misconstrued the nature of the self-reference. The sort of philosophical explanation of language (propositions, words) to which Wittgenstein was referring is quite clear when one examines the original context of the remarks in MS 110. *PI* §120 was originally written in the general context of a discussion of psychological concepts such as 'intending' and 'meaning' (both *meinen* and *Bedeutung*). On the page preceding his entry of the remark, Wittgenstein had asserted, "It is important to express generally the error that I am inclined to make in all these reflections. The false analogy from which it originates."[168] Then on the next page, *immediately* preceding the first draft of *PI* §120, he explicitly identified the "error" to which he was referring:

> I believe that error lies in the notion that the meaning [*Bedeutung*] of a word is an idea [*Vorstellung*] that accompanies the word.
> And this notion again has to do with (is connected with) that of consciousness [*Bewußtsein*]. That which I always called "the primary" ["*das Primäre*"].[169]

Wittgenstein then jotted down the first draft of PI §120. However, a mere page and a half after jotting it down he further remarked,

> For the issue is precisely whether by the "sense [*Bedeutung*] in which one uses a word" must be understood a process that we experience while speaking or hearing a word.
> The source of the mistake seems to be the notion of *thoughts which accompany the sentence* [*Satz*]. Or which precede its ~~symbolic~~ expression. . . .[170]

The explanations to which Wittgenstein is referring in PI §120 are those sorts of philosophical explanations toward which he himself was inclined (and to which he succumbed at some earlier point in his career): namely, explanations of language (words, sentences, and so on) by means of an hypothesized psychological substratum that lies in the psyche behind language: explanations such as those that treat 'the sense in which one uses a word in a sentence' as constituted by a process of thought that accompanies the sentence; explanations such as the account of the 'meaning' of a *word* as an idea (*Vorstellung*) that accompanies it. Wittgenstein caricatures for us quite graphically what he once meant by *Vorstellung*, for later in this same manuscript volume he divulges "idea [*Die Vorstellung*] in the sense in which I formerly had spoken of it, is like an image [*Bild* picture] with the subscript 'likeness of N. N.'."[171] We see quite clearly here what Wittgenstein is up to in the last paragraph of PI §120 (see the MS 110 version cited q. 163). "One . . . thinks of the meaning [of a word] as a thing [*Sache*] of the same kind as the word, though also different from the word. Here the word, there the meaning": here the word; there the meaning as a thing of the mind, an 'object' of the mind or of thought. "The money, and the cow that you can buy with it": the word, and the *Vorstellung* that one can conjure with it. The last paragraph of PI §120 points to the false analogy that is at the basis of the sort of 'philosophical explanations' Wittgenstein is concerned with, explanations which he himself apparently once offered and now is repudiating.

These sorts of explanation are quite familiar to us by now. They are the sort of views Wittgenstein was repudiating in the context of his rejection of 'metalogic'. We have been led from PI §120 right back again into the heart of Wittgenstein's repudiation of the metalogical interpretation of psychological concepts. Clearly the metalogical view of psychological concepts was part and parcel of his attempts sometime earlier in his career *to explain* language. And clearly the stress on ordinary language that we find in PI §120 is the suggestion, a distinct echo of which we have already encountered in the context of his rejection of metalogic, that talk about language (words, sentences, and so on), the concepts in terms of which we try to explain language ('meaning', 'thought', 'understanding', and the like) are *expressions*, symbols, terms of our everyday language – "words like *any* others". As Wittgenstein suggests in *PI* §124, in the end we can only describe "the actual use of language" – that is, describe the actual use of those expressions and terms of our everyday language in which our very questions about language are couched. It is such descriptions which constitute what Wittgenstein refers to in *PI* §120 as the "obvious things about language". It is such expositions (*Ausführungen*) or descriptions, and not philosophical explanations (*Erklärungen*), that seem as if they might not satisfy us (see q. 163, or *PI* §120 in German).

But here one comes to something which is still unclear about the relationship between Wittgenstein's shift to ordinary language and his repudiation of the metalogical view of psychological concepts. In *PI* §120, and even more explicitly in the MS 110 version (q. 163), one finds Wittgenstein raising the issue of whether ordinary language is "somehow too coarse, material, for what we want to say", and raising the question of whether there might be a better one. What is still not clear is just how the issue of the adequacy or inadequacy of ordinary language is related to Wittgenstein's rejection of a metalogical interpretation of psychological concepts. We have, however, already been provided with the clue which will resolve this ambiguity. The reader will recall that in the context of his first (1930-1) draft of *PI* §120, Wittgenstein identified the error he was inclined to make as the view that the meaning of a word is an accompanying mental image or idea, a 'thought' behind the signs – and he indicated that this notion had to do with what he used to call "the primary" (i.e. consciousness; see q. 169). In what way might an earlier view that Wittgenstein had of 'consciousness' or "the primary", as he says he called it, have brought into question the adequacy of ordinary language?

The answer to this question has in effect already been adumbrated in some of the passages cited earlier. We have already been presented with a conception of consciousness that brings into question the adequacy of ordinary language. It is a conception of consciousness that Wittgenstein was repudiating in his rejection of the metalogical interpretation of psychological concepts, as when he spoke of

> the error that to believe, to mean, to know, to wish, to search for, to think, etc. are *states* and that in thinking, behind the symbolic processes, there must be something of a different kind which contains the sense [*Sinn*] of a sentence, as it were, in amorphous form, that is to say intuitively, like having in mind an invariant picture.... (See n. 146)

Such a view of consciousness or "the primary" leads one to "regard understanding as the essential thing, and signs as the inessential" (see q. 140).

This view of consciousness leads one to consider 'thought' as a "secret – and vague – process of which we only see intimations in language", or thinking as a "momentary process or perhaps an enduring state, of which words are just a clumsy reproduction" (qq. 148, 147). Quite clearly the notion of consciousness implicit in the metalogical view of psychological concepts carries with it the implication that our ordinary (spoken/written) language is derivative (or secondary) and to some extent inadequate at expressing those 'thoughts' and 'ideas' allegedly lying "behind" it. There is hypothesized, as it were, a language of consciousness (thoughts, ideas, immediate experiences) which is fundamental to our secondary and derivative ordinary one – perhaps the sort of dichotomy mentioned in *PI* §512, between a word language (*Wortsprache*) and a language of ideas or mental images (*Sprache der Vorstellung*; cf. MS 114, p. 121, published in *PG*, pp. 128–9).

It is presumably this whole viewpoint that Wittgenstein is rejecting when he asserts in the "Idealism" chapter of TS 213 that "There is not – as I used to believe – a primary language as opposed to our ordinary one, the 'secondary' one. ..."[172] There is an indication here that at some earlier point in his career Wittgenstein saw it as his goal to construct a sort of "primary language" or, as he in retrospect also refers to it, a "phenomenological language". Again, presumably he had in mind an attempt to construct a system of signs which would manage to express clearly and without confusion that (consciousness: 'thought', 'ideas', 'meaning') which it seems ordinary language only manages to express so clumsily. Almost immediately upon his return to philosophy in 1929–30, we find Wittgenstein denouncing what he refers to as his previous "goal" of constructing a "phenomenological language". Even more interesting for the purposes of our present concern, however, is the fact that almost invariably, along with his denunciation of his earlier goal, we find him stressing that his concerns now (post-1929) have shifted to the domain of ordinary language – viewed not merely as the *source* of philosophical confusion (this may always have been his view) but also as the *means* by which philosophical confusions are to be eliminated. For example, in late 1929 or early 1930 he wrote,

> I do not now have phenomenological language, or 'primary language', as I used to call it, in mind as my goal. I no longer hold it to be possible [*möglich*]. All that is possible and necessary is to separate what is essential from what is inessential in *our* language.[173]

Earlier in the same notebook he even more emphatically remarked,

> The assumption that a phenomenological language would be possible and that it would really first say that which we must (want

to) express in philosophy is – I believe – absurd. We must make do with our ordinary language and just correctly understand it. That is to say, we shouldn't allow ourselves to be seduced by it into talking nonsense.[174]

Precisely what Wittgenstein meant by 'phenomenological' or 'primary' language and just what such a language would look like are not very clear. It seems that he never got very far beyond merely *presuming* the possibility of such a language, for he only refers to it as having previously been his "assumption" and his "goal". Circumstantial evidence gives us a vague idea of what he might have had in mind by a 'phenomenological language', in that many of his references to it crop up in the general context of a discussion of 'sense perception', the 'visual field' or the theory of 'sense-data'.[175] In one such context he gives us virtually a definition of 'phenomenological language' – though it is still not clear just what such a language would look like. In the "Idealism" chapter of TS 213, having repudiated his earlier belief in a 'primary' or 'phenomenological' language (see q. 172), and having embarked on a "critique of the word 'sense-datum'", Wittgenstein explicitly indicates what he seems to have meant by 'primary' or 'phenomenological' language: "Phenomenological language: the description of immediate experience, without hypothetical additions [*Zutat*]."[176] This would suggest that he had in mind a system of signs that would succinctly express what might be the most elemental components of consciousness or thought. In which case, it would perhaps be better to translate *phänomenologische Sprache* as 'phenomenal language' (see my discussion in n. 175). There is little doubt that it is this sort of 'phenomenal' concern that Wittgenstein generally referred to in 1933 as

> that dead-end in philosophy, where one believes that the difficulty of the task consists in our having to describe phenomena that are hard to get hold of, the present experience that slips quickly by, or something of the kind. Where we find ordinary language too crude, and it looks as if we were having to do, not with the phenomena of every-day, but with ones that "easily elude us, and, in their coming to be and passing away, produce those others as an average effect".[177]

There is another matter that sheds a little more light on Wittgenstein's early notion of *das Primäre* (consciousness) and his early goal of constructing a primary or phenomenal language. The reader will recall that, in order to explain how the issue of the inadequacy of ordinary language may have arisen, serving as a clue was Wittgenstein's admission in MS 110 that his inclination to consider the meaning (*Bedeutung*) of a word as an accompanying idea or image (*Vorstellung*) was linked to his earlier notion of consciousness (*Bewußtsein*) or, as he used to refer to it, *das Primäre* (see q. 169). In the version of this remark found in TS 213 (p. 154) the German word for consciousness appears in a peculiar form – namely, *Bewußt-Sein*. This gimmick of using hyphenation to stress the meaning of the components of a word, though a common practice with many philosophers (especially those of continental European extraction), is quite untypical of Wittgenstein. What the hyphenation does to the word *Bewußtsein* is to transform it into the furcated expression 'consciousness of – Being', thus stressing that what Wittgenstein called *das Primäre* was taken in relation to 'Being' (reality/world?). With such an emphasis, it would seem that the perceived inability of the sentences of ordinary language adequately to express their sense or thought (the ethereal something lying in the psyche behind the signs) could at the same time be viewed as a perceived inability on their part adequately to express possible (conceivable) situations or states of affairs in the world (possible or thinkable features of 'Being', if you will). The earlier goal of a 'primary' or 'phenomenal' language, then, in that it was an attempt to remedy a perceived clumsiness of ordinary language in expressing thought (about the world or *Sein*), can be viewed as an attempt to remedy the clumsiness of ordinary language in expressing possible or conceivable states of affairs. This of course seems highly conjectural, but, consistent with this conjecture, we find Wittgenstein in 1936 making the following comment about his old notion of a 'primary' or 'phenomenal' language:

> "Phenomenal [*phänomenologische*] language"
> Belief in its necessity. It seems as if our language is, somehow, *crude*, an imperfect [*unvollkommene*] presentation of states of affairs [*Sachverhalte*] and only to be taken as a crude, imperfect likeness [*Abbild*, copy]. As if philosophy must improve, refine, it in order to be able to understand the structure of the world [*Bau der Welt*]. *Then* it becomes c̲l̲e̲ar that you must understand, i.e. recognize, language as it is, because the goal is not a new clarity that the (old) language doesn't (didn't) provide, but rather the elimination of philosophical puzzlement (bewilderment).[178]

Wittgenstein's earlier goal of a 'phenomenal language', it seems, *in that* it was an attempt to correct for the perceived inability of ordinary language to express thought clearly, was an attempt to express more clearly *possibilities* about the world. However, the perceived inability of ordinary language adequately to express possibilities about the world, to present *Sachverhalte* (see n. 178), indeed the very goal of a 'phenomenal language', were clearly the by-products of his (earlier) 'metalogical explanation' of language – what he referred to in *PI* §94 as "the subliming of our whole account [*Darstellung*]. The tendency to assume a pure intermediary between the propositional *signs* [*SatzZEICHEN*] and the facts [*Tatsachen*]."

One page after the above reference to 'phenomenal language', Wittgenstein quite explicitly acknowledged the 'metalogical' roots of his early dissatisfaction with ordinary language and his quest for a purity and perfect clarity in our sentences:

> I had of course formerly struggled against the idea that there isn't perfect [*vollkommenen*] order in logic. "Every sentence [*Satz*] has a *precise* sense [*bestimmten Sinn*]"; "In logic there can't be unclarity, for otherwise after all there would be no clarity (and thus also no unclarity)"; "A logically unclear sentence is (would be) one which has no precise sense, thus *no* sense" – Here always lurked the idea of the ethereal sense [*Sinn*] (sense of a proposition [*Satzsinnes*]), of that which one *meant*, of mental [*geistigen*] processes.[179]

Let us turn now to *PI* §108, to see whether it too provides evidence and any further insights that support our account of Wittgenstein's shift to an emphasis on ordinary language as the proper domain of logic. As previously indicated, paragraphs 2–4 of *PI* §108 are included virtually verbatim in TS 213. As they appear there, they are worded and arranged as follows:

> I don't believe that logic can talk about sentences [*Sätzen*] in a sense other than we ordinarily do, when we say "Here is a written sentence", or "No, that only looks like a sentence, but isn't one", etc. etc.
>
> The question "What is a word?" is wholly analogous to "What is a chess-piece?"
>
> We talk of course about the spatial and temporal *phenomenon* of language. Not about some non-spatial and non-temporal phantasm [*Unding*]. But we talk about it as we do about the pieces in chess, in that we tabulate rules for them, not describing their physical properties.[180]

The first two of these remarks were originally drafted on the same page in late 1929 or early 1930 (MS 107, p. 240). The last remark was drafted over a year later (early 1931) in a different notebook (MS 110, p. 221). The very early dates of these remarks indicate (though this really no longer needs saying) that, to the extent that Wittgenstein is identifying a shift which has occurred in his thinking, this shift had for the most part already taken place when he returned to philosophy in 1929–30.

Examining the MS 107 context first, one finds that, immediately prior to stating that he believed logic could only talk about sentences in an ordinary sense, Wittgenstein had remarked,

> Here we come to the apparently trivial question, what does logic understand by a word – is it an ink-mark, a sequence of sounds, is it necessary that someone should associate a sense with it, or should have associated one, etc, etc.? – And here, the crudest conception must obviously be the only correct one.
>
> And so I will again talk about 'books'; here we have words; if a mark should happen to occur that looks like a word, I say: that's not a word, it only looks like one, it's obviously unintentional. This can only be dealt with from the standpoint of normal common sense. (It's extraordinary that that in itself constitutes a change in perspective.)[181]

The indication is that viewing sentences in a very ordinary down-to-earth sense was in fact a "change in perspective" for Wittgenstein. The important question for *us*, here, is: a change in perspective *from what*? Obviously, it must have been a shift away from viewing sentences as in some sense extraordinary, but what more precisely might this other view of *Sätzen* have been? In a stretch of text written some time between 1934 and 1937, Wittgenstein addresses this issue directly:

> *One person* might say, "A sentence [*Satz*] is the most ordinary thing [*das Alltäglichste*] in the world." And *another*, "A sentence – that's something very queer!"
>
> And he can't simply look and see how a sentence functions [*funktioniert*], because the forms that we use in expressing ourselves about sentences, thought, etc., stand in the way.[182]

As for just what sort of misconception might be involved when a person views a sentence as "something very queer", Wittgenstein elaborates,

> For if he doesn't see it as something wholly ordinary [*ganz Alltägliches*], then that means he sees *something behind the sentence*.
> (It is something very queer, here already lies the whole mistake.)
> Herein already lies the ethereal, metaphysical.[183]

The notion of 'something behind the signs' is of course precisely what Wittgenstein was repudiating in his rejection of his own 'earlier' metalogical explanations of language. We have again found that the "change in perspective" involved in Wittgenstein's shift to a concern with ordinary language has its roots in his repudiation of metalogic.

Now let us examine the MS 110 context of the third paragraph of *PI* §108. This not merely provides further corroboration of points already made, but also gives us a firmer grasp of the relation between Wittgenstein's repudiation of metalogic and his shift to ordinary language. As it was originally drafted in early 1931 in the context of the remarks immediately preceding and succeeding it, the third paragraph of *PI* §108 read as follows:

> Can one thus say, "It is quite enough if philosophy makes its remarks about the expressions in the German language, about the language of chemists, etc."? That is to say, philosophy makes its remarks about expressions in various languages not about one overall conception [*Begriff*] placed above these.
>
> We talk about the spatial and temporal *phenomenon* of language. Not about some non-spatial and non-temporal phantasm [*Unding*]. But we talk about it as we do about the pieces in chess, in that we tabulate rules for them, not describing their physical properties.
>
> Dogmatism in philosophy arises by [consists in] assertions being made which are not about any recognized grammatical rules of one's expressions (of one's language). In this way the illusion is again conjured that we must in philosophy construct and make *new* discoveries [*Entdeckungen*], discover uniformities [*Zusammenhängen auffinden*].[184]

In this context Wittgenstein contrasts his own concern with language, as constituted by the actual expressions we use (inclusive of the 'language' used in chemistry, mathematics, etc.), with a concern that, as it were, neglects the grammatical rules of our expressions and instead attempts to make *new* discoveries (*Entdeckungen*). But what sort of "discoveries" is Wittgenstein referring to here? There is nothing here to indicate that he is referring to his earlier assumption that a 'phenomenal language' was discoverable. Rather he speaks more broadly of discovering "uniformities" and a general conception of language over and above our actual expressions in various linguistic contexts. We need to clarify what sort of "discoveries" Wittgenstein has in mind here; what sort of "uniformities" and 'general conceptions'. Where might one look for examples of philosophy which neglects the grammatical rules of our expressions and strives to "discover uniformities" or form a 'general conception' of language? As it so happens, Wittgenstein as he so often is, is quite accommodating on the matter. A few months earlier, in winter 1930, he had jotted down a remark that mentions a book in which we might find attempts to offer "discoveries" about language:

> In my former book the solution of problems was still far too little presented in a plain manner [*hausbacken*]. It still appeared too much

as though discoveries were necessary in order to solve our problems and everything was still too little conveyed in the form of the grammatically obvious [*grammatischen Selbstverständlichkeiten*] in ordinary language. Everything still appeared too much like discoveries.[185]

Wittgenstein has sent us to the *Tractatus* as an example of a work in which one appears to be making "discoveries" and fails sufficiently to approach things as a grammatical matter-of-course in ordinary language. It may be fairly obvious what sorts of views expressed in the *Tractatus* would count as apparent "discoveries" of uniformities or general conceptions about language, but there is no need to leap to speculation on the matter. The temptation to predicate comments on the emergence of Wittgenstein's later philosophy on any *presuppositions* about his views in the *Tractatus* has so far been avoided. Rather than abandon this strategy, let us allow *Wittgenstein*, who has sent us to the *Tractatus*, to give us some clues as to what in that work might count as examples of apparent "discoveries" of uniformities. In MS 110, following on from the previously cited passage (q. 184) giving the original context of *PI* §108, para. 3, Wittgenstein remarks,

> the illusion is again conjured that we must in philosophy construct and make *new* discoveries, discover uniformities.
> In logic we (indeed) seem to have to do with '*all propositions*'. But we only construct a calculus and leave use to its own devices.
> In philosophy we work with languages but just those that we use, for of course the rules of *their* use we want to (should) determine.
> In philosophy we work with languages, the everyday forms – – –
> In philosophy also we couldn't attain any greater *generality* than in what we say (express) in life and science. (That is to say also here we leave everything as it is.)
> Thus a sensational definition of number [*Zahl*] is no (not the) task of philosophy.
> Philosophy has to do with existing languages and should not pretend [*vorzugeben*] that it must deal with an abstract language.[186]

There seem to be two clues here concerning what might count in the *Tractatus* as apparent "discoveries" of uniformities. One clue is Wittgenstein's reference to "a sensational definition of number [*Zahl*]". The other clue is the reference to a concern with the construction of a calculus that deals with "*all propositions*" – to the neglect of the way our everyday expressions are actually used. These clues seem to point to Wittgenstein's own earlier efforts to define, by means of an abstract, symbolic language, the general form of a 'proposition' (*Satz*) and the general form of a 'number' (*Zahl*). In *Tractatus* 6.0 Wittgenstein had offered the symbolic expression '[p̄, ξ̄, N(ξ̄)]' as the general form of a proposition – thus defining a proposition as a function of 'elementary propositions' (see n. 176); and in *Tractatus* 6.3 the symbolic expression '[0, ξ, ξ + 1]' had been offered as the general form of a number.

Wittgenstein's shift to ordinary language, then, was at least in part an abandonment of his earlier quest for *generality* (for example, the general form of a proposition, the general form of a number). Such apparent "discoveries" he no longer (by the early thirties) considered the task of philosophy. Furthermore, he seems to have abandoned his earlier pretensions that the proper concerns of philosophy (the solution of philosophical confusions) involve and require the construction of an abstract, i.e. formal, language. In the *Tractatus* it seems he had in mind an abstract symbolism along the lines of Russell's and Frege's conceptual notations.[187]

This sheds a little more light on the nature of Wittgenstein's shift to ordinary language, but it is still unclear how, or even *that*, this aspect is related to his repudiation of metalogic. Might his earlier metalogical explanations of language be linked to his inclination to answer questions such as 'What is language?' ('What is a proposition?', 'What is a word?') by giving general (formal) definitions that stand, as it were, as an abstraction over and above the actual cases? The idea that this inclination is what Wittgenstein was repudiating in his shift to an emphasis on ordinary language as the proper domain of logic was suggested by *PI* §108, para. 3, as it appeared in its original context in MS 110. Wittgenstein provides us with a hint, however, that this paragraph is linked also to his repudiation of the metalogical view of psychological concepts. In the margin next to this paragraph in TS 213 (p. 71) he identified a topic with which he felt this remark properly belonged – thus indicating that he was thinking of transferring the remark to another section or chapter of TS 213. His marginal note reads, "Properly belongs with: 'Understanding' is no act while talking, etc." This, of course, we recognize not only as a general reference to the chapter headed "Understanding" (*Verstehen*), but also more specifically as a reference to his repudiation (in that chapter) of his earlier metalogical view of 'understanding' (see, for example, qq. 133–4). The marginal note provides fairly good evidence that Wittgenstein considered *PI* §108, para. 3, to be tied in with his repudiation of metalogic.

It has already been observed that this paragraph is at least in part a rejection of his earlier inclination to answer questions such as 'What is a proposition?' by giving general (formal) definitions that stand as abstractions over and above the actual cases. Now the indication is that this is somehow bound up with his earlier metalogical view of 'understanding'. But *how* so? The reader will recall that, according to the metalogical view, 'understanding' is some sort of psychic substratum fundamental to language – a psychological state or activity of 'grasping' the meaning (*Bedeutung/Sinn*) of words and sentences, i.e. grasping the ideas (*Vorstellungen*) or thoughts (*Gedanken*) which, as it were, lie *behind* (*hinter*) the signs. It would seem that anyone subscribing to such a view would tend to presuppose that a question such as 'What is a proposition?' is answerable in terms of a formulation of some pure, general conception or 'idea' of the nature of a proposition – one would tend to presuppose that, whether or not there appears to be any overall homogeneity or clear uniformity in the expressions we actually use in ordinary language, in our 'understanding' there is some pure 'idea' of a 'proposition' and all we need to find is an adequate – perhaps logical (formal), abstract – means of expressing this 'idea'. Thus the metalogical view of psychological concepts, which was fundamental to Wittgenstein's early view of language, could itself have been the basis of his early inclination to offer a pure, abstract, general conception of language (propositions, words).

In *PI* §102 he confesses as much. As first formulated in 1937 in its original bed of ideas, this section read as follows:

> What has become of the crystalline clarity? It becomes a form of presentation, nothing more.
>
> Understanding is no pneumatic [*pneumatischer*, spiritual, ethereal] process.
>
> The concept of family drives against the – – –
>
> It became clear of course that I didn't *have* a general concept of a proposition and of language.
>
> I had to recognize this and that as signs (Sraffa) and yet couldn't provide a grammar for them. Understanding and knowing the rules.
>
> The pneumatic with respect to understanding completely vanished and with it the pneumatical in sense [*das Pneumatische des Sinns*].
>
> At first the strict rules seemed as something (still) in the background [*Hintergrund*] hidden in the medium of the understanding; and one might say, "They *must* be there" – or "I see them, so to speak, through a thick medium, but I see them." They were thus *concrete*. I had used a metaphor (of the projection method, etc.) but through the grammatical illusion of homogeneous ideas [*einheitliche Begriffes*] it didn't seem to be a metaphor. The word 'real' [*eigentlich*].
>
> The moment this illusion becomes obvious, the moment it becomes clearer that language is a family, the more clear it becomes that that was fictitious concreteness, an abstraction, a form, and that, if we pretend after all that they are present, our assertions become queer and senseless. Thus we no longer play logical tricks.

We see that we must cling to examples in order not to meander about aimlessly.

Our reflections though don't now lose their importance, but rather this shifts completely to the misunderstandings that mislead us.[188]

Unfortunately, this rambling passage inundates us with themes having to do with Wittgenstein's later thinking – many of which will receive scrutiny in subsequent chapters.[189] For present purposes the reader is asked to focus on the passage as a statement about the relation between Wittgenstein's early metalogical view of 'understanding' and his inclination (in the *Tractatus*) to try and specify in abstract, formal terms such things – or, rather, such *Undingen* (phantasms; see qq. 180 and 184, and *PI* §108, para. 3) – as the 'general form of a proposition'.

First of all, in the above passage one finds coupled together both a denial of the metalogical view of understanding (here referred to as the view that understanding is a "pneumatic" process) and a recognition by Wittgenstein of the failure of his early attempt to offer a 'general conception of a proposition' (and of language). In addition, though, an account is given of *how* his early (Tractarian) quest for a 'general conception of a proposition' was related to his metalogical view of understanding. In the paragraph beginning "At first the strict rules . . ." (the original draft of *PI* §102), Wittgenstein indicates that his pursuit of a general conception (the strict rules for what counts as a proposition) was based on the assumption that there *must be* such a general conception hidden in the medium of the understanding – or, as he put it in *PI* §102, hidden in the medium of the understanding there must be "strict and clear rules of the logical structure of propositions [*Satzbaues*]". The *Hintergrund* of which Wittgenstein speaks is of course a reference to the psychological substratum that he previously considered to be fundamental to language and to lie "behind" (*hinter*) the signs. In this manner, Wittgenstein's Tractarian quest for 'discovered' uniformities or general conceptions (for instance, the general form of a proposition) was linked to his early metalogical view of psychological concepts.

We have found, then, that Wittgenstein's repudiation of his early metalogical view of psychological concepts was a major theme in the emergence of his later *Denkweise*. Apparently, early in his career (pre-1929) he had considered such concepts as 'understanding', 'meaning', 'thinking' and '(intentionally) depicting' as lying outside logic and referring to psychological states or processes which lie 'behind' language. However, this early view of psychological concepts, in spite of their 'extra-logical' status, seems to have been fundamental to his attempts early in his career *to explain* language.[190] Furthermore, his early metalogical view of psychological concepts seems also to have been intimately linked to his early attitude to ordinary language as somehow inadequate and not up to the task required of it by philosophy. In turn this attitude to ordinary language was tied in with his self-proclaimed early tendency to neglect the actual use of our everyday expressions and instead (1) attempt to construct some sort of 'primary' or 'phenomenal' language by means of which the 'sense' of meaningful propositions could be distinctly expressed, and (2) try to discover formal, abstract uniformities (such as the general form of a proposition) which express the general nature of language.

With his return to philosophy in 1929–30, however, Wittgenstein seems to have abandoned the metalogical view of psychological concepts that had been so fundamental to his early *explanations* of language, and instead began to consider them as "words like *any* others", words to be investigated by examining their role as terms in everyday discourse. This of course coincided with a restriction of the proper concerns of philosophy (logic) to the domain of ordinary language. With his shift to an emphasis on ordinary language and the abandonment of the metalogical view of psychological concepts came the recognition that his previous views concerning such concepts as 'meaning', 'understanding' and 'thinking' (and, for that matter, his previous view of language itself) were mistaken. Consequently Wittgenstein's early metalogical view of psychological concepts and metalogical *explanations* of language were bound up both with a misapprehension of the proper domain of logic, and with his own failure to grasp the 'logic' of psychological concepts. The evidence has demonstrated that by the early 1930s Wittgenstein had already shifted to ordinary language as the proper domain of logic and repudiated his earlier metalogical views, thus 'opening the gates' to the logical investigation of psychological concepts which so preoccupied him during the last two decades of his life.

3

Language Games:
the Heuristic Role of the 'Ideal'

"One cannot do so much with language games":[191] this is Rush Rhees' concluding remark in his Preface (1958) to *The Blue and Brown Books*. The remark seems to be an assessment of Wittgenstein's notion of a 'language game'. Were it that, there would be little harm in it; though one might wish that Rhees had elaborated a bit on the inadequacies of the notion. However, in this remark Rhees is not really offering his own assessment, but rather seems to be attempting to offer an *interpretation* of Wittgenstein's attitude toward 'language games'.

In his 1969 Preface to Wittgenstein's revised German version of the 'Brown Book', Rhees reveals to us what seems to have been the basis for his puzzling conclusion to his 1958 Preface. Much of the 'Brown Book' is a sequential examination of a number of hypothetical language games, and it seems that Rhees was aware that Wittgenstein, in reference to his attempt to revise the 'Brown Book', had written, "This whole 'attempt at a revision' ... is *worthless*."[192] After citing this remark in his 1969 Preface, Rhees then suggests that by this assertion Wittgenstein "certainly didn't mean that it [the revision] contained no worthwhile discussions or remarks. Perhaps there was something wrong with the whole attempt."[193] Explaining what he means by this, Rhees boldly suggests that Wittgenstein "seems to have had the impression that something was wrong with the method followed in it [the 'Brown Book']."[194] Rhees is correct in what he thinks Wittgenstein did *not* mean, for significant stretches of this 'Brown Book' revision were later included in *Philosophical Investigations*.[195] But Wittgenstein's assertion that his whole revision of the 'Brown Book' was worthless need not be taken to imply that he felt his 'method' in the 'Brown Book' was wrong; and it certainly does not imply that he felt "One cannot do so much with language games", as Rhees put it in his 1958 Preface. The remark Rhees cites from Wittgenstein's *Nachlaß* does not support such a bold conclusion – a conclusion which, not incidentally, is all too conveniently consistent with Rhees' theory that Wittgenstein's 'later' approach to philosophy was emerging during the 'Blue and Brown Books period'.

Rhees does, however, finally get around to telling us just what did lead him to offer such a bold interpretation, for he goes on to claim that once, in reference to the 'Brown Book' and the pre-war version of the *Investigations*, "[G. E.] Moore said Wittgenstein declared to him that in the Brown Book he had followed the wrong method, but in contrast in this manuscript [the pre-war *Investigations*] he had employed the right method. Moore indicated he didn't know what Wittgenstein meant by that."[196] Rhees tells us that Moore told him that Wittgenstein told Moore that.... The present study has so far refrained from appealing to second- or third-hand accounts of the views Wittgenstein allegedly expressed to people. The dangers of placing too great an importance on such reports, however well intentioned, are fairly obvious. Rhees claims Moore told him this in 1938, over three decades before Rhees recorded it for posterity in his 1969 Preface, though presumably Rhees had made a note of it in 1938. There probably is at least one point in Rhees' report that is accurate, and that is that Moore "indicated he didn't know what Wittgenstein meant". In his 1969 Preface, Rhees wisely confessed, "I don't know either."[197] It is a pity that Rhees was not as candid in his 1958 Preface, where he instead presented us with his mystifying conclusion that "One cannot do so much with language games."

The sorts of 'hypothetical' language games that so extensively populate the 'Brown Book' are not first introduced there, and the use to which Wittgenstein puts them there is not something he abandoned in subsequent writings. One finds such hypothetical games prior to the so-called 'Blue and Brown Books period', and one finds them throughout his writings after that period. In fact some of the very same 'language games' in the 'Brown Book' were included by Wittgenstein in *Philosophical Investigations*.[198] What *is* unique about the 'Brown Book' is that nowhere else in his later writings did Wittgenstein so exclusively restrict his flow of thoughts to a sequential appeal to hypothetical language games. The fact that in this latter respect the 'Brown Book' conspicuously stands apart from the other materials in his *Nachlaß* may bring us as close as we can come to a solution to what Wittgenstein might have meant when he indicated to Moore that there was something 'methodologically' amiss in the work – if he actually did say such a thing.

It is quite possible that the report Rhees passes on to us in his 1969 Preface is a rendition, albeit faded by time and the retelling, of something Wittgenstein had said to Moore in a letter written in late November 1936. Comparing his 'Brown Book' revision (begun in August 1936) and his recently commenced (November 1936) new effort (his first draft of the pre-war *Investigations* in MS 142; see n. 107), Wittgenstein declared,

My work isn't going badly. I don't know if I wrote to you that when I came here I began to translate into and rewrite in German the stuff [the 'Brown Book'] I had dictated to Skinner and Miss Ambrose. When about a fortnight ago, I read through what I had done so far I found it all, or nearly all, boring and artificial. For having the English version before me had cramped my thinking. I therefore decided to start all over again and not to let my thoughts be guided by anything but themselves. – I found it difficult the first day or two but then it became easy. And so I'm writing now a new version and I hope I'm not wrong in saying that it's somewhat better than the last.[199]

In all likelihood, it was when he "read through" the revision on the occasion mentioned in this letter that Wittgenstein wrote in MS 115 that his "whole attempt at a revision ... is *worthless*" (see n. 192). Even if this letter is not the ultimate source of the report passed on to us by Rhees, it is quite likely that this is the sort of point Wittgenstein was trying to convey. Here, however, there is no mention of any significant philosophical sense in which his efforts in the 'Brown Book' were methodologically wrong; rather Wittgenstein suggests that the way he went about things tended to constrain his thinking and resulted in a boring and artificial end-product. This is more a stylistic and/or procedural matter than a substantive methodological one. And there is not even a hint that he felt there was something methodologically inadequate about his notion of a 'language game'.[200]

The notion of a 'language game' is central to Wittgenstein's later *Denkweise*. It is the task of this chapter, as well as the following one, to uncover the way in which this notion came to hold a prominent place in his later approach to philosophy. The concern of the present chapter is with the sort of hypothetical ('constructed') langauge games one so plentifully finds in the 'Brown Book'. The next chapter considers 'language games' *qua* loci of *extant* linguistic practice.

In order to grasp how the notion of a hypothetical ('constructed') language game emerged as a significant feature in Wittgenstein's later philosophy, it is not only important but perhaps indispensable to come to grips with the crucial shift that took place in Wittgenstein's thinking concerning the proper role of the 'ideal'. To uncover what this shift was and how it is related to the emergence of hypothetical language games as a prominent feature in his later philosophy, let us work backwards (chronologically) through Wittgenstein's *Nachlaß*: first considering his latest characterizations of the place held by hypothetical language games in his philosophical deliberations, and then journeying back through his notebooks to the manuscripts of the early 1930s in order both to find out when such characterizations were originally proffered and to search for clues as to how his new view emerged.

Sprinkled throughout Wittgenstein's writings during the last decade of his life (the 1940s) are characterizations of the importance and role of hypothetical (constructed) language games in his later approach to philosophy. In late 1947, for example, right before describing a hypothetical language game, he explained what purpose the language game was to serve: "What I do here is really to point to a language game which demonstrates the difference between the concepts."[201] He then went on to present the language game: "Think of this language game: Determine how long an impression [*Eindruck*] lasts by means of a stop-watch. The duration of knowing, being able to, understanding could not be determined in this way."[202]

Since this latter remark was presented in the broader context of a contrast between concepts such as 'knowing' ('understanding', 'being able to') and concepts such as 'seeing' and 'hearing', it is fairly safe to assume that by 'impression' (*Eindruck*) Wittgenstein meant something along the lines of an auditory or visual impression. Though he did not give a name to the hypothetical language game he introduces here, one might call it 'timing the duration of a state of consciousness'. The suggestion is that, by introducing this hypothetical language game, a significant conceptual (logical) distinction is demonstrated between a concept such as 'knowing' and one such as 'hearing'. If one tries to play this language game, one finds that it makes sense to speak of timing one's visual or auditory impressions: for instance, we can tell someone to time the ringing in his ears after being subjected to a brief percussive outburst from a blaring loudspeaker. We can tell someone to attend to a sound and to inform us how long the sound lasts, when it begins to alter or fade, and when it stops.[203] If one paid attention to one's impressions one could time them with a stop-watch, though, of course, one might be distracted or interrupted and fail to notice when, as in the example just given, the sound altered or stopped. But Wittgenstein claims that, when we try to carry out the language game with concepts such as 'knowing' or 'understanding', we find that the game is no longer applicable – it does not make sense to speak of determining the duration of knowing or understanding in this way. Although one can pay attention to a visual or auditory impression and clock when it fades or ceases, one cannot (as Wittgenstein put it in a neighbouring remark in the same notebook) "follow with attention the forgetting of what one knew or the like".[204]

In this stretch of text, then, Wittgenstein was trying to point out a logical distinction between concepts such as 'knowing' and 'understanding' and those that might be called 'states of consciousness' – and he was trying to do so by means of a hypothetical language game. For our purposes, what is important in the example is not whether Wittgenstein is *convincing* in his attempt to show that 'knowing' and 'understanding' are not properly speaking 'states of consciousness'. Actually, he himself probably did not find his remarks wholly satisfactory, for he wrote on the cover page of this notebook, "In this volume no more than *one* halfway decent section comes out of each ten or twenty pages."[205] If one wanted to assess whether or not Wittgenstein has succeeded here in logically differentiating 'knowing' and 'understanding' from 'states of consciousness', one would have to examine carefully the whole nest of remarks dealing with this issue in this stretch of his manuscript – many of which remarks further buttress his position.[206]

What *is* of importance for our purposes is the light that the example sheds on Wittgenstein's use of hypothetical language games. By introducing a hypothetical notion (the game 'timing one's states of consciousness') Wittgenstein has tried to point out a logical difference between certain concepts. Roughly a year earlier (late 1946) in a different notebook, he had characterized generally the sort of role that hypothetical constructions play in his philosophy: "The investigation of language in philosophy is a describing and comparing of concepts, with the help also of concepts set up (constructed) *ad hoc*."[207] This is the sort of role that the hypothetical notion of 'timing one's states of consciousness' served. The suggested upshot of this particular game is that concepts such as 'knowing' or 'understanding' are not logically characterized by the sort of duration one would expect of psychological states (or processes), and thus are distinguishable from what one might call 'states of consciousness', such as hearing or seeing.

It is noteworthy that in this particular case one can characterize the 'logic' of Wittgenstein's methodological use of the hypothetical language game as a form of *reductio* reasoning. The concepts 'knowing' and 'understanding' are, of course, recognizable as among those concepts Wittgenstein earlier in his career viewed as 'metalogical' (see chapter 2): concepts which he took as designating psychological states or processes that lie behind the signs and which served as part of his early philosophical attempts to *explain* language. In effect what he has done with the hypothetical language game 'timing one's states of consciousness' is take this philosophical view of 'knowing' or 'understanding' and attempt to carry out its implications by means of an *ad hoc* language game. If 'knowing' or 'understanding' were a psychological *state*, then it should make sense to speak of 'timing its duration' in the sense in which one can time the duration of 'states' (for example visual or auditory impressions). Since it does not make sense to do this, 'knowing' and 'understanding' are not what we would call 'psychological *states*'. In this case the hypothetical language game is a projection of how things should be (what should make sense) *if* the philosophical view of 'knowing' or 'understanding' is correct.

Once one has set up the hypothetical language game, however, one finds that our conceptual world is not like that at all: though the game 'timing one's states of consciousness' makes sense with respect to such concepts as 'hearing' and 'seeing', it does not make sense with respect to such concepts as 'knowing' and 'understanding'.

Wittgenstein not only utilized this form of reasoning in his appeal to hypothetical language games, but seems to have explicitly recognized it as a methodological feature of his investigations, for he appears specifically to identify it in the following remark:

> A principle of our investigation: ~~construct the~~ describe in practical details and objectively how a reality looks which corresponds to the general world-description [*Weltbeschreibung*] of philosophers. You then at the same time clearly see that the world doesn't look like that and which part of the world actually does look like that.
>
> Take the general (vague) talk (chatter [*Gerede*]) of philosophers seriously and make a practical application of it!²⁰⁸

The hypothetical language game 'timing one's states of consciousness' seems to have been generated in just this manner. Wittgenstein took the philosophical chatter (to which he himself once contributed) about 'understanding' and 'knowing' as 'states of consciousness' and tried to construct a practical application for it – to describe how things should be if 'knowing' or 'understanding' were 'states of consciousness'. The indication was that 'knowing' and 'understanding' are not what we would call 'states', whereas perhaps 'seeing' and 'hearing' are.

Although the sort of reasoning involved in Wittgenstein's use of this particular hypothetical language game can perhaps be viewed as a prominent 'principle' in his investigations, a tactic maybe operative with many of the games he constructs, it is not the case that all of the hypothetical language games he introduces involve this sort of *reductio* pattern of reasoning. However, the feature of the particular example that *is* generalizable as a characteristic of Wittgenstein's overall employment of hypothetical language games is the general role that the hypothetical construction serves: namely, to help us clarify our own concepts.

The importance of the general role served by his introduction of hypothetical language games is perhaps most emphatically expressed in a remark Wittgenstein entered in one of his notebooks in 1948, when he went so far as to claim that "Nothing is more important for teaching us to understand our own concepts than constructing fictitious ones."²⁰⁹ A few months earlier (in the same notebook) he had explained,

> Why then do I generally want to construct variations on our concepts //on our conceptual world [*Begriffswelt*]//? Isn't it in order to

accentuate differences, and sometimes similarities, which were until now obliterated?

We build (draw) new boundaries //party walls//, demolish old ones, in order to (?) escape the hypnosis of an habituated kind of presentation. (?)[210]

And in a similar vein in late 1940 Wittgenstein had written, "One of the most important methods I use is to imagine a historical development for our ideas different from what actually occurred. If we do this we see the problem from a completely new angle."[211]

The following language game, also a product of the 1940s, is perhaps another good illustration of one of Wittgenstein's constructed variations on our 'conceptual world'; in particular it is a hypothetical variation of the 'historical development of our ideas'. It is an illustration which does not seem to involve a *reductio* pattern of reasoning as did the previous example.

> You must consider that a language game is possible, 'continuing a series of numerals', in which no rule, no expression of a rule is ever given, but the learning is done *only* by means of examples. So that the idea that each step can be justified by a something – a kind of model – in our mind would be entirely alien to these people.[212]

The particular way in which this hypothetical language game 'works' (might be taken to 'work'), the way it sheds light on our own concepts, is quite different from that of the previous example. The 'philosophical' view with which Wittgenstein is contending here seems to be the view one finds him struggling against in several other contexts:[213] namely, the view that 'knowing how to continue a series', 'knowing how to go on' designates a psychological state of having in one's mind some sort of model, rule or formula, and that continuing a series involves and is justified at each step in terms of the application of this 'model in one's mind'. The hypothetical language game Wittgenstein introduces this time, however, is not an attempt to construct the sort of conceptual microcosm that is *implied* by the philosophical view under consideration, and in the process finding out that our own conceptual world is not like that at all (thus shedding light on just what we *do* mean by certain expressions). Rather, quite the opposite strategy is used here: Wittgenstein now points out that one can imagine a hypothetical language game played by a hypothetical group of people (he sometimes refers to such groups as 'tribes') in which the 'philosophical view' does *not* come into play *at all*. The suggestion is that, even were the use of a model (*qua* rule or formula) never to come into play in learning the game 'continuing a series of numerals', so that the notion of a model (rule or formula) *in one's mind* would be entirely alien also, it would *still* be possible, it would *still* make sense to say, that the people in question *know* how to 'continue the series' so long as they are able to carry on in a certain way. This hypothetical language game sheds light on our own concepts in that it shows us that the notion of a 'model in one's mind' is not *logically* essential to our concept '*knowing* how to continue a series' – one can, as it were, play the game 'continue a series' *without* the notion of having a 'model in one's mind'.

Again, what is important for our purposes is not whether Wittgenstein is correct in this particular case, but rather what sort of purpose the hypothetical language game seems to be serving. And, again, it is not the *specific* way in which this language game '*works*' that is typical of his use of such language games, but rather its general role as a way of helping us to get clear about our own (ordinary) concepts and dispel philosophical misconceptions. The primary function of such games, then, is a heuristic one.

Such is the general role played by hypothetical language games in Wittgenstein's writings during the 1940s. That he considered hypothetical constructions of this sort to be of prime importance in his later philosophy is beyond question. To determine when, and more importantly *how*, hypothetical language games emerged as a prominent feature in Wittgenstein's philosophy, one has to go back to the manuscripts of the 1930s.

Thus far in the present discussion of the role of hypothetical language games scant mention has been made of *Philosophical Investigations*. The reason for this is that so much of the *Investigations*, especially part I, where Wittgenstein was more inclined to discuss his philosophical method, was originally written not in the last decade of his life, but rather in the 1930s. As soon as one moves to the manuscripts of the 1930s, and thus to some of the remarks published in part I of the *Investigations*, one is struck by clues as to how the use of hypothetical language games emerged as a prominent feature of his new *Denkweise*. Almost invariably these clues have to do with the notion of the 'ideal' and its role in philosophy.

What Wittgenstein identified in the 1940s as the general heuristic role played by hypothetical language games in his philosophy is also clearly expressed in *PI* §130. This remark, as it appears in the pre-war version of the *Investigations* (*c*.1937 or 1938), is linked to a discussion of the notion of an 'ideal':

> It is not our aim to refine or complete the system of rules for the use of our words in unheard-of ways.
> How should we have to imagine a complete list of rules for the employment of a word? – What do we mean by a complete list of rules for the employment of a piece in chess? Couldn't we always construct doubtful cases, in which the normal list of rules does not decide? Think e.g. of such a question as: how to determine who

moved last, if a doubt is raised about the reliability of the players' memories.

The regulation of traffic in the streets permits and forbids certain actions on the part of drivers and pedestrians; but it does not attempt to guide the totality of their movements by prescription. And it would be senseless to talk of an 'ideal' ordering of traffic which should do that; in the first place we should have no idea what to imagine as this ideal. If someone wants to make traffic regulations stricter on some point or other, that does not mean that he wants to approximate to such an ideal.

Likewise our exact [*exakten*] language games are not preparatory studies for some future regularization of language – as it were first approximations, ignoring friction and air-resistance. This view leads to inadequacies [*Ungerechtigkeiten*] (Nicod and Russell). The language games are rather set up as *objects of comparison* [*Vergleichsobjekte*] which are meant to throw light on the facts of our language by way of similarities and dissimilarities.

For the clarity we are aiming at is indeed *complete* clarity. But this simply means that the philosophical problems should *completely* disappear.[214]

The fourth paragraph (a version of *PI* §130) obviously points out what Wittgenstein considered to be the general heuristic role served by the "exact" or, as he put it in his 1943 revision of TS 220 (see TS 239, p. 85), the "clear and simple" language games he introduces. The key term is *Vergleichsobjekte*: hypothetical language games are to serve as "*objects of comparison*" which shed light on our own concepts. This is the same general role as we found Wittgenstein stressing in the 1940s. The clue to how his view of hypothetical language games may have emerged lies in what it is to which he *contrasts* his own approach to such games – the role he claims they do *not* serve. Wittgenstein claims he sets up his "exact" language games as 'objects of comparison' to shed light on the facts of our own language, and *not* as an attempt to offer a refined and complete system of rules for the use of words – *not* as an "'ideal' ordering" to which our language must approximate. He suggests that he is indeed introducing hypothetical language games with the aim of achieving "*complete* clarity"; but what he envisages here is not a *complete* system of rules for the use of words, but rather the *complete* elimination of philosophical misconceptions. Thus it is in their heuristic capacity as *Vergleichsobjekte* that "exact" ("clear and simple") language games serve to achieve complete clarity.

The suggestion seems to be that to set up an exact language game and take it as an 'ideal' to which language must approximate – as a complete system of rules for the use of words – leads to inadequacies. Although

Wittgenstein cites the views of the logicians Nicod and Russell as having led to inadequacies, he also felt his own earlier views were faulty in this way. The contrast we find here between the heuristic use of exact language games and the logician's regulatory use of exact games as a complete system of rules for the use of words is echoed also in Wittgenstein's 1936 revision of the 'Brown Book', except that there the logician he cites is himself. After having examined several hypothetical language games he wrote,

> Reflections such as these can show us the ~~infinite~~ enormous multiplicity of the medium [*Mittel*] of language [in the 'Brown Book' (*BBB*, p. 83), "the function of words in propositions"]; and it is striking (interesting) to compare what ~~we see (observe) here~~ becomes evident to us here with ~~the simple and strict rules which~~ what logicians have said about the structure of all propositions. (Compare also //This goes also for// what I myself said (wrote) in the *Tractatus*.)[215]

What Wittgenstein said in the *Tractatus* about the "structure of all propositions" concerned his general conception of a proposition as truth-functionally analysable in terms of 'elementary' ones. It seems that the inadequacies to which the logicians' (including Wittgenstein in the *Tractatus*) use of the 'ideal' (the exact game) lead stem from their taking the simple and strict rules of the 'ideal' game (perhaps the strict rules for truth-functional composition) as a complete system applicable for *all* propositions – thus failing to do justice to the "multiplicity" of language. However, the 'ideal' (the exact game), taken as a heuristic device, might serve to reveal that multiplicity rather than neglect it.

The 1937–8 context of *PI* §130, as previously cited from the pre-war version of the *Investigations*, links the notion of hypothetical language games to some sort of shift in Wittgenstein's thinking concerning the role of *das Ideal*. Much of that context, however, itself stemmed from remarks Wittgenstein had made in connection with TS 213 §58 (see n. 214), entitled

> Strict Grammatical Game Rules and Vague Language Use.
> Normative Logic.
> In What Way Do We Talk about Ideal Cases, an Ideal Language? ("Logic for a Vacuum")

The remarks in this section of TS 213 take us deeper into the nature of the shift in Wittgenstein's thinking concerning the role of the 'ideal'.

The shift to a heuristic use of exact language games as 'objects of comparison' involved an abandonment of his attempts earlier in his career to offer a refined and complete system of rules for the use of words (an 'ideal' order to which our language must approximate), but this should not be taken to imply that he was no longer concerned with 'rules of use' in his later philosophy. Rather there was a *change* in his concern with such rules. This comes out fairly clearly in TS 213 §58. After a lengthy presentation of an example of a name being used "without a fixed meaning", where "we are prepared to change the game-rules as required (make the rules as we go along)",[216] Wittgenstein wrote,

> And here I recall that Ramsey once emphasized that logic was a "normative science". If one means by that it sets up an ideal to which reality only approximates, then it must be said that this 'ideal' interests us only as an instrument for the approximate description of reality. It is of course possible to describe a calculus exactly, namely for the purpose of roughly characterizing a group of other calculi. If for example someone wanted to know what a board-game [*Brettspiel*] is, then I could by way of explanation exactly describe draughts and then say, "You see any board-game <u>functions</u> about like this." – Wasn't it then a mistake (for so it seems to me now) to assume that one who uses language always plays *one precise game* [*ein bestimmtes Spiel*]. For wasn't this the sense of my remark that everything in a proposition – however roughly it might be expressed – "is in order"? But didn't I want to say: everything must be in order, if someone says a sentence and employs it? Though thereby after all neither is something in order nor in disorder. – It would be in order if one could say: even this person plays a game according to a precise, fixed system of rules.[217]

The allusion to his previous 'mistaken' view, that anyone who uses language plays "*one precise game*" and in this sense the propositions of our language are "in order", is perhaps a reference to *Tractatus* 5.5562–3, where Wittgenstein suggested that there must be elementary propositions and that all of the propositions of our ordinary language, however vaguely expressed, are in perfect logical order – i.e. analysable in terms of elementary propositions. In which case, the 'one precise game' Wittgenstein alludes to is again that game implied by his Tractarian notion of the 'general form of a proposition', which in effect specified that whatever is to count as a 'proposition' must either be an 'elementary' proposition or be truth-functionally analysable in terms of elementary propositions.[218]

In the above passage Wittgenstein's critique of his earlier view seems to be twofold. On the one hand he seems to be making a point similar to that expressed in the previously cited remark (q. 215) in which reference was made to the *Tractatus*: namely, that there is not uniformity but rather multiplicity in language and thus logicians (including Wittgenstein), in their general characterizations of the "structure of all propositions", have erred in assuming that *one* game is played. On the other hand, there also seems to be a criticism of the notion that in language one always plays a *precise* game according to a precise, fixed system of rules. These criticisms are introduced after his having stressed that he is interested in the 'ideal' (the ideal, exact game) not as a requirement to which our real language must conform, but rather only as an instrument for the description of that reality (language). With the shift in his view of the role of the 'ideal' came the abandonment of both the requirement that language must involve one overall game and that that game must be according to a strict and precise system of rules. Thus, a page after the above cited passage from TS 213, we find Wittgenstein, by way of an analogy, elaborating on the change in his attitude to the notion of 'rules' of language:

> Doesn't the analogy between language and games throw light here? We can easily imagine people amusing themselves in a field by playing with a ball so as to start various games in a series, not playing to the end and perhaps in between even aimlessly throwing the ball, catching it, letting it fall, etc. Now someone says: the whole time they are playing a ball-game and following precise rules at every throw.... We could say: we investigate language in terms of its rules. If here and there it has no rules, then *that* is the result of our investigations.[219]

The 'ideal' game, when taken as a standard to which reality *must* conform, would lead one to claim in the above analogy that one *must* be "following precise rules at every throw" (this seems to have been an analogue to a view of language Wittgenstein held earlier in his career). However, if one takes the ideal, the exact game, as a heuristic instrument (an object of comparison) for investigating language, one is open to the possibility (and Wittgenstein came to the realization) that language is not, as it were, a uniform and exact game played according to fixed and precise rules. Thus there is still a concern with 'rules of language', but a uniform and precise system of rules is no longer a requirement of his investigation.

For Wittgenstein one of the symptoms indicating that an 'ideal' (ideal game, ideal calculus) has played an improper role in one's investigation is that one tends to assume that it (the ideal) *must* be applicable to what one is investigating (in Wittgenstein's case, 'language'), yet one does not seem to be able to specify concretely its application. There is another passage in TS 213 §58 which, when read in conjunction with a parenthetical insert Wittgenstein wrote a few years later, unequivocally points to the *Tractatus* as having manifested precisely such a symptom (see also my discussion in n. 228):

It is of the utmost importance that for a calculus of logic we always imagine an example in which the calculus actually is applied, and not examples of which we say they are not really the ideal, this though we don't have yet. That is the sign of a completely false view. (Russell and I have in different ways laboured under it. Check what I say in the *Tractatus* about elementary propositions and objects....[220]

The role that the ideal played in his old (Tractarian) approach to language was that of a requirement which, as it were, imposed itself on 'reality'. This was explicitly elaborated upon a few years later (1937) in a stretch of text which Wittgenstein indicated was an attempt to characterize in one quick stroke the protracted transitions "from the old to the new ways of thinking [*Betrachtungsweisen*]".[221] It is no coincidence that the dominant subject of discussion in this stretch of text is the shift in his view of the role of the 'ideal'. Concerning his earlier (Tractarian) attempts to "grasp the essence of language" he wrote,

> Language it seems must possess a kind of ideal order. An ideal rule-governed [*geregelte*] grammar. And we are inclined to speak of the totality of rules which govern the use of a word (and to ask what this totality looks like).
> It seems to us that super-order [*Über-Ordnung*] *must* be found in the actual [*wirkliche*] language. So we also ask ourselves what is the *real* [*eigentliche*, authentic] word, the *real* proposition of our language, for the written and uttered words and propositions don't possess in their nature the clarity that the sublime language requires. So we search for the real word and believe we find it perhaps in the idea [*Vorstellung*] of the word [cf. *PI* §105].
> And so it happens that we have a conception of an ideal and say it *must* be applicable to the reality of language, but we can't say how (without being able to say – how).[222]

Having a notion of an ideal and assuming it must be applicable to the reality of language but not being able to say *how*, is, of course, what we found Wittgenstein (in reference to the *Tractatus*) identifying as symptomatic of a false view (see n. 220). In particular, it seems he had earlier in his career assumed there was an ideal order in language – as it were, a sublime, clear essence of language (the *real* word, the *real* proposition) as opposed to the vague written and uttered words and propositions of ordinary discourse. Evidently, however, he had come to the realization that the 'ideal order' which he thought *must* be in language, was merely an abstraction he had imposed on language.

In MS 157, after the above passage, Wittgenstein next, in a staccato manner, ran through a series of examples of how in his earlier thinking an 'ideal' conception had, as it were, been dogmatically imposed on the reality of language. He mentions, for instance, the 'ideal' notion of a 'name' and asks, "(The *ideal* name) What was it that was false about this notion?"[223] He later continued,

> The ideal name should function like this: 'This name corresponds to *that*', and the '*that*' should be simple [*einfach*], completely simple.
> ... But why does one now believe that there must be (found) something corresponding to this construction? ...
> Why do I say the proposition *must* be built up [*gebaut sein*] in such and such a way?[224]

What Wittgenstein is questioning here is fairly obvious. In the *Tractatus* (see 3.202 and 4.22ff.) 'names' were those hypothesized "simple signs" (*einfachen Zeichen*) which were allegedly the constituents of 'elementary propositions'. And, as has been previously noted (see, for instance, n. 222), 'elementary propositions' were those hypothesized basic 'propositions' in terms of which anything that is to count as a proposition (meaningful statement) is in principle analysable. In the *Tractatus* 'names' and 'elementary propositions' were taken as, to use Wittgenstein's own self-deprecating expressions (see q. 222 and *PI*§105), the *real* (*eigentliche*, authentic) words and *real* propositions comprising, so to speak, the essence of language. Such are examples of how in his earlier thinking an 'ideal' (an abstraction, or, if you will, a hypothetical, exact game) was imposed on the reality of language.

Similarly, alluding to the Tractarian 'picture theory' and his early notion of a 'general form of proposition', he wrote,

> "If *one* sentence is a picture then every sentence must be a picture, for they must all be essentially the same. Every sentence says: this is how things are [*es verhalt sich so und so*]." Here we also have such an ideal, that forces its way on the phenomena.[225]

And a few paragraphs later he further explained,

> The idea of the essence [*Wesen*], when we wanted to state the essence of a proposition, was not simply a description of what one calls a proposition (what one signifies with this word), but rather it was to express an ultimate [*ein Letztes*], to provide the ultimate clarity about something incomparable [*das Unvergleichliche*]. To present it (no description) clearly once for all.

How have you come by this ideal?
The ideal is unshakable. You can never get outside it. You must always turn back. There is no outside; outside you cannot breathe. Where does this come from? //Where does this feeling come from?//
... It is as if we don't recognize a form of expression as a form of expression.
(Or almost as if we took the colour of the glasses, or a mark on the glasses through which we see, for the colour or a characteristic of the thing we look at.)
For example, "Every proposition after all says: This is how things are." That is such a pair of glasses.[226]

The expression "This is how things are" is, of course, Wittgenstein's characterization in the *Tractatus* (4.5) of the 'general form of a proposition'. For present purposes it is not necessary to speculate in any detail about what exactly the Tractarian 'picture theory' was, or what exactly the Tractarian notion of an ideal 'name' was and how such names were thought to serve as constituents of 'elementary propositions' (see n. 228), or just how Wittgenstein's formal notion of a 'general form of a proposition' amounted to a stipulation of the truth-functional analysability of 'propositions' in terms of 'elementary propositions'. Rather it suffices to point out that Wittgenstein himself cites such notions as examples of how earlier in his career he had offered an ideal (an abstract, pure, simple game or calculus) as some sort of sublime 'essence' of reality (language), and in so doing ignored the actual characteristics of language – offering, for example, some sort of general essence of a proposition (or of a word, a name) instead of just describing the 'propositions' of our everyday language. The role the 'ideal' case played in the *Tractatus* was a dogmatic one – that of the imposition of an abstraction onto reality. This role, in terms of the 'glasses' metaphor introduced above, led to the mistaking of features of that (the ideal case) through which one might examine language for fundamental (essential) features of language itself.

As one might suspect, the shift in Wittgenstein's thinking concerning the proper role of the 'ideal' is intimately tied in with his shift to an emphasis on ordinary language as the proper domain of logic. In the preceding chapter (see pp. 61-3) we found, for instance, that Wittgenstein's shift to an emphasis on ordinary language was at least in part a shift away from his Tractarian attempts to 'discover' uniformities – for example, the construction of a calculus which deals with "all propositions" (but which neglected the grammar of our everyday expressions). The sorts of 'uniformities' or 'general conceptions' that Wittgenstein strove to discover (for instance, the 'general form of a proposition') we now find him identifying as examples of the dogmatic imposition of an 'ideal' calculus on the reality of language.

Wittgenstein's shift to a concern with ordinary language, then, coincided with (and was bound up with) a shift to a concern with the 'ideal', not as an abstract, precise rule-governed grammar (see q. 222) which was presupposed as expressing the formal unity of language (the '*real*' essence of language), but instead as a *hypothetical* exact grammar which, *in its heuristic role*, does *not* neglect but rather serves to reveal the actual use (the actual grammar) of our everyday expressions. Inasmuch as Wittgenstein 'constructs' simple, exact language games in his later philosophy, he is in effect setting up hypothetical, exact grammars. Such 'ideal' grammars, however, are not put on a pedestal and offered as what is most 'concrete' or 'real', but, rather, are discarded once they have served their heuristic function of shedding light on the use (grammar) of our *everyday* expressions. (See the next chapter for a discussion of Wittgenstein's later notion of grammar.)

Just how central the shift in Wittgenstein's view of the role of the 'ideal' was for the emergence of his new *Denkweise* – and, for that matter, *that* this shift was bound up with his emphasis on ordinary language – is indicated by some of his other remarks in this same manuscript (MS 157). In the preceding chapter, among the texts examined in the account (see pp. 59ff.) of Wittgenstein's shift to an emphasis on ordinary language was *PI* §108 (paras 2–4). The first paragraph of this section, however, was not discussed. Actually, in the pre-war version of the *Investigations* the second to fourth paragraphs were not combined with the first (see TS 220, p. 76): Wittgenstein did not link them until his 1943 (TS 239, p. 74) revision of TS 220. Unlike paragraphs 2–4, which were initially drafted in 1929–31, much of the first paragraph was initially drafted in MS 157a (1937) in the midst of Wittgenstein's discussion of the shift in his thinking concerning the role of the 'ideal'. That this material was combined in one section (§108) in *Philosophical Investigations* is a good indication that Wittgenstein considered his emphasis on ordinary language to be intimately bound up with this shift, the centrality of which is obvious when one examines the context of the first paragraph of *PI* §108 as initially drafted in fragmentary form in MS 157a. In the context of a discussion of his early (Tractarian) requirement of complete clarity and exactness in 'logic', and again utilizing the game analogy, Wittgenstein wrote,

> "But still it isn't a game, if there is some vagueness in the rules." – But *does* this prevent its being a game? – "Perhaps you'll call it a 'game', but at any rate it certainly isn't the ideal (an ideal //pure//) game." This means: it is an impure game and I am interested in *that* which is pure. But the ideal is your form of expression and (a misunderstanding) seduces you *falsely to employ* the ideal.
> It is as if you said, 'The circumference of this wheel is *really* πd" (so precisely is it made).

The complete purity and clarity (crystalline clarity) of logic: it must be a crystal, *nothing amorphous in it*. . . .

But it isn't now like *this*; that we could stop dealing with that crystalline purity! The *preconceived idea* [*Vorurteil*, prejudice] which lies in it can only be removed by turning round our whole examination [*Betrachtung*, way of thinking]; and thereby give that purity a different place //and thereby put that purity in another place.

But also it is not like this, that one could say, "The preconceived idea is that the ideal *exists*. While we must only strive after it. //while we ourselves (reality) only approximate it.//" For also *in this* lies the (a) misunderstanding. The role of the ideal is thereby not grasped.

One might say: The examination must be turned round [*Die Betrachtung muß gedreht werden*], but about the fixed point of our real need.[227]

These remarks clearly indicate that the shift in the role of the 'ideal' is primarily what Wittgenstein was alluding to in *PI* §108 in his reference to 'turning round his whole examination or way of thinking [*Betrachtung*]'. The 'ideal', the formal unity, the exact calculus or game, is no longer to be dogmatically presupposed as constitutive of some sublime 'essence' of language. There is a recognition that language is not a 'formal unity', but rather is, as Wittgenstein put it in the first sentence of *PI* §108, a "family of structures more or less related to one another" (cf. q. 188). He suggests, however, that turning his way of thinking around does not involve the abandonment of the 'ideal' (the pure game, the calculus with precise rules); rather, the 'ideal' has a new 'place' in his philosophy, it plays a different role.

Several pages later in the same notebook, Wittgenstein more specifically identified what that new role of the 'ideal' is:

For we can avoid inadequacy [*Ungerechtigkeit*] or emptiness in our assertions only by, in our examination [*Betrachtung*], presenting (viewing) the ideal [*das Ideal*] as what it *is*, namely as an object of comparison [*Vergleichsobjekt*] – (so to speak) as a measuring rod – and not (instead of) as the preconceived idea [*Vorurteil*] to which everything *must* conform. The latter of course is (Herein lies) the dogmatism into which (our) philosophy can so easily fall.

But what then is the relation between a view like Spengler's and mine?

The inadequacy in Spengler: the ideal doesn't lose any of its majesty when it is presented as the principle of the form of reflection. A good unit of measure – –

Russell – Nicod[228]

The first paragraph in the above passage is clearly a version of *PI* §131. We find here many of the key terms we have already encountered. The new role of the 'ideal' is that of a *Vergleichsobjekt*: an "object of comparison" is of course precisely what Wittgenstein identified in *PI* §130 (cf. q. 214) as the role played by the ('ideal') exact language games he sets up in his later philosophy. This new role of the 'ideal' is contrasted to the 'dogmatic' application of the 'ideal' as a "preconceived idea" (cf. q. 227) to which everything "*must*" conform (cf. qq. 222, 224, 225). Also again there is reference to "inadequacies" resulting from a false view of the role of the ideal, and mention of Russell and Nicod in this connection (cf. q. 214).

What is genuinely new to us in the above passage is Wittgenstein's somewhat equivocal reference to Spengler. In the pre-war version of the *Investigations* (TS 220) only the first of the above paragraphs was included, but Wittgenstein parenthetically added a reference to Spengler right after his statement of the new role that the 'ideal' was to serve in his own philosophy: "(I am thinking of Spengler's way of thinking)". (See n. 228 for the whole passage.)

In *both* the MS 157b and TS 220 versions though, the reference to Spengler is somewhat equivocal; there is both a suggestion that there may be an affinity between Spengler's way of thinking and the role that the 'ideal' plays in Wittgenstein's own new *Denkweise*, and an indication that Spengler's way of presenting an 'ideal' may be somehow inadequate. Although it would be interesting to know what, if anything, Wittgenstein got out of Spengler and how he got it, when dealing with an intellect such as Wittgenstein's it is hazardous and may well be completely unproductive to speculate on such matters (as noted in chapter 1; see pp. 12–14). However, if Wittgenstein himself volunteered an account of *what* he had gleaned from Spengler, then even if we should not wish to hazard a guess as to *how* in the world he gleaned it, such an account might certainly shed some light on or help us to date the emergence of an important aspect of Wittgenstein's own new *Denkweise*.

Wittgenstein does indeed volunteer an account of *what* he gleaned from Spengler, though unfortunately he does not inform us *how* he gleaned it. In TS 213 §58, the section in which Wittgenstein explains the way he "talks about ideal cases, an ideal language" and from which several passages have already been cited (qq. 216, 217, 219 and 220), he noted the following about Spengler:

> Spengler could be better understood if he said: I am *comparing* different cultural epochs with the lives of families; within a family there is a family resemblance [*Familienähnlichkeit*], though you will also find a resemblance between members of different families; family resemblance differs from the other sort of resemblance in such and

such ways, etc. What I mean is: we have to be told the object of comparison [*Vergleichsobjekt*], the object from which this way of viewing things is derived, otherwise the discussion will constantly be affected by distortions [*Ungerechtigkeiten*]. Because willy-nilly we shall ascribe the properties of the prototype [*Urbild*] to the object we are viewing in its light; and we claim, "It *must always* be . . .".

This is because we want to give the prototype's characteristics a purchase on our way of representing things. But since we confuse prototype and object we find ourselves dogmatically conferring on the object properties which only the prototype necessarily possesses. On the other hand we think our view will not have the generality we want it to have if it is really true only of the one case. But the prototype ought to be clearly presented for what it is; so that it characterizes the whole discussion and determines its form. This makes it the focal point, so that its general validity will depend on the fact that it determines the form of discussion rather than on the claim that everything which is true only of it holds too far all the things that are being discussed.[229]

Here again we find many of the key terms that have dominated Wittgenstein's discussion of the proper role of the 'ideal'. There is mention of an ideal, here referred to as a "prototype" (*Urbild*; see n. 229) but in the 1943 version of *PI* §131 as a "model" (*Vorbild*; see n. 228) – a prototype which should be viewed as an *object of comparison* (*Vergleichsobjekt*). There is the suggestion that failure properly to view the ideal in its role as an object of comparison will result in inadequacies (*Ungerechtigkeiten*) because one would tend "dogmatically" to claim that the features of the ideal "*must*" be found in reality – one would tend dogmatically to impose on reality (the 'objects' one is examining) features which are true only of the ideal or prototype. There is also mention of a perhaps misbegotten desire for "*generality*" (something true of all cases, a uniformity), and this in contrast to a theme of 'multiplicity' as evoked by the metaphor of a "family": in a family there are resemblances and dissimilarities, but there is no pure uniformity (recall the preceding comments on q. 227 [*PI* §108] and cf. also q. 188). In the above passage, however, these themes are presented in reference to Spengler, the suggestion being that, although Spengler may not have adequately spelled out the role that an 'ideal' ("prototype") played in his examination of cultural epochs, one could better understand him if one viewed the role of an 'ideal' in his discussion as that of an "object of comparison". There is not much to go on here concerning just *how* Wittgenstein managed to find such themes in Spengler (see n. 230), but there is no doubt that what Wittgenstein saw in Spengler's thinking bears a striking resemblance to Wittgenstein's accounts of his own thinking concerning the role of the 'ideal'. In fact there is virtually nothing in what Wittgenstein says about Spengler that we have not already encountered in some form or another in Wittgenstein's comments about his own thinking.

The shift in Wittgenstein's thinking concerning the role of the 'ideal' clearly seems to have been inspired at least in part by Spengler. And, although the reference to Spengler does not shed any *new* light on the role of the 'ideal' in Wittgenstein's later philosophy, it does help us date the shift that took place in his thinking on the subject. Given that this shift was partly inspired by Spengler, and given that the discussion of Spengler cited from TS 213 was *originally* drafted in 1931 (see n. 229), it is evident that the change in Wittgenstein's thinking concerning the proper role of the 'ideal' had already taken place by the *early* thirties – prior to the so-called 'Blue and Brown Books period'. Consistent with this is Wittgenstein's acknowledgement of Spengler in 1931 as one of the thinkers in whom he found a *Gedankenbewegung* (tactic or manoeuvre in thinking) and, as he put it, "simply straightaway seized on it with enthusiasm for my work of clarification".[230]

If one keeps in mind the fundamental shift that took place (by the early 1930s) in Wittgenstein's thinking concerning the role of the 'ideal', it becomes quite clear what he means in the passages (sprinkled throughout his later writings) where he suggests that he '*constructs*' an ideal language or ideal languages'. These constructed ideal languages are the hypothetical language games, the simple, exact calculi (there will be a discussion of Wittgenstein's notion of 'calculi' in the next chapter) which are to serve as 'objects of comparison' to shed light on our actual language. As such, Wittgenstein *does* 'construct ideal languages', in his later philosophy, but he does so for a heuristic purpose, not a reformative one[231] (as, for instance, he formerly assumed one should be able to construct a precise 'primary'/ 'phenomenal' language that would more clearly and exactly express what is so clumsily expressed in ordinary language; see chapter 2, pp. 55–9).

In TS 213 §58, where Wittgenstein specifies the way in which he is concerned with "ideal cases, an ideal language", he explicitly cautions us not to misconstrue his concern. Directly after his lengthy discussion of Spengler and account of the proper role of the 'ideal' as a *Vergleichsobjekt* (see q. 229) he continued,

> How strange if logic were concerned with an 'ideal' language and not with *ours*, for where should we get this ideal language? And what should this ideal language express? Presumably, what we now express in our ordinary language; in that case this is the language logic must investigate. Or something else: but, then, how would I have any idea what that would be? – Logical analysis is the analysis of something we have, not of something we don't have. Therefore it is the analysis of

propositions *as they stand* [*wie sie sind*, as they are]. (It would be odd if the human race had been speaking all this time without ever putting together a genuine proposition.)

It is not true that what I say //we say// only concerns (or would have value for) an 'ideal language'; but perhaps one might say that we construct an ideal language in which then everything that can be said in other //non-ideal// languages is translatable.

If someone speaks of an ideal language, then one must ask: in what respect 'ideal'?[232]

The first paragraph of the above passage is also to be found in *Philosophical Remarks* (*PR*, p. 52) and thus stems from the very early 1930s. We find here (as we did in some of the passages examined in the preceding chapter) an emphasis on ordinary language as the proper domain of logic. The suggestion is that, instead of striving for some 'ideal' (for instance, perhaps the "*real* proposition", the "*real* word or name", see q. 222 and *PI* §105), 'logic' should concern itself with "the analysis of propositions *as they stand*".[233] But this shift in emphasis need not entail the abandonment of the 'ideal case, ideal language'; rather, as Wittgenstein suggests, the crucial question is how one is to take the 'ideal', what role it is to serve (see q. 227).

The second paragraph of the above passage was originally drafted in 1931 (MS 153a, pp. 129-30; see also the version in MS 111, p. 107) and was immediately preceded by the following remark: "Isn't then my expression that the proposition is a picture a false [*schiefer*, distorted] expression which pushed a certain analogy too far?" The 'picture theory' is, of course, one of the examples Wittgenstein gives of how in the *Tractatus* he had employed an 'ideal' dogmatically (see q. 225). One can *construct* an ideal language (calculus) in terms of which another (non-ideal) language – our ordinary one, for example – is to be understood or translated; however, whether or not our actual language (the real domain of our concern) does *in fact* wholly conform to this 'ideal' is not to be dogmatically presupposed (as it was in the *Tractatus*) but is rather to be determined by taking the 'ideal' as an 'object of comparison'. For this reason it is crucial to ask how one is taking the 'ideal' (ideal case, ideal language). As Wittgenstein admitted in some of his other remarks in TS 213 §58 (see qq. 217, 219 and 220), upon taking the 'ideal' as an 'object of comparison' rather than as something to which language "*must*" conform, he realized that ordinary language does *not* in fact conform to an 'ideal' – or, as he also put it, he was *mistaken* in thinking that "one who uses language always plays *one precise game*" (see q. 217).

To the extent, then, that Wittgenstein can be said to '*construct* an ideal language or ideal languages' in his later philosophy, such (exact, simple) 'languages' are to be taken not as ends in themselves, but rather are of importance only in their heuristic capacity. Thus one finds Wittgenstein in *Philosophical Grammar* asserting,

> We examine language *from the point of view* [*unter dem Gesichtspunkt*] of a game with fixed rules. We compare it with, measure it against, such a game.
> ... It can't be said that logic depicts an idealized reality, or that it holds strictly only for an ideal language, and so on. For where do we get the concept of this ideal?! The most that could be said is that "we are *constructing* an ideal language" which contrasts with ordinary language; but it can't be said that we are *saying* something that would hold only of an ideal language.[234]

Clearly, the suggestion is that we can say Wittgenstein is "constructing an ideal language", but such a language with fixed rules is set up as a game that "contrasts with ordinary language"; something with which to "compare" ordinary language, something against which to "measure" it.

In a similar vein in the 'Blue Book' he indicated,

> It is wrong to say that in philosophy we consider an ideal language as opposed to our ordinary one. For this makes it appear as though we thought we could improve on ordinary language. But ordinary language is all right. Whenever we make up 'ideal languages' it is not in order to replace our ordinary language by them; but just to remove some trouble caused in someone's mind by thinking that he has got hold of the exact use of a common word. That is also why our method is not merely to enumerate actual usages of words, but rather deliberately to invent new ones, some of them because of their absurd appearance.[235]

And in the final version of *PI* §81 one also finds Wittgenstein accepting the expression "*constructing* an ideal language", but again there is the warning not to misconstrue the role of the ideal:

> and the most that can be said is that we *construct* ideal languages. But here the word 'ideal' is liable to mislead, for it sounds as if these languages were better, more perfect, than our everyday language; and as if it took the logician to shew people at last what a proper sentence looked like.

Wittgenstein, then, '*constructs* an ideal language' in the sense that he sets up or imagines a hypothetical game which as an 'object of comparison' serves a heuristic, not a reformative, function *vis-à-vis* our ordinary language.

The so-called 'Brown Book' can and *should* be viewed as a *collection* of such 'constructed, ideal languages' or hypothetical language games. Granted, in the 'Brown Book' some of the ideal cases or games seem to have been 'constructed' by varying a game that had already been presented, and one might consider some (though not all) of the variants more 'complex' than the games of which they are a variation, but the linkage of games in this manner is in all likelihood little more than a stylistic device used to facilitate the smooth transition from one conceptual concern to another – a stylistic device which, incidentally, Wittgenstein seems to have found too artificial and constraining (see *PI*, Preface, paras 1–2; and q. 199). It would be a mistake to take the 'Brown Book' *as a whole* as an attempt to construct a language or some sort of overall 'uniform system'. Garth Hallett, for instance, after citing from the 'Blue Book' the remark "We recognize in these simple processes forms of language not separated by a break from our more complicated ones. We see that we can build up the complicated forms from the primitive ones by gradually adding new forms",[236] – then suggests that "This is what he [Wittgenstein] set out to do in the *Brown Book*" and that it was an attempt to build a "uniform system".[237] It is quite possible to recognize that some of our complicated forms of language (language games) might be built up out of simpler ones (as one might, for example, be able to build up more complicated forms out of the primitive "forms of language with which a child begins to make use of words": see 'Blue Book', *BBB*, p. 17), but it does not follow from such a recognition that what Wittgenstein was trying to do in the 'Brown Book', or for that matter anywhere in his post-1930 writings, was to construct one overall "uniform system" of language in this way.

Why Hallett would cite a remark from the set of class notes known as the 'Blue Book' to explain what Wittgenstein was doing in a manuscript (the 'Brown Book') that had not even been written at the time, *instead of* citing Wittgenstein's explanation *in* the 'Brown Book' itself, is not very clear. In the 'Brown Book' Wittgenstein makes it quite explicit that the simple language games he introduces should *not* be viewed as 'parts' of an overall 'system' of language that has been built out of them. After having presented the first five language games of the 'Brown Book' he explained,

> Systems of communication as for instance 1), 2), 3), 4), 5) we shall call 'language games'. They are more or less akin to what in ordinary language we call games. Children are taught language by means of such games. We are not, however, regarding the language games which we describe as incomplete parts of a language ["parts of a whole, '*the* language'" in MS 115, p. 126, published in *S*, vol. 5, p. 121], but as languages complete in themselves, as complete systems of human communication. To keep this point of view in mind, it very

often is useful to imagine such a simple language to be the entire system of communication of a tribe in a primitive state of society. ...²³⁸

Actually the very notion of 'building up a language' out of simpler forms (simple language games) seems wholly antithetical to the fundamental shift that by the early 1930s had already taken place in Wittgenstein's thinking concerning the proper role of the 'ideal' (ideal case, ideal language). To describe Wittgenstein's later writing as an attempt to *build up* our complicated language out of simple or primitive cases seems to differ only terminologically from attributing to him the view that language is a "uniform system" *analysable in terms of* simple or primitive cases. Under either description, however, one not only seems to be mistakenly attributing to Wittgenstein the view that language is a 'uniformity' (rather than a "multiplicity", a "family"), but also is grossly misconstruing (in terms of Wittgenstein's old thinking) the *heuristic* role that the ideal case plays in his *new Denkweise*.

That one would be grossly misconstruing Wittgenstein in this way if one took him to be attempting to 'build up a language' by means of the simple language games he introduces comes out quite vividly in a remark Wittgenstein made around 1933–4:

> When I describe precise [*bestimmte*] simple language games, this is not in order gradually to describe [*beschreiben*] with them (in terms of them) the (actual) processes of the ~~ordinary~~ developed language, which only would lead to inadequacies [*Ungerechtigkeiten*] (Nicod and Russell). ~~But rather I put forth the language games as objects of comparison [Vergleichsobjekte]~~ Rather we let the language games be what they are. They should simply shed their light on our problems.²³⁹

Obviously Wittgenstein is claiming that there is a correct and an incorrect way of taking the simple language games (ideal languages) he introduces. He does not intend, and we should not take, them as an attempt gradually to describe or construct (see q. 240) our more complicated ordinary language. The mention that this would lead to "inadequacies" and the reference to Nicod and Russell we should recognize by now (cf. qq. 214, 228 and 229) as a clear indication that one would be misconstruing the role of the 'ideal' in Wittgenstein's later philosophy if one interepreted his simple (ideal) language games in this way. The correct approach to the simple language games he introduces would be to take them in a purely heuristic way as hypothetical 'objects of comparison' which are to shed some light on our (conceptual) problems. What Wittgenstein specifies as the *correct* way of viewing the hypothetical (ideal) language games is, of course, precisely the point we found him making in *PI* §130 (cf. q. 214).

It is significant that the above passage, in which Wittgenstein explicitly explains what methodological purpose hypothetical language games serve (and do not serve) in his (new) philosophy, was *not* a first draft. Rather it was part of his 1933-4 revision of TS 213 material. Thus one finds virtually the same remark in TS 213 §46, entitled "The Functioning of Propositions Clarified [*erläutert*] by a Language Game [*Sprachspiel*]". In this section, in the midst of a discussion of a hypothetical language game, he cautioned,

> When I describe precise [*bestimmte*] simple games, this is not in order to construct [*aufzubauen*] with them gradually the actual processes of language – or of thinking – which only leads to inadequacies [*Ungerechtigkeiten*], but rather I set forth the games as such, and let them shed their light on the particular problems.[240]

Furthermore, this remark, as well as the rest of §46, was *originally* written in late 1931 or early 1932 (see n. 240). Thus, not only are there examples of hypothetical language games in the early thirties prior to the 'Blue and Brown Books period', but the role that such games or 'ideal cases' were to serve in his philosophy was also well defined by then.

A prevailing view, championed by G. P. Baker and P. M. S. Hacker, is that "the notion of a language game is introduced only [first] in the *Blue Book*" and "It is only in the *Brown Book* that the language game *method* achieves maturity (and perhaps is used to excess). There is no deep difference between its use there and in the *Investigations*."[241] Baker and Hacker are quite correct in suggesting that there is no significant difference between Wittgenstein's use of hypothetical language games in the 'Brown Book' and his use of them in the *Investigations*. However, they are mistaken in their claim that Wittgenstein's "language game *method*" was not in place prior to the 'Blue and Brown Books period'.

It should be quite clear from the evidence examined thus far that, as far as the heuristic role played by hypothetical language games (the simple, exact, 'ideal' cases or languages Wittgenstein 'constructs') is concerned (i.e. their role as *Vergleichsobjekte* – and *this* is generally speaking his "language game *method*"), the so-called 'Blue and Brown Books period', hitherto taken as distinguished by Wittgenstein's introduction of 'language games', is little more than a figment of the imaginations of those of Wittgenstein's pupils who happened to have copies of the class notes he dictated in 1933-4, and it is *not* a distinct period in the development of Wittgenstein's 'new' approach to philosophy (an approach which in the *Nachlaß* is already in place by the early 1930s). This finding, of course, would not be of very much consequence were it not for the fact that misconceptions about the emergence of Wittgenstein's new *Denkweise* seem to have led to such grievous editorial blunders as the decision to publish *Philosophical Grammar* instead of TS 213 – a blunder which in my opinion has deprived the general public of a vital key for unlocking the secrets of Wittgenstein's new *Denkweise* and has thus deprived them of what is perhaps one of the most important mansucripts in Wittgenstein's *Nachlaß* (see the remarks on TS 213 in the last section of chapter 1).

There is, however, one important bit of evidence that has not been sufficiently scrutinized. In the early stages of my account of the methodological role played by hypothetical language games in Wittgenstein's new *Denkweise*, a couple of concrete examples of language games were given and it was shown how they were employed in a heuristic capacity to shed light on or help clear up a philosophical (conceptual) problem. These examples, however, were taken from the manuscripts of the 1940s, and, although it has been indicated *that* there are examples of hypothetical language games in the manuscripts of the *early* 1930s, prior to the so-called 'Blue and Brown Books period' (for instance, in TS 213 and its manuscript sources), an early example has not yet been concretely examined and shown to have in fact been employed in a heuristic capacity. The present chapter will now conclude with just such an example.

Perhaps the most well-known hypothetical, ideal cases or languages introduced by Wittgenstein anywhere in his later philosophy are the variations of the 'builders' language game that he constructs as illustrative of the 'primitive' Augustinian view of the nature of language. (It has previously been suggested that this view should be taken as a 'parody' of Wittgenstein's own Tractarian views; see n. 228.) However, the primitive Augustinian view of language and the hypothetical 'builders' language game concocted as illustrative of it are not only to be found at the beginning of the 'Brown Book' (*BBB*, p. 77) and *Philosophical Investigations* (*PI* §§1–4), but also near the beginning of TS 213 (pp. 25–30). (Much of this TS 213 material, incidentally, was copied with virtually no changes into MS 114 and thus has been published in *PG*, pp. 56–8.) Furthermore, most of this stretch of TS 213, the precise wording of which is much closer to the *Investigations* than is the 'Brown Book' version, was originally written in 1931 (cf. MS 111, pp. 15–18). Even if one were not familiar with Wittgenstein's *Nachlaß*, though, the very existence of a version of the 'builders' language game in *Philosophical Grammar* should have signalled that there was something suspect about the prevailing view that hypothetical language games first emerged as a methodological feature in Wittgenstein's writings during the 'Blue and Brown Books period'. But the problem with taking the 'builders' game introduced in TS 213 (and *Philosophical Grammar*) as our example, and perhaps this is the reason it has not struck scholars as an anomaly, is that in TS 213 (and *Philosophical Grammar*)

Wittgenstein does not actually *call* the 'builders' game a 'language game', though this should be of little consequence if, as is the case, the 'game' plays the same methodological role in TS 213 (and *Philosophical Grammar*) as it does in the 'Brown Book' and the *Investigations*. In any event, the manuscripts of the early 1930s contain other examples of 'constructed', 'ideal' cases or languages to which Wittgenstein *does* actually refer as "language games" (*Sprachspielen*). So to avoid getting bogged down in a trivial controversy over the label 'language game', it is one of the latter, clear-cut cases that will now be examined. The familiar 'builders' language Wittgenstein presents in TS 213 *is*, however, a perfectly suitable example, and in fact the specific language game to be examined was considered by Wittgenstein to be "equivalent" to one of the variants of the 'builders' language game.

In MS 152 (1936), most of which consists of drafts of remarks for the pre-war version of the *Investigations* (TS 220), there is a page on which Wittgenstein wrote a list of about twenty topics that he wished to deal with in the *Investigations*. Virtually all these topics are readily recognizable as the subject of remarks in the published version of *Philosophical Investigations*. One of the topics listed is "Language game 'light–dark' or equivalent".[242] Wittgenstein did not include the 'light–dark' language game in *Philosophical Investigations*, but, as we shall see, he did include an equivalent. The 'light–dark' language game happens to be the one Wittgenstein presented in the previously mentioned §46 of TS 213, entitled "The Functioning of Propositions Clarified by a Language Game". Thus, not only was the 'light–dark' game originally drafted in the early thirties, but it is from a section of TS 213 in which we found one of Wittgenstein's explicit statements of the heuristic role of language games (see q. 240). The 'light–dark' language game is particularly suitable as an example because it *is* "equivalent" to a variant of the 'builders' language game found in *Philosophical Investigations* (and the 'Brown Book'): "equivalent" both in that the same philosophical (conceptual) problem is dealt with, and in that the hypothetical language games shed light on this problem in the same *way*, i.e. 'work' in the same way.

The 'light–dark' language game presented in TS 213 is as follows:

(An elliptical sentence: how does the grammar work when you say "'Hat and cane!' actually means 'give me my hat and my cane!' "?)
   This for example is a simple language game [*Sprachspiel*]: one says to a child (it can also be an adult though), while one turns on the light in a room, "Light", then, while turning it off, "Dark"; and does that perhaps several times with emphasis and varying durations. Then one perhaps goes into the next room, first turns on the light out there, and then brings in the child in order to inform him whether it is light or dark. // . . . to inform, "Light" or "Dark".

Should I now call "Light" and "Dark" 'propositions'? Well, as I wish.²⁴³

Wittgenstein uses this language game to shed light on more than one philosophical problem (see n. 244). One of these problems is illustrated by the following further remarks from the same section of TS 213:

> One might say, though, "The words 'light', 'dark' are meant here as propositions and not single words." That is to say, they are not used here as we use them in ordinary language (although we also actually often talk *like this*). Though, if I suddenly for no evident reason say the word 'Light' in isolation, then one will of course say, "What does that mean? That's no proposition [*Satz*, sentence]", or "You said 'Light', now what should I make of that?" The assertion of the word "Light" is in this case, so to speak, (?–) not yet a (<u>complete</u>) move of the game that we assume the other person plays (–?).
>
> But how does "Light", when it expresses the desire [*Wunsch*] for light, differ from "Light" when it states that it is light in the room? That we in each case *mean* it differently? And in what does that consist? In certain processes which accompany the expression, or in a certain behaviour that precedes it, perhaps accompanies it, and follows it?
>
> ... I say the word "Light!" – the other person asks me, "What do you mean?" – and I say //answer//, "I meant you should turn on the light." – How were things when I *meant* it? Did I silently say the "complete proposition" in the imagination [*in der Vorstellung*], or something corresponding to it in another language? (Yes, that *might* happen or also it might not.) The conditions that one <u>connects</u> with the expression "I meant" are *very diverse*.
>
> Now one can easily assume that "I meant you should turn on the light" means that thereby a mental picture swam before my mind of you doing this activity, and, also, that the sentence means that thereby the words of the whole sentence were present in the imagination, or that one of these two was the case – only I must recognize that I have made a stipulation about the words "I meant", and one that is more narrow than that which corresponds to the actual common use of the expression.²⁴⁴

The general philosophical view Wittgenstein seems to be dealing with here is the notion that what is most fundamental or essential to language (propositions, words) is mental states or processes that lie in the psyche, so to speak, 'behind' the signs. More specifically he seems to be addressing the view that what makes an utterance a 'proposition', and indeed what makes an utterance one particular proposition rather than another, is particular psychological phenomena that accompany it. In chapter 2 it was noted that Wittgenstein, in rejecting the metalogical view of 'psychological' concepts, was repudiating precisely the above sort of conception of the nature and functioning of language. The 'light–dark' language game addresses this philosophical problem by raising the question of whether, in this game, the expression "Light" is an elliptical *proposition* asserting 'it is light in the room'. Furthermore he asks, if "Light" is an elliptical proposition, what would differentiate the utterance "Light" as the assertion 'it is light in the room' from the same utterance when it 'expresses the desire for light'? The obvious answer to such queries is that the utterance "Light" is an elliptical *proposition* if what one *means* by it is 'it is light in the room'; and "Light" as the assertion 'it is light in the room' differs from the same utterance when it 'expresses the desire for light' in that in each case we *mean* it differently. Here lies the central philosophical (conceptual) problem. The philosophical view that what is most essential to language is mental states or processes that accompany the spoken or written signs has succumbed to the temptation to take a concept such as 'meaning' (*meinen*) as designating certain psychological states or processes. Thus, according to the philosophical view, *meaning* the proposition 'it is light in the room' when one asserts "Light" *consists in* a particular psychological process – perhaps silently saying the *complete* proposition in one's imagination as one utters the word "Light". Similarly, according to the philosophical view, *meaning* that one should turn on the light (rather than that it is light in the room) when one says "Light" *consists in* the particular psychological state or process accompanying the utterance – perhaps having a mental picture of the addressee engaged in the activity of turning on the light. Wittgenstein, however, points out that, although it might very well happen that when one said "Light" and meant 'you should turn on the light' one had a mental picture swim before one's mind or said the 'complete proposition' in one's head, it does not much matter which happened and it is quite conceivable that there were no such psychological accompaniments. Wittgenstein, therefore, is not denying that there might be such psychological accompaniments, but rather suggesting that they are not logically essential to the concept of 'meaning' (*meinen*). Thus the implication is that one has misconstrued the use of the expression "I meant . . ." if one takes it as a report about specific psychological processes or states that accompanied the utterance (in this case "Light") that is being explained or elaborated upon.

The heuristic role played by the hypothetical 'light–dark' language game is quite clear. The game serves to shed light on our concept of 'meaning' (*meinen*) and in so doing attempts to point out inadequacies in a certain philosophical view (misconception) of the nature and function of language (propositions, words).

It is easy to pick out which language game in the *Investigations* Wittgenstein considered "equivalent" (see q. 242) to the 'light–dark' language game. The "equivalent" game is the variant of the 'builders' language game one finds in *PI* §§19 and 20 (this game is also in the 'Brown Book', *BBB*, p. 78). It should be fairly obvious that Wittgenstein could (as he in fact does) make the same sorts of points about the concept 'meaning' (*meinen*) and the functioning of language if he used a different expression as a hypothetical example of a possible elliptical sentence. The expression Wittgenstein uses in *PI* §§19–20 (and the 'Brown Book', *BBB*, p. 78) is the utterance "Slab!" (or "Brick!") rather than "Light!" However, he goes on to raise virtually the same issues (How is it that the utterance "Slab!" might be an elliptical *proposition*? What is it to say "Slab!" and *mean* "Bring me a slab"? What differentiates "Slab!" as an elliptical form of one particular propostion rather than some other one?); and he goes on to suggest the same sorts of conclusions about the concept 'meaning' (*meinen*) and the functioning of language (for instance, that 'meaning' is not a mental state or process accompanying our utterances and serving as some sort of essential psychological substratum of language).

The 'light–dark' language game of TS 213, then, is not only a good illustration of Wittgenstein's employment of a hypothetical language game in a heuristic capacity *prior* to the 'Blue and Brown Books period', but it is an example that is especially telling because Wittgenstein himself considered it to be "equivalent" to a language game he introduces in *Philosophical Investigations* (and the 'Brown Book'). There is no doubt, therefore, that hypothetical language games, or "ideal cases, ideal games", as he was sometimes inclined to refer to them, were already a methodological feature of his philosophy by the early 1930s, and precisely in the sort of heuristic capacity that one finds them being used in the manuscripts of the 1940s and in *Philosophical Investigations* (the 'work' universally recognized as most representative of Wittgenstein's 'later' philosophy).

Of more importance than these findings concerning the chronology of Wittgenstein's thinking, however, is the fact that it has proved possible, primarily on the basis of *Nachlaß* material from the early and middle thirties, to reconstruct roughly *how* hypothetical language games (ideal languages) came to play such an important heuristic role in his post-1930 philosophy. It seems that, partly inspired by reading Spengler, though it is not very clear (and does not much matter) precisely how Spengler served as an inspiration, Wittgenstein had by the early thirties already come to the realization that the conception of language in the *Tractatus* was an 'ideal' conception, an abstraction, a hypothetical game that had been employed dogmatically and to the neglect of the multifarious grammar of our actual language. Instead of abandoning the employment of any such ideal, hypothetical languages, however, he apparently saw that the 'ideal' ("ideal cases, ideal games") could have a new place in his philosophy, employed not dogmatically but rather in a purely heuristic capacity as *Vergleichsobjekte* to shed light by way of similarities and dissimilarities on the actual 'games' of everyday language – thus the crucial shift in his thinking concerning the proper role of the 'ideal' in his philosophy, a shift that was so central to his new *Denkweise* that he referred to it as a matter of "turning round our whole examination [*Betrachtung*, way of thinking]" (see q. 227). As Wittgenstein was well aware, though, the term 'ideal' can be misleading, and a failure on the part of his readers to grasp fully the crucial shift that took place in his thinking concerning the 'ideal' might very well lead to a misunderstanding of the proper sense in which he can be said to "*construct* ideal languages" in his post-1930 writings (for example, in the so-called 'Brown Book').

It has been shown *how* hypothetical language games emerged as a prominent feature of Wittgenstein's later philosophy. As noted at the beginning of this chapter, however, the term 'language game' is used by Wittgenstein not only in reference to the hypothetical, ideal games he constructs, but also in reference to extant loci of linguistic practice. It is 'language games' of the latter sort that will be the subject of the next chapter.

4

Language Games: the Logical *versus* the Magical Views of Signs

It has become fairly commonplace to speak of Wittgenstein's 'abandonment' of the calculus model or conception of language in his later philosophy. Usually the claim is that he subscribed to a 'calculus model' of language in both the *Tractatus* (though he does not use the term 'calculus' there) and in the manuscripts of the early 1930s (where the term is frequently used), but that he later (by the mid-1930s, by the end of the so-called 'Blue and Brown Books period') repudiated the calculus view of language.[245] An attempt has also been made to explain the *emergence* of Wittgenstein's notion of 'language games' (of the non-ideal or non-hypothetical variety) by suggesting that the 'language-game model' *replaced* the calculus conception of language that Wittgenstein rejected.[246] However, the general view that Wittgenstein *abandoned* the calculus model of language, as well as the view that the 'calculus model' was *replaced* by a new 'language-game model', runs foul of the following generally ignored but grossly anomalous facts about Wittgenstein's later writings. First, by the early 1930s he had already clearly in a sense abandoned what might be called 'the *Tractatus* calculus model', yet he continued to use the term 'calculus' in a positive way to characterize language and he did so well into the 1940s, long after the so-called 'transitional period' of the early 1930s. This would suggest that, although he may very well have abandoned 'the *Tractatus* calculus', there is a different (perhaps looser, more flexible) 'calculus' conception operative in the post-1930 manuscripts which was not abandoned and may have been fundamental to his later *Denkweise*. Secondly, there is the oddity that, although Wittgenstein came to prefer the term 'language game' (or simply 'game'), he not only did not abandon the term 'calculus' but, from roughly 1930 on, tended to use these terms virtually *interchangeably*. This would seem to indicate that, although there may have been a shift in *terminological preference* for the term 'language game' (as opposed to 'calculus') in the post-1930 manuscripts, such a shift was not indicative of a *substantive* change in his view of language *during* the 1930s.

An *adequate* account of the *emergence* of Wittgenstein's notion of 'language games' would have to be of such explanatory power or scope that it could also explain the apparent anomalies just mentioned. The task of the present chapter is to offer an account of the emergence of his notion of language games (*qua* loci of *extant* linguistic practice) that *will* explain these apparent anomalies. It will be demonstrated that, to the extent that Wittgenstein endorses a 'calculus model' in the post-1930 manuscripts, it is not 'the *Tractatus* calculus' (which indeed had in a sense already been abandoned by the early thirties); and thus, unless he is alluding to a view to which he does not subscribe, the term 'calculus' (as with the term 'analysis'; see n. 233) in the post-1930 manuscripts should not be taken in a Tractarian sense. Furthermore, it will be shown that Wittgenstein does in fact use the terms 'calculus' and 'language game' virtually interchangeably in the post-1930 manuscripts, and hence the notion of a language game was not replacing an 'old' calculus view of language to which he still subscribed during the early 1930s, but rather was simply another, perhaps preferable, way of stating the sorts of points he was trying to make in his post-1930 use of the term 'calculus'.

This means that any *adequate* account of the emergence of the notion of 'language games' (of the non-hypothetical variety) must in effect be an account of the emergence of the post-1930 'calculus/language-game' conception, since the terminological variance does not represent a substantive philosophical change in Wittgenstein's thinking after 1930. It will then be shown that in the post-1930 manuscripts Wittgenstein used the terms 'calculus', 'language game' and at times 'system' in an attempt to characterize what might be called a 'logical' view of signs, and that he offered this 'logical' view in opposition to what might be called a 'magical' (or, perhaps less sensationally, 'psychological') view of signs. The emergence of the 'calculus/language-game' conception will thus be grasped in terms of this latter opposition; an opposition which was constituted not only, to a certain extent, by a clash between Wittgenstein's post-1930 approach to language and that of the *Tractatus*, but also, and perhaps to a much greater extent, by his attempts to criticize in general the sorts of accounts of language propounded in the publications of several of his contemporaries or near contemporaries, such as William James, Bertrand Russell, C. K. Ogden and I. A. Richards.

Before carefully examining Wittgenstein's post-1930 notions of 'calculus' and 'language game', let us first simply establish that in his later writings there are indeed remarks inconsistent with the standard views that during the 1930s he abandoned the 'calculus conception' of language and replaced it with a new 'language-game model'.

The remarks Wittgenstein thought fit for inclusion in *Philosophical Investigations* are universally acknowledged as representative of his 'later' thinking, yet in several passages in the *Investigations* a positive use of the term 'calculus' is clearly still operative. *PI* §559, for example, reads as follows:

> One would like to speak of the function of a word in *this* sentence. As if the sentence were a mechanism in which the word had a particular function. But what does this function consist in? How does it come to light? For there isn't anything hidden – don't we see the whole sentence? The function must come out in the course of the calculus [*im Laufe des Kalküls*]. ((Meaning-body.))[247]

In its original manuscript version (see n. 247) the expression *im Laufe des Kalküls* was actually written as an afterthought, as an alternative to the simpler expression *im Kalkül* ("in the calculus"). The positive use of the term 'calculus' unfortunately is lost in Anscombe's translation of *im Laufe des Kalküls* as "in operating with the word", though her free translation may better present the sort of point Wittgenstein was trying to make than would a more literal translation – at least for readers unfamiliar with Wittgenstein's post-1930 use of the term 'calculus' in the *Nachlaß*. In anticipation of issues to be dealt with later in this chapter, it should perhaps be pointed out that (1) the very *appropriateness* of Anscombe's 'free' translation of *im Laufe des Kalküls* as "in operating with the word" is an indication that Wittgenstein's post-1930 conception of 'calculus' may indeed differ from that of the *Tractatus*; and (2), as will be shown, the parenthetical expression "Meaning-body" (*Bedeutungskörper*) is used by Wittgenstein to refer to an aspect of what he calls the 'magical' view of signs to which he contrasted his own post-1930 'logical' view.

Another example of Wittgenstein using the term 'calculus' positively in *Philosophical Investigations* is the following remark. Having raised the question of whether 'red' could be defined by pointing to something that was *not* red, he wrote,

> But it might well be asked: are we still to call this 'definition'? – For, of course, even if it has the same practical consequences, the same *effect* [*Wirkung*] on the learner, it plays a different part in the calculus [*im Kalkül*] from what we ordinarily call 'ostensive definition' of the word 'red'.[248]

Again in anticipation of subjects to be dealt with later, it should be pointed out that Wittgenstein's attempt to distinguish in the above passage between the 'effects' (*Wirkungen*) of language and the 'role played by words in a calculus' is fundamental to his post-1930 attempts to differentiate between a 'magical' view of signs and his own 'logical' view.

Even quite late in his life, after most of what we know as part I of *Philosophical Investigations* had already been written, he continued to use the term 'calculus' positively in his characterizations of language. In 1946, for example, he wrote,

> One says, 'Had I not asked him then, no one would have known what he had felt."
> Now, this sentence has use in the calculus of language [*im Kalkül der Sprache*].[249]

This was among the remarks originally written between what have since been published as §§161 and 162 of *Remarks on the Philosophy of Psychology* (*RPP*, vol. I). What is of interest to us at the moment, however, is not so much the specific context of such remarks and the specific philosophical point Wittgenstein was trying to make, but, rather, simply the fact that even at this late date he was still using such an expression as "the calculus of language" in a positive way. Such passages certainly do not sort well with the claim that Wittgenstein abandoned the 'calculus conception' during the 1930s.

Also inconsistent with the claims that Wittgenstein abandoned the 'calculus conception' during the 1930s and that he replaced it with a substantially different 'language-game model' is the fact that in his post-1930 writings he tended to use these terms interchangeably. The best evidence of this sort of anomaly comes from the manuscripts of the 1930s, where his *terminological preference* for the expression 'language game'/ 'game' over 'calculus' began to assert itself. Were the shift of terminological preference indicative of a *substantive* shift in his thinking, one would expect, if not the complete abandonment, at least the extensive revision of remarks in which the concept of a 'calculus' is prominent. What one finds, however, is either (1) that within the same remark Wittgenstein shifts back and forth between the terms *Kalkül* and *Spiel* as if they were interchangeable, or (2) that, when there is revision, this often consists of little more than the *substitution* of one term for another, with no further changes in the remark. Take the following remark from TS 213:

> I want to say that the word 'chess' is just (only) a piece [*Stein*] in a game that we play.
> ~~calculus~~. If the calculus is to be described, then we would have to tabulate the rules //to have the rules tabulated before us//, but, if it is employed, then we are proceeding now according to the one then according to the other rule, and therewith their expression may swim before our mind, or also it may not.[250]

In the above remark Wittgenstein's only revision was to cross out the first 'calculus' and write instead 'game that we play'. Given that there is only a terminological substitution rather than a more substantive revision of the remark, it would seem that Wittgenstein's 'revision' was simply a restatement of the *same* point but in different terminological garb, rather than an attempt significantly to alter the basic point being made. It appears, therefore, that Wittgenstein was attempting to make the *same* basic point when referring to a *word* as, on the one hand, a "piece in a calculus" and, on the other, a "piece in a game that we play". This is especially evident given the fact that he did not bother to change 'calculus' on its second occurrence in the above remark – thus suggesting that the terms 'calculus' and 'game' were so interchangeable that he could simply shift from one to the other within the same remark with no loss in the coherence of the overall point being made.

Another example of the apparent interchangeability of the terms 'calculus' and 'game' for Wittgenstein is the following remark written around 1932–4: "Though isn't it *only* like this, that just the aspect of language which is a calculus, a game, is of concern to me?"[251] Such remarks from the early to middle thirties were obviously made during a period in which a clear terminological preference for one term over the other had yet to assert itself. But that the crux of the matter is precisely that, a mere *terminological* preference rather than a substantive shift in his thinking, is perhaps most explicitly indicated in a remark he made in one of his revisions of TS 213 during roughly the same period.

> I can only describe language games or calculi; whether one still wants to call them calculi is of course a matter of indifference [*gleichgültig*] provided that we don't let the use of the general terms [*Sammelnamen*] prevent us from investigating each particular case we wish to judge.[252]

Clearly, Wittgenstein is claiming that he is employing the general terms 'language game'/'game' and 'calculus' in such a way that it matters little which of the two he uses. Only if this were the case could he still on occasion (see qq. 247–9), long after his terminological preference for the expression 'language game' had asserted itself, employ the term 'calculus' in his characterizations of language without this constituting an abrogation of the 'new' conception of language in his later *Denkweise*.

Yet a further good illustration of the interchangeability of the terms 'calculus' and 'language game'/'game' for Wittgenstein is the following remark he wrote late in 1937 in his reworking of TS 213 material – and this, recall, is after the so-called 'Blue and Brown Books period' and his first draft in MS 142 of the pre-war version of the *Investigations*:

What does it mean "to discover that a sentence has no meaning [*Sinn*]"?

And what does this mean: "If I mean something by it, it must surely have a meaning [*Sinn*]"?

The first of course means: not letting oneself be misled by the appearance of a sentence and investigating its use ~~in the calculus~~ in the language game.

And "If I mean something by it" – does this mean soemthing like "If I imagine something with it"? – Well, if it is the (whole) purpose of the sentence that it arouse in you an image [*Vorstellung*], then one could say it has meaning. But ordinarily that is not everything that one requires of a sentence.[253]

Still suspending any comment on the philosophical point being made in such passages, here again one finds Wittgenstein simply crossing out the expression "in the calculus" (*im Kalkül*) and replacing it with "in the language game" (*im Sprachspiel*) – the latter expression obviously being another, perhaps better, way of making the same point as he wished to make by using the former.

As previously mentioned, there is yet a third term that Wittgenstein tended to use virtually interchangeably with the terms 'calculus' and 'language game'/'game'. That term is 'system'. For example, right after the previously cited remark (q. 251) in which he seemed to suggest that he is only concerned with language as a calculus or game he continued,

"The sentence [*Satz*] makes sense" can of course mean it is a term [*Glied*] of a system; but how then could "*I* understand it" mean that, for the system of language after all is in any case independent of the person?

One says, "I have said the sentence quite thoughtlessly", "said it quite mechanically without thereby imagining something". Or, on the other hand (also), "No, I *meant* what I have said." *Here* is where it is as if the sentence as it were took hold [*eingriffe*] in us.

But also "I mean something by it" could mean: the sentence is part [*Teil*] of a system familiar to me. *I* play the game of which it is a part [*Teil*].[254]

Ignoring for the moment what the overall thrust of the passage is, it is clear that when Wittgenstein speaks of a sentence as being 'part of a game (or calculus)', he is doing little more than simply reiterating, albeit in different terminological garb, the same basic point as he is trying to make in speaking of a sentence as "part of a system".

The virtual interchangeability of the terms 'system' and 'game' is similarly illustrated in the following passage from TS 213:

> "I understand these words" (that I perhaps say to myself), "I mean something by them", "They have a sense" must always mean the same as "They are not *ad hoc* invented sounds, but rather signs in a system." I play a game with them.[255]

Here again the shift from one notion ('system') to the other ('game') seems to have only a reiterative purpose. The terminological shift seems to be an attempt to *restate* his basic point rather than an attempt to make a radically *new* point.

The following passage from TS 213 is yet another clear indication that Wittgenstein introduced his 'game' conception of language *not* by way of a rejection and radical break with the 'calculus' and 'system' conceptions so prominent in his writings of the early thirties, but rather simply in an attempt to state more clearly his basic position.

> The sign in so far as it influences the mind by suggestion [*es suggeriert*], thus in so far as it has an effect [*es wirkt*], doesn't interest us. It interests us only as a move [*Zug*] in a game, term [*Glied*] in a system, that is autonomous [*selbständig*] //term in a system, that has its meaning in itself.// term in a system, that is intelligible in itself [*selbstbedeutend*]; that has its meaning in itself.//[256]

If, as it appears, Wittgenstein's 'game' conception was simply another way of formulating the same basic point about language that he was trying to make by way of his post-1930 notions of a 'calculus' and a 'system', it would seem to follow that these two terms too were for him virtually interchangeable. This in fact was the case, as *PI* §3 demonstrates quite vividly. As it was first drafted in 1931, the first sentence of this section read,

> I want to say: Augustine does describe a calculus, only not everything that we call language is this calculus.[257]

This sentence, as well as the rest of the section, crops up repeatedly in Wittgenstein's manuscripts and typescripts (see n. 257) and with virtually no changes, except that in the form in which it was finally published in *Philosophical Investigations* one finds that there has been a terminological substitution:

> Augustine, we might say, does describe a system of communication; only not everything that we call language is this system.

Wittgenstein has simply substituted for the term 'calculus' the term 'system (of communication)'. However, aside from the significance of the two specific terms involved, this example differs from the previous illustrations offered by showing just how *broadly* interchangeable the terms 'system', 'calculus' and 'game' were for Wittgenstein. The concern of the present chapter is with 'language games' of the *non*-hypothetical variety. But the last example cited could justifiably be taken as an illustration of the interchangeability of these terms also in the context of a discussion of *hypothetical*, 'ideal' cases, such as were considered in chapter 3. For Wittgenstein, the Augustinian 'calculus' or 'system of communication' was an 'ideal' (exact, simple) calculus or game which, when compared with our everyday language, perhaps turns out to be consonant with part, though not all, of what we call language. Thus for Wittgenstein even in the domain of 'ideal' cases (hypothetical language games) the terms 'game', 'calculus' and 'system' were virtually interchangeable. The example from *PI* §3 has illustrated this for the terms 'system' and 'calculus'; let us now consider some explicit examples of the interchangeability of the other two terminological combinations ('calculus'–'game' and 'system'–'game') in the hypothetical, 'ideal' domain.

Though the interchangeability of the terms 'game' and 'calculus' in the context of a treatment of 'ideal' cases should be quite obvious from the discussion of hypothetical language games in chapter 3, an illustration that allows us to see this at a glance is provided by the following textual revision in TS 213. The revised remark is reproduced here from the typescript itself, to show just how purely terminological the shift was in some of Wittgenstein's revisions involving the concepts 'calculus' and 'game'.

Die Aristotelische Logik ist ein Spiel, das sich auf Sätze anwenden lässt.
  The syllogism   calculus
Aristotelian logic is a game that *may* be applied to propositions.[258]

Here, in reference to the 'ideal' game which is Aristotelian syllogistic logic, the terms 'calculus' and 'game' are quite obviously being used interchangeably. Of interest is the fact that in the above passage, though the word 'game' was not crossed out in favour of the term 'calculus' (but see n. 258), it at least temporally preceded it – thus apparently standing on its head the bogus conventional view that Wittgenstein's 'calculus conception' was anterior to and replaced by his 'game model'.

To illustrate the interchangeability of the terms 'system' and 'game' in the domain of hypothetical, 'ideal' cases, there is no better example than the following passage from the 'Brown Book'. After presenting five such hypothetical cases, Wittgenstein explained, "Systems of communication as for instance 1), 2), 3), 4), 5) we shall call 'language games'."²⁵⁹ In this remark the terms 'system'/'system of communication' and 'game'/'language game' are virtually defined in terms of each other.

It is evident, therefore, that, both in reference to hypothetical, 'ideal' cases and when dealing with extant cases, Wittgenstein used the terms 'calculus', 'game'/'language game' and 'system'/'system of communication' interchangeably. Given this finding, however, what then is one to make of the occasional passage in Wittgenstein's later writings where he seems to be criticizing a 'calculus' conception of language? For instance, in the 'Blue Book' one finds him reminding us that

> in general we don't use language according to strict rules – it hasn't been taught us by means of strict rules, either. *We*, in our discussions on the other hand, constantly compare language with a calculus proceeding according to exact rules.
>
> This is a very one-sided way of looking at language. In practice we very rarely use language as such a calculus....²⁶⁰

It is fairly clear that the kind of 'calculus' of which Wittgenstein is speaking here is the 'ideal', exact kind considered in chapter 3. The italicized pronoun '*We*' presumably refers generally to 'we philosophers', but perhaps more specifically to 'we logicians' (particularly Wittgenstein *himself* in the *Tractatus*). That it is more specifically the sort of 'ideal' calculus one finds in the *Tractatus* that is being criticized in such remarks comes out quite clearly in *PI* §81, where Wittgenstein also speaks of the fact that "in philosophy we often *compare* the use of words with games, calculi which have fixed rules" and where he also critically refers to the need to "become clear what can lead us (and did lead me) to think that if anyone utters a sentence and *means* or *understands* it he is operating a calculus according to precise [*bestimmte*] rules". It is significant that in both the pre-war version of the *Investigations* (TS 220) and his 1943 revision of it (TS 239), the parenthetical phrase "(and did lead me)" read, "(and did lead me (*Tractatus*))". Thus, when Wittgenstein is critical of a calculus conception of language, it is with reference to a calculus of an 'ideal', 'exact' sort, and more specifically the sort of *role* that such an 'ideal' calculus played in the *Tractatus*.

In chapter 3 it was shown (see pp. 75–81) that what might be called '*the* (ideal) *Tractatus* calculus' was indeed abandoned, at least to the extent that it was no longer offered by Wittgenstein after 1930 as a model *of* language (expressing what is *essential to* language). As we have seen, after 1930 an ideal, exact, simple calculus (or game) was no longer a requirement of his investigations and no longer dogmatically offered as constitutive of the essence of language, but rather such simple, exact calculi or games were recognized as purely hypothetical and were employed in a purely heuristic capacity as 'objects of comparison' to help throw light on the characteristics of our extant language by way of similarities and dissimilarities (thus being introduced sometimes "because of their absurd appearance"[261]). Of course, *in* the *Tractatus* itself Wittgenstein did not view the '*Tractatus* calculus' as a *hypothetical* game (or calculus), but rather mistook it for an expression of the essence of language – feeling that language *must* conform to such an exact calculus (see q. 222) and that in using language one *must* be playing *one precise game* according to fixed and exact rules (see q. 217).

It is perhaps the temptation to take the term 'calculus' as implying a set of fixed and exact rules that eventually led Wittgenstein to prefer the word 'game' – although, as chapter 3 showed, the term 'game' itself is not absolved from precisely the same sort of undesirable misinterpretation; i.e. one might claim that, if what is played is not according to fixed and exact rules, then it is not a 'game' (see qq. 219, 227). But, clearly, the positive use to which Wittgenstein put the notions of 'calculus' and 'game' (and 'system') in his post-1930 writings is not a Tractarian attempt to characterize language as being rule-governed in an *exact* and *precise* manner, for, as pointed out in chapter 3, by the early thirties a uniform and precise system of rules was *no longer* a requirement of his investigations and he had *already* come to the realization that it is not the case that in language "*one precise game*" is played according to fixed and exact rules (see pp. 77–8).

Given that by the very early thirties Wittgenstein had already rejected the '*Tractatus* calculus' (or, more specifically, the *role* that calculus played in his early philosophy), his post-1930 criticism of that calculus and the role it played in his early philosophy cannot be offered as evidence that *during* the 1930s there was a substantive change in his thinking such that the 'calculus conception' *per se* was rejected and a new 'game model' introduced in its place. Indeed, it has already been demonstrated in this chapter that the notion of a 'calculus' was alive and well not only in his writings of the 1930s, but even in those of the 1940s, and what shift did take place *during* the 1930s seems not to have been a substantive one, but rather a shift in terminological preference for the 'game' idiom over the 'calculus' and 'system' idioms.

Since it has been shown that the shift in terminological preference for the expression 'language game' (as opposed to the terms 'calculus' and 'system') was not indicative of a substantive shift in Wittgenstein's thinking *during* the 1930s, and since the emergence of his notion of *hypothetical* language games or calculi has already been explained (in chapter 3), the task that now remains is to explain how the notion of *extant* language games, calculi or systems of communication, i.e. what might loosely be called the 'calculus/game/system' conception of language, emerged as an essential feature of Wittgenstein's post-1930 philosophy. For, granting that by the early 1930s

Wittgenstein had critically repudiated what might be called '*the* ideal *Tractatus* calculus' and in particular the role that that calculus played in his early philosophy, there remains the question of what he was up to with his *post-1930* 'calculus/game/system' conception of language and how this conception emerged.

A significant clue to how it emerged is to be found in TS 213 §10, from which a passage has already been cited (q. 256) to illustrate Wittgenstein's tendency to use the terms 'system' and 'game' interchangeably. Wittgenstein, having proclaimed that the psychological effect a sign has on the mind does not concern him, and that a sign is of interest to him "only as a move in a game; term in a system" (see q. 256), went on to elaborate,

> It would be characteristic for a specific erroneous view if a philosopher believed a sentence would have to be printed in a red colour, since only in this way would it completely express what the author wants to say. (Here we would have the magical view of signs instead of the logical one.)
>
> The investigation of whether the meaning [*Bedeutung*] of a sign is its effect is a grammatical investigation.
>
> I believe that to the causal theory of meaning one can simply answer that if someone received a push and fell, we don't *call* [*nennen*] the fall the meaning [*Bedeutung*] of the push....
>
> The sense [*Sinn*] of language is not determined by its ~~purpose~~ effect. Or what one calls the sense [*Sinn*], the meaning [*Bedeutung*] in language is not its effect.
>
> What we investigate is actually "the meaning of meaning" [the quoted phrase was written in English]: namely //or// the grammar of the word 'meaning' [*Bedeutung*].²⁶²

Wittgenstein's expressed disinterest in the psychological effects that signs have on the mind seems to be an explicit attempt to point out a view of signs from which he wishes to disassociate himself and in contrast to which he seems to be offering his own view of signs as 'only moves in a game' or 'terms in a system'. Given that much of the above passage was first drafted in 1930-1 (see n. 262), it strongly suggests that his own view of signs had already (by the early thirties) emerged as at least in part a reaction to a view of signs to which he took exception. Although it is somewhat ambiguous from the passage precisely what his own view of signs is and precisely what view he is opposing, this much is clear: (1) that he considered his own view of signs to be in some sense a 'logical' one, and (2) that the (no doubt derisively labelled) 'magical' view of signs that he was opposing he equated with a view that was perhaps generally known by the early 1930s as 'the causal theory of meaning' and which involved an account of 'meaning/

sense' in terms of the psychological effects that signs have on the mind. Presumably the 'magical' view of signs considers it the task of language to affect the mind; as a drug might produce certain hallucinations or feelings, language conjures up mental impressions. One has used a sign appropriately if the sign produces in the hearer or reader the mental impression one wishes to convey.

Wittgenstein's use of quotation marks in the above passage, and the fact that the quoted phrase "the meaning of meaning" was cited by Wittgenstein in English rather than in the language (German) in which he was writing, points the way toward an elucidation of the sort of 'magical' view of signs or 'causal theory' of meaning to which he was reacting. Actually, the very title of this section of TS 213 is itself an assertion in quotation marks which clearly demarcates the subject of his critique in the section: "The meaning [*Bedeutung*] of a sign is given by its effect (the associations that it causes)."[263]

There certainly is no scarcity in Anglo-American literature of 'causal theories' concerning the nature of signs or meaning. For the purposes of giving an account of the emergence of Wittgenstein's own post-1930 view of signs, however, it is important that one identifies the specific sort of 'causal theory' that he was opposing. Thus, given his apparent disinclination toward historical scholarship (see pp. 13–14), one would probably be off the mark if one were to suggest that Wittgenstein's own view of signs emerged in direct opposition to the accounts one finds in the associationist psychology of, for example, Locke or Hume. This, of course, is not to say that Wittgenstein's own view might not *serve as* a critique of the 'British Empiricists' of the seventeenth and eighteenth centuries; indeed it might, since, as will be obvious from the following discussion, the specific views that Wittgenstein was in fact opposing were of a philosophical lineage directly descendant from the views of the British Empiricists.[264] Similarly, it might well prove very interesting to contrast Wittgenstein's own views not only to the 'causal theories' propounded by thinkers of an obvious associationist bent but also to other and more recent varieties of 'causal accounts of signs', such as Kripke's 'causal' account of names.[265] However, for the purposes of an exegetical elucidation of the emergence of Wittgenstein's post-1930 philosophy, such a contrast would surely be an anachronistic digression.

The most conspicuous 'causal theory' of meaning in Anglo-American writings of the period immediately preceding Wittgenstein's return to philosophy in 1929–30 is to be found in a work co-authored by C. K. Ogden and I. A. Richards and first published in 1923. The full title of that work is *The Meaning of Meaning: a study of the influence of language upon thought and of the science of symbolism*.[266] This work was generally known under simply its main heading *The Meaning of Meaning*, which of course is the self-same English phrase that Wittgenstein quoted in TS 213 §10 (see q. 262), where he indicated that he was himself investigating "the meaning of meaning", but in a manner starkly contrasting with the sort of approach involved in the so-called 'magical' or psychological view of signs. The suggestion is that for him 'the *meaning* of meaning' – or, for that matter, whatever other *concept* one might wish to take as an instantiation of a phrase of the form 'the meaning of *x*' – is what he calls a 'logical/ grammatical' issue (to be further discussed presently) rather than a causal one having to do with the psychological effect that a sign has on the mind.

The title Ogden and Richards chose for their work, however, was not very original, a symposium entitled "The Meaning of 'Meaning'"[267] having been held three years prior to the publication of their book. The focus of the debate at that symposium was a paper Bertrand Russell had presented at a meeting of the Aristotelian Society in 1919, entitled "On Propositions: what they are and how they mean".[268] In his paper Russell had introduced a 'causal theory' of meaning which he elaborated upon a couple of years later (1921) in his book *The Analysis of Mind*.[269] In fact, there is a 'causal theory' also offered by Ogden and Richards in their book (1923) and it is so similar to the one propounded by Russell that Ogden and Richards considered their position on the whole compatible with Russell's, with the exception that they felt they had "refrained from making images a corner-stone" of their view. Otherwise they go so far as to recommend that Russell's account of meaning "be consulted by those who desire a more simple discussion of the part played by Mnemonic causation in knowledge than our brief outline provides".[270]

The above mentioned works of Russell, the symposium "The Meaning of 'Meaning'" and the book of the same title by Ogden and Richards were all published during the 'lost decade' between the authorship of the *Tractatus* and the manuscripts of 1929–30. It is uncertain, though also to a certain extent irrelevant, precisely *how* and to what degree Wittgenstein was cognizant of and had access to such material during the 'lost decade': for example, whether he got wind of this flurry of philosophical activity that took place in England in the early twenties by way of Frank Ramsey, who on more than one occasion visited Wittgenstein in 1923–4 at Puchberg (Austria), where Wittgenstein was teaching elementary school (though Ramsey's philosophical discussions with Wittgenstein probably centred on the *Tractatus* and the philosophy of mathematics), or whether Wittgenstein was perhaps more directly exposed to the issues and publications during his own visit to England (at Keynes' behest) in 1925.[271] However, since it is argued here that the emergence of Wittgenstein's post-1930 'calculus/ game/system' conception was to a large extent a reaction against the 'causal theory' of language propounded by the likes of Russell and Ogden, it *is* relevant to establish the fact *that* before starting to work out the 'calculus/

game/system' conception in 1929–30 Wittgenstein was at least *aware* of the philosophical activity in England during the 1920s concerning "the meaning of meaning" (the focus of which concern was the so-called 'causal theory').

Although there is no record of any philosophy produced by Wittgenstein during the 'lost decade', this is not to say that he was philosophically isolated and wholly out of touch with the English philosophical community. This much is obvious from his trip to England in 1925 and his contact with Ramsey. There is, however, concrete evidence which leaves no doubt whatsoever *that* during the 'lost decade' Wittgenstein was in fact specifically aware of the philosophical activity in England concerning "the meaning of meaning".

It seems that C. K. Ogden, and perhaps also Russell, at one point were of the opinion that the 'causal view' they shared provided a better understanding of signs and symbols than did Wittgenstein's *Tractatus*. In a letter to Russell dated 5 November 1921, in reference to an offprint of the Ostwald edition of the *Tractatus* (Ogden was at the time preparing the first English edition for Kegan Paul), Ogden wrote,

> Looking rapidly over the off print in the train last night, I was amazed that Nicod and Miss Wrinch had both seemed to make so very little of it. The main lines seem so reasonable and intelligible – apart from the Types puzzles. I know you are frightfully busy at present, but I should very much like to know why all this account of signs and symbols cannot best be understood in relation to a thorough-going causal theory. I mean the sort of thing in the enclosed: – on "Sign Situations" (= Chapter II of the early Synopsis attached). The whole book which the publishers want to call *The Meaning of Meaning* is now passing through the press; and before it is too late we should like to have discussed it with someone who has seriously considered Watson. Folk here still don't think there is a problem of *Meaning* at all, and though your *Analysis of Mind* has disturbed them, everything still remains rather astrological.[272]

It is ambiguous from the wording of this letter whether Ogden considered the 'better understanding' of signs that the causal theory allegedly provides to be compatible with or alien to the views expressed in the *Tractatus*. (From Ogden's comments on the *Tractatus* in *The Meaning of Meaning*, it seems that he may have considered the 'causal theory' to be an alternative to, rather than a refinement of, Wittgenstein's views – Ogden having assessed Wittgenstein's Tractarian account of signs as "unplausible [*sic*]" and "highly improbable".[273]) Russell, in his reply to Ogden (8 November

1921), seems (at least at the time) to have been more expansive in his estimation of the merits of the 'causal theory':

> I haven't had time to read your "Sign-Situations" yet, but I think probably the causal treatment of meaning does give the solution. It was because I thought so that I started working on "Analysis of Mind", which grew out of the problem of meaning.[274]

Now, this exchange between Ogden and Russell may well have been nothing more than a case of collegial backscratching (see q. and n. 276); however, *prima facie* it seems that Ogden and Russell at the time considered their 'causal theory' if not opposed to, at least an improvement on, Wittgenstein's views. Obviously, one would not expect Wittgenstein to have been aware of Ogden's and Russell's convictions about the 'causal theory', unless of course Russell discussed with Wittgenstein in Innsbruck nine months later (August 1922; see n. 271) the 'solution' that the causal theory purported to offer. However, Ogden apparently thought enough of the 'causal theory', and of its relevance to Wittgenstein's thinking, to send Wittgenstein a copy of *The Meaning of Meaning* as soon as it was published (1923). We know this from Wittgenstein's letter to Ogden of March 1923, in which Wittgenstein acknowledged,

> I have just got your P. C. dated March 17. "The meaning of meaning" reached me a few days ago.... I have not yet been able to read your book thoroughly. I have however read in it and I think I ought to confess to you frankly that I believe you have not quite *caught the problems* which – for instance – I was at in my book (whether or not I have given the correct solution)....[275]

There is no question, therefore, of *whether* during the 'lost decade' Wittgenstein was in fact *aware* of the philosophical activity in England concerning "the meaning of meaning", and that he identified this phrase with, if not the symposium on the subject published in *Mind* (see n. 267), certainly Ogden and Richards' book and Russell's work during that period (since Ogden and Richards in their book identify their 'causal theory' with the position Russell maintained in his *The Analysis of Mind*).

Wittgenstein not only had a copy of Ogden and Richards' *The Meaning of Meaning*, but seems also to have discussed the work with Ramsey – even going so far as to have Ramsey find out from Russell what he thought of the book, for in a letter dated 20 February 1924 one finds Ramsey reporting back to Wittgenstein, "He [Russell] does not really think *The Meaning of Meaning* important, but he wants to help Ogden by encouraging the sale of it. He wrote a review of it, from which the quotation you saw was taken, in a political weekly."[276]

Language Games: logical vs magical views

Given Wittgenstein's exposure to and curiosity about the sort of philosophical (or should one say psychological?) speculation about language that was going on in England (and elsewhere[277]) during the lost decade (epitomized by the 'causal theory' advanced by Russell and Ogden), it is quite clear that it was perhaps precisely the sorts of views propounded by Ogden in *The Meaning of Meaning* and Russell in *The Analysis of Mind* that Wittgenstein was alluding to in 1930–1 (see q. 262) as the 'magical' (or psychological) view of signs, the 'causal theory of meaning', and in contrast to which he distinguished his own 'logical' view (the post-1930 'calculus/game/system' conception).

It is consonant with Wittgenstein's awareness of the tenor of philosophical developments in England during the 'lost decade' that a good deal (though not all[278]) of his philosophical energies during the early years after taking up writing philosophy again was spent criticizing and working out alternatives (among which is his post-1930 'calculus/game/system' conception) to views found in the aforementioned works of Russell and Ogden. In Wittgenstein's manuscripts from these early years immediately following his return to philosophy one finds not only *indirect* allusions (such as in q. 262) to tenets propounded by Russell and Ogden, but also fairly frequently *explicit* critical reference to the views of these authors, thus leaving no doubt whatsoever that views *such as* (though not restricted to) those propounded by these specific authors served as a major focal point of his critical philosophical efforts during this period. A good example of an explicit reference to these authors, and in particular to their 'causal theory' of meaning, which Wittgenstein seems to have considered paradigmatic of the sort of psychological or 'magical' view of signs in contrast to which his own post-1930 view of language emerged, is the following pair of remarks he wrote in a notebook in 1930:

> The thought [*Gedanke*] is completely described by its expression [*Ausdruck*]. A description which lies outside of the expression of the thought doesn't concern us for it belongs to psychology or physiology.
>
> Thinking means using propositions [*Sätze*] but the use of the propositions is presupposed in any explanation. The only thing that one can clarify about language is its structure (the grammar). For the use evades our explanation – unless its use is for producing certain effects [*Wirkungen*], thus its causal relations. But these interest the psychologist, not us. To that extent Ogden and Richards are right with their causal view, except that they don't see the other aspect.[279]

This explicit reference to Ogden and Richards' 'causal view' quite distinctly echoes the sorts of points we found Wittgenstein making when trying to contrast his 'logical' view of signs with what he called the psychological or 'magical' view (cf. q. 262). Here again he tries to demarcate between, on the one hand, a psychological/physiological investigation concerned with 'causal relations' and the 'effects' of language (on the mind), and, on the other hand, a (logical) investigation of what he calls 'grammar' or the 'structure' of language. There is a recognition that one can indeed investigate language from a psycho-physical perspective and that in such an investigative domain the 'causal theory' of Ogden and Richards may be tenable; however, there is also the suggestion that Ogden and Richards fail to recognize and thus perhaps confuse the logico-grammatical aspects of language as distinguished from the causal, psycho-physical aspects. A few months later (February 1931), and apparently in the same vein, Wittgenstein made an even more explicitly indicting critical reference to Ogden and Russell's views, parenthetically remarking that "Ogden and Richards and Russell's theory of meaning rests on a confusion, or conflation, of motive and cause."[280]

Hitherto in the present study for the most part no appeal has been made to sources outside the central corpus of Wittgenstein's later writings in an attempt to explain the emergence of features of his later thinking (an exception, of course, is the excursus on Spengler in n. 228). However, since it is incontrovertible not only that Wittgenstein was aware of Russell's and Ogden's work during the 'lost decade', but also that their work both served as a major focal point of his critical efforts after his return to philosophy and, more importantly for our purposes, seems to have provided part of the general backdrop against which the emergence of his post-1930 'calculus/game/system' conception of language is to be understood, a brief account of some of Russell's and Ogden's views during the period immediately prior to Wittgenstein's return to philosophy will prove useful, helping to point out the contrast between the 'logical' and 'magical' (or psychological) views and thus facilitate a better appreciation of the emergence of Wittgenstein's post-1930 'logical' view of signs.

Around the turn of the century or shortly thereafter, Russell began, as he put it, "to emerge from the bath of German idealism" and experienced "intense excitement ... to be able to believe again that there really were such things as tables and chairs".[281] Unfortunately, this apparently exhilarating achievement was not long-lived. It seems that Russell was unable to resist creeping back into an 'idealistic bath' of another (though today less infamous) variety: namely, the sort of 'idealism' one finds in the British Empiricists of the seventeenth and eighteenth centuries (especially Berkeley and Hume), for he later confessed, "Bit by bit, chiefly under the influence of physics, this delight has faded, and I have been driven to a position not unlike that of Berkeley, without his God and his Anglican complacency."[282] (How the popularity of the sundry idealistic bath-houses frequented by an indulgent generation can vary! As is well known, Russell's wanderings were symptomatic of the general shift of philosophical patronage that occurred among Anglo-American philosophers after the turn of the century.) "Berkeley, without his God and his Anglican complacency" is, of course, a long-winded way of saying 'Hume'. This second, albeit different, 'bath of idealism' was apparently Russell's indulgence during the years between the world wars – beginning perhaps in 1918–19 during the peak of his interest in the philosophical implications of Einstein's theory of relativity (see n. 282) and continuing at least through to the publication in 1940 of his book *An Inquiry into Meaning and Truth* (which Russell has appropriately characterized as "Hume plus modern logic"[283]). This period coincided with and was inextricably linked to his concern with "problems connected with meaning", a concern which was initiated during his incarceration in 1918, was the impetus for his book *The Analysis of Mind* (1921) and several articles, and to which he returned in lectures during the 1930s (published in 1940 as *An Inquiry into Meaning and Truth*).[284] It was during this period, which for Russell was a period of distinctly Humean bent (and for Wittgenstein included the 'lost decade'), that Russell propounded the 'causal theory of meaning' and the general account of language (signs) against which Wittgenstein was in part reacting when he took up writing philosophy again in 1929–30 and proceeded, during the thirties, to expatiate upon his 'new' approach to language.

'Meaning' was defined by Russell in terms of 'associations' (images, sensations) aroused by a given (in the case of words) linguistic-stimulus situation. With what he called the "narrative use" of language (as opposed to the "demonstrative use of language to point out a feature in the present environment",[285] i.e. what now might be called the 'non-ostensive' as opposed to the 'ostensive' use of language), the "essence of the narrative 'meaning'" of a word is what he called an "imagination-image".[286] As he put it a little later in the same discussion, "words used demonstratively describe and are intended to cause sensations, the same words used in narrative describe and are intended to cause images".[287] Furthermore, "a word is used 'correctly' when the average hearer will be affected by it in the way intended"[288] – i.e. when the average hearer would have the same association ("imagination-image") as the speaker. (In such a philosophical bath-house we might very well, as Wittgenstein intimates, encounter someone who believed that in writing about, for instance, a 'wonderful red sunset' one could be correctly understood (the right 'image' would be conjured) only if one's words were printed in red – and just the right shade of red at that (recall Wittgenstein's remark in q. 262).)

As with the "narrative use" of individual words, Russell characterized the 'meaning' of "word-propositions" as follows: "A word-proposition, apart from niceties, 'means' the corresponding image-proposition, and an image-proposition has an objective reference dependent upon the meanings of its constituent images."[289] (Incidentally, for Russell, following Hume, an 'image' or 'idea' is generally speaking a "copy of sensations".[290] The 'meaning' of an image is that sensory-stimulus configuration or 'object' of which it is a copy.)

Following, and to a certain extent improvising on, Semon (see n. 277), Russell considered 'meanings', *qua* 'image associations' that a word produces, to be what he called "mnemic phenomena" – that is to say, "responses of an organism which, so far as hitherto observed facts are concerned, can only be brought under causal laws by including past occurrences in the history of the organism as part of the causes of the present response".[291] Apparently reluctant to play physiologist (though not, it seems, to play psychologist[292]), Russell ignored the predominantly physiological emphasis of Semon's theories and reduced Semon's "Law of Engraphy" and "Law of Ekphory" to a single general psychological law of "mnemic causation" that he felt would explain the causal nature of 'meaning':

> If a complex stimulus A has caused a complex reaction B in an organism, the occurrence of a part of A on a future occasion tends to cause the whole reaction B.[293]

Russell did not elaborate in any great detail concerning how this law is to be applied to specific "mnemic phenomena"; however, given his definition of meaning in terms of 'associations' (images, sensations) this general law of "mnemic causation" can be more explicitly understood as a causal explanation of 'meaning' in the following manner. Assume that in the history of an individual a complex stimulus A has occurred (presumably with an appropriate frequency and duration), and that this *complex* stimulus A was composed of two primary parts (call them A_1 and A_2) of which one part (A_1) was a specific linguistic stimulus (a word) and the other (A_2) a different stimulus configuration (an 'object'). Assume also that the *complex* stimulus A has had a specific effect (complex reaction B) on the individual. The specific composition of this complex reaction we might designate as $B_{(A1, A2)}$, i.e. the roughly simultaneous sensations of a specific 'word' and a specific 'object'. According to Russell's general law of mnemic causation, if at a later point in the history of this individual only part of the complex stimulus A occurs – let us say, only the linguistic stimulus (word) A_1 – then there will take place the *whole* of complex reaction $B_{(A1,A2)}$, i.e. not only the sensation (B_{A1}) of the word, but also, if not the sensation of an object, since there is no occurrence here of a stimulus-object (A_2), a copy (image) of the sensation (B_{A2}) of a stimulus-object (A_2). Thus, according to Russell, the 'meaning' of a word is the effect it has on the 'mind' (the image associated with the word) and this effect is more broadly explainable by way of "mnemic causation" in terms of the history of the individual.²⁹⁴

It is not necessary here to give a complete account of Russell's philosophical views during this period, but there are at least two other aspects of his overall account of language that deserve mention as part of the backdrop against which Wittgenstein's post-1930 'calculus/game/system' conception of language emerged: namely, Russell's account of what he called "propositional attitudes" (for instance, believing, wishing, expecting) and his account of what he later called "logical words" (terms that Aristotle would have classified as 'syncategorematic': 'but', 'and', 'or', and the like).

Russell considered 'belief' to be "the central problem in the philosophy of mind". ²⁹⁵ In keeping with his overall "neutral monist" thesis during this period, he was of the opinion that this aspect of 'mind' could be nothing more than sensations or images (the stuff out of which 'mind' is allegedly composed). Thus, one finds him suggesting that in the main the following view (which he cites from William James) seems inevitable: "*In its inner nature, belief, or the sense of reality, is a sort of feeling more allied to the emotions than to anything else.*"²⁹⁶

Russell, though, tended to use the term 'belief' somewhat more broadly as a generic term designating a wide range of mental 'occurrences' that he called "propositional attitudes" – which in effect were various kinds of 'feelings' that are not part of but rather attach to the 'meaning' (image-proposition) of word-propositions.²⁹⁷ As he admitted in *The Analysis of Mind*, however, "The view of belief which I have been advocating contains little that is novel except the distinction of kinds of belief-feelings such as memory and expectation."²⁹⁸

At around the time that he wrote *The Analysis of Mind* Russell seems not to have been very sure just how many kinds of "belief-feelings" he had discovered, but speculated that there might well be a wide spectrum of such "belief-feelings" that can attach to an "image-proposition", including such occurrences as "or-feelings" and "if-then-feelings":

> It seems to me that there are various feelings that may attach to a [image-]proposition, any one of which constitutes belief. Of these I would instance memory, expectation, and bare non-temporal assent. Whether there are others, I do not know. . . . Possibly disjunctions and implications may involve other kinds of belief-feelings.²⁹⁹

By the time he published *An Inquiry into Meaning and Truth* Russell was less inclined to lump the latter so-called 'occurrences' under the general rubric 'beliefs', preferring instead to distinguish more starkly between "propositional attitudes" (belief, desire, and so on) and what he now called "logical words" ('or', 'not' and the like).[300] He did, however, continue to consider all "logical words" as designating "experiences" and being "indispensable for the description of certain mental facts".[301] For the purposes of what he called his "psychological theory of the meaning of logical words",[302] Russell dismissed the logician's definitions of logical words in terms of truth conditions as a "short circuit", and indicated, for example, with respect to the word 'or', that

> We wish to know what are the occurrences that make the word 'or' useful. These occurrences are not to be sought in the facts that verify or falsify beliefs, which have no disjunctive quality, but are what they are. The only occurrences that demand the word 'or' are subjective, and are in fact hesitations. In order to express a hesitation in words, we need 'or' or some equivalent word.[303]

Russell considered it likely that an analogous account in terms of 'experiences' or mental 'occurrences' could be given of the meaning of all "logical words"[304] (or, for that matter, any word whatsoever) – asserting, for instance, that

> 'not' must derive its meaning from experiences of rejection, and 'or' from experiences of hesitation. Thus no essential word in our vocabularly can have a meaning independent of experience. Indeed any word *I* can understand has a meaning derived from *my* experience.[305]

As with his general account of 'belief' (see q. 296), Russell's "psychological theory of the meaning of logical words" seems for the most part also to have been inspired by William James, James too having contended that

> There is not a conjunction or a preposition, and hardly an adverbial phrase, syntactic form, or inflection of voice, in human speech, that does not express some shading or other of relation which we at some moment actually feel to exist between the larger objects of our thought.... We ought to say a feeling of *and*, a feeling of *if*, a feeling of *but*, and a feeling of *by*, quite as readily as we say a feeling of *blue* or a feeling of *cold*.[306]

These, then, are some of the prominent features of Russell's approach to language, especially in those works (such as *The Analysis of Mind*) to which Wittgenstein had indirect, if not direct, exposure during the 'lost decade'. Russell's view of language, and in particular his 'causal theory' of meaning, was for the most part simply reproduced by Ogden and Richards in their work *The Meaning of Meaning*, only with less stress on 'images', with

Language Games: logical vs magical views

different terminology, and in a manner that perhaps lent itself more readily to a 'behaviourist' reading. Ogden and Richards' account (and their terminology) has come to be recognized by linguists as the classical account of meaning or 'signification'.[307] Figure 4.1, reproduced from *The Meaning of Meaning*, clearly illustrates Ogden and Richards' version of the 'causal theory'.[308]

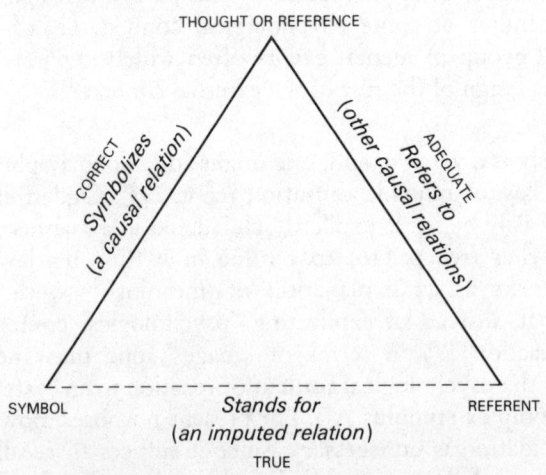

Figure 4.1

According to their view there are "three factors involved whenever any statement is made, or understood": *thoughts* (or 'references' – they use this term in a very peculiar way), *symbols* (or 'words') and *referents* (or 'things').[309] As one can see, in place of Russell's mentalistic talk about 'images', Ogden and Richards prefer to speak of 'thoughts' – though, as Russell noted,[310] 'thoughts' is an equally mentalistic expression. For Ogden and Richards the 'meaning' of a symbol (word, sentence) is the 'thought' caused by the symbol. Also similar to Russell's account (cf. q. 288), they define a 'correct' symbol as one which "will cause a similar reference [= 'thought'] to occur in a suitable interpreter".[311] And, of course, "An incorrect symbol is one which in a given universe of discourse causes in a suitable interpreter a reference [= 'thought'] different from that symbolized in the speaker."[312] It becomes quite clear what Ogden and Richards are up to in speaking of an 'interpreter' in such passages, given their definition of 'interpretation': "Our interpretation of any sign is our psychological reaction to it, as determined by our past experience in similar situations, and by our present experience."[313]

Here there is evident a Russellian emphasis on the 'mnemic' history of the individual as the broader causal context in terms of which 'meaning' is

120   *Language Games: logical vs magical views*

to be understood. However, Ogden and Richards did not adopt Russell's term "mnemic causation" to denominate their broad causal explanation of 'meaning' (or 'reference'), instead preferring to call it the "contextual theory of reference or meaning",[314] which they explain as follows:

> Behind all interpretation we have the fact that when part of an external context recurs in experience this part is, through its linkage with a member of some psychological context, i.e. of a causally connected group of mental events often widely separated in time, sometimes a sign of the rest of the external context.[315]

This obviously is a version, and, one might add, a poorly phrased version, of Russell's law of mnemic causation (cf. q. 293). Ogden and Richards' version can easily be more explicitly elucidated in a manner analogous to that used earlier (see p. 116) to outline how Russell's law of mnemic causation works as an explanation of 'meaning' – with the obvious exception that, instead of explicating "psychological context" (Russell's "complex reaction B") in terms of 'images', one must now speak of 'thoughts' as the psychological context or reaction to an "external context" (Russell's "complex stimulus A"). For present purposes, however, a more detailed elucidation is unnecessary, since it suffices to recall Ogden and Richards' acknowledgement of their debt to Russell (cf. q. 270). Having pointed out that they had managed to "refrain from making images a cornerstone" of their view, Ogden and Richards admitted,

> It is mainly on this point that the view here developed differs from Mr Russell's account of meaning, which should, however, be consulted by those who desire a more simple discussion of the part played by Mnemonic causation in knowledge than our brief outline provides.[316]

Such, then, were some of the main aspects of the views concerning meaning and language propounded by Russell and Ogden in works published during Wittgenstein's 'lost decade' – works to which he was exposed during those years. Given the nature of those views and the fact that Wittgenstein himself alludes to the inquiries into the subject of language that characterized philosophical activity in England during this period, there can be no doubt whatsoever that it was precisely views such as those of Russell and Ogden (in particular the law of mnemic causation offered by them as an explanation of 'meaning') about which Wittgenstein in January 1930, soon after taking up writing philosophy again, disparagingly remarked,

There is a kind of philosophy – one might call it psychologistic [*psychologistische*] philosophy but I haven't yet found a really good name for it – which always speaks of associations and the simultaneous or vaguely simultaneous occurrence of events A, B and C; of similar constituents of two events having the consequence that the whole occurs [to the mind; *einfallen*] when a part comes before our eyes. A typical philosophical dead-end. The combination of strived-for exactness and factual irrelevance.[317]

Clearly, not only was Wittgenstein aware of the philosophical activities and views of such thinkers as Russell and Ogden during the 'lost decade', but aspects of their thought such as the law of mnemic causation served as a subject of his critical efforts upon his return to philosophy in 1929–30. Let us now return to the *Nachlaß* and examine more carefully particular remarks in which Wittgenstein seems to be formulating his post-1930 'logical' view of signs, his 'calculus/game/system' conception of language – thereby to establish definitively whether his 'logical' view did in fact at least in part emerge in opposition to the sort of 'psychological' view one finds in the works of Russell and Ogden, and in the process come to a better appreciation of the post-1930 'calculus/game/system' conception itself.

Many passages have already been cited in which Wittgenstein discusses what we have called the 'calculus/game/system' conception of language, but these passages were cited only so as to establish that his use of the 'game'/'language game' idiom (as opposed to the 'calculus' and 'system' idioms) constituted merely a *terminological* and not a substantive shift in his view of language *during* the 1930s. It is testimony to the validity of the central thesis of the present chapter that in many of these same passages contrasting themes and issues are present which are now readily identifiable as aspects of the 'psychological' view of language found in the works of Russell, Ogden and James. Let us then briefly review some of the passages in question, only this time with an eye open for aspects of the 'psychological' view in contrast to which Wittgenstein's 'logical' view may have emerged.

A contrast between Wittgenstein's 'calculus/game/system' conception and the 'psychological' view of signs is readily detectable in the passage from around 1932-4 (q. 254) in which Wittgenstein suggests that the expressions "I understand [a sentence]" and "I mean something by [a sentence]" need not be taken as claims that the sentence had somehow taken hold in us, that we thereby imagined something, but rather could simply mean that the sentence is "part of a system familiar to me. *I* play the game of which it is a part." Here one can now recognize that Wittgenstein is contrasting the 'system/game' conception to a viewpoint identifiable as the 'psychological' or 'magical' view of language. It is the psychological view that holds that when we 'understand' or 'mean something by' a sentence the sentence, as it were, takes hold in us, we thereby imagine or think something. For Ogden, for example, to 'understand' a sentence is to 'interpret' it, i.e. to have "a psychological reaction to it [a 'thought'] as determined by our past experience in similar situations" (see n. 309 and q. 313). Similarly, for Russell (the Russell of the early 1920s) 'understanding' a sentence would consist in experiencing an appropriate "image-proposition".

A second obvious example is the passage from TS 213 (q. 256) in which Wittgenstein quite explicitly states that he is not interested in a sign "in so far as it influences the mind by suggestion, thus in so far as it has an effect" (this clearly is an allusion to the 'psychological' or 'magical' view of signs), but rather he is interested in a sign "only as a move in a game; term in a system, that is autonomous". Here again it is clear that the 'calculus/game/system' conception has been introduced to counter the 'psychological' or 'magical' view.

Such a contrast is also reflected in the passage from Wittgenstein's 1937 revision of TS 213 (q. 253) in which we found him simply substituting the phrase "in the language game" for "in the calculus". In that passage he seemed to be offering the general suggestion that 'meaning' (the 'meaning (or lack of it) of a sentence' and 'meaning something by a sentence') is to be accounted for or investigated in terms of the use of the linguistic expression in the calculus or language game, *rather than* in terms of accompanying or aroused images. The latter, of course, is now recognizable as the sort of psychological account that, in particular, Russell gave during the early 1920s.

This contrast comes out somewhat more vividly in TS 213 §20, of which the previously cited passage from MS 116 (q. 253) was a partial revision. In that section, entitled "The sense of a sentence is no *soul*", one finds the explicit assertions that

> The sense of a sentence is not pneumatic, but rather is what is given as an answer to a request for an explanation of the sense. And – or – one sense differs from another, as the explanation of the one from the explanation of the other.
> The role the sentence plays in the calculus, that is its sense.
> The sense (therefore) doesn't stand *behind* it (as the psychic occurrence of images [*Vorstellungen*] etc.).[318]

And finally there is the remark from *Philosophical Investigations* cited (q. 247) as evidence that the 'calculus' conception was alive and well in Wittgenstein's later works. In *PI* §559 he again stresses that the function of a word (in a sentence) is not something *hidden*, but rather comes out in the course of the calculus – thus again contrasting the calculus conception to a view of the function of words in terms of something 'hidden'. It is not very clear from the wording of this section just what the hidden something might be which, according to the contrasting view of language, accounts for the function of words, but Wittgenstein seems to have given us a hint with his parenthetical expression "Meaning-body" (*Bedeutungskörper*). Given our knowledge of the philosophical views to which he was exposed during the 'lost decade', there is little difficulty in identifying the sort of view of language that fits the bill here. The 'pyschological' (or 'magical') view of signs accounts for the function of words in terms of something hidden, and according to that view the 'something hidden' is the sensations and images conjured by a sentence. Recall that it is sensations and images that Russell and James considered to be the 'meaning' of words and which they were also inclined to call the 'stuff' (see n. 283) out of which mind (and the world) is allegedly composed. Such 'meaning-stuff' (a sensation or image) is very likely the sort of 'hidden something' that Wittgenstein was tempted to allude to as a "Meaning body".

Actually, there is quite explicit evidence in the *Nachlaß* linking the term 'meaning-body' to the 'psychological' or 'magical' view of signs and, in at least one case, specifically to the views of William James. In TS 213, two pages after a stretch of text in which Wittgenstein explicitly distinguishes between the 'magical' view of signs and his own 'logical' view (see q. 262), and in the section (11) entitled "Meaning [*Bedeutung*] as a feeling standing behind the word; which is expressed by a gesture", one finds the following reference to the views of William James:

> Anybody who reads and understands a sentence perceives the words //the different types of words [*Wortarten*, parts of speech]// in different ways, although the visual form [*Bild*] and sound [*Klang*] of the types doesn't differ. We completely forget that *nicht*, *Tisch* and *grün* viewed as articulations or written forms don't differ essentially from each other and we see that clearly in a language foreign to us. (James.)[319]

In TS 213 there were three handwritten annotations to this paragraph which shed light on what Wittgenstein was up to. First, in the margin he had noted that the paragraph should be "as a quotation" (*als Zitat*), thus indicating that the remark was not so much his own pronouncement, but rather the sort of remark someone else might be likely to make. Given the parenthetical reference to James, there is little doubt that Wittgenstein considered it the sort of pronouncement William James might make. This is even more evident in a later revision (MS 114, 1933-4) of TS 213 in which the parenthetical reference to James is expanded to "(Compare William James on the feelings that correspond to words like 'not', 'but', and so on.)"[320] As we know from our survey of some the philosophical literature to which Wittgenstein was exposed (whether indirectly or not) during the 'lost decade', James, whose views on such matters seem to have inspired Russell (see q. 305), was of the opinion that it is the accompanying experiences that really differentiate between words. (Recall James' suggestion that "We ought to say a feeling of *and*, a feeling of *if*, a feeling of *but*, and a feeling of *by*, quite as readily as we say a feeling of *blue* . . ." – q. 306.) Presumably it is because different types of words can look and sound so similar (especially in a language which is foreign to us; see n. 319) that one may be inclined (as James was) to think that what really differentiates between words is the feelings accompanying them.

The second illuminating annotation to the paragraph cited above (q. 319) is the parenthetical expression "Meaning-bodies". This was placed right next to the parenthetical reference to James and thus constitutes a quite straightforward attempt to identify 'meaning' in the Jamesian (and Russellian) sense of, as Wittgenstein put it in the title of this section (TS 213 §11), "a feeling standing behind the word". This point comes out even more clearly in his MS 114 revision of TS 213, where instead of the simple parenthetical annotation "Meaning-bodies" one finds the expanded remark "(The metaphor [*Das Gleichnis*] of meaning-bodies which stand behind the word imposes itself upon us here.)"[321]

And, finally, the third illuminating annotation is the apparently insignificant instruction that the remark (q. 319) should be transferred to another (specified) place in the typescript, directly following the statement, "The difference between types of words [*Wortarten*] is like the difference between pieces in a game [*Spielfiguren*], or like the even greater difference between a game-piece and the chess-board."[322] It seems that what Wittgenstein planned to do here is what we have already found him doing in so many other instances – namely, juxtaposing the psychological view of signs and his own view of signs as 'pieces or parts in a game (system/calculus)'. Again the suggestion is that it is not some feeling or 'meaning-body' associated with or conjured up by the pieces (types of words) that differentiates them, but rather their role in the (language) game.

Wittgenstein did in fact carry out his intention to juxtapose his own 'logical' view of signs and the remark (q. 319) suggestive of a Jamesian 'psychological' view. This was done in both his 1933–4 (see n. 322) and his 1937 reworkings of TS 213. In the 1937 revision the clash between the Jamesian 'psychological' view and his own is even more pronounced:

> One who reads a sentence in his mother tongue perceives the individual words, as they follow one another, each in a (completely) different way. We completely forget that *nicht* and *mich* and *sieht*, as articulations or written forms, don't differ essentially from each other

//are not *so very* different from each other//. In a language completely foreign to us we ~~perceive~~ notice the real uniformity of words. – Could one not talk (even) about the pieces of a game in a wholly analogous way? Though also (for example) about tools ~~in a toolbox~~ (the instruments [*Instrumenten*] of a dentist) (perhaps); one who doesn't know their purpose (use) perceives (on̲ly̲) long and short, sharp and dull (thick and thin) ~~pieces of metal [Stahlstücke]~~ rods [*Stäbe*]. For the one who uses them, they above all each have their (a) *meaning* //they above all have meanings//.

In so far as (to the extent that) (according to James) there is an if-feeling, an or-feeling, etc., there is for the chess-player (surely) (a̲l̲so̲) a king-feeling, a bishop-feeling, etc. But is it these feelings that is what really matters with a chess-game?[323]

Wittgenstein's answer to this last question would be an emphatic 'NO' – and with such an answer he would not be denying that 'feelings' might accompany a word (or, analogously, accompany a piece in a chess-game), but rather attempting to demarcate between a 'psychological' and a 'logical' concern with words; to demarcate between a Jamesian psychological concern with 'meaning' in terms of the 'feelings' accompanying a word and his own 'logical' concern with the 'meaning' of a word in terms of its role in a language game (calculus/system). (With respect to the chess analogy, one might speak for instance of the 'logic' or 'grammar' of a chess-piece, as opposed to the feelings that might be associated with the piece. 'Grammar' will be discussed shortly.)

The term 'meaning-body' is, then, quite definitely Wittgenstein's way of generally alluding to the 'psychological' or 'magical' view of signs. Furthermore, with both of the passages where we found him using the term 'meaning-body' there was clearly an intention to contrast his own post-1930 'calculus/game/system' conception of language with the 'psychological' view – hence reinforcing the account offered here of the emergence of his post-1930 'logical' view of signs.

Thus far, two fundamental points have been established. First, it has been demonstrated that the terminological variance between the expressions 'calculus', 'game'/'language game' and 'system'/'system of communication' that one finds in Wittgenstein's post-1930 writings is not indicative of a series of transformations in his view of signs or conception of language after 1930. On the contrary, such terms have been found to be roughly interchangeable for Wittgenstein during this period and simply were terminologically different ways of formulating a single uniform conception of language (*not* a conception of language as uniform; see chapter 5) which remained constant in his post-1930 writings. This uniform view has been referred to as the 'calculus/game/system' conception of language or, more simply, the post-1930 'logical' view of signs. Secondly, it has been shown, primarily on the basis of the very same passages used to establish the first point, that to a great extent Wittgenstein's 'calculus/game/system' conception of language or 'logical' view of signs emerged as a reaction to the sort of 'psychological' (or, as he derisively called it, 'magical') view of signs he had encountered in the works of some of his contemporaries during the 'lost decade'.

Having established the above points, much of the task of the present chapter has been accomplished. However, at the beginning of this chapter it was suggested that, although to a great extent Wittgenstein's 'calculus/game/system' conception emerged in opposition to, generally, the sorts of psychological accounts of language propounded during the 'lost decade' in the publications of some of his contemporaries, it was *not only* the views of his contemporaries to which he was reacting, but also to a certain extent his *own* earlier views. The latter point has not yet been demonstrated. In order to do so, it will be necessary to explore in more depth at least some of the aspects of Wittgenstein's post-1930 'logical' view of signs.

There are many important features of this 'logical' view that deserve more careful scrutiny, and some will be the subject of the next chapter. For the remainder of this chapter there will be a focus on some of the aspects which offer an insight into how his post-1930 'calculus/game/system' conception may to a certain extent have emerged as a reaction to his *own* earlier views about language.

Since it has already been established that there is indeed a single 'calculus/game/system' conception of signs operative in Wittgenstein's post-1930 writings, there is no longer any need to restrict ourselves to passages from the *Nachlaß* which clearly illustrate the interchangeability of the terms 'calculus', 'game'/'language game' and 'system'/'system of communication'. As a result, the resources to which appeal can be made are greatly enhanced. One very important clue to how Wittgenstein's post-1930 'logical' view of language may have emerged in part as a reaction to some of his own earlier views is his post-1930 conception of 'grammar'.

The concept of 'grammar' has come to the fore in some of the passages already cited from the *Nachlaß*. For instance, in one of the remarks in which Wittgenstein was clearly attempting to demarcate between his own approach to language and that of Ogden and Richards there was the suggestion that, unlike Ogden and Richards' causal theory, which was concerned with the psycho-physical aspects of language, his own concern was with 'grammar' or the 'structure' of language (see q. 279).

Similarly, in the significant remark from TS 213 where Wittgenstein was found differentiating between what he called the 'magical' and 'logical' views of signs (and recall that this remark appears on the same page where he explicitly asserted that he was interested in a sign "only as a move in a game, term in a system, that is autonomous" (see q. 256), there again was an attempt to demarcate between a concern with the causal aspects of language and an investigation of 'grammar' – one of the suggestions being that it is not by way of an investigation of the effects that the word 'meaning' has on the mind that one can determine the meaning of 'meaning', but rather by way of an investigation of "the grammar of the word 'meaning'" (see q. 262).

There is an interesting annotation in TS 213 right next to the paragraph (q. 262) in which Wittgenstein distinguishes between the 'magical' and 'logical' views of signs: namely, an indication that perhaps the paragraph should be transferred to TS 213 §14, entitled "That which interests *us* about signs; the meaning which for *us* is decisive, is that which is laid down in the grammar of the signs." Furthermore, within this section the remark in which Wittgenstein differentiated between the 'magical' and 'logical' views of signs was to have been placed immediately preceding the following explication of what he means by 'grammar':

> Grammar (– I might //one could// say –) is the account books [*Geschäftsbücher*, transaction legers] of language; from them everything, which doesn't concern (vague) *feelings* but rather (actual) facts, must be learned.[324]

What Wittgenstein means here by 'facts' as opposed to 'feelings' is quite clear from some of his revisions of this remark. In one of his revisions there is the following illuminating alternative wording for part of the remark: "everything, which concerns the (actual) *transactions* [*Transaktionen*] with our words and not mere (certain) vague feelings that the words evoke".[325]

The 'facts' of which Wittgenstein speaks are, then, 'facts' about language, our actual linguistic transactions, and these as opposed to the 'feelings' that might accompany or be conjured by words. In his chapter entitled "Philosophy" he even went so far as to specify that for him "The method of philosophy [is] the perspicuous [*übersichtliche*] presentation of grammatical //linguistic [*sprachlichen*]// facts."[326] It would have been appropriate for him to transfer the remark in which he differentiated between the 'logical' and 'magical' views of signs and place it in the text next to the above-cited (q. 324) explication of what he means by 'grammar', because in his explanation of his use of the term 'grammar' he is in effect delineating the concerns of his 'logical' view of signs, and doing so in such a way as to distinguish these concerns from the concerns of the 'magical' or psychological view. Grammar is, as it were, the ledger of our actual linguistic transactions, and it is the actual transactions with words (what we do, what we say, how we use them) that is the concern of the logical view of signs – not the feelings evoked by words. It is in terms of the actual transactions with language that the meaning/sense of words/sentences is to be understood. As Wittgenstein stressed immediately after yet another draft of his explication of the term 'grammar' (in q. 324), "How do you use the word, what do you do with it? – this will teach me how you understand it."[327] This is so presumably *not* because we do not have more direct access to the pneumatic or spiritual accompaniments of discourse and thus must settle for observable 'manifestations', but because, even if there were such pneumatic accompaniments, it is not these that determine the meaning of words – rather it is the actual linguistic transactions that are constitutive of their meaning, and one's 'understanding' of a word is constituted by the transactions that one is able to carry out with it. It might of course be quite nice (from a speaker's standpoint) if the meaning of words were their psychological accompaniments, for at least then – if language were not an 'autonomous system or calculus' (cf. q. 256) – it would be logically impossible to lie: lying would presumably be 'thinking one thing but saying another'; yet, if the *meaning* of what one says is the psychological accompaniment of one's words, then there would be no lies, just *misunderstandings* on the part of those who hear us speak. And, as Wittgenstein intimated in a similarly humorous vein, if 'meaning' is the psychological accompaniment of words, 'Why might one not be able to have a full-blown language with only one word?' – a form of economy, incidentally, that would make learning that language a delightfully simple affair: one would need only learn how to utter or write the single word and one could then say all one wanted simply by varying the psychological accompaniments. This somewhat humorous suggestion was hinted at in TS 213 §10, entitled "The sense of a sentence is no *soul*", from which a passage has already been cited (q. 318). Having claimed that the meaning of a sentence (or words) is not 'pneumatic', not something imagined along with it, but rather is "the role the sentence plays in the calculus" or, as he put it in his MS 116 revision (see q. 253), its "use in the language game", Wittgenstein later, no doubt tongue in cheek, interjected,

> Of course one could also put our question in a very elementary way: why isn't a language possible //couldn't come about// with merely one word, for after all it certainly happens that a word (in a language) has several meanings. (Why then not all [meanings]?)[328]

This was one of the few passages in this section of TS 213 that Wittgenstein crossed out. It is likely that he did so for the following reasons. On the one hand, someone might answer, "Well one *can* after all have a very *simple* language with only *one* word, just as one can have a very simple game with only one kind of piece (e.g. draughts)." Such an answer would be uninteresting and would miss the point Wittgenstein was trying to make. Or, on the other hand, someone might give the unfortunate and, for Wittgenstein, absolutely misbegotten answer, "Why of course we *can't* have a *full-blown* language with only one word; no one would be able to figure out what we were imagining each time we uttered it."

The passage in TS 213 was perhaps crossed out precisely because a person might be inclined to give *such* answers (answers which either miss the point of the remark altogether or simply reinforce the misconception he wishes to dispel), *instead of* acknowledging what Wittgenstein would want a reader to acknowledge, namely:

> "Obviously there could not be a full-blown language with only one word for the same sort of reason that there couldn't be chess with only one kind of piece (a physically uniform set of pieces) – we would have no way of keeping their different roles distinct; no way of distinguishing which kinds of moves belonged to which pieces."

Grammar (as Wittgenstein uses the term in his post-1930 writings), in that it is the ledger of our actual linguistic transactions, is, as it were, the ledger of the sorts of moves that are (can be) and are not (cannot be) made in a given 'language game'; the ledger of what is a part of (and what is excluded from) a given 'system of communication'; the ledger of what is a step in (and what is a misstep in) a given kind of 'linguistic calculation', a given 'calculus of language'. Thus one finds Wittgenstein making the following sorts of parallel claims about 'grammar'. In 1930–1 he wrote, "Grammar of course describes the meaning of signs."[329] Or, as he also put it in the same notebook, "Grammar describes how the signs are being used. Though not how they are being used as a result of a series of observations, but rather the use in each particular case."[330] And again in the same notebook, except now in terms of the 'system' idiom, one finds the remark that "Grammar describes the system, the space [*Raum*] in which a place [*Stelle*] for the symbol (sign) is indicated."[331] Similarly, in terms of the 'game' idiom and with respect to an example of a sentence that could be taken as a statement about 'grammar', he once explained, "that sentence is a grammatical one, one which describes the language game".[332]

In such passages as these there is a clear linkage of the notion of 'grammar' to the 'calculus/game/system' conception of language. 'Grammar' is, as it were, a description of the role that a sign plays or the 'place' of a sign within a particular 'language game', 'system of communication' or 'calculus'. Notice that in q. 331 Wittgenstein uses the expression "the space" as another way of designating the system (i.e. calculus, language game) in which a given sign has a 'place' and in terms of which the meaning of the sign is to be understood. Throughout his career Wittgenstein used spatial metaphors in his characterizations of language. His use of spatial metaphors in his post-1930 writings, however, can and should be taken not in a formal and abstract sense,[333] but rather as a figurative way of referring to concrete domains or loci of actual linguistic practice: our actual linguistic 'transactions', 'language games', 'calculi' or 'systems of communication'. There is quite a wide variety of spatial metaphors used by Wittgenstein in his later writings in the context of his discussions of 'grammar'. Instead of speaking of the 'grammar' of concepts, he sometimes speaks, for instance, of their 'geometry', or their 'geography', or their 'physiognomy' (see n. 230), or their 'structure'. All such metaphors in his post-1930 writings should be taken in the light of his post-1930 conception of 'grammar' as the 'ledger' of our actual linguistic transactions and his post-1930 conception of language games (linguistic calculi, systems of communication) as domains or 'loci' (itself a spatial metaphor) of extant linguistic practice.

A good illustration of Wittgenstein's post-1930 use of spatial metaphors in his discussion of the 'grammar' of signs is his occasional metaphorical use of the term 'geometry'. In 1930–1, for example, in the context of a comparison of 'gestures' [*Geste*] with signs, and a discussion of the sense in which 'grammar' would be essential for their intelligibility, he wrote, "I could also not understand a gesture if I didn't see it as a possibility within a specific space [*Raum*]. And thus there is also a grammar of gestures (that is to say, their geometry)."[334] One finds Wittgenstein using such a 'geometry' metaphor even as late as 1948, when, in the context of a discussion of colour concepts, he suggested,

> "There is no bluish yellow." This is like "There is no regular biangle"; one might call it a proposition of colour-geometry, i.e. it is a proposition that gives a conceptual specification [or determination: *ein begriffsbestimmender Satz*].[335]

"There is no bluish yellow." This for Wittgenstein is a statement about 'grammar', a statement about the use of our concepts. It is not one of those risky empirical generalizations that might some day be refuted by a new discovery about the world (as opposed to realizing a fact about our language): we shall not some day discover in a corner of some energetic painter's palette a patch of 'bluish yellow'; and this presumably not because our artists could never be clever enough, or because it would be one of those mysterious little bands in the colour spectrum that we just cannot *see* (such as 'ultra-violet'), but rather because, whatever wavelength on the spectrum and however ingenious our artists, there is no 'colour' we would *call* 'bluish yellow'. Observe the parallel ways in which Wittgenstein could

Language Games: logical vs magical views 131

formulate such a *grammatical* point as "There is no bluish yellow" by using spatial metaphors and his 'calculus/game/system' terminology:

- 'Bluish yellow' is not a possibility within colour-space.
- 'Bluish yellow' is not part of (or is not a term of, or does not have a place in) the system of colour-concepts.
- 'Bluish yellow' is not a step in the calculus with colour words.
- 'Bluish yellow' is not a move in our language games with colour words.

In the same notebook in which the above reference (in q. 335) to 'colour-geometry' occurs, Wittgenstein went so far as to state the goals of philosophy in terms of another, but similar, spatial metaphor: "The philosopher wants to master the geography of concepts: to see each place [*Ort*] in its nearest and in its farthest (broadest) environs. //to understand each place (site) in its nearest, and also in its broadest environs."[336] The reference to "the geography of concepts" in this passage does not at all invoke a formal conception of language, but rather fits in quite clearly with the 'calculus/game/system' conception of language in terms of, as I have put it, 'loci of extant linguistic practice'.

Perhaps the most puzzling spatial metaphor used by Wittgenstein, and the one most likely to seduce one into interpreting his post-1930 conception of 'grammar' as a formal pursuit along the lines of the *Tractatus* (see n. 333), is his expression 'structure'. Recall that we have already encountered this term in a manuscript from the year 1930, in which context he specified that he is not interested in the psycho-physical aspects of language, as were Ogden and Richards, but rather in clarifying "its structure (the grammar)" (see q. 279). This is no relic of his Tractarian concerns with formal logic. Even as late as 1946-7 one still finds him on occasion characterizing 'grammar' in terms of the description of "the structure of our concepts":

> If we can find a ground for the structure of concepts [*Begriffsbildung*] among the facts of nature (psychological and physical), then isn't the description of the structure of our concepts really disguised natural science; ought we not in that case to concern ourselves not with grammar, but with what lies at the bottom of grammar in nature?[337]

Disregarding Wittgenstein's efforts to differentiate between his concern with 'grammar' and the concerns of natural science (see n. 337), it is fairly clear that there is here, as in the remark from 1930, an identification of 'grammar' with a concern for "the structure of our concepts". That what he might be up to with his reference to "the structure of our concepts" is quite consistent with his post-1930 conception of 'grammar' as the 'ledger' of our actual linguistic transactions comes out very clearly in another remark he made late in his career (1947):

> "I know", "I can", "I believe" don't express a 'content of experience' [*Erlebnisinhalt*]: how is this apparent in the structure of the language game [*Struktur des Sprachspiels*]? How is it apparent that 'knowing' is not an experience; or, what do the various forms of experience have in common with each other and not with 'knowing'? Is it something which, for example, the acoustical experience has in common with the acoustical idea [*Gehörsvorstellung*]? What then are 'states of consciousness'? ...
> You must basically learn afresh the use of words.[338]

Wittgenstein's advice on how one might "learn afresh the use", how one might obtain a clear idea of the 'grammar' or "structure of the language game", would be, as he indicated in one of his revisions of TS 213 material,

> the word 'know' doesn't designate a state of consciousness. That is to say, the grammar of this word ['know'] isn't that of a 'state of consciousness'. But rather a different one. And there is only one way to learn to recognize it: to look at how the word is actually used.[339]

There is no doubt whatsoever that the spatial metaphor 'structure' is being used by Wittgenstein in his post-1930 writings not in a formal sense, but rather figuratively, in reference to the characteristics or constitution of language games, extant loci of linguistic practice: what moves can be made and what moves cannot, what we can say and what we cannot (what makes sense and what does not) within a given language game. This is not to suggest that in his later writings Wittgenstein felt that formal logic might not be used to help shed some light on the 'grammar' of our concepts,[340] but rather that in his post-1930 writings the concept 'grammar' (as well as 'structure') did not designate some sort of abstract, formal, logical structure of language (see n. 333).

One finds Wittgenstein's use of 'spatial metaphors', his emphasis on 'grammar' as a ledger of our actual linguistic transactions and his 'calculus/game/system' conception all coalescing within a single stretch of text in one of his revisions of TS 213, but in addition it is quite evident from this passage that the backdrop against which his post-1930 notion of 'grammar' (and in general his post-1930 'logical' view of signs) emerged was the 'magical' or psychological view of signs:

I want to say: the place of a word in grammar is its meaning.
But I might also say: the meaning of a word is what the explanation of its meaning explains [cf. n. 318].
The explanation of the meaning explains the use of the word.
The use of a word in the language is its meaning.
Grammar describes the use of words in the language.
So it has somewhat the same relation to the language as the description of a game, the rules of a game, have to the game.
Meaning, in our sense, is embodied in the explanation of meaning. If, on the other hand, by the word 'meaning' we mean a characteristic sensation connected with the use of a word, then the relation between the explanation of a word and its meaning is rather that of cause to effect.[341]

The last paragraph of this passage is clearly recognizable as an allusion to the psychological view of signs and in particular to the 'causal theory' of meaning. The import of such a passage, the fundamental clash between his post-1930 'logical' view and the 'psychological' view in opposition to which his own view emerged, is perhaps nowhere more bluntly stated than in the following notebook entry (May 1938) where Wittgenstein, almost imploringly, wrote,

Your (my) game remains (takes place) completely in language....
I would like you to be aware that words are only words. "That no magic power dwells in them", I might say. That is, I would like you to ask, "Yes this is what I *say – and what else?*" ...
I would like you to make the transition from the soul of a sentence to its function in the language game.[342]

"Yes, this is what we *say*, and also *this*, and sometimes *that*.... These are the moves we make in the *language game* with the word; such are the steps in this *calculus* of language; this is and that is not part of the *system* of communication – such is the (grammar) ledger of our actual linguistic transactions." But now where do we find ourselves? Where has Wittgenstein taken us with his 'logical' view of signs, his post-1930 notion of 'grammar' as the ledger of our actual linguistic transactions, his 'calculus/games/system' conception of language as loci of extant linguistic practice? We find ourselves in the domain of ordinary language. The domain delineated by Wittgenstein's post-1930 conception of 'grammar' is the very domain to which, as has been demonstrated (see chapter 2), Wittgenstein himself had shifted when taking up writing philosophy again in 1929–30. It is at this juncture, if the reader has not already surmised the connection, that it becomes evident how Wittgenstein's post-1930 'calculus/game/

system' conception of language was not only a reaction to the views of some of his contemporaries, but also at least in part a reaction to his own earlier views. As was demonstrated in chapter 2, Wittgenstein himself at an earlier point in his career, before taking up philosophy again in 1929-30, had dabbled in 'psychological' speculation about the nature of language; he himself considered such concepts as 'understanding', 'meaning' (*meinen* and *Bedeutung*) and 'thinking/thought' as designating psychological states or processes which lie 'behind' language and constitute some sort of psychological substratum fundamental to language. This of course is not to suggest that Wittgenstein at some earlier point in his career held precisely the *same* views (for instance, the 'causal theory' of meaning) as he was criticizing in the works of Russell, Ogden or James, but rather that some of his own earlier conceptions were such that they too constituted a 'psychological view' of signs – a view which was perhaps in some (though certainly not all) respects similar to the 'psychological' views of Russell, Ogden and James.

There is a passage in the 'Blue Book' which indicates that his 'calculus/game/system' conception of signs emerged as a reaction to psychological views *in general*, including those views shown in chapter 2 to be what Wittgenstein later in his career referred to as his *own* early 'metalogical' views about psychological concepts:

> I have been trying in all this to remove the temptation to think that there '*must* be' what is called a mental process of thinking, hoping, wishing, believing, etc., independent of the process of expressing a thought, a hope, a wish, etc. And I want to give you the following rule of thumb: If you are puzzled about the nature of thought, belief, knowledge, and the like, substitute for the thought the expression of the thought, etc. The difficulty which lies in this substitution, and at the same time the whole point of it, is this: the expression of belief, thought, etc. is just a sentence; – and the sentence has sense only as a member of a system of language; as one expression within a calculus.[343]

Here the 'calculus/game/system' conception has been introduced not in opposition to *specific* views which are identifiable as those of his contemporaries, but rather, apparently, in opposition to the *general* tendency to view such concepts as 'thinking' and 'knowing' as designating 'mental processes' – a tendency of which, as demonstrated in chapter 2, he himself was guilty at an earlier point in his career. Recall, for instance, that Wittgenstein himself once considered 'thoughts' and 'meaning' to be "psychical constituents" lying behind language (see, for example, pp. 53-4 and n. 149).

In the 'Blue Book', right after the above-cited passage in which the conceptions of a 'calculus' and 'system of language' were introduced, Wittgenstein furthermore went on to warn the reader not to misconstrue the conception of a 'calculus' as designating some sort of "permanent background to every sentence" which lies there in a lump "in the mental act of thinking".[344] This admonition seems to be an implicit suggestion that the concept of a 'calculus' should not be misconstrued in terms of the sort of 'ideal', strict, rule-governed calculus or grammar that one finds in the *Tractatus*. Recall that early in his career his view was that 'hidden in the medium of the understanding there *must be* strict and clear rules of the logical structure of propositions' (see chapter 2, esp. pp. 61–5; cf. also chapter 3, pp. 78–80). This sort of 'psychological' aspect to his earlier conception of an 'ideal grammar' is perhaps most explicitly acknowledged in TS 213 §39, headed, "Grammatical rules – and the meaning of a word. Is the meaning, when I understand it, grasped 'all at once'; and as it were laid out in the grammatical rules?" In this section one finds the confession that

> In my view the grammatical rules appear as the display in separation [*Auseinanderlegung*, taking to pieces] of what I experience all at once in the use of the word. So to speak (only) results of, expressions of the properties I experience all at once while understanding. This must of course be nonsense.[345]

It is fairly obvious that Wittgenstein does not still advocate the view he refers to as "my view" in this passage, since he considers it nonsense. "My view", therefore, must refer to a position he held at some earlier point in his career. This is more explicit in his MS116 revision of the remark, where he simply drops his assessment of the view as nonsense and instead begins the remark as follows: "I formerly (once) thought that grammatical rules were the display in separation of . . ."[346]

Further on in TS 213 §39 Wittgenstein again refers to this misconceived psychological conception of 'grammar'. Having claimed that *understanding* an 'act of pointing' as a 'sign' is not a process in the mind that accompanies the pointing, he then parenthetically interjected,

> (The notion is here again and again that the meaning, the interpretation, is a process that accompanies the pointing and so to speak gives it a soul (without which it would be dead). There it can especially appear that a sign seems to include the complete grammar, that the grammar were contained in it like a string of pearls in a box and we had only to pull it out. (But this picture is just what misleads us). As if understanding were an instantaneous grasping of something

from which later only consequences are drawn; that is, these consequences already exist in an ideal [*ideellen*] sense before they are drawn....)[347]

Given this sort of self-criticism on Wittgenstein's part, at least one of the passages previously cited as evidence of the interchangeability of the 'calculus' and 'game' idioms in his writings is now recognizable as an instance of his introducing the 'calculus/game/system' conception not in opposition to the views of his contemporaries, but in opposition to his own earlier view that 'meaning', a "complete grammar" (an exact and complete set of 'grammatical rules'), is experienced "all at once" when we use and 'understand' a word. The passage in question (q. 250) is from TS 213:

> I want to say that the word 'chess' is just (only) a piece in a ~~calculus~~. [game that we play.]
> If the calculus is to be described, then we would have to tabulate the rules //to have the rules tabulated before us//, but, if it is employed, then we are proceeding now according to the one then according to the other rule, and therewith their expression may swim before our mind, or also it may not.

The suggestion here is that a word, viewed as "a piece in a calculus" or "a piece in a game that we play", could be used/understood and yet not necessarily involve the 'rules of the game' all swimming before one's mind. In fact this very passage, both as it is situated in TS 213 and as it was originally drafted in MS 110 (1930–1), is very clearly introduced in the overall context of a criticism of Wittgenstein's own earlier 'metalogical' inclinations, the context of which has to some extent already been discussed in chapter 2. It was in this context that, for instance, the following remarks discussed in chapter 2 appeared:

> It is important to express generally the error that I am inclined to make in all these reflections. The false analogy from which it originates.
> I believe that error lies in the notion that the meaning [*Bedeutung*] of a word is an idea [*Vorstellung*] that accompanies the word.
> And this notion again has to do with (is connected with) that of consciousness [*Bewußt-Seins*]. That which I always called 'the primary' [*das Primäre*].[348]

Given what we saw in chapter 2 to be the nature of Wittgenstein's early 'metalogical' views, views he repudiated upon his return to philosophy in 1929–30, it is clear that his post-1930 'calculus/game/system' conception emerged at least to some extent also as a reaction to his *own* earlier view of 'meaning' (and 'understanding') and the apparently correlative notion (see q. 188) of an 'ideal pure grammar' "hidden in the medium of the understanding".[349]

It has been shown, then, that, contrary to the standard accounts of the emergence of Wittgenstein's so-called 'language-game model' of language, there was what might be called a single 'calculus/game/system' conception of language which, in spite of some shifting about in terminological preference over the last twenty years of his life, was already in place by the early 1930s soon after his return to philosophy. Furthermore, that this 'calculus/game/system' conception of language or 'logical' view of signs was already in place by such an early date was due both to the fact that Wittgenstein's view had emerged to a great extent as a reaction to the 'psychological' accounts of language propounded by his contemporaries during the 'lost decade' (accounts to which he had been exposed *during* that period) and to the fact that his post-1930 'logical' view emerged to some extent by way of repudiation of several of his own earlier notions.

The account given in the present chapter is, of course, not a full explanation of Wittgenstein's post-1930 'logical' view of signs. What has been offered is, however, an elucidation of one very important theme in the emergence of that view. The following chapter will examine another such theme and its bearing on the emergence of Wittgenstein's later *Denkweise*.

5
Wittgensteinian Relativism and the Dynamic View of Language

In the preceding chapter the emergence of Wittgenstein's post-1930 'logical' view of signs, his view of signs as moves in a language game or extant locus of linguistic practice, was explained as having been to a great extent a reaction to the sort of psychological accounts of language found in the works of several of his contemporaries, accounts which explained the 'meaning' of signs in terms of mental entities ('ideas', 'feelings' or, as Wittgenstein derisively put it, 'souls') lying in the psyche behind language. In addition, it was shown that the emergence of his post-1930 'logical' view of signs was also to a certain extent a reaction to some of his own earlier views about language. This point linked the emergence of his 'logical' view to some of the issues discussed in chapter 2: namely, Wittgenstein's own inclinations earlier in his career to view 'understanding', 'meaning', 'thinking', and, in general, what might be called 'psychological' concepts, as 'metalogical' concepts designating mental events, states or processes which lie 'behind' language. In chapter 2 it was shown that upon his return to philosophy in 1929–30 he repudiated his own earlier 'metalogical' views of 'psychological' concepts and began treating such concepts as "words like any others" (see chapter 2, q. 134 and pp. 48–9, 54–5), thus embarking on an investigation of the 'logic' of psychological concepts, the role of such concepts in ordinary language – in the 'language games', if you will, one plays with them. His concern with these matters persisted over the last twenty or so years of his life.

With this shift away from a 'metalogical' view of psychological concepts to his post-1930 'logical' view of signs came a very fundamental shift in Wittgenstein's orientation toward language, a shift which can with some justification be likened to a shift away from an absolutistic, static and perhaps in part mentalistic conception of language to a 'logical' (in his post-1930 sense), relativistic and dynamic conception. This shift was so basic that it might even be called (to borrow a Kuhnian turn of phrase) a 'paradigm shift', resulting in a host of new categories which were, if not wholly incommensurate with, at least novel in relation to and representative of a radical break from, his own earlier conceptions. The notion of a 'language game' is one such new category or conception. The purpose of the present chapter is to examine a few further 'new' conceptions (for instance, Wittgenstein's perception of his approach to signs as involving a sort of linguistic 'relativity theory' and the correlative notion of 'forms of life') that were ushered in by his fundamental change in outlook, and to show how these new conceptions emerged as prominent features of his later *Denkweise*.

Shortly after his return to philosophy in 1929–30 Wittgenstein indicated in several places in his notebooks that his approach to language now involved a sort of 'relativity theory'. Early in 1930, for instance, one finds him stressing that "A step is necessary which is analogous to that of relativity theory."[350] And later the same year he admitted, "We have here a sort of relativity theory of language before us. (And the analogy is nothing (not) fortuitous.)"[351] Almost invariably such comments were made in the context of a discussion of 'psychological' concepts, the very sorts of concepts he once considered 'metalogical' but which upon his return to philosophy in 1929–30 he began to treat as "words like any others", investigating their 'logic' as expressions in ordinary language. Just what the 'logic' of such concepts is was a matter that he spent much of his last twenty years thrashing out. However, that 'psychological' concepts are not to be assumed to be names for ethereal mental processes but, rather, are to be investigated as expressions whose sense is constituted by their 'grammar' in ordinary discourse (see chapter 4, pp. 126–34) involved a fundamental shift in his thinking which was already in place by the early 1930s and which tended to 'relativize' such concepts – that is to say, deal with them as everyday linguistic expressions which are intelligible only relative to the specific language games, calculi or systems of communication constitutive of their sense.

In the chapter of TS 213 entitled "Expectation, Wish, etc." one finds Wittgenstein suggesting that there is a similarity between his own views and that of relativity theory:

> It is – I think – important to recognize that, if I perhaps believe that someone will come to me, my enduring state has nothing to do with what is in question and the other elements of the thoughts – that is to say, it doesn't *contain* them. The same applies though for expectation, wish, etc., etc. If I expect someone, then I don't think during this whole time that he will come, or suchlike. Yes, even if I just thought of it, then this process is of course nothing amorphous as perhaps that of pain, but consists only in that I perhaps just now say the sentence

"He will come." One can't *amorphously* see that something is the case, believe that something is the case, wish, fear, think, etc.
The expression of expectation is the expectation.
The anticipation [*Vorbereitung*] is as it were itself language and cannot go outside of itself. (In the 'not being able to go outside of itself' lies the similarity of my views and that of relativity theory.)[352]

It is not evident from these remarks precisely what Wittgenstein means by comparing his views to 'relativity theory'. The following suggestions, however, are fairly clearly present in the passage. First, his views of 'believing', 'wishing', 'expecting', 'thinking', and so on, now involve an approach which deals with them as fundamentally linguistic matters rather than in terms of amorphous psychic phenomena that might precede or accompany speech. Secondly, in treating 'believing', 'expecting', and so on, as linguistic matters rather than extra-linguistic phenomena he in effect views them as in some sense or other meaningful only relative to language. Furthermore, there seems to be the outright negative suggestion that an assertion such as 'I expect (or I believe) he will come' is not a *statement about* (does not report, is not concerned with) an enduring psychological state that one might be experiencing at the time of the utterance. Wittgenstein does not explain here what such assertions *do*, if they do not report on psychological states, though he does suggest that in some sense the expression of expectation is itself the expectation, the anticipation itself is in some sense language.

In the above-cited passages Wittgenstein, as so often in his writings, seems much more concerned to dispel what he considered a misconception (i.e. that expressions of 'expectation', 'belief', and so on, are reports about one's psychological states) than to give an exhaustive positive characterization of the particular concepts under consideration. The specific section (76) of TS 213 in which these passages appear was of course drafted in the very early thirties soon after his return to philosophy (for instance, the paragraph in which he compares his views to 'relativity theory' was drafted in 1929–30; see n. 352), and thus, even if he had given a thorough positive characterization of the concepts he mentions ('expecting', 'believing', 'wishing', 'thinking', and so on), one would hardly expect that doctrinally his early analyses of such concepts would have survived the years of further scrutiny and exploration he devoted to them. However, the 'relativistic' character of his general approach to such concepts could (and did) remain constant throughout his later years, even though doctrinally his specific accounts of some of these concepts may have varied from one probing to the next (indeed, perhaps within the same notebook) – though, as will be seen by way of illustration, even some of the doctrinal details of his very early accounts of some of these psychological concepts survived the years of further investigation and revision leading up to his last draft of *Philosophical Investigations*. Yet this chapter is not concerned with the doctrinal (and historical) details of his accounts of specific concepts such as 'expecting', 'wishing' and 'thinking', but rather with his general suggestion that his overall approach to such psychological concepts involves a sort of linguistic 'relativity theory'. To the extent that doctrinal details of his accounts of some of these concepts are introduced in the course of this chapter, they are offered *only* as an *illustration* of a more general point about the (for example, 'relativistic') character of his later *Denkweise*. These details, therefore, will be offered neither as 'correct' doctrines nor as accounts which constitute Wittgenstein's final doctrinal resting-place with respect to a given psychological concept or expression.

Wittgenstein's repudiation of the view that concepts such as 'expecting', 'believing' and 'thinking' report inner psychological states or experiences is by now quite familiar territory for us. In fact the section (76) of TS 213 in which the repudiation cited above (q. 352) was found is in several ways quite explicitly linked to passages and themes that have already been examined in preceding chapters. For instance, marginal notes Wittgenstein made in this section of TS 213 indicate that he intended to insert here some further remarks from p. 154 of the typescript. In the latter stretch of TS 213 we find two key themes that have already been the subject of discussion. It was on p. 154 of the typescript, in the midst of an examination of other 'psychological concepts' (such as 'intending', as in 'intending to play chess'), that Wittgenstein made the following confession (see chapter 2, qq. 168–70, and the discussion on pp. 53ff and 58ff):

> It is important to express generally the error that I am inclined to make in all these reflections. The false analogy from which it originates.
> I believe that error lies in the notion that the meaning [*Bedeutung*] of a word is an idea [*Vorstellung*] that accompanies the word.
> And this notion again has to do with (is connected with) that of consciousness [*Bewußt-Sein*]. That which I always called 'the primary' [*das Primäre*].
> ... The source of the mistake seems to be the notion of *thoughts which accompany the sentence*. Or which precede its expression. ...

There seems, then, to be a link between Wittgenstein's claim that his view of 'psychological' concepts involves a sort of linguistic 'relativism' and what we found in chapter 2 to be his repudiation of a 'metalogical' view of such concepts. This linkage is clearly echoed even in the very passage (q. 352) in which he likens his views to 'relativity theory', for the negative suggestion that an assertion such as 'I expect he will come' is not a report about an enduring psychological state accompanying the utterance is obviously in keeping with his repudiation of a 'metalogical' view of psychological concepts.

The second key theme present in that part of TS 213 from which Wittgenstein intended to draw remarks for inclusion in §76, where he speaks of the 'relativistic' character of his views, is that expressed in another passage already cited (see q. 250 and the discussion on pp. 135–7):

> game that we play.
> I want to say that the word 'chess' is just (only) a piece in a ~~calculus~~. If the calculus is to be described, then we would have to tabulate the rules //to have the rules tabulated before us//, but, if it is employed, then we are proceeding now according to the one then according to the other rule, and therewith their expression may swim before our mind, or also it may not.

It will be recalled that this is one of the remarks examined in the preceding chapter in relation to Wittgenstein's post-1930 'logical' view of signs or 'calculus/game/system' conception of language. Thus there is perhaps also a specific connection between that conception and the linguistic 'relativism' of which he speaks.

These same two themes to which Wittgenstein's 'relativism' seems to be linked are also present in the original manuscript source where he drafted his 'relativity theory' remark (q. 352). For example, several pages after drafting that remark, one finds the following, now familiar, sort of repudiation (see n. 149 and the discussion on p. 47ff):

> One doesn't have thoughts, and *alongside* language.
> It isn't like this: that one has signs for others, but for oneself one has a mute thought. As it were, a gaseous or ethereal thought in contrast to visible and audible symbols.

And also from this same general stretch of the notebook where the 'relativity theory' remark was drafted one again finds a remark having to do with the 'calculus/game/system' conception of language (see n. 153):

> One can also put it this way: if one always expresses oneself in a system of language and thus what a sentence means is only explained through sentences of this system, then after all meaning [*Meinung*] falls completely out of language, thus out of consideration, and language remains the only thing we can consider.

Here the suggestion is that, if the sense of a sentence is to be explained only in terms of the system of language to which it belongs, then 'meaning' in the sense of a 'psychological accompaniment of discourse' falls out of consideration (see the previous discussion of this on p. 48ff). This suggestion is at the heart of Wittgenstein's post-1930 'logical' view of signs, his 'calculus/game/system' conception of language. Thus it seems that what he alludes to as the 'relativistic' character of his views may indeed somehow be connected with, or is perhaps a by-product of, both his 'calculus/game/system' conception of language and his repudiation of the psychological view of signs to which his own 'logical' view was a reaction.

A clue to the nature of the linguistic 'relativism' involved is provided by the context of the above remark in which Wittgenstein seems to stress that what a sentence means is only explained in terms of a system of language, and not in terms of psychological accompaniment. On the same page in the notebook he had previously written,

> But if one says, "How am I to know what he means, when I see nothing but the signs he gives?", then I say, "How is *he* to know what he means, when he has nothing but the signs either?"
> The question "*How* is that meant [*gemeint*]?" only makes sense when it means "Is it meant '*thus*' [*so*]." This *thus* is a linguistic expression.[353]

There seem to be two interrelated points here, both of which are suggestive of a sort of linguistic 'relativism'. On the one hand there seems to be the point that a question about the meaning of signs is a question about language (the usage of signs), not a question about psychology (a psychological occurrence accompanying speech). And Wittgenstein tries to make this point by way of a further point about language, about the verb 'to mean' (*meinen*): namely, that asking someone "*How* is that meant?" is a question about the use of language, a question in answer to which one expects a linguistic explanation of the signs, *not* an account of the workings of a psychological mechanism or *how* one managed to execute some sort of psychological activity or process.

The first of the above paragraphs, although drafted in 1929–30 in the same stretch of text as one of Wittgenstein's 'relativity theory' remarks, was reproduced in numerous other manuscripts and typescripts (see n. 353), including TS 213 and *Philosophical Investigations*. In both of these contexts it was paired with a familiar, previously cited remark that sheds additional light on the way in which the 'relativistic' character of Wittgenstein's approach is linked to the 'calculus/game/system' conception of language. As it appeared in TS 213 (but cf. *PI* §503), the remark in question read as follows:

> If I give anyone an order I feel it to be *quite enough* to give him signs. And I would never say: this is only words, and I have got to get

behind the words. Equally, when I have asked someone something and he gives me an answer (i.e. a sign) I am content – that was exactly what I expected – and I don't raise the objection: but that's a mere answer. It is clear that nothing else could be expected and that the answer presupposes the use of language //a language// //specific language game//. As everything that is to be said //we could say//.[354]

The suggestion here seems to be that, if an order is given – let us say, of the form 'Bring me an x' – this is a move in a language game, and what is meant, what is to count as carrying out the order, is relative to, for example, what is *called* 'bringing' and what is *called* an 'x'. The order 'Bring me an x' does not mean 'Do what occurs in my mind's eye when I say "Bring me an x"' – after all, if that is what an order means, then all one might have to do to carry it out is repeat the order (assuming of course that our psychological apparatuses tend to work in the same way). Nor does it mean 'Do what I picture *you* doing when I say "Bring me an x"' – one can give orders without picturing someone else carrying them out, and very rarely is what one happens to picture when one gives an order a very good facsimile of what one wants done. Yet, even if one were very good at picturing things as one gave orders, such mental occurrences are not essential to the language game of giving orders and obeying them. As Wittgenstein put it, the words are "*quite enough*". When we learn such a language game as 'Bring me an x' we are not taught to read minds; rather, we are taught what it is to fetch things. If it is not clear from the specific order just what it is (for example) that should be brought, and we ask what is meant by an 'x' (or perhaps what it means 'to bring something'), then we are asking for a definition, not a description of a state of mind: we are quite content with an *answer*, i.e. with another sign that can take the place of the word 'x' in the order 'Bring me an x' (or perhaps a demonstration of what it is 'to bring something') – this would be an explanation of the meaning of 'x' (or of the order) and would in part specify what is to count in this case as an execution of the order. The 'relativism' involved, then, is such that it views the question about the 'meaning' of a sign (for instance, the question 'How do you mean the order "Bring me an x"?') as a question not about the psyche but about language, and more specifically about the system of language, the language game, which is determinative of the sense of the sign.[355]

This sort of linguistic 'relativisim' is presumably applicable both to expressions involving psychological concepts, such as 'meaning' (*meinen*), 'expecting' and 'wishing', and to signs in general (including 'orders') – and indeed it is by clarifying psychological concepts in terms of the various language games constitutive of *their* sense that Wittgenstein tries to convince us of the applicability of his linguistic 'relativism' to signs in general. The reason for this latter strategy is presumably that it is precisely a misunderstanding of the language games involved with such concepts as 'meaning', 'expecting' and 'wishing' that has led to a misbegotten general view of the meaning of signs in terms of hidden psychic accompaniments lying behind language. Thus in both TS 213 and *Philosophical Investigations*, shortly after the above-cited passages (qq. 353-4) Wittgenstein illustrates how a concept such as 'meaning' (*meinen*) might tempt one to adopt a psychological view of signs:

> "I am not merely saying this, I mean something by it." – When we consider what is going on in us when we *mean* (and don't merely say) words, it seems to us as if there were something coupled to these words, which otherwise would run idle. – As if they, so to speak, connected with something in us.[356]

Misled, according to Wittgenstein, by a misconstrual of the expression 'to mean something by a word', one is inclined to think that the meaning of an utterance or written sign is a psychological occurrence in us that accompanies the sign – that it is a psychological accompaniment that differentiates between a meaningless sound or mark and a meaningful word; it is the psychological accompaniment that, as it were, gives a sign its life and without which it would be dead. In contrast to this view, Wittgenstein proposes a sort of linguistic 'relativism' which amounts to the suggestion that signs have meaning only relative to language games, systems of communication or linguistic calculi and that these are in effect a form of life constitutive of the meaning of signs. Wittgenstein's linguistic 'relativism', by way of its linkage with his post-1930 'calculus/game/system' conception of language as 'loci of extant linguistic practice' (see the discussion in chapter 4), is then his answer to the question 'What gives signs their life?' – and it is an answer offered in stark contrast to the sorts of answers one finds in psychological views of signs, such as Russell's and some of Wittgenstein's own earlier 'metalogical' speculations about language.

It is necessary, however, both to establish more concretely the fact that Wittgenstein's 'calculus/game/system' conception of language served as an answer to the question 'What gives a sign its life?' (an answer at variance with the psychological view of signs), and to obtain a clearer idea of the 'relativistic' implications of his answer. To a certain extent the first of these tasks has already been accomplished in chapter 4, since the demonstration that Wittgenstein's post-1930 'calculus/game/system' conception emerged as a reaction to a 'psychological' view of signs was in effect a demonstration that he was giving an alternative answer to the question 'What gives a sign its life?' In that context, though, the question was not formulated in this way, but rather as 'What constitutes the "meaning" of signs?' – in answer to which question Wittgenstein offered his 'logical' view of signs in opposition to a causal, psychological account. It is important, however, to recognize both that the question concerning the 'meaning' of signs can be formulated as 'What gives a sign its life?' and that Wittgenstein himself was often wont to couch the question in such terms. Thus his own answer to the question – namely, that the 'life' of a sign is constituted by the 'loci of extant linguistic practice' (the language games, calculi or systems of communication) of which it is a part – would tie in the whole issue of the relativistic character of his 'calculus/game/system' conception to the familiar Wittgensteinian notion of a 'form of life'. Langauge games (systems of communication/linguistic calculi) can be said to be 'forms of life' in two senses: (1) they are *activities*, i.e. loci of extant linguistic practice (this is Wittgenstein's point in *PI* §23); and (2) it is these activities which are constitutive of the 'life' of signs, not some sort of auxiliary psychological accompaniments that lie behind language. The latter sense suggests that at least some of the philosophical roots of the notion of a 'form of life' lie in Wittgenstein's repudiation of a psychological view of signs.

Concrete evidence that Wittgenstein tended to couch the question concerning the meaning of signs in terms of the formulation 'What gives a sign its life?' can be had simply by examining the sorts of issues in the context of which he tended to make his point about the 'relativistic' character of his approach to signs. For example, the previously cited 'relativity theory' remark from TS 213 was originally drafted around 1929–30 in the following specific context:

> My whole idea is always that if someone could see the expectation he would necessarily be seeing what was expected.
>
> (My ideas shove themselves pell-mell, the one drives out the other, pushes itself forward, etc. like so many crabs in a basin.)
>
> The anticipation is as it were itself language and cannot go outside of itself. (In the 'not being able to go outside of itself' lies the similarity of my views and that of relativity theory.)
>
> One could say, whether an expectation is fulfilled I determine like this: if the expectation was expressed by the proposition that p will be the case and the occurring state of affairs [*Tatbestand*] is described by the sentence 'p' then the expectation is fulfilled.[357]

The third paragraph is obviously Wittgenstein's draft of the 'relativity theory' remark which he later included in TS 213 (see q. 352). The parenthetical aside offered in the second paragraph is of interest not only because it is a fairly clear indication that even as early as 1929–30 Wittgenstein himself viewed his philosophical deliberations as involving a rapid, almost chaotic, displacement of his previous ideas, but also because the remark seems to suggest that the 'relativism' involved in his succeeding claim that "The anticipation is as it were itself language" (or, as he also put it in TS 213, "The expression of expectation is the expectation") is an outlook which either displaces the statement expressed in the preceding paragraph or at least offers a new way of interpreting it. That is to say, there seems to be an indication that the 'relativistic' suggestion "The expression of expectation is the expectation" either displaces or offers a new interpretation of his own preceding idea that "if someone could see the expectation he would necessarily be seeing what was expected". The fourth paragraph appears to try to point out how this might be so: namely, how it might be that, given that "The expression of expectation is the expectation", in seeing the expectation (i.e. expression of expectation) one would be seeing what is expected. If we saw (heard) the expression 'I expect that p will be the case', we should see that 'p' was what was expected. Now the question is, how might Wittgenstein's suggestion involve a displacement of view-points and how might the new position involve a sort of linguistic 'relativism'?

The position apparently being displaced is the assertion (or an interpretation of the assertion) "if someone could see the expectation he would necessarily be seeing what was expected". Just what view is being displaced is fairly clear both from the overall problem with which Wittgenstein is wrestling and from the context of discussion of the view in subsequent manuscripts. In the original MS 108 context (as well as in subsequent contexts) there is an overall concern with the issue of how to decide what is to count as the fulfilment of an expectation, the fulfilment of a wish, the execution of a command, the realization of a belief, and so on. Utterances of belief, wishes, expectations, commands seem to require something else which, as it were, satisfies or completes what is expressed in the utterance. They seem to require a means of comparing them with reality, a means for deciding what is to count as '*that* which is expected', '*that* which is ordered', '*that* which is believed', '*that* which is wished' and so on. The view that "if someone could see the expectation he would necessarily be seeing what was expected" can be construed as a way of dealing with the issue of how one is to decide what fulfils the expectation. In TS 213 this view surfaces in §87, headed, "Reality seems essentially to be able to correspond or not correspond with a proposition. It seems to require comparison with the proposition." In the latter context the overall issue of how one is to decide what fulfils the expectation is brought up by way of the simile of a proposition being laid against reality like a ruler. In terms of this simile, the overall issue is expressed as follows:

> Someone might say: lay a ruler against a body; it doesn't say that the body is of such-and-such a length. Rather it is in itself as it were dead and achieves nothing of what thought achieves. It is as if we had imagined that the essential thing about a living man were the outer

form and then made a block of wood in that form, and were abashed to see the dead block [*toten Klotz*], which had no similarity at all with the living being [*dem Leben*].[358]

It is after this remark in TS 213 that one finds the remark, "if someone could see the expectation he would necessarily be seeing what was expected". One way of taking this is in terms of the suggestion that just as with respect to a ruler, one may also be *tempted* to say of a proposition that it in itself seems dead and achieves nothing of what 'thought' achieves. It may seem that the mere words one sees or hears (as with the block of wood) are not in themselves alive, and that it would only be if one could *see* the mental processes behind the words that one could tell exactly *what* is expected, believed, ordered, or whatever – only if one could see the mental process of expectation could one really ascertain *what* was expected and thus determine what in reality would count as fulfilment of the expectation. For words to be laid against reality they seem to require mental processes, processes without which the mere words seem to be dead. As Wittgenstein put it in terms of another illustration of such a view in his MS 114 revision of TS 213, "When we give an order, it can look as if the ultimate thing sought by the order had to remain unexpressed, as there is always a gulf between an order and its execution. . . ."[359] And for *PI* §§431–2, part of which was drafted in his MS 116 (p. 22) revision of TS 213, he even more explicitly added,

"There is a gulf between an order and its execution. It has to be filled by the act of understanding."
"Only in the act of understanding is it meant that we are to do THIS. The *order* – why, that is nothing but sounds, ink-marks. –"
Every sign *by itself* seems dead. What gives it life? In use it is *alive*. Is life breathed into it there? Or is the use its life?

The sort of view being rejected rests on an interpretation of concepts such as 'understanding', 'expecting' and 'wishing' as reports about psychological processes. More broadly, however, it rests on a psychological view of the meaning of signs in general – that is, on a psychological answer to the question 'What gives a sign its life?'

In the above passage, Wittgenstein seems to be countering with the suggestion that perhaps it is not a psychological accompaniment but rather the *use* that is the life of a sign – though there seems to be the danger of misinterpreting this counter-suggestion as the claim that 'only there, when using the sign, does a psychological accompaniment breathe life into it'.[360] In TS 213 Wittgenstein countered as follows:

My notion is always: if someone could see the expectation he would necessarily be seeing //recognize// what was being expected.

But that is the case: if you see the expression of expectation you see what is being expected. And in what other way, in what other sense, could one see it?!³⁶¹

It is noteworthy that in his version of this remark in *PI* §452 Wittgenstein even more clearly formulated the psychological view he was challenging in terms of the assertion that, "If someone could see the expectation, the mental process [*geistigen Vorgang*], he would necessarily be seeing *what* was being expected." His counter to this, the suggestion that "if you see the expression of expectation you see what is being expected", is clearly a reiteration of what he elsewhere identifies as an example of his linguistic 'relativism' (i.e. the view that "The expression of expectation is itself the expectation", "The anticipation is as it were itself language" – see q. 352), and it is a reiteration of this 'relativism' theme in the context of a repudiation of a psychological answer to the question 'What gives a sign its life?'

Importantly, in place of a psychological answer to this question, Wittgenstein invariably introduces his 'calculus/game/system' conception of signs. In TS 213, for instance, shortly after his relativistic counter-suggestion that "if you see the expression of expectation you see what is being expected", he indicated,

> The awkwardness with which the sign tries to get its meaning across, like a dumb person who uses all sorts of suggestive gestures, disappears when we recognize that what is essential to the sign is the system to which it belongs....³⁶²

Similarly, in his MS 114 revision of TS 213 he again indicated,

> The appearance of the awkwardness with which a sign tries to get its meaning across, like a dumb person who uses all sorts of suggestive gestures – this disappears when we remember that the sign does its job [*seine Funktion hat*, has its function] only in a grammatical system.³⁶³

It is, then, only in relation to a system of language, a grammar, a locus of linguistic practice, that signs have 'life' – not by way of some sort of psychological accompaniment. The relativistic character of the claim that "The expression of expectation is the expectation" seems to involve a suggestion that an *expression* of (for example) the form 'I expect...' (as well as one of the form 'I order you to...') is to be taken as a linguistic move or act which performs a function, does a job, has a use within the context of a system of language, and it is there that the expression is alive, it is that which decides the *meaning* of the expression. Whether what is to be decided is just *what* is expected when someone says 'I expect x', or what is being suggested when one makes an assertion of the form 'I expect...', the decision is made in relation to a system of language, a locus of linguistic practice, in which, on the one hand, the term 'x', and, on the other, an expression of the form 'I expect...' are used.

Wittgenstein recognized that, if one misconstrues the meaning of an expression of the form 'I expect...', then one is likely to be misguided in answering the broader question 'What is the meaning of a sign?' (for example, 'x' in 'I expect x') or 'What gives a sign its life?' That is to say, if one takes 'I expect...' as a report about a state of mind, one is likely to think that a question about '*what* is expected' (i.e. the meaning of 'x' in 'I expect x') asks for a description of a state of mind, a description of the psychological process (perhaps a mental event of some sort) that accompanied the utterance 'I expect x' and which may constitute the 'life', so to speak, of the term 'x'. Thus one finds that, when trying to dispel the view that, in order really to decide *what* is expected (what would fulfil the expectation) when someone says 'I expect x', one would have to see the psychological process accompanying the utterance, Wittgenstein straightaway tries to point out that an expression of the form 'I expect...' is not a report about a psychological process. To point this out involves a clarification of the meaning of an expression of the form 'I expect...', i.e. a clarification of the grammar, the use of the expression, the role it plays in the language games or systems of communication constitutive of its sense. In *PI* §453, for example, right after a version of the 'relativistic' counter-suggestion "if you see the expression of expectation you see what is being expected" (previously cited from TS 213; see q. 361), Wittgenstein went on to explain,

> But to say that someone perceives an expectation *makes no sense*. Unless indeed it means, for example, that he perceives the expression of an expectation. To say of an expectant person that he perceives his expectation instead of saying that he expects would be an idiotic distortion of the expression.

Similarly, with respect to the example of orders, Wittgenstein would presumably claim that 'the expression of an order is the order. That someone perceives an order *makes no sense*, unless it means that he perceives the expression of an order. To say of someone who orders that he perceives his order instead of saying that he orders would be an idiotic distortion of the expression.' The claim seems to be that, if someone says, 'I order you to...' or 'I expect...', he is not reporting something that he perceives in his mind but rather is performing linguistic acts the meaning of which is constituted by the role of these acts in the language games or systems of communication to which they belong.

But now, although it is quite clear that one would call an expression of the form 'I order you to...' an order, it is not so clear that one would want to call an expression of the form 'I expect...' an expectation. The sense of Wittgenstein's suggestion that the expression of expectation is the expectation comes out rather more clearly in *Zettel* §65:

> If I say "I expect [*Ich erwarte*]..." – am I remarking that the situation, my actions, thoughts etc. are those of expectancy of this event; or are the words "I expect..." part of the process of expecting?
>
> In certain circumstances [*Umständen*] these words will mean (will be replacable by) "I believe such-and-such will occur." Sometimes also: "Be prepared for this to happen...."

One can perhaps speak of 'expectant behaviour', which might include such occurrences as picturing to oneself the expected circumstance, nervously fidgeting, checking one's watch, or an increase in one's blood pressure, but Wittgenstein seems to be suggesting in the above passage that such occurrences are not being *reported* when one says 'I expect...'. Rather, the expression 'I expect...' is, as it were, itself an act of expecting, and we might ascertain this by noticing that the utterance 'I expect...' in certain circumstances does the same sort of job as (means, is replacable by) the utterance 'I believe such-and-such will occur' or 'Be prepared for this to happen.' That an 'expression of expectation' might in certain circumstances involve the same type of linguistic move as an 'expression of belief' does not of course help us very much, given that one might just as well be tempted to view an 'expression of belief' as a report about psychological occurrences. 'Believing' has itself, along with the notion of 'expecting', been identified by Wittgenstein as problematic (see, for example, q. 352). But to recognize that in certain circumstances the expression 'Be prepared for this to happen' plays the same role, serves the same duty, as 'I expect...' is more directly helpful in that it is an indication that the linguistic job performed by 'I expect...' is not that of reporting about the occurrence of mental processes but rather a matter of offering some assurance of the likelihood of a predicted state of affairs (and perhaps a matter of offering a warning to that effect). To offer assurance or to forewarn that something will happen obviously has a quite different function from reporting what one is picturing in one's mind's eye, or one's nervous fidgeting or one's blood pressure. Thus the claim is that in some circumstances, although the expression 'I expect...' may seem to be a report about a psychological accompaniment to one's utterance, it in fact offers assurance or forewarns – and here it is clear why Wittgenstein might want to say that the expression of expectation is the expectation, for, if the language game actually being played were that of offering assurance or forewarning, clearly we would call an 'expression of assurance' an 'assurance' and an 'expression of warning' a 'warning'.[364]

In some cases, under certain circumstances, when we ask someone 'What do you expect?' we clearly are not asking him for a description of a state of mind, but rather asking him to say what in his estimation will be the probable course of events. And the answer we receive ('I expect...') will be a mild assurance (certainly not a guarantee) as to the probable course of events. Should we later return to that person and accuse him of having been wrong, we should not be claiming that he misidentified what was taking place when he said 'I expect...' (that what he was experiencing was not 'expecting' but rather perhaps 'wishing' or 'fearing' or 'hoping'; or that he misidentified what he was actually picturing at the time – say, it was not John he imagined coming through the door, but Henry); rather, we should be claiming that what *later* took place was not what he *said* (predicted) would take place ('giving a false expectation').

Interestingly, Wittgenstein's suggestion in Zettel §65 points out a sort of language game one plays with the concept 'expecting' which bears a marked resemblance to the sort of role that several other 'psychological' verbs play in certain circumstances. 'Wishing', 'believing', 'thinking', 'knowing' and 'fearing' each, under certain circumstances, perform an analogous sort of linguistic role. Under certain situations 'I believe...', 'I wish...', 'I fear...' and 'I know...' can be understood as involving gradations of assurance concerning the likelihood of a predicted state of affairs (plus perhaps, in the cases of fearing and wishing, also an implicit comment on the desirability of the forecast event). 'I know Bill will come' is a strong assurance that Bill will come. 'I expect he will come' and 'I believe he will come' offer some assurance, but not as much as 'I know...', suggesting that it is likely but not certain that Bill will come. The amount of assurance being offered by 'I expect...' as opposed to 'I believe...' may be different, but perhaps also in certain circumstances (as Wittgenstein seems to suggest in Zettel §65) the expressions may be roughly interchangeable (this because they offer the same assurance, not because they report the same psychological event). A certain degree of assurance is also involved when one says, 'I fear he will come' – it is a statement of the likelihood of the event, but in addition a comment on its undesirability; whereas 'I wish he would come' in some situations is a suggestion of the unlikelihood (thus the awkwardness of 'I wish he will come') but *desirability* of Bill's coming. When speaking of possible future events such are the sorts of functions performed by these 'psychological' concepts (assertions as to the likelihood and/or desirability of a forecast event), and such functions are quite different from the function of reporting one's state of mind.

For our purposes, what is important about Wittgenstein's suggestion in *Zettel* §65 (and its possible extension to other psychological verbs) is that it involves a stress on the *Umständen*, the circumstances of the loci of linguistic practice, as constitutive of the meaning or the 'life' of expressions such as 'I expect he will come' and 'I believe he will come.' When one examines such expressions relative to the loci of linguistic practice to which they belong (inclusive of, for example, the fact that and the extent to which a person can be taken to task for the strong assurance 'I know he will come' as opposed to the weaker assurance 'I expect he will come' or 'I believe he will come', should what that person *said* would happen not happen, and indeed how it is that an assurance proves to be false, when it is that we call an expression of expectation 'false' – these are among the *Umständen* of the language game), it becomes clear that the game played is not at all that of 'reporting about one's psychological states'. The recognition of this presumably frees us from the temptation to think that questions such as '*What* is expected?' or '*What* is believed?' (questions about the *meaning* of 'he will come') are questions about what is going on in one's mind as one utters the expressions 'I expect he will come' and 'I believe he will come.' Here, also, the 'life' of the specific sign 'he will come' is not to be understood in terms of some sort of psychological mechanism called 'believing' or 'expecting', but rather is constituted by the role of the expression 'he will come' in the loci of linguistic practice constitutive of *its* sense (by what is *called* 'he' and what is *called* 'coming') and thus is relative to language (in this case to the definitions of 'he' and 'coming'). For example, as Wittgenstein suggests in the chapter of TS 213 in which he made the previously cited 'relativity theory' remark (q. 352), if 'he' is explained by means of an ostensive definition (say, by pointing to Bill), then this ostensive definition would hold also for 'he' in the expression 'I expect he will come.'[365] Thus it is suggested that, just as it is not a mental image of Bill that one means when one says '*he* will come', it is not a *report* about the occurrence of a mental image that is being offered when one says 'I expect he will come.'

In his MS 114 revision of material from this same chapter of TS 213, Wittgenstein makes a similar point about the concept 'wishing' when he explains,

> What I really want to say is this: the wish that he should come is the wish that really *he* should really *come*. If a further explanation of this assurance is wanted, I would go on to say "and by 'he' I mean that man there, and by 'come' I mean doing this ...". But these are just grammatical explanations, explanations which create [*schaffen*] language.
>
> It is *in language* that it's all done [*ausgetragen*, decided].[366]

By "grammatical explanations" and "explanations which create language" Wittgenstein presumably means explanations which involve not descriptions of states of mind but definitions or descriptions of the use of signs, as in the above case perhaps ostensively defining the word 'he' and the word 'come'. Thus, also in the case of the 'expression of a wish', the connection between the 'wish' and '*what* fulfils the wish' is a connection set up within language. This is the import of Wittgenstein's claim "It is *in language* that it's all done", and it is an import that clearly invokes a sort of linguistic relativism.

This claim recurs time and again in the chapter of TS 213 containing Wittgenstein's 'relativity theory' remark (q. 352). Elsewhere in the chapter, for instance, he wrote,

> If I say, "The proposition determines in advance what will make it true", then, certainly, the proposition 'p' determines that p must be the case in order to make it true; but that is all one can say about that and this just means, "The proposition p = the proposition that the fact p makes true."
> It is *in language* that it's all done.[367]

Similarly, in his MS 114 revision of this passasge he added,

> And the statement that the wish for it to be the case that p is satisfied by the event p merely enunciates a rule for signs: (the wish for it to be the case that p) = (the wish that is satisfied by the event p).
> Like everything metaphysical the harmony between thought [*Gedanken*, thoughts] and reality is to be found in the grammar of the language.[368]

By 'thoughts' in the second paragraph Wittgenstein does not mean a mental entity of some sort, but rather the 'content' of a proposition, i.e. something asserted *in* language. The term 'thought' is being used here as in the expression 'This book contains a lot of interesting thoughts', i.e. Wittgenstein is making a statement about linguistic assertions or claims rather than about some hypothesized mental events that might take place between dustcovers (or between one's ears). Consistent with this is the fact that the title of the section (43) of TS 213 from which Wittgenstein drew the remark about the "harmony between thoughts and reality" was alternately, and more explicitly, worded, " 'The connection between language and reality' is //presented// made by the definitions of words, which again belong to grammar [*Sprachlehre*]. So that language remains self-contained, autonomous."[369] Wittgenstein's emphasis here on 'grammar' as the basis for "The connection between language [or 'thoughts'] and reality" is, of

Wittgensteinian Relativism 155

course, to be taken in the sense discussed in chapter 4: namely, as designating the language games, systems of communication or linguistic calculi constitutive of the sense of signs. Thus in this same section of TS 213 Wittgenstein had intended to stress that

> I could say: only the *content* of a proposition interests me. And the content of a proposition is in it. The proposition has its content as a term of a calculus.
> Is then 'to understand a proposition' of the same sort as 'to be master of [*beherrschen*] a calculus'? Thus like: being able to multiply? That's what I believe.[370]

The harmony or connection between thoughts (language) and reality, then, according to Wittgenstein, lies in grammar: the connections between an order and '*what* is ordered', between a wish (= expression of a wish) and '*what* is wished', between an expectation (= expression of an expectation) and '*what* is expected' and so on, are connections belonging to language, to the language games involved in one's use of expressions such as 'I order you to ...', 'I wish ...', 'I expect ...', and so on. And this 'connection' is language-dependent (relative to language), rather than a matter of psychology, in a twofold way: (1) the *meaning* of an utterance, as, for instance, of the form 'I wish ...' (i.e. what it is 'to wish'), is decided by the language game to which the expression belongs – 'I wish ...' is, as it were, a move in a game (a term in a calculus or system) the intelligibility of which move (term) is relative to the game (calculus, system of communication) to which it belongs; and (2) the *meaning* of '*x*' in, for example, an expression of the form 'I wish *x*' (i.e. *what* it is *that* is wished), is itself relative to language (a language game, calculus, system) – relative to what is *called* '*x*'. The connection between language (thoughts) and reality, therefore, in that it lies in 'grammar', rests on the language games (calculi, systems of communication) constitutive of the meaning of signs. Thus in MS 109, where Wittgenstein first drafted his claim that "the harmony between thoughts and reality is to be found in the grammar of the language" (see q. 368), he went on a few pages later to stress that "grammar is the life of propositional signs [*Satzzeichen*]",[371] and then subsequently reiterated,

> The relation, connection, between thoughts and reality is given by language through the common possession of expressions [*die Gemeinsamkeit des Ausdrucks*]. This relation cannot be presented otherwise.
> We have here a sort of relativity theory of language before us. (And the analogy is nothing (not) fortuitous.)[372]

Again, then, Wittgenstein's relativity theory of language seems to rest on his answer to the question 'What gives signs their life?', and his answer to this question is proffered in terms of his post-1930 'logical' view of signs.

Wittgenstein's linguistic 'relativism', his insistence that it is *in language* that it is all done, and the way in which this relativism, by way of his post-1930 'calculus/game/system' conception, served as a *logical* rather than psychological answer to the question of the relation between language and reality is not a fleeting stance that he briefly held during the early thirties, but rather was quite clearly a fundamental position he maintained throughout his later life. For instance, a little over a page after the 'relativity theory' remark (q. 372) from 1930, Wittgenstein went on to emphasize more specifically with respect to the relation between 'expectation' and 'what is expected' that "It is *in language* that an expectation and event make contact."[373] Virtually the identical point is also later made about the concept 'wishing' in Wittgenstein's draft of material for his MS 114 revision of TS 213, where, after saying, "If I imagine the expression of a wish as the act of wishing, the problem appears solved, because the system of language seems to provide me with a medium in which the proposition is no longer dead",[374] he several pages later re-emphasized, "(It is in language that wish and fulfilment meet). Remember that the expression of a wish can be the wish, and that the expression doesn't derive its sense from the presence of some extraordinary spirit!"[375]

It should come as no surprise that this sort of more specific rendering of his linguistically relative approach to the issue of the relation between language (thoughts) and reality, as this issue applies specifically to concepts such as 'wishing' and 'expecting', is to be found in several other manuscripts and typescripts, including both the chapter of TS 213 (see n. 373) from which another of Wittgenstein's 'relativity theory' remarks (q. 352) has been cited and, *much later*, even his final draft of *Philosophical Investigations*. The 1930 remark about 'expecting' (q. 373), for example, is clearly an early version of what we now recognize as *PI* §445. The context of one of Wittgenstein's early versions of the specific claim made in *PI* §445 provides an appropriate summary statement of the linguistically relativistic import of his view that "It is *in language* [grammar] that it is all done":

> What then should it mean that in language it is all done [*ausgetragen* decided]? *For us* everything is done [*ausgetragen*, decided] in language.
> Language appears to me as, so to speak, a ruler against which one measures facts and where their difference or correspondence is decided [*ausgetragen*]. In this way expectation and fulfilment are matched in language.
> In what respect then does grammar describe language? It says that such-and-such word combinations [*Wortverbindungen*] are permis-

sible. Also that this word means the same as that one. It is therefore actually a gathering of recollections [*Sammelerinnern*] about rules. It consists of agreements [*Vereinbarungen*] about language.[376]

The reference to 'rules' here should be taken in the sense suggested in chapter 4 (see n. 341): namely, as a reference to 'statements which specify the sorts of moves that can and cannot be made within a given language game, calculus or system of communication'; and these are statements about the loci of linguistic practice which are constitutive of the meaning or 'life' of, in this case, an expression of the form 'I expect . . .' or the sign 'p' in 'I expect p' (see also my discussion of rules in nn. 376 and 360). It is evident, then, that Wittgenstein's linguistic 'relativism' as it found specific expression also in the *Investigations* is both central to his post-1930 'logical' view of signs and was introduced in opposition to a 'psychological' answer to the question 'What gives signs their life?'

Let us turn now to another remark where Wittgenstein seems to advocate a sort of linguistic relativity theory, and see whether again his relativism is intimately linked to both the general question 'What gives signs their life?' and his 'logical' (as opposed to 'psychological') answer to this question by way of his post-1930 'calculus/game/system' conception. In considering this remark, the particular object will be to make still more explicit the relationship between Wittgenstein's post-1930 linguistic 'relativism' and the emergence of the notion 'forms of life', in order ultimately to achieve a fuller understanding of the emergence of these aspects of Wittgenstein's later *Denkweise* also as they more concretely came into play in his critique of particular features of his own earlier philosophy.

In the very early thirties, Wittgenstein wrote the following remark in one of his notebooks:

> To me it is always as if I could show that the word 'thought' is used incorrectly (when I say the thought is unsatisfied). That when I call thoughts unsatisfied I must use the word, as, so to speak, a function in a sentence in which it is to be satisfied by something else. I might then say, the word is used not absolutely but rather relatively.[377]

That the 'relativity' suggested here is a *linguistic* one comes out fairly clearly in a remark he made on the preceding page in this notebook. In response to the issue of how one is to decide how an order is employed, how it anticipates its execution (cf. my discussion on pp. 143–4), Wittgenstein emphasized that "only the use of language can show how it is employed".[378] And a few pages later he similarly stressed that "the place of (a) word in the language is its meaning"[379] (recall my discussion in chapter 4 of Wittgenstein's use of 'spatial metaphors'; see p. 129ff). Here again, the linguistic relativism seems to hinge on a 'logical' response to the question of 'meaning', the question of what determines/constitutes the meaning of a sign, whether that sign be an 'order', a 'wish' (which incidentally is also one of the examples Wittgenstein deals with in this stretch of text[380]), an 'expectation' or, indeed, any other proposition (thought) one might utter. As Wittgenstein re-emphasized on the next page in his notebook, "Again, one can only make explicit the grammar of the word 'wishing'. (And similarly the word 'thinking' etc.)"[381]

Linking the above 'relativity' remark (q. 377) to the issue of 'meaning' as formulated specifically *in terms of* the question 'What gives signs their *life*?' is quite straightforward. Several remarks from the same stretch of notebook were included in the chapter of TS 213 entitled "Thought, Thinking". For example, the emphasis that "one can only make explicit the grammar of the word 'wishing' . . . 'thinking' etc." is to be found in that chapter (see n. 381). The first section of the chapter is headed, "How does one think the sentence '*p*', how does one expect (believe, wish) that *p* will be the case? Mechanism of Thinking." In this section Wittgenstein's primary concern was to delineate how one might go astray with such concepts. Among the remarks one finds here are, for instance, the following:

> If it is asked, "How does the thought //sentence// manage to represent?", then the answer might be: "Do you (really) not know? You certainly see it when you think //when you use it." For nothing is concealed.
>
> How do sentences do it? – Don't you know? For nothing is hidden.
> . . .
> But to the answer "You surely know how sentences do it, for nothing is concealed" one would like to say, "Yes, but it all goes by so quickly and I should like to see it as it were laid open to view."[382]

Wittgenstein seems to be identifying here a temptation to think that sentences manage to represent only by virtue of subtle psychological mechanisms constitutive of the sense of the sentences, and that it is such mechanisms which are being reported in utterances of the form 'I think that *p*', 'I believe that *p*', 'I expect that *p*', 'I wish that *p*' and so on. There seems to be the suggestion that we are mistakenly tempted to say 'Yes, but such psychological processes all go by so quickly and we should like to see them as it were laid open to view.' As Wittgenstein similarly phrased this misconception on the following page of TS 213,

> We feel – as was indicated – that thoughts occur to us like a landscape that we have seen and are supposed to describe, but we don't

remember exactly enough to be able to describe them in all their connections. Thus, we believe, we can't describe thinking after the event because a̲l̲l̲ the ~~many~~ d̲e̲l̲i̲c̲a̲t̲e̲ processes have then been lost sight of.

We would like as it were to see these intricacies under the magnifying glass.[383]

The tendency of which Wittgenstein speaks here is perhaps even more clearly identified several pages later in TS 213, when he parenthetically refers to our being "accustomed to thinking of it [thought] as something ethereal and s̲t̲i̲l̲l̲ unexplored; as if we were dealing with something whose exterior alone is known to us, but whose essence is still unexplored, perhaps like (that of) our brain."[384] Wittgenstein minced no words when expressing his opinion of such a view of the notion of 'thought' as it relates to the issue of the signification of signs, bluntly stating elsewhere in the same chapter of TS 213 that "One of the most dangerous ideas is, oddly enough, that we think with our heads or in our heads"[385] and "To say thinking is just an activity of the mind, as speaking is of the mouth, is a travesty (o̲f̲ ̲t̲h̲e̲ ̲t̲r̲u̲t̲h̲)."[386] In his drafts of material for his MS 115 revision of TS 213 he just as bluntly alluded to the sort of error involved here as "that dead-end in philosophy where one believes that the difficulty of the task consists in our having to describe phenomena that are hard to get hold of, the present experience that slips quickly by or something of the kind".[387]

The specific connection between this sort of erroneous tendency and the question 'What gives signs their life?' is pointed out quite explicitly in his MS 114 reworking of material from this chapter of TS 213:

> One might say: in all cases what is meant by 'thought' is what is alive [*das Lebende*] in the sentence. That without which it is dead, a mere succession of sounds or written shapes.
>
> If however I were to speak in the same way about a something that gives meaning to a configuration of chess pieces, that is to say distinguishes them from any old arrangement of bits of wood, I might mean all sort of things! The rules that make the arrangement of pieces a situation in a game, the specific experiences we link with such game situations, the use of the game.
>
> Or similarly if we were to speak of a something that distinguishes paper money from mere printed bits of paper and gives it its meaning, its life!
>
> When we speak of thoughts and their expression, the thought is not a kind of state of mind [*Stimmung*] that is brought about by the sentence, as by a potion. And communication by language is not a process by which I use a drug to bring about in others the same pains as I have.[388]

The suggestion is that, given our (misbegotten) inclination to view 'thoughts' (wishes, beliefs, and so on) as subtle psychological processes or mechanisms, we are seduced into thinking that in general what gives signs their 'life' is such psychological processes. But Wittgenstein is quick to point out that there might be an altogether different sort of answer to the question 'What gives signs their life?' It is evident from the last paragraph in the above quotation that the answer he *rejects* – namely, the view that the life of a sign is its psychological accompaniment (perhaps an accompanying experience) and that one communicates with others by using signs as it were as 'potions' to conjure in others the same psychological accompaniments that one has oneself – is the sort of answer proffered by the 'psychological' or 'magical' view of signs (discussed in chapter 4). Wittgenstein, however, suggests an altogether different answer by raising the analogous questions 'What gives a chess arrangement life?' and 'What gives paper money its life?'

What is it that renders an arrangement of pieces a meaningless collection of bits of wood as opposed to a situation in a game? Assuming that the pieces are physically differentiated so that one can distinguish their roles (see the discussion in chapter 4, p. 128ff), Wittgenstein's answer seems to be that what gives an arrangement of wood life is not the psychological accompaniment that the situation evokes, but rather, perhaps, the system of rules for what is to count as a meaningful arrangement (caution, however, should be exercised with respect to Wittgenstein's notion of 'rules', see my discussion in nn. 341, 360 and 376). If during a game of chess (perhaps with a neophyte) one's opponent moves his bishop onto the same square as his pawn, what results is a meaningless arrangement of the pieces. The neophyte might plead that his bishop is quite thin and could easily share a space with his pawn or that it was only a temporary arrangement and that the bishop was just passing through on his way to a more noble engagement, but this would not render the arrangement any more meaningful – and this is not because the neophyte (or I) could not have the appropriate accompanying experiences (perhaps a 'bishop-feeling' and a 'pawn-feeling' in spatial communion), but because the rules of the game are such that two pieces cannot occupy the same space (however slender they are) and bishops cannot pass through the space occupied by another piece (though knights can). This is not to say that it is physically impossible for chess-pieces to occupy the same space or that the neophyte and I are not free to do what-so-ever we please, but rather it is to say that there are no such moves, there are no such arrangements *in this game*, the game *called* 'chess' (cf. *Zettel* §134).

Similarly, in terms of Wittgenstein's suggested money analogy, one can experience anything one wants when one passes a mere printed or blank slip of paper (perhaps picture to oneself a valuable plot of country real estate or a million ounces of gold), but for all that the blank slip of paper will not get one very far; and this is not because one did not picture things vividly enough or because others are incapable of being equally imaginative, but, rather, because the blank slip of paper has no role in the commercial marketplace, it has no use, there are no rules of exchange governing the value of blank slips. One can of course set up a *system* of exchange for blank slips of paper – for instance, in a poker-game the players may agree that each blank slip counts as one dollar, but it is the *system* of exchange that decides the value of the slip. If, when it comes time to settle accounts at the end of the game, one finds that one has lost one's shirt, one cannot very well plead, 'Ah, but I only *imagined* a penny when I passed most of *my* slips of paper.' One can of course *say* this, but will probably be risking more than one's shirt if one does so.

It is Wittgenstein's view that also the 'life' of *signs* lies in the (linguistic) system to which they belong, in their role in, so to speak, the linguistic 'marketplace', in the rules governing which moves can and which cannot be made with the signs in the language games of which they are a part. The irony of the overall problem with which he is wrestling, the problem of what constitutes the 'life' of signs, is that one is not very likely to see the validity of the sort of answer he provides unless one has already obtained a clear understanding of the 'life' (language games, calculi, systems of communication) which constitutes the 'meaning' of the signs involving *psychological* concepts – expressions such as 'I think ...', 'I believe ...', 'I mean ...', 'I wish ...' and so on. As previously suggested (see p. 150), confusion about the 'life' of these latter sorts of signs leads one to adopt the (allegedly mistaken) psychological view of what constitutes the 'life' of signs in general. It is for this reason that in the context of one of his 'relativity theory' remarks (q. 377) and then also in the "Thought, Thinking" chapter of TS 213 (q. 381) Wittgenstein stressed that "Again one can [and needs] only make explicit the grammar of the word 'wishing'. (And similarly the word 'thinking' etc.)"

The diagnosis of the overall problem of the signification of signs and the way in which Wittgenstein's solution to it rests on the latter sort of linguistically relative, 'logical' approach to the more specific question of what is the 'life' that constitutes the meaning of specific *psychological* concepts is perhaps nowhere more vividly pinpointed than in the "Thought, Thinking" chapter of TS 213 and his subsequent reworkings of it. In TS 213, again citing an erroneous or misleading view of the notion of 'thoughts' as it relates to the signification of signs, Wittgenstein commented, "'How does thought work, how does it use its expression?' – this is //sounds// analogous to the question 'How does the Jacquard loom [*Musterwebstuhl*] work, how does it use the cards?'"[389] The loom of which Wittgenstein speaks is a mechanism for weaving figured fabrics and involves a chain of variously perforated cards that determine the figure patterns. One is tempted to think that 'thought' is, as it were, the inner mechanism of a loom, and we wonder how it works, how the mere written marks or verbal sounds (the cards) manage to produce a significant sentence. Wittgenstein next goes on in TS 213 to illustrate more specifically this sort of misconception in terms of the psychological verb 'to believe:'

> The feeling is that with the sentence 'I believe that p is the case' the process of belief isn't described (that only the cards of the loom are given and everything else is merely hinted at). That one could replace the description 'I believe p' by the description of a mechanism wherein then p, that is to say now the series of words 'p', would only occur as *one* component like the cards in the loom. But here is the error: whatever this description includes, besides just the sentence 'p' *with its grammar*, would be worthless for us. That [its grammar] is as it were the real mechanism in which it [the sentence 'p'] lies embedded.[390]

One finds two (by now quite familiar) basic points being made here: (1) an expression of the form 'I believe p' *tempts* one to think that a hidden psychological mechanism or process is being reported but not described in its inner workings, and that it is these inner workings that are constitutive of the signification of the sentence 'p'; and (2) it is however *not* the inner psycho-physical goings-on that are determinative of the sense of the sentence 'p', but rather the *grammar* of the sentence, and to the extent that one can talk of the sentence being linked to or embedded in a 'mechanism' (the term becomes awkward here) *grammar* is that 'mechanism'. Recall at this juncture that Wittgenstein's post-1930 conception of 'grammar' was in terms of 'loci of extant linguistic practice', the language games, linguistic calculi or systems of communication constitutive of the meaning of signs (see my discussion in chapter 4, p. 126ff). Thus, consistent with this, in his MS 114 revision of the above passage (q. 390), Wittgenstein simply concluded, "And the sentence itself remains the only thing that interests us – not as part of a mechanism [i.e. psycho-physical mechanism], but as part of a calculus."[391]

Now observe how in his MS 117 reworking of this material Wittgenstein merely translates the above discussion (the overall problem of the signification of signs and his suggested solution by way of his 'calculus/game/system' conception or 'logical' view of language) into the *Leben* idiom:

> "How does thought work, how does it use its expression?" on the analogy: "How does the Jacquard loom work, how does it use the cards?"

The philosophical confusion concerning the idea of thinking together with the problems of psychology, is presented to us by the picture of a hidden (invisible) mechanism.

This mechanism: is perhaps the picture the brain, translated into something ethereal.

It seems: 'believing' describes something which occurs with the sentence – as 'digesting', something which occurs with the meal.

One could then understand the belief if one knew what really went on at the time. One would then have analysed the 'process of belief'.

... It is absolutely not unexplored processes of belief that interest us, the mechanism which we don't understand is no mental but rather the use [*Gebrauch*] of our well-known processes of belief, e.g. of the expression of the sentence 'I believe. . . .'

To the question "How does one do that?", the one who answers perhaps through introspection will not come up with anything useful an answer that one could use. It is reported at the time: I say this, I imagine such and such, and the like.

The mechanism which we don't understand is not anything in our soul [*Geiste*], but rather that of the life [activity, *Leben*] in which this expression swims. //but rather of the life [activity, *Leben*] that surrounds [*umgeben*] this expression.// //but rather that of the life of this expression.//[392]

This passage is clearly a reworking of the text previously cited from TS 213 (see qq. 389 and 390). Notice that, in the last paragraph, what Wittgenstein had previously identified as the real subject of interest, what really is determinative of the meaning of the sentence '*p*' and indeed expressions of the form 'I believe *p*', 'I expect *p*', and so on – namely, the 'grammar' or the 'calculus' (see his MS 114 revision cited in q. 391) in which the expressions are embedded – he now simply refers to as the 'life' of the expressions, the 'life' which surrounds the expression. One of the senses of the German word *Leben* is in fact 'activity', and quite obviously the 'life' of which Wittgenstein is speaking here is the *linguistic activity* or locus of linguistic practice (the language game, calculus or system of communication) which is determinative of the 'grammar' of the signs. It is the language game (calculus, system of communication) that is a form of life; and it is in relation to this *activity*, not to some ethereal hidden psychological mechanism, that one is to understand the signification of signs. There is no doubt, therefore, that Wittgenstein intended his 'calculus/game/system' conception as an emphasis upon the forms of 'life', the forms of activity or loci of linguistic practice constitutive of the meaning of signs, and that this emphasis involved, as he saw it, in effect a sort of 'linguistic relativity theory' of the signification of signs.

The identification of language games (calculi, systems of communication) as forms of 'life', forms of linguistic 'activity', an identification documented above in Wittgenstein's reworking of TS 213 material, is, as was previously suggested (see p. 146), in part precisely the point Wittgenstein makes in *PI* §23 when he asserts that

> the term 'language *game*' is meant to bring into prominence the fact that the *speaking* of language is part of an activity, or of a form of life [*Lebensform*].
> Review the multiplicity of language games in the following examples, and in others:
>
> Giving orders, and obeying them –. . . .

In the same section Wittgenstein went on to list several language games, forms of 'life', forms of linguistic activity. As might be expected, his first draft of this list and the original wording of his recommendation that we ponder this list, the suggestion "Let's think about the (great) multiplicity of language games: . . .", were written in the margins and on the *Rückseiten* (versos) of TS 213 in the immediate vicinity of the above-discussed remarks in which he stressed that his interest was not in a psychological mechanism, but in the expression itself "*with its grammar*" – with what he called in his MS 114 revision the 'calculus' and to which he later (MS 117) referred as the 'life' (activity) constitutive of the meaning of the expression.[393] The list of language *games* Wittgenstein gives in *Investigations* §23 is quite clearly to be taken as an enumeration of 'forms of life', an enumeration of some of the various loci of linguistic practice that can be determinative of the 'life' (meaning) of signs.

Lest there be any doubt about such an identification, one needs only to note the fact that some of the specific language games listed are also included elsewhere in Wittgenstein's notebooks when he offers us an *enumeration* of examples of different forms of life. Examine, for instance, the following notebook entry:

> Were we to come to an unknown land with [an] unknown (language and unknown) customs, it would sometimes (in many cases) be easy to find (see) a language and form of life [*Lebensform*] which we would call 'ordering' [*Befehlen*] and 'obeying;' perhaps though you would observe no language and form of life which would wholly correspond to our 'ordering', etc. As also there is perhaps a people who possess no <u>form of life</u> corresponding to our '*greeting*' [*Grüßen*] //who possess nothing corresponding to our '*greeting*'.
> The common behaviour of mankind is the system of reference by means of which we interpret an unknown language.[394]

What Wittgenstein identifies here as *forms of life* ('ordering' and 'greeting') are the very same loci of linguistic activity that he identifies elsewhere as 'language games' (both of these examples in fact are included in all of his versions of the *PI* §23 language-game list, even in his first draft of this list in TS 213; see n. 393). The above passage is quite obviously an initial draft of what later was published as *PI* §206 (see n. 394).

Similarly, in another manuscript written in the late 1940s Wittgenstein gives the following list of what ostensibly he considered examples of 'forms of life':

> Instead of the unanalysable, specific, indefinable: the fact that we act in such-and-such ways, e.g. *punish* certain actions, *establish* the state of affairs thus and so, *give orders*, report [*berichten*] (e.g.) describe colours, take an interest in others' feelings. What has to be accepted, the given – one might say – is *forms of life* [*Lebensformen*]. //is facts of living [*Tatsachen des Lebens*].//[395]

In the manuscript source Wittgenstein had for emphasis underlined the expression 'forms of life'. 'Facts of living' was introduced as shown above *after* the main text and within double obliques, indicating a possible alternative wording. Here again, at least three of these so-called 'forms of life' ('giving orders', 'reporting' and 'describing') are also included in *PI* §23 in Wittgenstein's list of language games – though, granted, 'describing colours' may be taken as a form of life or locus of linguistic practice different from 'describing the appearance of objects' (cf. *PI* §23, but cf. also the passage cited in n. 394 where Wittgenstein simply speaks generally of 'describing'). The above passage is readily recognizable as the broader context in which Wittgenstein first drafted what was later published as *PI*, p. 226, para. 3. It is quite clear, then, that what he elsewhere (*PI* §23) has listed as language games are to be taken as an enumeration of a variety of forms of life – a sampling from the multiplicity of loci of linguistic practice which are constitutive of the 'life'/meaning of signs.

There is little doubt that Wittgenstein's linguistic 'relativism' and the notion of a 'form of life' emerged as features in his later philosophy by way of the problem of signification, the question of what constitutes the 'life' or meaning of signs. His references to the multiplicity of 'forms of life' both in the above passage (q. 395) and in *PI* §23 further corroborate this account of the emergence of these themes and they do so in such a way as to add another dimension to our grasp of that emergence. In the above passage (q. 395) Wittgenstein *contrasts* an emphasis on the multiplicity of *forms of life* or loci of linguistic activity (language games) to a concern with "the unanalysable, specific, indefinable". In the manuscript source this remark was first drafted in the context of a discussion of the claim that "Thinking is something specific", that it is something specific which happens inside of us. This broader context of discussion is fairly clearly an echo of the sort of theme with which Wittgenstein wrestled in his chapter of TS 213 entitled "Thought, Thinking" (see the previous discussion on p. 158ff), where the issue of an account of 'thinking' or 'thought' was discussed with respect to the problem of the signification of signs, the question of what constitutes the 'life' of a sign. In the above passage (q. 395), however, one finds Wittgenstein suggesting that an emphasis on 'forms of life' should replace the notion of "the unanalysable, specific, indefinable". This suggestion points in the direction of another very interesting dimension to the emergence of his linguistic 'relativism' and the notion of 'forms of life', a dimension which, as this study has found to be the case with the emergence of so many of the essential features of Wittgenstein's later *Denkweise*, shows these themes as having at least in part emerged in critical reaction to a recognizable feature of his earlier (*Tractarian*) philosophy.

The reference (in q. 395) to a notion of indefinables, things specific and unanalysable, very obviously evokes a conception of 'simples' or 'objects' in a Tractarian sense (and their corresponding simple 'names') – those supposed fundamental elements which are unanalysable but in terms of which any *meaningful* proposition can be analysed. Wittgenstein's apparent contrast of his notion of the fundamental character of 'forms of life' (the loci of linguistic practice he calls language *games*) with the notion of the analysability of the meaningfulness of propositions in terms of 'simples' appears to be precisely the sort of contrast he also introduces in *PI* §23 where, having given a list of various language games and suggested that we view them as activities or 'forms of life', he then counsels the reader to compare this "multiplicity of tools in language and the ways they are used [in the MS 152 (p. 48) draft, 'multiplicity of tools in language and language games'], multiplicity of kinds of words and sentences, with what logicians have said about the structure [*Bau*] of language. (Including the author of the *Tractatus Logico-Philosophicus*.)."[396] The allusion here to his Tractarian view of the 'structure of language' again evokes a conception of the determination of the meaning of a sign (sentence) by way of its analysability in terms of 'simples', i.e. the analysability of a sentence in terms of 'elementary propositions' and their purely 'simple' constituents ('names'). *Such* an approach to the signification of signs obviously rests on a conception of 'simples' ('names' and their corresponding bearers or 'objects', as Wittgenstein called them) as something "unanalysable, specific, indefinable" (cf. q. 395). These supposed 'names' (and their combination into 'elementary propositions') were taken to be the essence of language, and the 'objects' or bearers corresponding to 'names' were taken to be the primary constituents of reality – this not in the sense that one can say of these objects that they do or do not exist, but rather in the sense that these so-called 'objects' are, as it were, the (perhaps 'phenomenal'; see my discussion in chapter 2, pp. 56–9 and nn. 175–6) primary constituents of *possible* states of affairs; thus a proposition can be 'meaningful' whether or not it is true, i.e. even when there is no state of affairs in the world corresponding to it (forthcoming below is an account of Wittgenstein's own explanation in *PI* §39 of what led him to postulate 'names' *qua* 'simples'). Wittgenstein's suggestion (in q. 395 and *PI* §23) that instead of 'simples' or 'the unanalysable' one should speak of the structure of language in terms of the multiplicity of forms of life or language *games* is clearly a suggestion that the notion of 'language games' as constitutive of the 'life' or meaning of signs has *displaced* his old Tractarian atomistic approach to 'meaning' in terms of 'names' (and their corresponding bearers or 'objects'). It is not, however, immediately evident that and how this suggestion ties in with the account given in this chapter of the emergence of Wittgenstein's notion of 'forms of life' and of its link with the linguistic 'relativism' he considered to be characteristic of his later approach to signs. This connection of themes must now be demonstrated.

It has previously been pointed out that in the *Tractatus* Wittgenstein assumed the possibility of a purely simple (or 'primary') language in terms of which meaningful propositions could be completely 'analysed', but he never managed actually to construct such a language – viewing it instead as the task of further logical analysis to discover the supposed real 'names' and purely primary constituents to which he referred as 'objects' (see n. 228 and q. 220). The 'bearers' of these 'names' could not be things in the world, 'objects' in the ordinary sense of the word, because that would imply, as Wittgenstein retrospectively explained in *PI* §39, that a sentence such as "Excalibur has a sharp blade", which clearly does make sense, could not make sense if the sword did not or ceased to exist as an 'object' in the world. Wittgenstein first put the matter in terms of this specific example in 1930 soon after his return to philosophy when he wrote,

(The) Meaning (of a word) could can only be what we explain in the explanation of a word.
One always has the false idea that the meaning of a word is a question of only an object, that is to say a thing in the sense in which the sword Excalibur would be the meaning of the word 'Excalibur'. But also here something is amiss, for if I then however say "Excalibur no longer exists", is perhaps here 'Excalibur' meaningless just because the sword no longer exists?[397]

The account in *PI* §39 of what tempted him in the *Tractatus* to postulate 'simples' was first drafted in his MS 115 *Umarbeitung* of the 'Brown Book', where he quite explicitly pointed to the nature of the errors on which such reasoning was founded:

> If one does not want to call the proper name of a man or one like 'Excalibur' names in the 'strict logical' sense of the word, then this is because a *name* must designate something *simple* [*etwas Einfaches*]. – The sword Excalibur however consists of parts combined in a particular way. If they are combined differently Excalibur does not exist. But it is clear that the sentence "Excalibur has a sharp blade" makes *sense* whether Excalibur is still whole or is broken up. But if 'Excalibur' is the name of an object, this object no longer exists when Excalibur is broken in pieces; and as no object would then correspond to the name it would have no meaning. But then the sentence "Excalibur has a sharp blade" would contain a word that had no meaning, and hence the sentence would be nonsense. But it does make sense; so there must always be something corresponding to the words of which it consists. So the word 'Excalibur' must disappear when the sense is analysed and its place be taken by words which name simples. It will be reasonable to call these words the real names. – This reasoning rests on various errors: (a) that a word must 'correspond' to an object, whereby it has meaning, the confusion of the meaning with the bearer of a name; (b) a false conception of the philosophical or logical analysis of a proposition, as if it were analogous to chemical or physical analysis; (c) a false view of 'logical exactness', ignorance of the concept of 'family'. – [398]

The error with which we are concerned at present is the error of assuming that the meaning of a word is an 'object' corresponding to it, the error of confusing "the meaning with the bearer of a name." Wittgenstein explicitly repudiated such a view soon after his return to philosophy. As early as 1931, for instance, one finds him making such unequivocal statements as

> It is true: names can represent things [*Dinge vertreten*]; but they don't represent their meaning; and to call the things (perhaps spatial objects) the meaning of the words is absurd.
> Doesn't that mean: the bearer of the name is not its meaning?[399]

The sort of 'simples' Wittgenstein had envisioned had to be such that one could not say of them that they exist or do not exist, and they had to be so purely simple that they could, as it were, serve as elemental nuggets of sense in terms of which an ordinary object – for example, a sword – or a state of affairs could be analysed. It has already been noted that the primary language of simple signs, which he postulated (though never realized) as the goal of logical analysis, was in all likelihood what he also later on occasion referred to as his 'earlier goal of a phenomenal language' (see my discussions in chapter 2 pp. 56–9 and nn. 173–6). The concern of this chapter is not, however, with the precise 'phenomenal' nature of the 'primary language' of simples Wittgenstein envisioned (cf. my discussion of his abandonment of the goal of a phenomenal language in n. 176): that is a hazardous and inherently vague subject for speculation, given that Wittgenstein never actually came up with such a language, and later, in order to criticize his notion of 'simples', was forced to do so by way of parodistic illustrations such as Augustine's account of language (see n. 228). Rather, the concern here is to show that and how *Wittgenstein* in retrospect considered his repudiation of the fundamental error *underlying* his notion of simples (that is, the identification of meaning with the 'bearer' of a name) to be linked to his shift to a linguistically relative view of language games as constitutive of the life of signs – and this can be gleaned purely on the basis of Wittgenstein's *post-1930* remarks in the *Nachlaß*.

First of all, the psychological view of signs in contrast to which his post-1930 linguistically relative, logical view emerged can be considered as involving a conception of 'meaning' in terms of 'objects' or 'bearers' of a mentalistic variety. This, incidentally, would after all have been a natural direction for Wittgenstein to have taken earlier in his career (Russell seems to have taken it and he also is serving as the brunt of Wittgenstein's criticism here; see n. 405 and my discussion of Russell in Chapter 4), given that 'objects' in the ordinary sense (things in the world) would not do as an account of the meaning of signs (for the sort of Tractarian reasoning cited in q. 398). That Wittgenstein himself considered the error of identifying meaning with an object to be connected to an erroneous *psychological* view of signs is quite explicitly pointed out in the very first chapter of TS 213, where he asserts,

> The difficulty is to see clearly the grammar of the word 'to mean' [*meinen*] ... The use of the nouns 'sense' [*Sinn*], 'meaning' [*Beudeutung*], 'interpretation' [*Auffassung*] and other words misleads us to believe that this sense etc. stands opposite the signs like the word – the name – of a thing that is its bearer. Such that one might say, "The arrow (sign) has a completely precise meaning, is meant in a completely precise way, which I *faute de mieux* must again express through a sign." The meaning [*Meinung*], the intention would be as it were its soul, which I would ideally like to show directly, but to which I unfortunately can only indirectly point through its body.
> If I (in order to explain the sense of an arrow) say, "I mean this arrow such that one follows it by a movement in the direction from the tail to the point", then I give a definition (I substitute one sign for

another), although it seems as if I had so to speak completed the assertion //statement// of the arrow (which the arrow makes). I have replaced the arrow by a new sign that we are able to use instead of the arrow. – *Able to use* [*Gebrauchen können*] – Although it *seems* as if the arrow itself were essentially incomplete, in need of completion [*ergänzungsbedürftig*], and as if I had now given the needed completion [*Ergänzung*]. As one recognizes a description of an object as incomplete and can complete it. As if the arrow had begun the description and we completed it by the sentence. – Also like this: if as before I say, "I mean this arrow such that …", then it gives the impression that I had just now described what was essential [*das Eigentliche*], the meaning [*Meinung*]; as if the arrow was, as it were, only the musical instrument [*Musikinstrument*], but the meaning [*Meinung*, *qua* psychological accompaniment] the music, or better yet: the arrow, – that is to say in this case – the sign, the cause of inner, psychical processes, and the words of explanation just the description of these processes. Here haunts the view of the sentence as a sign of the thought [*Gedanken*]; and the thought as a process in the soul, or in the head.[400]

Recall at this juncture that in the *Tractatus* (3.1) it is claimed that a proposition (sentence) is where "a thought finds an expression that can be perceived by the senses" and that at the time it was Wittgenstein's view that a 'thought' (*Gedanke*) consists of "psychical constituents" (see n. 149). Now, given that Wittgenstein never managed to specify what the elemental psychical constituents of the 'sense' of signs are, never managed to construct a 'primary or phenomenal language', as he was also inclined to put it, how was he to set about demonstrating the erroneousness of the view of meaning in terms of the psychical bearers of names, and show the correctness of his post-1930 linguistically relative, logical' approach to the meaning of signs in terms of language *games*, a multiplicity of 'forms of life' constitutive of the meaning of signs? The most pervasive strategy in his writings is to clarify the language games, the grammar, involved with those very concepts (including, for instance, the noun *Bedeutung*) that mislead us into thinking of the meaning/sense of a sign as the psychological accompaniment or bearer of the sign. The most misleading concepts are, of course, the psychological verbs (to understand, mean [*meinen*], think, believe, wish, etc.) which in gerundial from ('understanding', etc) seem to be *names* of psychological processes and when appearing in regular conjugated form in utterances seem to report the occurrence of psychological processes. The latter strategy and the way in which it manifests a sort of linguistic 'relativism' have already been discussed earlier in this chapter.

Wittgensteinian Relativism

But there is another strategy employed by Wittgenstein and it speaks more directly to the notion of 'simple' or 'primary' signs *per se*, i.e. it shows *how* the linguistically relativistic notions of a multiplicity of language games or forms of life are conceptions which displace his earlier notion of simples. Again, since in his earlier view there was no specification of just what the "psychical constituents" are, no concrete examples of the supposed primary signs in terms of which the sense of our ordinary meaningful propositions was to be analysed, the critical strategy must of necessity be of a parodistic nature (cf. n. 228). As this issue was previously adumbrated in n. 176, what Wittgenstein tries to show is that ultimately the analysability or definability of one sign in terms of another, as *definiendum* and 'elemental' or 'simple' *definiens*, only makes sense in the context of a language game. What is ultimately fundamental or primary is not a hypothesized psychic substratum or a system of signs which seem to express 'elemental' or 'atomic' 'ideas' or 'thoughts', but rather the loci of linguistic practice involving conventions and rules of use which in some cases, under some situations, might prescribe the relation of one concept to another as that of 'primary' (simple) to 'secondary'. The strategy, the way Wittgenstein tries to show this, is more clearly described in the 'Blue Book' and carried out time and again in *PI* §§47–64 and elsewhere. In the 'Blue Book' Wittgenstein advises,

> There is one way of avoiding at least partly the occult appearance of the processes of thinking, and it is, to replace in these processes any working of the imagination by acts of looking at real objects. Thus it may seem essential that, at least in certain cases, when I hear the word 'red' with understanding, a red image should be before my mind's eye. But why should I not substitute seeing a red bit of paper for imagining a red patch.[401]
>
> If the meaning of the sign (roughly, that which is of importance about the sign) is an image built up in our minds when we see or hear the sign, then first let us adopt the method we just described of replacing this mental image by some outward object seen, e.g. a painted or modelled image. Then why should the written sign plus this painted image be alive if the written sign alone was dead? – In fact, as soon as you think of replacing the mental image by, say, a painted one, and as soon as the image thereby loses its occult character, it ceases to seem to impart any life to the sentence at all. (It was in fact just the occult character of the mental process which you needed for your purposes.)
>
> The mistake we are liable to make could be expressed thus: We are looking for the use of a sign, but we look for it as though it were an

object *co-existing* with the sign. (One of the reasons for this mistake is again that we are looking for a 'thing corresponding to a substantive'.)[402]

The strategy suggested here is to take the philosophical notion of the meaning or life of a sign as psychological constituents and suppose that in place of these hypothesized psychic constituents we simply had a (somewhat primitive) language in which the words stood for real painted or modelled images. Wittgenstein indicated that this strategy would lead to the following linguistically relativistic conclusions concerning the signification of signs:

> if we had to name anything which is the life of the sign, we should have to say that it was its *use*.[403]
>
> The sign (the sentence) gets its significance from the system of signs, from the language to which it belongs. Roughly: understanding a sentence means understanding a language.
> As a part of the system of language, one may say, the sentence has life....[404]

The strategy offered and its suggested upshot seem to bear more generally on the error of viewing meaning as the psychological bearer of signs. The basic strategy, however, can be and is in *PI* §48 applied specifically to the notion of simples.

PI §48 is on the surface of it directed against a view offered in Plato's *Theaetetus*. The *Theaetetus* account, however, is of interest to Wittgenstein only because (as with Augustine's account of language) it is a reflection of views he himself held earlier in his career, in particular his Tractarian notion of 'objects' as primary constituents (*Grundbestandteilen* or *Urelementen*) of reality and about which one could assert neither existence nor non-existence (see the discussion in n. 228, and especially the passage cited there from Wittgenstein's 1936 revision of the 'Brown Book', where incidentally he also cites Russell's notion of 'individuals' as illustrative of the sort of view he is criticizing). *PI* §48 is therefore intended primarily as a critique, albeit a somewhat indirect one, of his own Tractarian notion of simples. He suggests that we imagine a (hypothetical) language in which letters (= words = names) stand not for psychical constituents but rather for coloured squares ('R' = red square, 'G' = green square, 'W' = white square, 'B' = black square). A sentence would be a concatenation of letters (= names) and would serve to describe the arrangement or complex of coloured squares on a surface. The example he gives is the sentence "RRBGGGRWW" and this sentence would describe the following sort of complex:

R	R	B
G	G	G
R	W	W

Wittgenstein explains that the sentence describes the arrangement of the squares in the order

$$\begin{array}{ccc} 1 & 2 & 3 \\ 4 & 5 & 6 \\ 7 & 8 & 9 \end{array}$$

Though Wittgenstein does not note this, obviously the latter stipulation is already a stipulation about the language game involved, as it were a stipulation about the 'grammar' of concatenations of names in a sentence, and thus from the outset introduces a linguistically relative features to the signification of signs in this primitive language. Without these initial 'grammatical' rules, the sentence "RRBGGGRWW" might just as well be read from right to left as in Arabic script (this would be a description of the same complex upside-down), or for that matter, even if read from left to right, the sentence might be taken to describe an arrangement of squares in another order – for instance,

$$\begin{array}{ccc} 1 & 2 & 3 \\ 8 & 9 & 4 \\ 7 & 6 & 5 \end{array}$$

in which case the sentence would describe the following quite different complex:

R	R	B
W	W	G
R	G	G

Thus at the very outset there are already 'rules' of the language game which determine what is to count as the complex of squares that satisfies or corresponds to a given concatenation of names.

Wittgenstein, however, has introduced the game in *PI* §48 as a way of criticizing his Tractarian notion of 'simples' and showing that, instead of such a notion, one should regard the language game or locus of linguistic practice as *primitive* and thus the ultimate arbiter of the signification (meaning/life) of signs. Consequently, the linguistically relative features that *he* points out about the game introduced in *PI* §48 more directly show that, in this illustration, what *counts as* 'simple' is a function of the game – there is no *absolute* bedrock of 'simples' or *Urelementen*, but rather the simple/composite distinction is itself relative to the language game or locus of linguistic practice constitutive of the meaning of the signs. Wittgenstein, therefore, goes on in *PI* §48 to point out a *multiplicity* of language games, relative to each of which *different* notions of 'simplicity' and 'complexity' would be involved:

> The primary elements are the coloured squares. "But are these simple?" – I do not know what else you would have me call 'the simples', what would be more natural in this language game [*Sprachspiel*]. But under other circumstances [*Umständen*] I should call a monochrome square 'composite', consisting perhaps of two rectangles, or of the elements colour and shape. But the concept of complexity might also be so extended that a smaller area was said to be 'composed' of a greater area and another one subtracted from it. Compare the 'composition of forces', the 'division' of a line by a point outside it; these expressions shew that we are sometimes even inclined to conceive the smaller as the result of a composition of greater parts, and the greater as the result of a division of the smaller.
> But I do not know whether to say that the figure described by our sentence consists of four or of nine elements! Well, does the sentence consist of four letters or of nine? – And which are *its* elements: the types of letters, or the letters? Isn't it irrelevant which we say, so long as we avoid misunderstanding in any particular case! [Anscombe's translation of this last sentence has been modified so that it better fits both the rhetorical and *emphatic* character of the original German. Cf. *PI* §48]

As emphasized in the last paragraph, the issue of 'simples' can in many (indeed, perhaps most) cases be for the most part irrelevant to the signification of signs. The force of the first of the above paragraphs, however, is to demonstrate that, to the extent that it makes sense to speak of 'simples' and 'composites', or of signs as being related to each other as primary and secondary signs, such distinctions are meaningful only *relative to* a language game and there might be any number of language games in the context of each of which a wholly different sort of 'simple/complex' distinction is involved. For instance, the first of the host of different alternatives Wittgenstein mentions is that under other circumstances (*Umständen*) a monochrome square might not serve as a 'simple' at all, but rather as a 'composite' consisting of two rectangles or of the elements colour and shape. It is also pointed out that in some cases one even speaks of something smaller as a result of a composition of greater parts; for example, one can speak of a force vector as a result of a composition of greater (but directionally conflicting) forces:

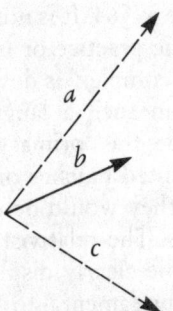

Here force vector *b* is the result of the composite action in somewhat counter-directions of forces *a* and *c*. *In this game*, vector *b* is as it were 'composite' and is *analysable* in terms of the resultant action of two greater forces.

Wittgenstein's reference in the above passage (*PI* §48) to different *Umständen* is recognizable as a reference to the different conditions of other loci of linguistic practice or language games constitutive of the 'life' of signs. In *PI* §64 (drafted in 1936 in MS 152 [p. 67], as were most of the remarks between *PI* §48 and §69; cf. MS 152, pp. 56–75) a similar point is made by way of yet another alternative locus of linguistic practice relative to which again there is a wholly different sense of what is to count as 'simple':

> Let us imagine language game (48) altered so that names signify not monochrome squares but rectangles each consisting of two such squares. Let such a rectangle which is half red half green be called 'U'; a half green half white one, 'V'; and so on. Could we not imagine people who had names for such combinations of colour, but not for individual colours? Think of the cases where we say: "This arrangement of colours (say the French tricolour) has a quite special character."
>
> In what sense do the symbols of this language game stand in need of analysis? Indeed, how far is it even *possible* to replace this language game by (48)? – It is just *another* language game, even though it is related to (48).

Unfortunately a language of 'names' of bi-coloured rectangles would not be capable of completely describing the complex in *PI* §48, because there is an *odd* number of colour squares in the figure and there would always be a remaining portion of the complex which had not been described however rich the language of names of *bi*-coloured rectangles – so a name of a *tri*-coloured rectangle (for example, black–green–white) would also *have* to be introduced in the language game of *PI* §64. Such a modification, however, would not in the slightest diminish the 'relativistic' force of the point Wittgenstein is trying to make in §64. It is not 'simples' which are primary, but rather the loci of linguistic practice or language games. The language game might be such that the 'complex' is described as *composed* of bi- and tri-coloured rectangles, and in such a language 'names' of bi- and tri-coloured rectangles would be the 'primary' linguistic units. Were the monochrome squares not painted patches on a paper surface but instead mental images of some sort, they would be no more *absolutely* simple or atomic than the 'real' patches. The relativistic notion of a *multiplicity* of language games or forms of life clearly displaces the notion of *absolutely* simple signs as that which is fundamental to Wittgenstein's account of the signification of signs. As he predicted in the 'Blue Book' (see qq. 401–4), what is demonstrated is that, "if we had to name anything which is the life of the sign, we should have to say that it is its *use*. . . . The sign (the sentence) gets its significance from the system of signs, from the language, to which it belongs." The 'system' or language game is the form of life constitutive of the meaning of the signs. This is what is 'primitive' or 'primary' (cf. my discussion in n. 176).

In TS 213 Wittgenstein also makes a parallel sort of linguistically relativistic point with respect to the notion that an example of a simple 'name' would be an ostensive gesture – saying 'this' and pointing to a (simple) 'object' of sense, such as a colour:

> You say pointing to a red object is the primary sign for 'red'. But the pointing to a red object is no more than a certain hand movement in the direction of a red object and except within a system is no sign at all. If you say you mean: the pointing, to a red object, *understood as a sign* – then I say, the understanding, that is of concern to us, is no process which accompanies the pointing (perhaps a process in the brain), and, if you nevertheless mean such a process, then this [process] in itself again is no sign. ((The notion is here again and again that the meaning, the interpretation, is a process that accompanies the pointing and so to speak gives it a soul (without which it would be dead) . . . .))[405]

In his first draft of this remark in 1930, instead of offering the latter parenthetical interjection Wittgenstein had subsequently continued, "One should now say: the ostensive hand movement is obviously in itself not primary (a primary sign) but rather perhaps within the system in which it is used...."[406] He had argued similarly several pages previously in this early manuscript, when he wrote in one of his characteristic hypothetical exchanges with an imaginary interlocutor,

> "Even if I (we) now say, the bearer of the name is not its meaning, then still the bearer determines the meaning, and if I, while pointing, say 'This is N' then the meaning of 'N' is determined."
>
> But the correct understanding of the word 'bearer' in the particular case (colour, form, tone, etc.) already decides here the meaning down to a last determination...
>
> The meaning of the name is its place (I mean, its function) in the game.[407]

The ostensive gesture "This is N" itself would make sense only *within* a language game. In terms of the illustration cited from *PI* §48 (and echoed above with the parenthetical reference to a multiplicity of particular cases) what is to count as the (simple) 'bearer' of the name 'N' if one pointed at something and said 'This is N' is itself ultimately a function of, and thus relative to, a game – say, the game of naming 'monochrome *squares*', as opposed to naming 'the *colour* of a square' or 'the *shape* of a square'. Ultimately it is the use or 'function' of the 'sign' in the *Umständen* of the language game that is the 'life' of the sign, and it is the 'game' that is ultimately determinative of its meaning – even in the cases (such as ostension) where one might want to call the sign a '*simple* name'. The fundamental point is that the very notion of 'simples' is itself *relative* to the language game.

In TS 213, immediately prior to the above-cited linguistically relativistic point (q. 405) concerning the notion of a simple 'name', Wittgenstein had made an interesting observation that in fact has served as the basis for the title of this chapter. His post-1930 linguistically relativistic approach to language and the issue of the 'meaning' or signification of signs, in that it involved, as has been shown, a shift away from an absolutistic conception of 'meaning' in terms of a bedrock of purely simple 'bearers' (whether mentalistic or otherwise) and their names as grounds of the 'analysability' of any meaningful proposition – a view of the analysis of language as analogous to the chemical analysis of compounds in terms of their elemental constituents (the second 'error' Wittgenstein mentions in q. 398; cf. my discussion in n. 233) – was in effect a shift away from a somewhat static conception of language to a *dynamic* one in which signs are viewed as *moves* in the specific *Umständen* of the multifarious (and indeed from an historical perspective *changing*; cf. *PI* §§23 and 18) language games or loci of linguistic practice constitutive of their meaning or 'life'. As Wittgenstein himself put it in TS 213 by way of an illustration with respect to signs for negation,

> Any sign of negation is equivalent to any other one, for $\begin{array}{c|c} P & \\ \hline T & F \\ \hline F & T \end{array}$ is a complex of lines just as is the word 'not', and it becomes a negation only by the way it *'works'* [*wirkt*] – that is to say, the way it is used in the game.
> I want to say: the sign only works dynamically, not statically.[408]

This is Wittgenstein's annotated version of the remark in TS 213. Significantly, in the orignal text of TS 213, which simply reproduced his 1930–1 draft of the remark in MS 110, he had gone on to explain, "But here is not meant the effect in the sense of psychology (the word 'effect' [*Wirkung*] thus is not meant causally). . . ."[409] Wittgenstein, understandably, wished to ensure that his readers would not take his reference to 'the way a sign works' as a reference to the psychological 'effects' that a sign might have on the mind; a view that, as we have found, was anathema from the perspective of his post-1930 'logical' view of signs. He explains that instead what he means by 'the way a sign works' is "the way it is used in the game", thus clearly introducing his 'calculus/game/system' conception as an explanation of the sense in which he considers signs to be 'dynamic' rather than 'static'. The life/meaning of signs is constituted by their use or function in the loci of linguistic practice in which they are embedded, and this Wittgenstein considered a 'dynamic' view of language – that is to say, a view of language *as* dynamic not static. As he similarly explained several pages later in MS 110, only in terms of his post-1930 notion of 'grammar' (*qua* ledger of our actual linguistic transactions; cf. the discussion in chapter 4, p. 126ff),

> Grammar describes the system, the space [*Raum*] in which a place [*Stelle*] for the symbol (sign) is indicated. . . .
> Thus a sign cannot exist without grammar.
> A sign without grammar would be 'static'.[410]

And then subsequently in the same manuscript he again reiterated, "Grammar describes how the signs are being used . . ." (see n. 330).

The word 'grammar' is being used somewhat equivocally in these two passages, but the equivocation is a perfectly natural and quite harmless one. In the first and last of the above cited sentences, 'grammar' is used to refer to the *description* of the use or function of signs in the systems or loci of linguistic practice constitutive of their meaning. In the second and third sentences, however, the word 'grammar' refers not so much to the *descrip-*

tion of the locus of linguistic practice in which a sign is embedded, as to the locus of linguistic practice *itself*. A sign exists, is meaningful *qua* sign, only as embedded in a 'grammar' *qua* system or locus of linguistic practice (cf. qq. 390–2); a sign which is not a move *within* a locus of linguistic activity (a language game) would be 'static' – and this point obtains whether or not one has ready to hand a 'grammar' *qua description* of that locus of linguistic practice (see also my discussion in n. 360). The emphasis on the locus of linguistic practice as constitutive of the life or meaning of a sign is, then, according to Wittgenstein, a view of language as dynamic rather than static – words are meaningful only as moves in the sundry forms of life or language games in which they are embedded.

Wittgenstein's post-1930 linguistic 'relativism' and his correlative emphasis on the multiplicity of the 'forms of life' or loci of linguistic practice constitutive of the meaning or 'life' of signs emerged, then, both as a reaction to mentalistic approaches to the problem of signification (particularly as these might rest on a 'metalogical' view of 'psychological verbs') and as a critique of his early Tractarian hypothesization of *absolutely* 'simple' signs in terms of which any meaningful utterance could be analysed. Furthermore, in his own words the fundamental shift that had taken place in his view of language can be characterized as having involved a change from a 'static' conception of language to a 'dynamic' one.

Given the account offered here of the emergence of Wittgenstein's post-1930 linguistic 'relativism' and his notion of 'forms of life', let us now consider its implications for some of the secondary literature, if not on his linguistic 'relativism' (nothing has been written about that), then at least on his notion of 'forms of life' (about which subject a considerable amount has been written).

Once one has grasped the emergence of Wittgenstein's notion of 'forms of life', there becomes apparent a rather glaring deficiency which unfortunately is shared by most of the various (often conflicting) interpretations of Wittgenstein's notion. Our focus will be upon this single deficiency since it in itself is significantly debilitating for many of the interpretations that have achieved currency in the secondary literature. First the deficiency will be defined, then a demonstration will be given of how it applies to, and in some cases devastates, several of the more prominent types of interpretation of Wittgenstein's conception of 'forms of life'.

The deficiency is what might be called the 'error of insufficient specificity'. It has been shown that there was a positive and a negative dimension to the emergence of Wittgenstein's linguistic 'relativism' and his correlative emphasis on a multiplicity of 'forms of life' as constitutive of the meaning or 'life' of signs. The negative dimension was the fact that the conception of a 'form of life' emerged as a repudiation of a psychological answer to the question 'What gives signs their life?' The positive dimension was that Wittgenstein's emphasis on the multiplicity of 'forms of life', by way of its connection with his calculus/game/system conception, provided a *solution* to the problem of signification or meaning – this both in the sense that it provided an answer to the question of what determines the meaning*fulness* of signs, and, even more importantly, in the sense that it provided a concrete basis for generating an account of the meaning or 'grammar' of *specific* signs. By investigating the 'forms of life,' the concrete *Umständen* of linguistic *activity*, the loci of linguistic practice (language games, calculi, systems of communication) constitutive of the 'life' or meaning of *specific* signs, one can generate a concrete description of their grammar, their meaning, their specific uses or functions in the linguistic marketplace. Remarkably, most of the more prevailing interpretations of Wittgenstein's notion of 'forms of life' fail to remain faithful to the features of this conception which distinguished it as a significant step forward in the emergence of his later *Denkweise* – and in particular fail to remain faithful to the role of the notion of 'forms of life' in providing a *concrete* means for ascertaining not just the meaningfulness but also the *meaning* of *specific* signs (whatever these signs may be; whether utterances involving psychological verbs ('I believe ...', 'I expect ...', 'I wish ...', 'I hope ...', and so on), logical symbols such as negation, mathematical symbols, or other types of sign). If an interpretation of Wittgenstein's notion of 'forms of life' does not present the notion as in principle specific enough to provide a concrete means for generating the grammar, use, meaning of *particular signs* (the conception, after all, was introduced by Wittgenstein as a *positive* alternative to a 'psychological' account of the signification of signs), then the interpretation will be said to suffer from the 'error of insufficient specificity' and thus be an inadequate account of Wittgenstein's conception.

Taking now a fairly representative sampling of interpretations (those of Gier, Hunter and Malcolm), it will be shown that they attribute to Wittgenstein views of 'forms of life' which suffer from the 'error of insufficient specificity' and thus are unfaithful to Wittgenstein's actual conception.

Nicholas Gier has suggested that for Wittgenstein there is an "equivalence of forms of life and cultural forms, styles and structures", [411] and by this he does not mean the concrete loci of linguistic practice that might be characteristic of a culture, but "a cultural style in general"[412] – sprinkling his account of Wittgenstein's notion of forms of life with such numbingly vague illustrations as "a religious 'style' of cosmology", "the latest scientific 'style'" and, lest the previous illustrations not be broad enough, "a western life-style".[413] Attempting to be more philosophically profound, Gier goes on to characterize for the reader what he considers to be Wittgenstein's "phenomenology of forms of life", and abruptly concludes,

Lebensformen are therefore primarily the formal conditions, the patterns in the weave of our lives, that make a meaningful world possible. They are the existential equivalents of Kant's *Bedingungen der Möglichkeit der Erfahrung*. Understandably, some commentators have proposed that forms of life perfom a transcendental function [Gier refers us here to the works of the following authorities: Peter McHugh, Stephen Erickson and Igance Verhack].

... The philosophy of the later Wittgenstein can therefore be characterized as a descriptive phenomenology of forms of life, i.e. the formal structures which make a meaningful life possible. In an illuminating article on Wittgenstein and Cassirer, R. S. Rajan proposes, as we cited at the beginning of the chapter, that philosophy for both thinkers "ultimately becomes phenomenological description of the forms of our lives".[414]

What is the meaning, what is the 'life,' of expressions of the form 'I expect ...', 'I hope ...', 'I order you to ...', and so on? Wittgenstein suggests that we examine these expressions as embedded in concrete loci of linguistic practice (language games, calculi or systems of communications) and it is these that are forms of life constitutive of the meaning of the specific signs. One could 'phenomenologically describe Western life-style in general' until one is blue in the face, even ornament what one has described with the grandiose label 'existential conditions for the possibility of experience', but this would *not* even approximate what Wittgenstein intended by introducing the conception of 'forms of life' into his later *Denkweise*. That is to say, a description, whether 'phenomenological' or otherwise, of 'Western life-style in general' (whatever that might be) would *not* provide a concrete solution to the problem of signification such as would enable one to generate non-psychological answers to questions about the meaning of *specific* signs. One must therefore reject Gier's interpretation of Wittgenstein's notion of forms of life as off the mark.

This is not to suggest that there are not perhaps some very interesting parallels to be drawn between Wittgenstein and Kant (or Cassirer, or whomever you please), but rather that, for such a comparison to be at all fruitful, one must first achieve a sound grasp of Wittgenstein (not to mention Kant or Cassirer) *in his own terms*. Gier has not done that.

Nor should a rejection of Gier's *broad* cultural interpretation of Wittgenstein's notion of forms of life be taken as a suggestion that Wittgenstein did not have broad reflections about culture and that his own philosophical deliberations were not intimately linked to such broader reflections (indeed they were; see the next chapter); rather, the point is that Wittgenstein was not engaged in such broad reflections on *general cultural life-styles* when introducing his conception of language games and referring to them as *forms of life* constitutive of the meaning of signs.

A somewhat more penetrating account of Wittgenstein's notion of 'forms of life', but nevertheless also deficient, is the so-called "organic account" offered by J. F. M. Hunter.[415] According to this account, what Wittgenstein is trying to get across with his notion of 'forms of life' is that language use *in general* (that is to say, speaking or talking – and writing, presumably) is just something that comes naturally to us as living beings, rather as digestion or defecation do – well, not quite that naturally: we do have to be trained through drill and the like to speak, to use language; but, once we have been so trained, it just comes, we 'just do it blindly' as an immediate response in a situation. By 'language use' Hunter is referrring not to the use (*Gebrauch*) or function of a word in a language game, but rather to the act *per se* of using language. A 'form of life' is, as it were, a "general competence".[416]

What is penetrating about Hunter's account is not the exegetical explanations he gives of Wittgenstein's specific references to 'forms of life', but rather what he offers (on the basis of the interpretation of passages independent of those references) as the "cash value of an organic account". This value, Hunter suggests, consists in the following three claims.

1 Language teaching is an *ad hoc* trial-and-error process designed to mould and shape a person until he uses an expression the way we do. It is not a matter of teaching the learner to guess something (for instance, something mental) that we cannot communicate to him directly.[417]
2 "Appropriate language use need not, and does not ordinarily involve even the most rudimentary mental act . . ., but comes as an immediate response of a person in a situation."[418]
3 Language is self-sufficient, which is to say, "whether in saying things meaningfully, or in understanding what other people say, or what we read, we do not need, and do not generally use, any logical [e.g. 'rules'] or psychological paraphernalia of any kind: the words themselves are quite sufficient."[419]

These are all for the most part negative points about language use: a denial that teaching and learning language is a matter of getting across, and getting the hang of guessing, things that cannot be communicated directly; a denial that mental acts are essential to appropriate language use; and a denial that the use of rules and/or psychological paraphernalia (for example, feelings, images, sensations, mental acts) is necessary for understanding language and speaking meaningfully. These three negative claims are not independent of each other, and perhaps there is some degree of redundancy, but it is quite clear that these are roughly the sorts of things Wittgenstein himself wished to deny in his repudiations of 'psychological' accounts of language and the signification of signs. Hunter has aptly characterized the sorts of views which, as we have found, Wittgenstein was trying to reject by way of his introduction of the notion of 'forms of life', and thus Hunter has, for the most part, captured the negative thrust of Wittgenstein's introduction of this notion in his later *Denkweise*.[420]

Given that Wittgenstein wished to make such or similiar negative claims about language use and that he in part introduced his notion of 'forms of life' by way of such repudiations, he certainly would not want to deny the sort of negative claims Hunter attributes to him, whatever other points he wished to make by calling linguistic expressions, or rather the language games they involve, 'forms of life'. But also, most certainly, such negative claims are not *all* Wittgenstein wished to get across by introducing his notion of 'forms of life'. As this chapter has demonstrated, Wittgenstein's notion of a 'form of life', especially by way of his identification of forms of life and language games (an identification Hunter fails to recognize[421]), emerged in his later *Denkweise* as a *positive alternative* to a psychological account of the meaning of signs – emerged as concrete means for explaining the meaning of specific signs. Hunter's "organic account" seems totally oblivious to this concrete positive function for which Wittgenstein introduced his conception of 'forms of life'. To say generally of a linguistic expression that 'It is just a *doing* that comes naturally to us' would tell us nothing about what the specific sign means other than, whatever it means, its meaning something does not rest on a psychological accompaniment of speech. Furthermore, such a general claim would provide no concrete means for generating a non-psychological account of the meaning of the given specific linguistic expression. Hunter's "organic account", therefore, also suffers from the 'error of insufficient specificity', and thus it is, though not a false characterization of Wittgenstein's conception of 'forms of life', certainly a deficient one.

A third interpretation of the notion of forms of life, and *prima facie* the most plausible one, is offered by Norman Malcolm in his 1954 review of *Philosophical Investigations*. It is a short and very sketchy treatment of the subject which for the most part simply repeats the identification Wittgenstein himself appears to make in *PI* §23 – that is, the identification of language games and forms of life:

> It [the term 'form of life'] is intimately related to the notion 'language-game'. His choice of the latter term is meant to "bring into prominence the fact that the *speaking* of language is part of an activity, or of a form of life" (23; cf. 19). If we want to understand any concept we must obtain a view of the human behavior, the activities, the natural expressions, that surround the words for the concept. What, for

example, is the concept of *certainty* as applied to *predictions*? The nature of my certainty that fire will burn me comes out in the fact that "Nothing could induce me to put my hand into a flame" (472). That reaction of mine to fire shows the *meaning* of certainty in this language-game (474). (Of course, it is *different* from the concept of certainty in, e.g., mathematics. "The kind of certainty is the kind of language-game" (p. 124).)[422]

Malcolm has strung together here enough quotations and paraphrases to ensure that he cannot be very far off the mark in his characterization of the views he attributes to Wittgenstein. As presented above, Malcolm's interpretation would seem to be wholly consistent with the findings of the present chapter – namely, that forms of life are the same thing as language games, and that Wittgenstein, by calling language games 'forms of life', has simply attempted to stress certain important characteristics of language games: (1) they are *activities* or loci of linguistic *practice*, and (2) it is the language games or loci of linguistic practice, *not* psychological accompaniments, that are constitutive of the meaning or 'life' of signs.

It seems, however, from some of Malcolm's comments on the subject in subsequent publications, where he has the occasion to give further illustrations of what he would call 'forms of life', that he has interpreted this identity (of language games and forms of life) in such a was as to vitiate any *concrete* role that the conception might serve in the determination of the meaning or 'life' of specific signs – and thus his interpretation of the notion of 'forms of life' turns out to fly in the face of precisely the role for which this notion was introduced in Wittgenstein's later *Denkweise*. For instance, in his memoir on Wittgenstein one finds Malcolm giving the following illustration of a 'form of life':

> I think that there was in him [Wittgenstein], in some sense, the *possibility* of religion. I believe that he looked on religion as a 'form of life' (to use an expression from the *Investigations*) in which he did not participate, but with which he was sympathetic and which greatly interested him.[423]

And similarly in his article "Anselm's Ontological Argument" Malcolm writes,

> At a deeper level, I suspect that the argument can be thoroughly understood only by one who has a view of that human 'form of life' that gives rise to the idea of an infinitely great being, who views it from the *inside* not just from the outside and who has, therefore at

least some inclination to *partake* in that religious form of life. This inclination, in Kierkegaard's words, is "from the emotions".[424]

If one asserts that there is an identity of language games and forms of life, and one gives 'religion' as an example of a form of life, then presumably one takes 'religion' as an example of a language game. Even if we accept Malcolm's suggestion that the full signification and intelligibility of signs (or arguments constructed out of them) required a sort of empathy felt "from the *inside*", it is quite clear that his conception of language games and forms of life here is so broad as to be no less impotent than Gier's interpretation for the purposes of clarifying the meaning or life of specific signs. To say of a specific religious sign or utterance that it is embedded in "that religious form of life" or 'the religious language game' would not provide us with any concrete means at all for determining specifically *what* is meant by the given sign. Furthermore, if the language game played (or form of life involved) is constitutive of the meaning of the specific sign and all religious signs or locutions involve this same language game or form of life (namely, 'the religious one'), then there is the rather absurd consequence that all religious signs have the same meaning. The latter, of course, is not something Malcolm would want to claim, but it is the consequence of applying his interpretation of Wittgenstein's notion of forms of life in the capacity for which Wittgenstein had introduced the notion – namely, for the purpose of generating concrete non-psychological accounts of the meaning or life of specific signs. Malcolm's 'language-game account' of the notion of forms of life, as elaborated in subsequent publications, must therefore also be rejected on the grounds that it commits the 'error of insufficient specificity'.

For Wittgenstein, in the domain of religious discourse there is no less a *multiplicity* of language games or forms of life – loci of linguistic practice – constitutive of the life or meaning of signs than in any other domain of discourse. To speak of '*the* religious language game or form of life' so levels and obliterates this multiplicity that it not only defeats the whole purpose for which these conceptions were introduced in the first place, but also in so doing runs counter to one of the dominant thrusts of Wittgenstein's later *Denkweise*.

There is in fact some indication that Wittgenstein was in a sense, if not sympathetic to, at least tolerant of and perhaps felt some compassion for religion – not, however, the philosophical/metaphysical speculations of natural theologians (as Malcolm would have us believe with his feigned Wittgensteinian reflections about Anselm's ontological argument), but rather the everyday religious *language* of common religious people. Such tolerance (and perhaps compassion) is illustrated in an interesting remark he wrote in 1947. This passage is of interest not only because it is an indication, albeit rare, of his tolerance of religious language, but also because it gives some clues as to how Wittgenstein might have applied his notion of 'language games' or 'forms of life' to religious expressions:

> The use [*Gebrauch*] of the word 'fate'. Our behaviour [*Verhalten*, attitude] toward the future and the past. To what extent do we hold ourselves responsible for the future? What do we think of the past and the future? If something unwelcome happens, do we ask, "Whose fault is it?", do we say, "It must be somebody's fault" – or do we say, "It was God's will", "It was fate"?
>
> Just as asking a question demands its answer, or not asking it a different behaviour, a different kind of activity [*Art des Lebens*, kind of life], *similarly*, in this sense, so also does an utterance like "It is God's will" or "We are not masters of our fate." What this sentence does, or at any rate something similar, a command [or order, *Gebot*] could also do! Including one which a person gives to himself. And conversely a command, e.g. "Don't complain!", can be expressed as the assertion of a truth.
>
> Now why am I so anxious to distinguish between these kinds of use [*Verwendungsarten*] of 'affirmative sentences?' Is it after all necessary? Have men really previously not correctly understood what they meant by a sentence? Is it pedantry? – It is only an attempt to procure for that sort [of sentence] its rights [or legitimacy: *zu ihrem Recht zu verhelfen*]. Thus indeed a reaction against the overrating of science. The use of the word 'science' for 'everything that can be meaningfully said', already expresses this overrating. For this actually means utterances fall into two classes: good and bad; and already therein lies the danger. It is as if one partitioned all animals, plants and minerals into advantageous and deleterious ones.
>
> But naturally the words 'procure their rights' and 'overrating' express my point of view. I of course also could have said, "I want then to procure for them respect again"; only I don't see it that way.[425]

Wittgenstein demonstrates here a tolerance of the religious expressions "It was God's will", "It was fate" (or "We are not masters of our fate"). Instead of dismissing such expressions as meaningless, he quite to the contrary tries to explain their meaning and in so doing demonstrate their meaningfulness. (Whether Wittgenstein is *correct* or not in his account of these expressions is irrelevant to understanding what he is doing here.) It is fairly clear that his *reason* for wanting to explain their meaning and demonstrate their meaningfulness, or, as he put it, "procure for that sort [of sentence] its rights [or legitimacy]", is more a desire to *react against* the "overrating of science" than a matter of holding religion (religious language) in any great esteem. By the "overrating of science" (see also my discussion in the next chapter) Wittgenstein explains he means the identification of meaningful discourse and science or scientific (empirical) assertions – and thus the partitioning of all discourse into either scientific/empirical claims or nonsense. Wittgenstein perhaps had in mind here the onslaught suffered by religion/religious language at the hands of the so-called 'logical positivists', who questioned the legitimacy and indeed meaningfulness of religious discourse.[426] It is likely, however, that here he also is at least in part reacting to views he himself had held earlier in his career – not that he himself had participated in the logical positivist onslaught against religious language, but rather that he himself in the *Tractatus* had sown the seeds of this onslaught by in effect defining "what can be [meaningfully] said" as "the propositions of natural science" (see *Tractatus* 6.53) and hypothesizing that the essence of language, the essence of a proposition, is that it is an empirical statement about the world, a statement of the form "this is how things are" (see *Tractatus* 4.5 and 4.1).

Yet what specifically does Wittgenstein try to demonstrate, in the above-cited passage, about the religious expression "It was God's will"? First notice that his point about the kind of activity or 'kind of life' involved in asking and answering a question, as opposed to a situation where a question has not been asked, demarcates between what he has explicitly identified in one of his drafts of *Investigations* §23 as language games or forms of life (see n. 394) – he does not describe above an example of another contrasting language game or form of life which would not involve asking and answering questions, but asking and answering questions is clearly itself something he has elsewhere labelled a 'language game' or 'form of life'. He suggests that there is perhaps a similar (not the same) demarcation to be drawn with respect to the utterance "It is God's will" – that is to say, another demarcation between language games or forms of life. And he goes on to draw precisely such a demarcation by pointing out that the 'affirmative sentence' "It is God's will" functions as, is used as, a sort of command or order, even though it has the form of a description of 'how things are', the form of an assertion of a truth (whether 'natural' or 'supernatural' is irrelevant here). This is an attempt on his part to explain the meaning, the use, of the assertion "It is God's will" by describing the language game or form of life constitutive of the meaning of the expression, and indeed distinguishing the language game or form of life involved (commanding or ordering) from another, different game or form of life (describing how things are) which one might be inclined to assume is involved because of the form of the expression. He thus distinguishes between "kinds of use of 'affirmative sentences'". One perhaps need not be reminded that 'commanding or ordering' and 'describing' are among the examples

Wittgenstein has given us of 'language games' or 'forms of life' (see n. 394, q. 395, and *PI* §23).

Under certain circumstances, in some situations, when confronted with the facts of a past (personally) tragic event or impending, unwelcome but unavoidable developments (perhaps a person has a terminal illness), if one says, "It was [or is] God's will", in spite of the putative 'affirmative' character of the sentence one is not describing 'how things are', not asserting a truth, not suggesting that one has inside information about the volitions of a supernatural being (or force: 'fate', if one says, "It is fate"), nor, as it were, answering the question, 'Whose fault is it?' Rather a very different language game is involved: the utterance "It was [or is] God's will" as it were *functions* as a command, an order, a request or perhaps a recommendation that one act or comport oneself in a certain way with respect to what did or will happen – the utterance says, 'Be resolute, don't complain, don't be resentful.' In certain circumstances if one consolingly but firmly says to a bereaved person, "It was God's will", it is out of place, it is a false move, it is to a certain extent incoherent to answer, 'How do you know?' or 'How could God will such a horrible thing?' And it would be *no less* out of place to go on, as no doubt a natural theologian would, to spin an elaborate philosophical theodicy. This not because there is no God, or one cannot really know the volitions of a supernatural being, or it is mysterious and beyond comprehension how a perfect God can will evil, but rather because, in a sense, when one has said, "It was God's will", one has said nothing *about* the volitions of a supernatural being. The appropriate response to a command or request is either to acquiesce in or to refuse to comply with the command or request (perhaps even to question the appropriateness of the requested behaviour), but *not* to raise questions of epistemology and truth about the states of affairs of this or any other world. Religious mythology here is itself, as it were, the *form* of expression of the language game or form of life involving, as Wittgenstein hints, a fundamental way of comporting oneself toward the future or the past.

Wittgenstein here is in no way offering a *justification* of religion or religious language, nor is he making the sweeping and vacuous suggestion that the meaningfulness or intelligibility of the utterance "It was God's will" requires an empathy with or partaking in the 'form of life' of a religious person – however one might wish to characterize '*the* religious form of life', whether in terms of conventional involvement in the institutional aspects of religion (church-going, participating in religious rituals and ceremonies, heeding pastoral advice on certain matters, and so on), or in more extreme terms such as evangelically crusading to save the souls of infidels, or even simply in terms of a belief in an infinitely great being and/or merely attempting to live 'by the Bible' (or some other religious work) when it comes to questions of morality and social conduct, and so on.

Rather Wittgenstein is offering an explanation of the meaning or grammar of the specific utterance "It was God's will" by *describing* the concrete language game constitutive of the sense or 'life' of the expression. The Catholic burial imposed on him by some of his 'inspired' students notwithstanding, it would be hard to imagine the so-called (in Malcolm's sense) 'forms of life' in which Wittgenstein partook being any further removed from that of a 'religious man' – certainly in any sense Malcolm might have in mind as necessary for fully understanding Anselm's ontological argument. But Wittgenstein does not need to 'be religious', he does not need to be inclined to 'partake in *the* religious form of life or *the* religious language game' in order to explain the meaning or grammar of the specific utterance "It was God's will", because such vague generalities are not what he would refer to as the 'language game' or 'form of life' constitutive of the meaning or signification of this or any other *specific* sign.[427]

The account that has been given in this chapter of the emergence of Wittgenstein's linguistic 'relativism' and the related notion of 'forms of life' has been, one could say, not so much an account of the historical origins of these conceptions as an account of the *logical* genesis of these features of Wittgenstein's later *Denkweise*. (Understanding this *logical* genesis has made it possible to recognize a serious, but unfortunately quite common, deficiency in several of the prevailing interpretations of Wittgenstein's notion of 'forms of life'.) There has been no attempt in this chapter, however, to explain *where* Wittgenstein got these ideas, and it has only been to a very limited extent that anything has been said about *when* he got them (it has merely been observed that thematically these ideas are to be found soon after his return to philosophy in 1929–30). No attempt has been made to determine what sort of exposure Wittgenstein had to the 'theory of relativity' *per se*; for example, whether he was *directly* in touch with and influenced by developments in the physical sciences after the First World War (after he had written the *Tractatus*) and in particular during the 1920s (during the 'lost decade'), when the impact of the apparent confirmation in 1919 of Einstein's 'general theory of relativity' was reverberating through the various strata of the intellectual community, or whether Wittgenstein was indirectly inspired perhaps by way of Russell, whose own thinking was influenced by this development in physics after the First World War (see n. 282). Nor has any attempt been made to give an account of *where* Wittgenstein got the notion of 'forms of life'.[428] This is not to suggest that one could not take an educated guess at the historical origins of such conceptions (see my discussion of Spengler in n. 428), but rather to underline that what is most important for understanding the emergence of such features is to uncover the philosophical/logical roots of these conceptions in the intellectual *Kampf* which spawned and indeed sustained Wittgenstein's later philosophy. The broader setting of this *Kampf* will be the subject of the final chapter.

6
Metaphysics and Wittgenstein's Struggle against the Intellectual Current of Our Times

Perhaps a necessary ingredient (though not the only one) for greatness in a thinker is the ability to maintain the distance and scope of vision necessary for the critical edge to cut through the minutiae and deadening mediocrity of the intellectual fashions of one's time. Wittgenstein had a broad scope of vision. There is a significant critical edge to his philosophical deliberations that sets his thinking apart from intellectual fashions and from those who are merely fashionable in their time but whose works are later cast onto the ash-heap of intellectual history. It is the purpose of this chapter to characterize the emergence of Wittgenstein's later *Denkweise* in the light of the broader scope of vision which was an underlying driving force behind his philosophical deliberations.

Wittgenstein considered himself an outsider to twentieth-century Western civilization – a civilization dominated by the methods and fruits of modern science; a civilization whose culture Wittgenstein felt to be in a state of disintegration. Born in 1889, he was not the only child of the turn of the century to feel this way, and it makes no difference what socio-psychological factors contributed to this feeling of alienation – for example, his background as a cultured aristocratic child of the dissipated Hapsburg Empire, his admixture of ethnic origins, his tormented unstable personality, his anomic social and behavioural peculiarities, his experience of being vocationally a German-speaking transplant in a strained Anglo-Saxon world before, during, between and after the two devastating world wars. For our purposes such factors are irrelevant. What is of importance is that he viewed his later *philosophical* deliberations as a struggle against dominant intellectual trends in our modern civilization and that at the heart of his *philosophical* enterprise is reflected this broader *Kampf* which characterized his overall outlook.

In late 1930, not long after his return to philosophy, Wittgenstein wrote, in the midst of drafts of material for TS 213, the following reflections he thought he might include in a foreword ("Zu einem Vorwort") for his projected 'book'. This draft of a foreword gives us both an indication of how broadly he construed the *Kampf* which was his later philosophy, and a clue as to the nature of the intellectual current against which he felt he was struggling:

> This book is written for those who are in sympathy with the spirit in which it is written. This spirit is, I believe, a different one from that of the main current of European and American civilization. The spirit of this civilization, whose expression is the industry, architecture, music, fascism and socialism of our time, is alien and uncongenial to the author. This is not a value judgement. It is not as if he believed that what today passes for architecture is architecture, and not as if he did not approach (without understanding its language) what is called modern music with the greatest suspicion; rather the disappearance of the arts does not justify any disparaging judgement about humanity....
>
> I realize then that the disappearance of a culture does not signify the disappearance of human value, but simply of certain means of expressing this value, yet the fact remains that I have no sympathy for the current of European civilization and do not understand its goals, if it has any. So I am really writing for friends who are scattered throughout the corners of the globe.
>
> It is all one to me whether or not the typical Western scientist understands or appreciates my work, since he will not in any case understand the spirit in which I write. Our civilization is characterized by the word 'progess'. Progress is its form, rather than making progress being one of its features. Typically it constructs. It is occupied with building an ever more complicated structure. And even clarity is sought only as a means to this end, not as an end in itself. For me on the contrary clarity, perspicuity are ends in themselves.
>
> I am not interested in constructing a building so much as in having a perspicuous view of the foundations of possible buildings.
>
> So I am not aiming at the same target as the scientists and my way of thinking is different from theirs.[429]

Clearly Wittgenstein felt estranged from contemporary Western civilization, but it is his claim that the 'spirit' of his *philosophical writings* is alien to the intellectual current of contemporary Western civilization – and this is of genuine interest. Furthermore there is the hint that more specifically it is the goals and 'scientific way of thinking' characteristic of the prevailing intellectual current of our times that are in conflict with his own *Denkweise*.

Wittgenstein apparently considered such a point about his later *Denkweise* of sufficient importance to stress it in his lectures during the early thirties. G. E. Moore, for example, in his notes on Wittgenstein's lectures during this period, recounts that Wittgenstein considered his new approach to philosophy, his "new method", to require "a 'sort of thinking' to which we are not accustomed and to which we have not been trained – a sort of thinking very different from what is required in the sciences".[430] Yet, if Wittgenstein's later approach to philosophy is to be understood as a struggle against a 'scientific way of thinking' which he considered to be the intellectual trend of our time, and if, as Moore reports, Wittgenstein viewed his post-1930 philosophy as involving a *new* approach, a different way of thinking, a "new method", then there arises the question of how to place Wittgenstein's *earlier* philosophy. Did his earlier (Tractarian) philosophy also run counter to the intellectual trend to which he refers as a 'scientific way of thinking' – or had he to a certain extent himself been swept up earlier in his career in what he later preceived as the scientific current of our times? It will be shown here that the latter was the case, and thus his later *Denkweise* can be grasped as having emerged not only as a reaction against a perceived general intellectual trend of our times, but also to this trend as it manifested itself in his *own* earlier philosophy.

First, however, let there be no doubt that these broader horizons in terms of which Wittgenstein viewed his philosophical struggles during the early thirties were fundamental to his outlook throughout his later life and permeated all aspects of his thinking. Roughly a decade later, in a period during the Second World War when he was writing fairly extensively on the philosophy of mathematics, Wittgenstein made a similarly combative and sweeping claim about his philosophical activity in general: "At present we are combating a trend. But this trend will die out, superseded by others, and then the way we are arguing against it will no longer be understood; people will not see why all this needed saying."[431]

Even as late as 1947, in a remark reminiscent of the draft foreword he had written nearly two decades earlier, though now, somewhat disconsolately, he expected the impact of his work to be negligible, he wrote,

> Nothing seems to me less likely than that a scientist or mathematician who reads me should be seriously influenced in the way he works.... The most I might expect to achieve by way of effect is that I should first stimulate the writing of a *whole lot* of garbage and that then this *perhaps* might provoke somebody to write something good. I ought never to hope for more than the most indirect influence.
>
> E.g. there is nothing more stupid than the chatter about cause and effect in history books; nothing is more wrong-headed, more halfbaked. – But what hope could anyone have of putting a stop to it just by *saying* that? (It would be like my trying to change the way women and men dress by talking.)[432]

Metaphysics and Wittgenstein's Struggle

What is of interest about this passage is that it is evidence that even in his later years he still viewed the spirit of his philosophical writings as running counter to the scientific current of his intellectual milieu. Around roughly this same period (the late 1940s), and apparently in one of his more pessimistic moods, Wittgenstein went even so far as to remark,

> The truly apocalyptic view of the world is that things do *not* repeat themselves. It isn't absurd, for example, to believe that the age of science and technology is the beginning of the end for humanity; that the idea of great progress is a delusion, along with the idea that the truth will ultimately be known; that there is nothing good or desirable about scientific knowledge and that mankind, in seeking it, is falling into a trap. It is by no means obvious that this is not how things are.[433]

There is little doubt that the sort of strong suspicion and antipathy expressed here toward the dominant scientific current of our age is an antipathy which coursed through the veins of the whole corpus of Wittgenstein's writings during the last twenty or so years of his life. Our task now is to demonstrate how this antipathy concretely manifested itself in some of the specific features of his later *Denkweise*.

Several prominent themes in the emergence of Wittgenstein's later *Denkweise* have already been characterized in previous chapters. If the 'spirit' of his later writings can, as he suggests, be broadly viewed as involving a struggle against a dominant 'scientific way of thinking' which is characteristic of the intellectual current of contemporary Western civilization in general (and thus also characteristic of its *philosophy* – the later Wittgenstein presumably exempted), then one would expect that this underlying struggle, which was the driving force for his later philosophical deliberations, would manifest itself in the very themes that have already been examined in earlier chapters of this study. This in fact is the case. Thus, much (though not all) of what is to follow will involve a recapitulation of some of the earlier themes, except now in the light of the broader horizon of concern that Wittgenstein claims is the 'spirit' of his later philosophical work.

One would not expect that in the notebook where Wittgenstein jotted down drafts of a foreword the specific philosophical remarks preceding and succeeding those drafts would in any way be connected with the sympathies expressed there, but in the case of the two 1930 drafts (see n. 429) of the 'counter to the spirit or main current of European and American civilization' foreword, there is a very definite connection. The subjects of his reflections prior to and in between the 1930 drafts seem to have *moved him* to express the very sympathies (or rather antipathies) one finds there, for in some of the preceding remarks and in those intervening Wittgenstein was engaged in a critique of a perfect instance of how the trend toward a 'scientific way of thinking' manifested itself in the philosophical inclinations and theories of his contemporaries. Furthermore, a few pages later, in his remarks immediately after the second draft of the foreword (the draft published with *Philosophical Remarks*; see n. 429), Wittgenstein criticized a perfect example of how he *himself* in his earlier philosophy had to a certain extent been caught up in the 'scientific intellectual current' of his time. Let us first examine how, in Wittgenstein's view, the trend toward a 'scientific way of thinking' manifested itself in the philosophical inclinations of his contemporaries.

Given the findings of chapter 4 of this study, it is significant that at the time when Wittgenstein was drafting his 1930 foreword he had been critically reflecting about the psychological, 'causal theory' of signs offered by Russell, Ogden and Richards. For instance, it was in the middle of drafting the foreword that he made the following previously cited comment (q. 279) about the 'causal view':

> The thought is completely described by its expression. A description which lies outside of the expression of the thought doesn't concern us for it belongs to psychology or physiology.
>
> Thinking means using propositions, but the use of the propositions is presupposed in any explanation. The only thing that one can clarify about language is its structure (the grammar). For the use evades our explanation – unless its use is for producing certain effects [*Wirkungen*], thus its causal relations. But these interest the psychologist, not us. To that extent Ogden and Richards are right with their causal view, except that they don't see the other aspect.

The reader will recall that the 'causal view' was, especially as Russell formulated it in the early 1920s, an attempt to give an *explanation* of the meaning or signification of signs, by way of associationist psychological laws (the "law of mnemic causation"), in terms of the 'effects' of language (on the mind), or, to borrow a humorous expression Wittgenstein used many years later, a 'peep-show of feelings'.[434] There is no need to repeat here the theories offered by Russell, James and Ogden (and Wittgenstein's criticism of them), but it is important to note the 'spirit' in which these *theories* were expounded.

Recall that Russell speculated about the number of kinds of "belief-feelings" he had *discovered* (see my discussion of qq. 298 and 299 on p. 117ff). Recall that Russell, reluctant to play physiologist, nevertheless was not reluctant to play psychologist by adapting Semon's physiological theories and formulating his own psychological "law of mnemic causation" to *explain* the meaning of signs (see my discussion of q. 293 on p. 116).

Metaphysics and Wittgenstein's Struggle

And recall that Russell first introduced his 'causal theory of meaning' with the ambition of emulating the methods of empirical science:

> I believe that there is one method of acquiring knowledge, the method of science; and that all specially 'philosophical' methods serve only the purpose of concealing ignorance.... Now meaning is an observable property of observable entities and must be amenable to scientific treatment. My object has been to endeavour to construct a theory of meaning after the model of scientific theories, not on the lines of traditional philosophy. [Cited in n. 292]

During this same period and also in a 'scientific' vein, Russell said regarding his Jamesian 'theory' of belief as a mental occurrence or 'feeling' (recall my discussion in chapter 4, p. 117ff), "The theory I wish to advocate ... is presented for acceptance on the ground that it accords with what can be empirically observed and that it rejects everything mythological or merely schematic."[435] And in the context of a discussion of the "meaning of 'meaning'" Russell similarly asserted about the concept of 'thought' or 'thinking' that he is "one who regards thought as merely one among natural processes, and hopes that it may be explained some day in terms of physics".[436] Such approaches to the conceptions of 'meaning' and 'thought' are quite in keeping with the sentiments Russell conveyed in his Herbert Spencer lecture at Oxford in 1914, where he enthusiastically spoke of a "scientific philosophy", "the adoption of scientific method in philosophy", "the [possible] victory of scientific method in the investigation of philosophical questions", and indicated that,

> A scientific philosophy such as I wish to recommend will be piecemeal and tentative like other sciences; above all, it will be able to invent hypotheses which, even if they are not wholly true, will yet remain fruitful after the necessary corrections have been made.[437]

Noteworthy is the fact that at around the time Wittgenstein was writing his 1930 draft foreword (q. 429) Russell referred to "scientific technique" as the "spirit which is characteristic of modern times".[438] Evidently Russell, unlike Wittgenstein, wholeheartedly embraced that spirit.

Ogden and Richards, not the sort to be left off the scientific bandwagon, express similar sentiments in the summary of their chapter entitled "Sign-Situations", the chapter in which they present their version of Russell's 'causal theory of meaning':

> In all thinking we are interpreting signs....
> Our interpretation of any sign is our psychological reaction to it, as determined by our past experience in similar situations and by our

present experience. [This invokes Russell's 'law of mnemic causation,' see my discussion of q. 313 on pp. 119–20.]

If this is stated with due care in terms of causal contexts or correlated groups we get an account of judgement, belief and interpretation which places the psychology of thinking on the same level as the other inductive sciences, and incidentally disposes of the 'Problem of Truth'.

A theory of thinking which discards mystical relations between the knower and the known and treats knowledge as a causal affair open to ordinary scientific investigation, is one which will appeal to common-sense inquirers.[439]

It will be recalled that, with respect to an account of the meaning or signification of signs, it was Wittgenstein's view that "one of the most dangerous ideas is, oddly enough, that we think with our heads or in our heads" (see n. 385) and "To say thinking is just an activity of the mind, as speaking is of the mouth, is a travesty (of the truth)" (see n. 386). It is quite clear, as it no doubt also was to Wittgenstein, that Russell's and Ogden's inclinations to offer such views of 'thought' or 'thinking' as part of their causal, psychological theories concerning language or the signification of signs were a direct product of their emulation of the methods of the natural sciences and showed how they had been caught up in the 'scientific spirit' of the age.

And then of course there was William James, who, although not quite a contemporary of Wittgenstein, seems to have served as such a major source of inspiration for Russell (see n. 437) and Ogden (see n. 296). Though much of the discussion in chapter 4 was devoted to Russell and Ogden, it was demonstrated there that the emergence of Wittgenstein's post-1930 'logical' view of signs was also in part a reaction to the 'psychological' view of signs as one finds it in James' work. It was perhaps from reading James' work that Wittgenstein came to realize just how pervasive was the trend toward 'scientific', psychological explanations of language.

James characterized his psychological investigations as "the science of finite individual minds" and indicated that in his book *Principles of Psychology*, much of which was first published in philosophical journals (for example, *Mind* and the *Journal of Speculative Philosophy*), he had "kept close to the point of view of natural science throughout".[440] With respect to such comments, Wittgenstein at one point remarked,

> How needed is the work of philosophy is shown by James' psychology. Psychology, he says, is a science, but he discusses almost no scientific questions. His movements are merely (so many) attempts to extricate himself from the cobwebs of metaphysics in

which he is caught. He cannot yet walk, or fly at all he only wriggles. [This sentence was written in English.] Not that that isn't interesting. Only it is not a scientific activity.[441]

One needs only to read James, as it seems Wittgenstein had, in order to realize that the explanation of language by means of causal associationist laws was a pervasive intellectual fashion of the day – a fashion perhaps best exemplified by some of the 'scientific' research in so-called 'psychometrics'. Interestingly, in his chapter entitled "Association" James gives both a brief history of 'associationism' and capsule accounts of associationist theories of 'memory', 'expectation', 'imagination' ('fancy'), 'belief', 'judgement', 'reasoning', 'fear', 'love', 'volition' and 'infinitude'. These theories in themselves, however sketchily summarized and whether or not Wittgenstein bothered to read the literature, could easily have provided (and probably did provide) Wittgenstein with enough fodder to sustain his philosophical deliberations over the last twenty years of his life. From this chapter alone, it would have been clear to Wittgenstein that (as Ogden later seems to have acknowledged[442]) the so-called "law of mnemic causation" or the "contextualist theory of reference" (as Ogden preferred to call it; see n. 314) can be understood as little more than the application in new terminological garb of common (and popular) associationist doctrines explaining the 'meaning' of signs. The versions of the law of association that James cites are those of David Hartley and Alexander Bain:

> Any sensations A, B, C, etc. by being associated with one another a sufficient Number of Times, get such a power over the corresponding Ideas a, b, c, etc., that any one of the sensations A, when impressed alone, shall be able to excite in the Mind b, c, etc., the ideas of the rest.[443]
>
> Actions, Sensations, and States of Feeling, occurring together or in close succession, tend to grow together, or cohere, in such a way that, when any one of them is afterwards presented to the mind, the others are apt to be brought up in idea.[444]

The applicability of such laws specifically to language was to James quite evident:

> the most notorious and important case of the mental combination of auditory with optical impressions originally experienced together is furnished by language. The child is offered a new and delicious fruit and is at the same time told that it is called a 'fig'. Or looking out of the window he exclaims, "What a funny horse!" and is told that it is a 'piebald' horse. When hearing his letters, the sound of each is repeated

to him whilst its shape is before his eye. Thenceforward, long as he may live, he will never see a fig, a piebald horse, or a letter of the alphabet without the name which he first heard in conjunction with each clinging to it in his mind; and inversely he will never hear the name without the faint arousal of the image of the object.[445]

There is perhaps no finer collection of psychologistic gems of 'scientific' *explanation* of language than this chapter on association in *Principles of Psychology*, the content of which chapter, the associationist "theory propounded", was first published by James in *Popular Science Monthly*.[446] Here one finds James admiringly citing some of the scientific 'discoveries' of (among others) Sir Francis Galton, Gabriel Valentin, J. M. Cattell and Wilhelm Wundt. For instance, having explained how the laws of association would be applicable to language (q. 445), James went on to recount some of Valentin's findings:

> Reading exemplifies this kind of cohesion [psychological association] even more beautifully. It is an uninterrupted and protracted recall of sounds by sights which have always been coupled with them in the past. I find that I can name six hundred letters in two minutes on a printed page. Five distinct acts of association between sight and sound (not to speak of all the other processes concerned) must then have occurred in each second in my mind. In reading entire words the speed is much more rapid. Valentin relates in his Physiology that the reading of a single page of the proof, containing 2629 letters, took him 1 minute and 32 seconds. In this experiment each letter was *understood* in 1/28 of a second, but owing to the integration of letters into entire words, forming each a single aggregate impression directly associated with a single acoustic image, we need not suppose as many as 28 separate associations in a sound. The figures, however, suffice to show with what extreme rapidity an actual sensation recalls its customary associates. Both in fact seem to our ordinary attention to come into the mind at once.[447]

It is no wonder that Wittgenstein took it upon himself in his *Umarbeitung* of the 'Brown Book' (later included in *PI* §156ff; see nn. 116 and 195) to discuss at length such an apparently odd philosophical topic as the concept of 'reading'. It seems that Valentin's bit of scientific wizardry was accomplished by timing how long it took to *read* a page of text and then cleverly dividing by the number of letters on the page. Alas, it is now clear that so many would have so much less difficulty *understanding* Wittgenstein's writings if they would just spend a little *more* time on their alphabet! What is amiss here is not only the view that 'understanding' a passage is the

Metaphysics and Wittgenstein's Struggle

aggregate of 'understanding' each of its letters, but also the very notion of 'understanding' as a psychological process or state the duration of which can be timed. Apparently some of the hypothetical language games that Wittgenstein concocted (because of their absurd appearance; see q. 235 and the related illustrations in q. 202, p. 70ff and n. 206) did not require very much imagination at all; he need only have read James' accounts of some of the scintillating 'progress' and 'discoveries' science had made concerning the human 'mind'.

James' citation of the work of Sir Francis Galton is equally scientifically spirited:

> The time-measuring psychologists of recent days have tried their hand at this problem by more elaborate methods. Galton, using a very simple apparatus, found that the sight of an unforeseen word would awaken an associated 'idea' in about 5/6 of a second.[448]

James refers us here to some of the findings Galton presented in his chapter "Psychometric Experiments' in *Inquiries into Human Faculty and its Development*. In that chapter Galton even "took pains to determine as far as feasible the dates of my life at which each of the associate ideas was first attached to the word".[449] (Galton was working with a "list of 75 words gone over 4 times", which list "had given rise to 505 ideas [but only 289 *different* ideas, you see there was some repetition] and 13 cases of puzzle".[450]) All of Galton's findings were of course impressively displayed in tables of data. With respect to the amount of repetition of 'ideas' he had discovered, he offered the following conclusions:

> I was fully prepared to find much iteration in my ideas, but had little expected that out of every hundred words twenty-three would give rise to exactly the same association in every one of four trials; twenty-one to the same association in three out of the four, and so on, the experiments having been purposely conducted under very different conditions of time and local circumstances. This shows much less variety in the mental stock of ideas than I had expected, and makes us feel that the roadways of our minds are worn into very deep ruts. I conclude from the proved number of faint and barely conscious thoughts, and from the proved iteration of them, that the mind is perpetually travelling over familiar ways without our memory retaining any impression of its excursions. Its footsteps are so light and fleeting that it is only by such experiments as I have described that we can learn anything about them.[451]

Russell's and Ogden's psychological speculations about language almost seem modest in comparison to Galton's explanations – this in spite of the fact that Galton embellished his explanations with concrete scientific data and statistics (psychometricians are far more statistically and methodologically sophisticated, if not more enlightening, today). Of course, one would not expect Wittgenstein to have read Galton thoroughly, if at all, but, since he did read James, he was thus perhaps at least aware of the following comments of Galton about language, most of which James found important enough to quote verbatim in "Association":

> On throwing these results into a common statistical hotchpot, I first examined into the rate at which these associated ideas were formed. It took a total time of 660 seconds to form the 505 ideas; that is, at about the rate of 50 in a minute [this is where James erroneously obtained the figure of 'about 5/6 of a second' for the formation of an associated idea; see q. 448] or 3000 in an hour. This would be miserably slow work in reverie, or wherever the thought follows the lead of each association that successively presents itself. In the present case, much time was lost in mentally taking the word in, owing to the quiet unobtrusive way in which I found it necessary to bring it into view, so as not to distract the thoughts. Moreover, a substantive standing by itself is usually the equivalent of too abstract an idea for us to conceive properly without delay. Thus it is very difficult to get a quick conception of the word 'carriage', because there are so many different kinds – two-wheeled, four-wheeled, open and closed, and all of them in so many different possible positions, that the mind possibly hesitates amidst an obscure sense of many alternatives that cannot blend together. But limit the idea to say a landau, and the mental association declares itself more quickly. Say a landau coming down the street to opposite the door, and an image of many blended landaus that have done so forms itself without the least hesitation.[452]

It is quite clear that Wittgenstein's post-1930 'logical' conception of language was wholly antithetical to such a psychological approach to the 'meaning' of signs (see the discussion in chapter 4). In fact, Galton's notion of an "image of many blended landaus" is most likely just what Wittgenstein was critically alluding to in the 'Blue Book' (*BBB*, p. 18) as a "Galtonian composite photograph".

James' citations of the work of Cattell and Wundt are along roughly the same psychologistic lines, though not nearly as entertaining as Galton's 'scientific' findings. For instance, reporting the findings of Wundt (a founding father of modern 'experimental' psychology) James writes,

> Wundt next made determinations in which the 'cue' was given by single-syllabled words called out by an assistant. The person experi-

mented on had to press a key as soon as the sound of the word awakened an associated idea. Both word and reaction were chronographically registered, and the total time-interval between the two amounted, in four observers, to 1.009, 0.896, 1.038, and 1.154 seconds respectively. From this the simple physiological reaction-time and the time of merely identifying the word's sound (the 'apperception-time', as Wundt calls it) must be subtracted, to get the exact time required for the associated idea to arise. These times were separately determined and subtracted. The difference, called by Wundt the *association-time*, amounted, in the same four persons, to 706, 723, 752, and 874 thousandths of a second respectively.[453]

After this account of Wundt's findings, James then quotes directly the following account of further 'discoveries' made by Cattell (formerly assistant in Wundt's psychological laboratories who had gone on to undertake his own research):

> When two or more letters are always in view, not only do the processes of seeing and naming over-lap, but while the subject is seeing one letter he begins to see the ones next following, and so can read them more quickly. Of the nine persons experimented on, four could read the letters faster when five were in view at once, but were not helped by a sixth letter; three were not helped by a fifth, and two not by a fourth letter. This shows that while one idea is in the centre, two, three, or four additional ideas may be in the background of consciousness. The second letter in view shortens the time about 1/40, the third 1/60, the fourth 1/100, the fifth 1/200 sec.
>
> I find it takes about twice as long to read (aloud, as fast as possible) words which have no connection as words which make sentences, and letters which have no connection as letters which make words. When the words make sentences and the letters make words, not only do the processes of seeing and naming overlap, but by one mental effort the subject can recognize a whole group of words or letters, and by one will-act choose the motions to be made in naming, so that the rate at which the words and letters are read is really only limited by the maximum rapidity at which the speech-organs can be moved. As the result of a large number of experiments, the writer found that he had read words not making sentences at the rate of 1/4 sec., words making sentences (a passage from Swift) at the rate of 1/8 sec., per word. Letters not making words were read in 1/40 sec. less time than words not making sentences; capital and small letters were read at the same rate, small German letters slightly and capital German letters considerably more slowly than the Latin letters. . . .[454]

"[T]he subject can ... by one will-act choose the motions to be made in naming", and all this in a few one-hundredths of a second – oh how "it all goes by so quickly" (see on p. 158ff the discussion of Wittgenstein's comments in q. 382)! Cattell, however, astute scientist that he was, cautioned at the outset of his published findings,

> Psychometry seems to be of as great interest as Psychophysics, but it has not been nearly so fully and carefully worked over. This is partly due to the difficulties which lie in the way of determining the time taken up by mental processes. . . . Considering therefore the difficulty of analysing the period measured, the inaccuracies of the recording apparatus, and the artificial often incorrect methods of making the experiments, we have reason to fear that the results obtained by the psychologist in his laboratory do not always give the time it takes a man to perceive, to will and to think.[455]

Would that Cattell had been as circumspect in his metaphysics as in his scientific method.

It is quite clear, then, not only that James (like Russell and Ogden) was caught up in the scientific current of the times, but also that Wittgenstein, having read James, would have been well aware just how strong and sweeping this current was.

The pretentious scientific (or pseudo-scientific) characteristics of Russell's, Ogden's and James' *explanations* of language (inclusive of their *theories* about the psychological phenomena they considered fundamental to language: 'thought', 'meaning', 'understanding', 'belief', and so on) and in general the 'scientific spirit' of their writings (for instance, their admissions that they were attempting to emulate a scientific way of thinking) seem to have been at least in part the sorts of things Wittgenstein was repudiating in, for example, the following methodological dicta fundamental to his later *Denkweise* – dicta oft repeated in his notebooks over the last twenty years of his life:

> (Just don't make any hypotheses!) [1930][456]

> We are not in the domain of explanations and any explanation sounds trivial for us. [1931][457]

> You want explanations instead of wanting descriptions. And you are therefore looking for the wrong kind of thing. [1931][458]

> Refrain from writing down any hypotheses and any vague general statements and you have made a philosophical investigation. [1931][459]

> Instead of restless suppositions and explanations, we want to give calm expositions (considerations) //statements// of linguistic facts. //we want calm confirmation of linguistic facts. [1931][460]

... we wrongly expect an explanation, whereas the solution of the difficulty is a description, if we give it the right place in our considerations. ... [1934]461

Our method is *purely descriptive*; the descriptions we give are not hints of explanations. [1934–5]462

(*Description*, not explanation, is what we want!) [1939–40]463

Describe – don't explain! [1940]464

Philosophical problems are solved not by explanations, but rather only by description. [1946]465

The search for an explanation obstructs [hinders] description //obstructs a full grasp of the facts, i.e. (thus) the *description*.//
   The preconceived hypothesis works like a filter that only admits into view //admits for our observation// a quite tiny part of the facts. [1946]466

What we do is the opposite of theorizing. Theory blinds. [1946–7]467

And then of course there are also the similar and quite familiar passages in *Philosophical Investigations*, where in at least one instance such methodological dicta have been unequivocally offered by Wittgenstein as concrete illustrations of how his antipathy to a 'scientific' form of reflection manifests itself at the heart of his approach to philosophy:

> It was true that our considerations must not be scientific ones. The empirical finding [*Erfahrung*] "that, contrary to our preconceived ideas, it is possible to think this or the other" – whatever that may mean – couldn't be of interest to us. (The pneumatic view of thinking.) And we may not advance any kind of theory. There must not be anything hypothetical in our considerations. All *explanations* must cease, and description alone take its place. And this description gets its light, that is to say its purpose, from the philosophical problems. These are, of course, not empirical problems; they are solved, rather, by looking into the workings of our language, and that in such a way as to make us recognize those workings: *in despite of* an urge to misunderstand them. The problems are solved not by giving new empirical data [*neuer Erfahrung*; in MS 152 also *neuer Erfahrungstatsachen*], but by arranging what we have always known. ... [First drafted c. 1936]468

Philosophy simply puts everything before us, and neither explains nor deduces anything. – Since everything lies open to view there is nothing to explain. For what is hidden, for example, is of no interest to us.

One might also give the name 'philosophy' to what is possible *before* all new discoveries and inventions. [First drafted in 1930–1][469]

Almost all of the above methodological dicta are obviously two-pronged: they both repudiate something methodologically characteristic of a scientific way of thinking, *and* suggest a methodological *alternative* which purportedly runs counter to the spirit of a scientific way of thinking. Wittgenstein rejects the offering of explanations and hypotheses, the advancing of theories, and the attempt to solve philosophical problems with new discoveries or the uncovering of *new* empirical data (*neuer Erfahrung*); and instead he suggests that we merely *describe* (and arrange) something well known to us. In what follows, it will become clear that the methodological *alternative* Wittgenstein offers is to be understood in terms of his post-1930 'logical' approach to the signification of signs, which approach, as this study has shown, itself emerged to a great extent as a reaction to the pseudo-scientific speculation about language offered by his contemporaries.

Not all of the above passages (qq. 456–69) were originally written in the context of Wittgenstein's criticism of contemporaries (on near contemporaries) such as Russell, Ogden or James (indeed, many of these methodological dicta were written in the context of Wittgenstein's criticism of features of his own earlier thinking – more about that presently), but at least some of the above passages were drafted in the general context of a criticism of his contemporaries and thus identify some of Wittgenstein's specific methodological proclamations as having in part emerged as a reaction to particular manifestations of a 'scientific way of thinking' in the works of his contemporaries.

The repudiation in q. 457, for instance, was quite clearly written at least in part with the 'causal theory of meaning' in mind. In MS 111 (1931), two pages prior to his assertion that "We are not in the domain of explanations and any explanation sounds trivial for us", Wittgenstein had made the following previously discussed comments explicitly about the 'causal theory of meaning':

> The meaning is a stipulation [*Festsetzung*, i.e. a conventional one], not an experience. And thereby not a causality [*Kausalität*]. . . .
>
> The sign in so far as it influences the mind by suggestion [*es suggeriert*], thus in so far as it has an effect [*es wirkt*] doesn't interest us at all.
>
> It interests us only as a move in a game: term in a system that is autonomous. //that has its meaning in itself// //. . ., that is intelligible in itself.[470]

As we know (see qq. 256, 262 and the discussion on p. 108ff) this passage was later included by Wittgenstein in TS 213 along with even more explicit references to the causal, psychological theory of signs offered by Russell and Ogden. Note that in the above passage Wittgenstein not only repudiates the causal *explanation* of meaning, but also offers an *alternative* means for giving an account of the meaning of signs; namely, in terms of his 'calculus/game/system' conception. The same sort of methodological repudiation and methodological alternative are to be found in Wittgenstein's MS 114 revision of TS 213, where, in the context of another version of q. 457, he rejects attempts to *explain* language (the signification of signs) in terms of purported psychological mechanisms such as 'thought' and 'belief', indicates that he is interested rather in signs as parts of a calculus, and then again claims that he is "not in the domain of causal explanations [*Kausalerklärungen*]".[471] Wittgenstein's reiterated insistence in the above methodological dicta (see qq. 458, 461–5, 468) on 'description' as an alternative to 'explanation' is to be taken as a reference to *description* of the calculi, language games or systems of communication constitutive of the meaning of signs – this is the alternative to the pseudo-scientific psychological *explanations* offered by the likes of Russell, Ogden and James. The point comes out even more clearly in MS 111, where Wittgenstein, having stressed that

> I should (can) say: language interests me only in so far as it is a calculus.
> Leave the grammar as it is[472]

and having warned that

> One of the most dangerous ideas is, oddly enough, that we think with our heads or in our heads. [Cited in q. 385; see chapter 5, p. 159ff]
> ... The idea of thinking as a process in the head, in a completely enclosed space, makes it something occult[473]

went on to state, "Philosophy is purely descriptive, and it just describes language. That is to say: it gives no foundations [*Gründe*]."[474]

Thus, when Wittgenstein offers 'description' as an alternative to psychological *explanation*, he is referring to description of *language*, and more specifically description of language *qua* calculus, language game or system of communication (see chapter 4). Furthermore, as is stressed by Wittgenstein's suggestion (in q. 472) that we should "Leave the grammar as it is", and as should be evident from the fact that his conception of grammar was in terms of '*extant* loci of linguistic practice', *description* of language *qua* calculus, language game or system of communication is a description of the *actual use* of language. Less than a year before (1930–1) Wittgenstein had stressed precisely this point in another manuscript:

> Philosophy may in no way interfere with the real (actual) use of language; it can in the end only describe it.
> For it cannot give it any foundation [*begründen*] either.
> It leaves everything as it is.[475]

This passage was included in the "Philosophy" chapter of TS 213, and obviously was (along with another remark) his first draft of *PI* §124. What is left as it is, what is just described, is the grammar, the actual use of language (though occasionally with the help of fictitious language games that serve as a foil to shed light on the actual use of language; see chapter 3, q. 207 for example). Recall that Wittgenstein in his later writings sometimes used the word 'grammar' to refer to the *description* of the use of signs, the *description* of the loci of linguistic practice (language games) constitutive of the meaning of signs (see chapter 4, qq. 329–32; and chapter 5, pp. 178–8). It is in this respect that 'description' is to be understood as a methodological alternative to the giving of pseudo-scientific, psychological *explanations* of the meaning of signs in terms of the effects they have on the mind. Thus the now quite obvious and explicit rendition of the 'description, not explanation' dictum one finds in *PI* §496: "Grammar does not tell us how language must be constructed in order to fulfil its purpose, in order to have such-and-such an effect on human beings. It only describes and in no way explains the use of signs."

Another clear illustration of the fact that Wittgenstein's methodological repudiation of 'explanation' was at least in part a reaction against the pseudo-scientific psychological accounts of language offered by some of his contemporaries is *PI* §126 (cited in q. 469). As it was first drafted in 1930–1, Wittgenstein's emphasis that "there is nothing to explain. For what is perhaps hidden is of no interest to us" was entered a couple of pages after he had made the related comment that "Only by the *complete* disregard of the psychological could we arrive at what is for us essential."[476] Yet it is precisely the hidden psychological effects of signs that Wittgenstein's contemporaries (especially Russell) and near contemporaries (especially James) seemed to place as the cornerstone of their accounts of language. Indeed it is evidently at least in part such explanations in terms of hidden (psychological) occurrences ('ideas', 'images', 'thoughts', and so on) that Wittgenstein is repudiating in *PI* §126, because it was a few pages after his 1930–1 draft of this repudiation that he had explicitly singled out for criticism the psychological, causal *theory* of the signification of signs offered by several of his contemporaries: "Ogden and Richards and

Russell's theory of meaning rests on a confusion, or conflation, of motive and cause" (cited in q. 280).

James' psychological explanations of language seem so to have irked Wittgenstein that even as late as 1946 he was moved during one period consistently, if intermittently, to criticize James over the span of roughly 120 notebook pages.[477] (Such persistent refocussing on the views of a single author is very rare in Wittgenstein's writings.) Here one finds the 'description, not explanation' dictum raised in objection to, specifically, aspects of James' attempts 'psychologically' to *explain* the 'meaning' of signs. In this context the methodological dictum was initially introduced prior to the lengthy critique of primarily Jamesian themes, when Wittgenstein first cautioned,

> The 'experience of meaning': don't forget that we haven't to *explain* a phenomenon, but merely to describe! Our enemy is the idea of a 'philosophical theory' //What we are not looking for is a 'philosophical theory'.[478]

Significantly, two pages later Wittgenstein indicated that the difficulty is to describe the familiar language games in which our 'psychological' expressions are used[479] – thus once again reiterating that the methodological alternative he is advocating is to be understood in terms of his calculus/game/system conception of language. It subsequently becomes clear that his words of caution here are intended to obviate specifically the sorts of psychological explanations and theories one finds in James:

> "Yes, I know the word. It's on the tip of my tongue. – " Here the idea forces itself on one of the gap which James speaks of, which only this word will fit into, and so on. – One is somehow as it were already experiencing the word, although it is not yet there. – One experiences a *growing* word. – And I might of course also say that I experienced a growing meaning, a growing explanation of meaning.
> . . .
> When I *was going* [*wollte*, *wanted*] to say it, *was able* to say it, I had not yet *said* it. . . .
> Of course there is something wrong too about the explanation that the meaning or its explanation has grown out of a certain germ. In fact we do not perceive such a growth; or at any rate only in very rare cases. And this explanation springs just from the tendency to explain instead of merely describing. . . .
> Of course the *meaning* occurred to me *then*! Not at the time when I reported it, nor in the interval.

This just is what one calls it: this just is the way we use the words "The meaning occurred to me" ("in this so-called twentieth century" [quoted in English]).[480]

Here quite obviously the 'description, not explanation' dictum is being introduced in opposition to James' inclinations to try to *explain* language psychologically. In fact Wittgenstein's criticism seems to be directed specifically at some of James' speculations in his chapter of *Principles of Psychology* entitled "The Stream of Thought", where James imaginatively explained,

> Suppose we try to recall a forgotten name. The state of our consciousness is peculiar. There is a gap therein; but no mere gap. It is a gap that is intensely active. A sort of wraith of the name is in it, beckoning us in a given direction, making us at moments tingle with the sense of our closeness, and then letting us sink back without the longed-for term. If wrong names are proposed to us, this singularly definite gap acts immediately so as to negate them. They do not fit its mould. And the gap of the word does not feel like the gap of another. ... But the feeling of an absence is *toto cœlo* other than the absence of a feeling. It is an intense feeling. The rhythm of a lost word may be there without a sound to clothe it; or the evanescent sense of something which is the initial vowel or consonant may mock us fitfully, without growing more distinct. Every one must know the tantalizing effect of the blank rhythm of some forgotten verse, restlessly dancing in one's mind, striving to be filled out with words.
> ... What is that first instantaneous glimpse of some one's meaning which we have, when in vulgar phrase we say we 'twig' it? Surely an altogether specific affection of our mind. And has the reader never asked himself what kind of a mental fact is his *intention of saying a thing* before he has said it? It is an entirely definite intention, distinct from all other intentions, an absolutely distinct state of consciousness....[481]

It was a page after these remarks that James cited in support of his views some of the 'scientific' findings of Sir Francis Galton (see my discussion in n. 448). And, incidentally, it was a few pages prior to this that James gave his theory of the 'meaning' of words such as 'if', 'but' and 'or' (i.e. in terms of 'if-feelings', 'but-feelings', and so on) – which theory Russell adopted and Wittgenstein took pains to criticize (see chapter 4, q. 306 and the discussion on p. 123ff).

There is absolutely no doubt, therefore, that Wittgenstein's methodological dictum 'description, not explanation', as well as his prohibition against theories, emerged in part as a reaction also to James' psychological explanations and theories about language – speculations that James offered in the 'spirit' of a 'scientific' approach to the problems. Actually it was near the beginning of the notebook (MS 130) in which Wittgenstein commenced the protracted critique of James under discussion that he drafted the version of the 'description, not explanation' dictum cited in q. 465. Having early in the notebook identified as a topic for discussion "The assumption of a 'feeling' as the means of philosophical explanation"[482] (a recognizable Jamesian and Russellian practice), he then a few pages later added,

The assumption of a 'feeling' for the removal of a philosophical problem.
Philosophical problems are not solved by explanations, but, rather, only by descriptions....
Philosophical problems can be solved //Philosophy can be carried on, i.e. philosophical perplexities removed, whatever the state of our natural-scientific, or mathematical knowledge....[483]

Clearly his subsequent critique of James' views was a follow-up on this issue.

Furthermore, neither is there any doubt whatsoever that, in the context of his criticism of James, as in that of his criticism of Russell (and Ogden), what Wittgenstein is offering as a methodological alternative to 'theories' and 'explanations' of language is the *description* of the actual use of signs in the language games constitutive of their sense. This is further corroborated by the fact that it was in MS 131, where Wittgenstein assailed James for having tried to explain rather than merely describe language, that he later exclaimed, "Perceive the word – the name of the sensation – as an instrument! That is to say, always ask yourself how this thing is used (employed) ..." (cited in n. 427). And early in the same manuscript Wittgenstein had stressed, "The investigation of language in philosophy is a *describing* [my italics] and comparing of concepts ..." (see chapter 3, q. 207). Similarly, a few years later (1949), and again in the context of a criticism of James on this score, Wittgenstein advised, "Let the use of words teach you their meaning."[484]

The spirit of Wittgenstein's post-1930 philosophy, then, constituted a struggle against the scientific intellectual current of his times, and particularly as this current was manifested in the attempts on the part of his contemporaries (and those who inspired them) to emulate a 'scientific way of thinking' by offering psychological *theories* and causal psychological *explanations* of language or the 'meaning' of signs. Moreover, it has been shown that this spirit of his later writings is evident in some of the methodological dicta and prohibitions so frequent in and fundamental to his later philosophy.

However, Wittgenstein's later philosophy was a struggle against the scientific intellectual current of the times not only as that current manifested itself in the psychological speculations of some of his contemporaries and near contemporaries, but also as it manifested itself in his own earlier thinking. The way in which his earlier thinking had itself succumbed to the scientific intellectual trends of the day is both more interesting and more complex.

It should be obvious from the discussion in chapter 2 that the 'metalogical' speculations or views espoused by Wittgenstein in his earlier writings themselves constituted an attempt to offer psychological *explanations* of the underpinnings of language. As demonstrated in that chapter, Wittgenstein earlier in his career had considered 'understanding', 'thought', 'meaning' (*meinen*), and so on, as 'metalogical' concepts designating psychological states and processes fundamental to language and the signification of signs. Of course, at the time of his early philosophical writings, although he attempted to offer such metalogical explanations of language, he nevertheless considered such speculation to fall outside the proper concerns of formal 'logic' – thus the designation of such views as 'metalogical'. It is from this point of view (i.e that of his early formal 'logical' concerns) that one is to interpret his very *early* methodological claims that the theories and hypotheses of natural science have nothing to do with philosophy, which he considered to be concerned with describing the 'logical form' of scientific propositions and logically clarifying the 'sense' of such propositions by analysing them in terms of primitive or elementary propositions.[485] It was perhaps in recognition of the fact that his 'metalogical' speculations about language fell outside the proper concerns of (formal) 'logic' that he acknowledged near the end of the *Tractatus* that his study of sign language seemed to correspond to the study of thought-processes (*Denkprozesse*) and ran the risk of getting involved in inessential psychological investigations.[486] As demonstrated in chapter 2, when Wittgenstein shifted to a concern with ordinary language and broadened his conception of 'logic', he came to reject his earlier 'metalogical' views and to recognize that those views rested on a misconstrual of the 'logic' (in a broad sense) of psychological concepts – that in his earlier philosophy he had indeed become involved in inessential psychological speculation about 'processes' lying 'behind' the signs. Thus in that respect he had himself been caught up in the scientific current of the times and, like Russell, Ogden and James, had indulged in psychological speculation.

Yet Wittgenstein also came to recognize that it was not only in his earlier 'metalogical' explanations of language that he had fallen prey to the dominant scientific intellectual trend of the times; he had done so even in the 'logical' aspects of his earlier philosophy. Wittgenstein identifies and repudiates several such aspects which are recognizable as characteristic of a 'scientific way of thinking'. Let us now return to the context of Wittgenstein's 1930 draft foreword, the 'counter to the spirit or main current of European and American civilization' foreword, and as our starting-point examine what he identifies as an instance of how he himself in his earlier work had been caught up in the scientific spirit of the times. Immediately after his second draft of the foreword (see n. 429), having, understandably, offered a short comment on the problem of bumping against the limits of one's own honesty,[487] Wittgenstein went on to offer the following contrast between the 'spirit' of his new projected work and his own earlier writings:

> This book I offer to all of those who are in sympathy with the spirit in which it was intended.
> In my former book the solution of problems was still far too little presented in a plain manner. It still appeared too much as though discoveries were necessary in order to solve our problems and everything was still too little conveyed in the form of the grammatically obvious in ordinary language. Everything still appeared too much like discoveries.[488]

The second of these paragraphs has already been discussed in the context of chapter 2, where it was demonstrated that among the apparent *discoveries* to which Wittgenstein alludes was his Tractarian postulation of the 'general form of a proposition' and the attempt to construct an abstract 'calculus' that deals with 'all propositions' (to the neglect of the actual use of our everyday expressions; see pp. 61–3). The attempt to solve philosophical problems by offering *discoveries* about the essence or form of language, the essence or general form of a proposition, is, then, acknowledged by Wittgenstein as an instance of how he himself in the *Tractatus* had been caught up in the scientific spirit of the times.

Wittgenstein's Tractarian postulation of such apparent 'discoveries' as the 'general form of a proposition' is intimately linked to two other respects in which he considered the 'logical' aspects of his earlier thinking to have fallen prey to the scientific intellectual trends of the day. On the one hand, his general conception of language, i.e. the nature of a proposition, constituted a definition of the essence of a proposition as involving a statement of the form "this is how things are" (see *Tractatus* 4.5 and 4.1) – that is to say, as involving an empirical statement about the world. This resulted in his Tractarian identification of "what can be [meaningfully] said" with "the propositions of natural science" (see *Tractatus* 6.53). Such an identification was of course subsequently naïvely embraced by the adherents of so-called 'logical positivism' and in particular some of the members of the 'Vienna Circle' with whom Wittgenstein came in contact during the lost decade. As pointed out in chapter 5 (see p. 186ff), Wittgenstein came to view the identification of meaningful discourse with the empirical propositions of natural science, an identification which he himself advocated in the *Tractatus*, as involving an "overrating of science". Thus his Tractarian speculations about the essence of language demonstrated a 'scientific spirit' not only *qua* alleged 'discoveries', but also in their tendency to result in an "overrating of science" – a glorification of science as constituting the sole domain of meaningful discourse. In chapter 5 it came to light that the linguistic 'relativism' of Wittgenstein's post-1930 philosophy, via his view of language games as 'forms of life' constitutive of the meaning of signs, served in part as a vehicle allowing him to react against the "overrating of science" which had resulted from his simplistic Tractarian speculations about the essence of language.

It was, however, in those of Wittgenstein's contemporaries who latched onto and championed his Tractarian identification of meaningful discourse with the empirical propositions of natural science that the "overrating of science" became most pronounced. Thus Wittgenstein was probably reacting as much to the legacy of his *Tractatus* in the hands of those who claimed to be championing some of its fundamental tenets as to the *Tractatus* itself. The members of the Vienna Circle, for instance, who were so enamoured of most of Wittgenstein's Tractarian views, were in a way caught up in the scientific spirit of the times every bit as much as were Russell, Ogden and James. The 'criterion of meaning' advocated by the 'logical positivists' or 'logical empiricists', as some of them preferred to be called, is a clear reflection of Wittgenstein's Tractarian view of meaningful propositions as being of the general form "this is how things are". Rudolf Carnap's version of a 'meaning criterion', for example, was that

> The meaning of a statement lies in the fact that it expresses a (conceivable, not necessarily existing) state of affairs. If an (ostensible) statement does not express a (conceivable) state of affairs, then it has no meaning; it is only apparently a statement.[489]

There is clearly a reduction, here, of meaningful discourse to empirical statements about the world amenable to scientific verification or refutation. In the hands of the members of the Vienna Circle, however, the Tractarian view of the 'general form of a proposition' was blown into an overall endorsement of what they like to refer to as their *wissenschaftliche Weltauffassung* (scientific world-view).[490] For Carnap in 1929, for instance, the focus of this world-view was the task of promoting what he called a "new scientific method of philosophizing" (*neue wissenschaftliche Methode des Philosophierens*).[491] Carnap was still inclined to use the expression "scientific method of philosophy" many years later in his "Intellectual Autobiography", where he fondly reminisces about some of his colleagues in the Vienna Circle as, among other things, being "thoroughly imbued with the scientific way of thinking", and having "shared our hopeful belief that the scientific way of thinking in philosophy would grow stronger in our era."[492] Similarly, in the Preface (1928) to his book *Der logische Aufbau der Welt* Carnap had emphasized that he and his colleagues in the Vienna Circle had in common a "basic scientific attitude" (*wissenschaftliche Grundeinstellung*), that for them "the strict and responsible fundamental orientation [*Grundhaltung*] of the scientific researcher is strived for also as the fundamental orientation for philosophical work", and that the "basic attitude and train of thought" of his book belonged to a certain "scientific atmosphere" – he even having gone so far as to suggest in the first sentence of his Preface that his book was a "scientific book".[493] It is perhaps no coincidence that the sentiments Wittgenstein expressed in his 1930 draft foreword (see q. 429) were almost a mirror opposite of the sentiments of the Vienna Circle as explicitly stated by Carnap two years earlier in the concluding paragraph of his 1928 Preface to *Der logische Aufbau der Welt*. Referring to the "basic scientific attitude" of his group, Carnap expansively wrote,

> We too have 'emotional needs' in philosophy; but they are filled by clarity of concepts, precision of methods, responsible theses, achievement through cooperation in which each individual plays his part.
>
> We do not deceive ourselves about the fact that movements in metaphysical philosophy and religion, which resist such an orientation, again exert quite a strong influence today. What then, in spite of that, gives us the confidence that our call for clarity, for metaphysics-free science will succeed? It is the insight, or, to put it more carefully, the belief, that those opposing powers belong to the past. We feel there is an inner kinship between the attitude on which our philosophical work is founded and the intellectual attitude which presently manifests itself in entirely different walks of life; we feel this orientation in artistic movements; especially in architecture, and in movements which strive for meaningful forms of personal and collective life, of education, and of external organization in general. We feel all around us the same basic orientation, the same style of thinking and doing. It is an orientation which demands clarity everywhere, but which realizes that the fabric of life can never quite be comprehended. ... Our work is carried by the faith that this attitude will win the future.[494]

The, no doubt intentional, clash between Wittgenstein's 1930 draft foreword and Carnap's is unmistakable (see the lengthy discussion in n. 494). And it comes as absolutely no surprise that, during his brief period of contact with some of the members of the Vienna Circle near the end of the 'lost decade', Wittgenstein expressed repugnance at the 'scientific attitude' of the members of the Circle (see n. 426). It seems quite likely that there is some truth in the suggestion of Herbert Feigl that Wittgenstein was spurred to take up philosophy again through his contact with the Vienna Circle.[495] Yet, if this is so, it seems highly likely that, however much the members of the Circle were indebted to the *Tractatus*, and indeed perhaps precisely because of that indebtedness, Wittgenstein's acquaintance with the views and basic orientation of the Circle stimulated him more through provocation than through inspiration (see n. 494). The Tractarian identification of 'meaningful statements' with the propositions of natural science, then, perhaps especially by virtue of the fact that this view was wholeheartedly embraced as a buttress for the *wissenschaftliche Weltauffassung* of the Circle, was one of the ways in which Wittgenstein felt that his earlier views, and to a certain extent he himself, had been caught up in the scientific spirit of the age. (Recall Wittgenstein's comments, discussed in n. 427, about the word 'soul' – a word which most certainly would have been on the *Index verborum prohibitorum* of even the more moderate adherents of 'logical positivism' during the 1920s and early 1930s.[496])

The second major, intimately linked offshoot of Wittgenstein's alleged Tractarian 'discovery' of the 'general form of a proposition' was its implied notion of philosophical (logical) analysis. Here too we find evidence of a 'scientific way of thinking'. It was noted in chapter 2 (see p. 63) that Wittgenstein's formal definition (in *Tractatus* 6.0) of the 'general form of a proposition' amounted to a definition of meaningful propositions as functions of 'elementary propositions' – these themselves allegedly being concatenations of purely simple signs ('names') designating simple 'objects' (not 'objects' in the ordinary sense of the word; see n. 228). Furthermore, it was pointed out that Wittgenstein seems to have envisioned elementary propositions and their purely simple constituents as comprising some sort of 'primary' or, as he sometimes referred to it, 'phenomenal' language (see pp. 56–7) – a primary language in terms of which the meaningful propositions of everyday language could in principle be *completely analysed*. He also was on occasion inclined to speak of the primary, phenomenal language of 'simples' and 'elementary propositions' as one out of which one could *build up* or *logically construct* the meaningful propositions of everyday language (see n. 176 and q. 224) Recall, however, that Wittgenstein never managed actually to come up with this 'primary' or 'phenomenal' language but merely assumed it as a goal possibly attainable in the future by way of further logical analysis (see chapter 2, pp. 56–7 and n. 228). It was, though, demonstrated in chapter 3 that Wittgenstein, upon his return to philosophy, rejected the notion of a primary language or 'ideal calculus' and the correlative notion of 'logical analysis' as a false 'ideal' dogmatically imposed on the reality of language (see p. 80ff); and in chapter 5 it was shown how his post-1930 'calculus/game/system' conception of language entailed a linguistic 'relativism' which displaced his earlier conception of the analysability of ordinary propositions in terms of a primary, ideal language of 'simple' signs (see p. 166ff and n. 176). As it turns out, the view of 'logical analysis' that Wittgenstein rejected upon his return to philosophy in 1929–30, and indeed the very attitude he had earlier maintained – namely, that, although he could not specify the primary language of simples, such a language was a goal and assumed discoverable upon further logical analysis – he came to recognize as characteristic of a *scientific* way of thinking and thus another instance of the way in which his earlier philosophy had participated in the scientific intellectual fashions of the age.

It was indicated earlier in this chapter that not all of Wittgenstein's familiar methodological dicta (qq. 456–69) reflective of his antipathy to a 'scientific' form of reflection were introduced in the context of a criticism of his contemporaries alone; rather, some of them occur in the context also of a criticism of aspects of his own earlier philosophy. A case in point is the remark cited in q. 460. As first drafted in 1931, it occurred in the context of the following remarks critical of a central aspect of his Tractarian notion of 'logical analysis':

> The false ring to the question of whether there must not be primary signs (ostensive gestures) whereas our language even could make do without the others (words) lies in one's expecting to get an *explanation* of the existing language instead of a mere description.
>
> (Instead of restless suppositions and explanations, we want to give calm expositions (considerations) //statements// of linguistic facts //we want calm confirmation of linguistic facts.)[497]

In TS 213 the first of these remarks appears in the section headed "Primary and Secondary Signs", whereas the parenthetical methodological dictum is included in the "Philosophy" chapter (see n. 497). Evidently Wittgenstein's methodological repudiation of 'explanations' is linked to his rejection of his hypothesization (earlier in his career) of 'primary signs' and a purely simple 'primary language' – which notions, though not concretely extrapolated, were fundamental to his early conception of 'logical analysis'. Given the link already established between his 'description, not explanation' dictum and his antipathy to the scientific spirit of our times, the very fact that he identifies the notion of 'primary signs' (and thus the notion of 'analysis') as a by-product of the attempt to give *explanations* indicates that he viewed such notions as manifestations of a 'scientific way of thinking' in his own earlier work. This comes out even more explicitly in another remark he wrote that same year (1931): "The error concerning primary signs is due to those who treat philosophy as a sort of physics, in which they (wish to) track down simple laws. Laws as in the sense of the Newtonian laws of motion."[498]

As previously suggested, if the notion of 'primary signs' or a 'primary language' came to be viewed by Wittgenstein as a misguided attempt on the part of philosophers to think in a scientific way, then he must have come to view the very notion of 'logical analysis' as similarly misguided. Later in the same notebook as includes the above remark he expressed precisely such a view, and in addition candidly mentioned two philosophers whose conceptions of 'logical analysis' he felt constituted a misguided emulation of science:

> The idea of constructing elementary propositions (as for example Carnap attempted) rests on a false notion of logical analysis. It views (the problem) this analysis as ~~one of the construction~~ that of discovering a *theory* of elementary propositons. It is modelled on what (in mechanics) takes place ~~for example in mechanics~~ when a number of fundamental laws are discovered from which ~~follow the propositions of mechanics~~ proceeds the whole system.
>
> My own view was false: in part, because I wasn't clear about the sense of the words "A logical product is *hidden* in a sentence" (and the like); ~~and~~ secondly, because I too thought logical analysis must bring to light hidden things (as chemical and physical analysis does).[499]

These remarks were later included by Wittgenstein in the "Elementary Propositions" section of TS 213 (see n. 499), where, incidentally, it is even more expressly the *Tractatus* notion of 'logical analysis' that is repudiated. It was of course a Tractarian conception of 'logical analysis' that Carnap adopted in his *Der logische Aufbau der Welt* and made a cornerstone of the Vienna Circle's *wissenschaftliche Weltauffassung* (see n. 494). Clearly Wittgenstein had come to think that in the *Tractatus*, indeed in the most central logical feature of his earlier philosophy – the notion of 'logical analysis' – he had been caught up in the scientific intellectual current of the times.

The *Tractatus* and the works of its Viennese disciples, however, are not by any means the only places where one finds a conception of 'logical analysis' modelled on a scientific way of thinking. A Tractarian conception of 'logical analysis', accompanied by a scientific fervour not present in the *Tractatus* but later exhibited in the Vienna Circle's *wissenschaftliche Weltauffassung*, is to be found in Russell's work. It has already been pointed out that, as early as his Herbert Spencer lecture at Oxford in 1914, Russell was peddling what he called "scientific philosophy" or "scientific method in philosophy" (see q. 437). Even at that time, a conception of 'logical analysis' was fundamental to the so-called "scientific philosophy" he advocated. That same year (1914), for instance, in his Lowell Lectures in Boston (published in *Our Knowledge of the External World as a Field for Scientific Method in Philosophy*), Russell spoke of a philosophy "genuinely inspired by the scientific spirit", a "genuinely scientific philosophy" which

> when purified from all practical taint, is to help us to understand the general aspects of the world and the logical analysis of familiar but complex things. Through this achievement, by the suggestion of fruitful hypotheses, it may be indirectly useful in other sciences, notably mathematics, physics, and psychology.[500]

In the Preface published with these lectures Russell explicitly identified 'logical analysis' as the central methodological feature of this "genuinely scientific philosophy" and acknowledged his indebtedness to both Frege's work and Wittgenstein's not yet published 'discoveries'.[501] By 1935, when in his address to the first international congress of scientific philosophy (organized by Carnap and others) he suggested that "scientific philosophy" was "perhaps destined to as great a career" as the empirical sciences themselves, the creed had become firmly entrenched.[502] Carnap in fact had begun his *Der logische Aufbau der Welt* with a citation of Russell's spirited canon that "The supreme maxim in scientific philosophizing is this: wherever possible, logical constructions are to be substituted for inferred entities."[503] Carnap had obtained this canon from Russell's 1914 article "The Relation of Sense-data to Physics", where there is an even more vivid illustration of what Russell's conception of 'logical analysis' was:

> The method by which the construction proceeds is closely analogous in these and all similar cases. Given a set of propositions nominally dealing with the supposed inferred entities, we observe the properties which are required of the supposed entities in order to make these propositions true. By dint of a little logical ingenuity, we then construct some logical function of less hypothetical entities which has the requisite properties. This constructed function we substitute for the supposed inferred entities, and thereby obtain a new and less doubtful interpretation of the body of propositions in question. This method, so fruitful in the philosophy of mathematics, will be found equally applicable in the philosophy of physics....
> A complete application of the method which substitutes constructions for inferences would exhibit matter wholly in terms of sense-data, and even, we may add, of the sense-data of a single person, since the sense-data of others cannot be known without some elements of

inference. This, however, must remain for the present an ideal, to be approached as nearly as possible, but to be reached, if at all, only after a long preliminary labour of which as yet we can only see the very beginning....⁵⁰⁴

A telling illustration of the possible Fregean roots of the notion of 'logical analysis' adopted by Russell is the following remark Frege made in 1892 in a journal entitled *Vierteljahrsschrift für wissenschaftliche Philosophie* ('Quarterly Review of Scientific Philosophy'). As part of a response to criticism of his *Grundlagen der Arithmetik*, he at one juncture maintained,

> One cannot require that everything shall be defined, any more than one can require that a chemist shall decompose every substance. What is simple cannot be decomposed, and what is logically simple [*einfach*] cannot have a proper [*eigentlich*] definition. Now the logically simple [*Logischeinfache*] is no more given us at the outset than most of the chemical elements are; it is reached only be means of scientific work. If something has been discovered that is simple, or at least must count as simple for the time being, we shall have to coin a term for it, since language will not originally contain an exactly corresponding expression. On the introduction of a name for something logically simple, a definition is not possible; there remains nothing other than to lead the reader or hearer, by means of hints, to understand what is meant [*das Gemeinte*] by the words.⁵⁰⁵

Now note that here in Frege the "scientific work" of analysing something (he was speaking of mathematical concepts) into *discovered* logically simple elements is introduced on analogy with chemistry (cf. q. 499). In Russell's (and later in Carnap's) hands such a method was obviously extended to apply to the propositions of physics. Also note with respect to Russell's account of his own method of "scientific philosophizing" (q. 504) that the 'simples' in terms of which propositions were to be 'analysed' were conceived in phenomenalistic terms – simple 'names' designating phenomenally simple 'objects' – but Russell could not specify the simples in terms of which a complete analysis was to be accomplished, postulating this as an "ideal ... to be reached, if at all, only after a long preliminary labour" (recall nn. 220 and 228).

Such a conception of analysis obviously also was Wittgenstein's view in the *Tractatus*, as he confessed in one of his reworkings of TS 213:

> If you want to use the appellation "elementary proposition" as I did in the *Tractatus Logico-Philosophicus*, and as Russell used "atomic proposition", you may call the sentence "Here there is a red rose" an

elementary proposition. That is to say, it doesn't contain a truth-function and it isn't defined by an expression which contains one. But, if we're to say that a proposition isn't an elementary proposition unless its complete logical analysis shows that it isn't built out of other propositions by truth-functions, we are presupposing that we have an idea of what such an 'analysis' would be. Formerly, I myself spoke of a 'complete analysis', and I used to believe that philosophy had to give a definitive dissection of propositions so as to set out clearly all their connections and remove all possibilities of misunderstanding. I spoke as if there was a calculus in which such a dissection would be possible. I vaguely had in mind something like Russell's definition of the definite article, and I used to think that one could and should use visual impressions, etc., to define the concept say of a ~~chair~~ [Sessel] sphere and thus exhibit once and for all the connections between the concepts, the source of all misunderstandings, etc. At the root of all this was a false, idealized picture of language and its use //the use of language//....[506]

It has previously been pointed out that upon his return to philosophy in 1929–30 the *assumption* of an 'ideal', 'primary' or 'phenomenal' language, whose precise composition was to be worked out in the future, was repudiated by Wittgenstein (see the discussion in chapter 2, pp. 56–7 and nn. 175–6). What is of interest for the purposes of the thematic concerns of the present chapter is that Wittgenstein considered *what* he was repudiating – namely, both the notion of 'logical analysis' and its correlative *assumption* of a 'primary', 'phenomenal' language – as involving a 'scientific way of thinking'. By way of a definitive demonstration of this fact, recall now the following explicit repudiation dating from 1931:

> It is of the utmost importance that for a calculus of logic we always imagine an example in which the calculus actually is applied, and not examples of which we say they are not really the ideal, this though we don't have yet. This is the sign of a completely false view. (Russell and I have in different ways laboured under it. Check what I say in the *Tractatus* about elementary propositions and objects....) [Previously cited in q. 220; see my discussion in chapter 3, p. 78ff, and cf. the lengthy discussion in n. 228; note also that what Wittgenstein is referring to here is very obviously illustrated in the last paragraph of the above quotation from Russell (q. 504)]

In the section of TS 213 in which Wittgenstein included the above passage, he had written in the margins of the typescript the following illuminating remark (later combined with the above passage in his MS 115 revision of TS

213) about his (and Russell's) conception of 'logical analysis', which *assumed* but could not concretely specify an ideal calculus of simples in terms of which meaningful propositions might be completely analysed (recall, incidentally, that this was also characteristic of Carnap's early *Konstitutionssystem*; see n. 220):

> Is the concept 'red' indefinable? By 'indefinable' one has in mind something like unanalysable; and indeed just as though there were here an unanalysable *object* (like a chemical element). Then logic would after all be a sort of *very* general natural science. –But the impossibility of analysis corresponds to one of our *assumed* ways of presentation.[507]

Not only is there a recognition here that his repudiated earlier conception of 'logical analysis' constituted an approach which involved a sort of 'scientific' mode of reflection, but again (cf. qq. 499 and 398) there is even explicit recognition of precisely the sort of 'chemical analogy' Frege had used to characterize his own "scientific work" (see q. 505). Furthermore, it seems that the scientific, 'chemical model' of logical analysis was linked to that more general feature of Wittgenstein's earlier outlook that he identified as symptomatic of a false view – that general feature which he perhaps most bluntly identified as 'scientific' in 1941 when he complained, "What a curious attitude scientists have: 'We still don't know that; but it is knowable and it is only a matter of time before we get to know it!' As if that went without saying."[508] This of course was Wittgenstein's own early attitude toward that postulated ideal calculus of simples, the discovery of which he saw as the task of future logical analysis (recall chapter 3, p. 78ff and the discussion in nn. 220 and 228 – especially the second passage cited in the latter note). The assumption of a *to be discovered* ideal, primary language of simples and elementary propositions, then, stemmed from a view of logical analysis as analogous to the task of *discovering* irreducible chemical elements.

Wittgenstein's recognition of and rejection of such 'scientific' features of his Tractarian philosophy seems to have even come across quite clearly in his lectures in the very early thirties. According to G. E. Moore, Wittgenstein, having stressed that he had found a "new method", went on expressly to indicate that "it was misleading to say that what we wanted was an 'analysis', since in science to 'analyse' water means to discover some new fact about it, e.g. that it is composed of oxygen and hydrogen, whereas in philosophy 'we know at the start all the facts we need to know'".[509] Another specific illustration of the sort of view Wittgenstein was repudiating is identified by him in the following remark he drafted in 1931. In the midst of a discussion of the relationship between a logical 'calculus' and our actual language he wrote,

This all is connected with the false notion of logical analysis which Russell, Ramsey and I had. Such that one expects a final logical analysis of the facts, as of a chemical compound. An analysis by which one then perchance really discovers a 7-place relation, like an element which actually has the specific weight of 7.[510]

Undeniably, Wittgenstein upon his return to philosophy in the early thirties had come to view both his earlier conception of 'logical analysis' and its correlative assumption of a discoverable primary language as instances of how some of the 'logical' aspects of his earlier philosophy involved a 'scientific way of thinking'. His rejection of the 'scientific' attempt to solve philosophical problems by means of 'discoveries' or the uncovering of 'new facts', therefore, applies not only, as we have seen, to 'psychological' attempts to explain (causally) the meaning of signs in terms of mental phenomena, but also to the 'logical' assumption of the 'analysability' of meaningful propositions in terms of *discoverable* simple signs, the uncovering of new facts about the elemental constitution of language. These two spheres might, of course, not necessarily be independent of each other, if, for instance, one were to give the conception of a 'primary language' a phenomenalist twist – as it seems Russell, Wittgenstein and at one point Carnap did.[511]

It should be emphasized that, although Wittgenstein repudiated the 'scientific' aspects of his earlier philosophy, he did so not *because* they were scientific. They were for the most part repudiated on independent grounds, such as that they were founded on a false conception of language and its uses. Wittgenstein's specific *reasons* for rejecting his earlier conception of analysis and his correlative notion of a 'primary language' of simple signs have already been discussed in previous chapters. What has been demonstrated here is Wittgenstein's recognition that his errors were to some extent the result of his having been caught up in the scientific current of the times – thus situating his rejection of those 'logical' aspects of his earlier thinking within the horizon of the broader *Kampf* which was his later philosophy as he perceived it.

There is a deep irony in Wittgenstein's struggle against the scientific intellectual fashions of our age – an irony easily overlooked, but perhaps even more easily misconstrued. A salient feature of the 'scientific' intellectual current of our century has been its opposition to traditional metaphysics. Without exception those of his contemporaries singled out by Wittgenstein for criticism considered their 'scientific' mode of reflection an indispensable means for ridding ('cleansing', 'purifying') our thoughts of all metaphysical elements. Given this, it would seem possible to interpret Wittgenstein's struggle against that 'scientific' intellectual current as an endorsement of metaphysics. Carnap, for instance, appears to have interpreted Wittgenstein in this way, suggesting that the repugnance he exhibited toward the views and 'scientific' attitude of the members of the Vienna Circle was due to a "love for metaphysics or metaphysical theology" (see n. 426). This, however, is grossly erroneous. To understand why it is one must come to an appreciation of Wittgenstein's post-1930 view of metaphysics in the light of his broader *Kampf* against the 'scientific' intellectual current of our times.

In Wittgenstein's later philosophy there is definitely an opposition to metaphysics, but it is an opposition which is wholly consistent with and indeed fundamental to his repudiation of a 'scientific way of thinking'. It was found earlier in this chapter that his opposition to such thinking involved a differentiation between logical/conceptual concerns with the meaning or use of our expressions (a concern to clarify the linguistic facts, if you will) and 'scientific' concerns about the nature of things – for example a concern with making discoveries and offering theories, (causal) explanations and hypotheses about phenomena (in particular the phenomena allegedly essential to the signification of signs). His post-1930 'logical' view of signs in effect constituted an alternative to the 'scientific ways of thinking' characteristic of the philosophical endeavours of his contemporaries. This very demarcation between 'scientific' or empirical concerns and 'logical' or 'grammatical' concerns with the elucidation of the *use* of the everyday expressions of our language was essential to his view of metaphysics in his later writings. This becomes evident when one notes his somewhat unconventional view of metaphysics. In a remark written in the spring of 1947 Wittgenstein characterized metaphysics in such a way as to distinguish it from what he considered to be the proper task of philosophy:

> Philosophical investigations: conceptual investigations. The essential thing about metaphysics: that the difference between factual and conceptual investigations is not clear to it. A metaphysical question is always in appearance a factual one, although the problem is a conceptual one.[512]

Although written late in his life, this remark echoes sentiments Wittgenstein apparently expressed well over a decade earlier. One of the students who took down Wittgenstein's dictation of the 'Brown Book', Alice Lazerowitz (*née* Ambrose), has noted that during the early thirties he claimed that "Philosophical questions have been approached as one would a scientific problem because they sound as though they are questions about facts of which we do not know enough rather than questions about language."[513] It would seem that Wittgenstein identified the tendency to treat philosophical questions as 'scientific' issues with the confusion of factual and conceptual concerns – the latter being precisely what he

Metaphysics and Wittgenstein's Struggle 223

considered to be the essential characteristic of 'metaphysics' (see q. 512). This comes out even more explicitly in another remark he made in the early thirties, when he charged that

> Philosophers constantly see the method of science before their eyes, and are irresistibly tempted to ask and answer questions in the way science does. This tendency is the real source of metaphysics and leads the philosopher into complete darkness. I want to say here that it can never be our job to reduce anything to anything, or to explain anything. Philosophy really is 'purely descriptive'.[514]

It is not the concern of this chapter to give an exhaustive account of Wittgenstein's post-1930 conception of metaphysics. An exhaustive account would have to deal at length with several issues outside of the proper scope of themes of the present volume. It *is* of concern here, however, to understand Wittgenstein's view of metaphysics *from the perspective of* his repudiation of a 'scientific way of thinking'. To this end, it is essential to note not only that a 'scientific way of thinking' is generally identified in the above passage as the source of metaphysics, but also that there is explicit mention there of the sorts of methodological features he considered to be the source of metaphysics – namely, the inclination to *explain* rather than describe, and the attempt to reduce (or analyse) things into something else (presumably more simple – on analogy with, for example, the reduction of a substance to its chemical elements). Both of the latter features have of course already been discussed at great length in the present chapter and have been shown to be features Wittgenstein considered fundamental to a 'scientific' mode of reflection.

It is especially telling that on two of the previous occasions in the present volume where the issue of 'metaphysics' has arisen, it has in fact been in the context of a discussion of these very same features of a 'scientific way of thinking' (though not there identified as such). In chapter 3 (n. 228) Wittgenstein was found to have identified his 'ideal' Tractarian conception of language as the source of the *metaphysical* use of several expressions (for example, 'object', 'name' and 'proposition'). It was his complaint that his conception of the essence of language, of the 'general form of a proposition', had entailed perceiving ordinary language (meaningful discourse) as reducible to (analysable in terms of) a purely simple or primary language of *real* 'names' and *real* 'propositions' designating the elemental constitution of the world ('objects' and their elemental 'complexes'). Furthermore it was his Tractarian uses of such words that were cited by him as prime examples of expressions in need of 'being brought back from their metaphysical to their everyday use' (see *PI* §116 and the discussion of this in n. 228). What has been demonstrated in the present chapter is that Wittgenstein came to recognize that the 'way of thinking' involved in his earlier philosophy – for instance, the attempt to discover the 'general form of a proposition' and the correlative notion that language could be reduced to or analysed in terms of discovered (or, rather discoverable) elemental constituents, a thinking which led to a false, 'idealized' conception of language that neglected and thereby did violence to the *multiplicity* characteristic of the actual use of our expressions – was a 'scientific' way of thinking (as identified for example in q. 514) and the *source* of his *metaphysical* Tractarian use of the expressions 'object', 'name' and 'proposition'. (This would also apply to Russell's 'logical atomism' and Carnap's *Konstitutionssystem*;[515] cf. nn. 228, 220 and 176.)

The issue of metaphysics also arose earlier in this chapter when Wittgenstein was cited as having charged that William James, his efforts at a 'scientific' mode of reflection notwithstanding, had not freed himself from "the cobwebs of metaphysics in which he is caught. He cannot yet walk, or fly at all he only wriggles" (see q. 441) – the suggestion being that James' own speculations (for example, about the nature of language and the human 'mind') were themselves characterized by and enmeshed in a form of *metaphysics* (see, for instance, n. 448). We saw that Wittgenstein considered James' 'scientific' or pseudo-scientific speculations to be prime examples of a misguided attempt to offer *explanations*. It is clear from q. 514 that Wittgenstein considered it precisely the tendency to think scientifically, by attempting to offer causal, psychological explanations, that to a certain extent was the *source* of some of the metaphysical cobwebs in which James was caught. (This obviously would also apply to Russell's and Ogden's causal explanations of language, as well as to some of Wittgenstein's own early 'metalogical' views; see q. 183.)

Such a point was also explicitly made in the 'Blue Book', though not with specific reference to James or Russell. In the general context of a discussion of questions concerning the 'meaning' of signs, Wittgenstein indicated that taking such questions (for instance, 'What is the meaning of a word?', 'What is the object of a thought?') as questions about special sorts of psychological *things* or processes, i.e. as questions to be answered by offering psychological (causal) explanations of the meaning of signs (words, sentences) in terms of accompanying (associated) 'feelings' or mental processes which take place in a hidden 'medium of the mind' is to take questions about language in a *metaphysical* way; it is to take questions about language, questions about signs (including questions about such signs as 'I mean . . .', 'I think . . .', 'I expect . . .', see the discussion of Wittgenstein's linguistic 'relativism' in chapter 5) as analogous to "a question of physics, like asking, 'What are the ultimate constituents of matter?'"[516] It is to take a question about language in a way that renders it "a typically metaphysical question; the characteristic of a metaphysical question being that we express an unclarity about the grammar of words [including the words 'I mean ...', 'I think ...', and so on] in the *form* of a scientific question."[517] For Wittgenstein, giving *explanations* (such as those offered by Russell and James) of the meaning of signs in terms of a queer "mechanism of the mind" that gives the signs their 'life', which mechanism "must be of a most peculiar kind to be able to do what the mind does", is to make

> two mistakes. For what struck *us* as being queer about thought and thinking was not at all that it had curious effects which we were not yet able to explain (causally). Our problem, in other words, was not a scientific one; but a [conceptual] muddle [for example, about such expressions as 'I think ...', 'I mean ...'] felt as a [scientific] problem.[518]

The contention here is not only that there is a mistake (a confusion) about concepts such as 'meaning', 'thinking' and 'understanding', but also that the problem, itself a conceptual one, has furthermore been mistaken for a *scientific* one requiring causal, psychological *explanations*.

It was *not*, therefore, out of any "love for metaphysics or metaphysical theology" (cf. n. 426) that Wittgenstein found the views and scientific attitude of the Vienna Circle repugnant. The scope of his conception of metaphysics was such that it encompassed not only traditional metaphysics, but also, and especially, the dominant mode of reflection of our own epoch; and it is primarily the latter, the 'metaphysics' of our own epoch, that constituted the intellectual current against which he was struggling. This broader struggle is reflected in the emergence of virtually every major theme of his later *Denkweise* examined in this study. For Wittgenstein, scientific reflection, instead of being free of metaphysics, is itself often a *form* of metaphysics, a *source* of the metaphysics of our epoch (this is the irony). For him, a 'metaphysician', defined in the terms most relevant to our own times and viewed from the perspective of that *Kampf* which was his later philosophy, is, as it were, a philosopher playing scientist – that is, a philosopher who treats a conceptual matter as if it were a factual one. Wittgenstein, therefore, far from having an emotional sympathy for metaphysics and metaphysical theology, would have *included* among those infamous volumes to be committed to the flames many of the tomes of those would-be 'scientific philosophers' of our era who would do the committing.[519]

But there is yet a deeper dimension to Wittgenstein's struggle against the scientific intellectual current of our times. There is yet a broader horizon in terms of which the *Kampf* which was his later philosophy is to be understood. An indication of this is the following remark he made in 1938:

"This expression made it seem as if . . ." – as if the impossible were the case? "This expression is misleading" – It leads us to take the *impossible* for the truth? Where does it lead us when it misleads us? – It leads us into philosophical uncertainties difficulties; it leads us to gaze [in astonishment, *anzustaunen*] at scientific windbags (inflated idols) and thoughtlessly haggle over certain (good-sounding) formulae (and the like).[520]

It would seem that the intellectual tendency toward a 'scientific way of thinking', which Wittgenstein considered characteristic of our age, *itself* was viewed by him as stemming from language, from the misleading expressions of language. He would thus seem to have viewed the ultimate source of the metaphysics of our times as lying in language itself, in so much as language itself lures us, tempts us, tricks us into confusing conceptual and factual matters. Thus the *Kampf* which was his later philosophy, a *Kampf* against the scientific intellectual fashions of the day, seems to have been perceived by him within the even broader horizon of a *Kampf* against language. As he explicitly phrased this broader point in 1933–4 (not surprisingly, in the general context of a repudiation of the talk of some philosophers about 'analysing' the meaning of words as if such an effort were "a kind of scientific investigation into what the word *really* means"[521]), "Philosophy, as we use the word, is a fight against the fascination which forms of expression exert upon us."[522] And similarly in the context of his familiar (*PI* §109; see q. 468) repudiation of a scientific way of thinking, he again more broadly stressed that "Philosophy is a struggle [*Kampf*] against the bewitchment of our understanding by means of our language."[523]

The metaphysics of our epoch, and the 'scientific way of thinking' from which it is derived, were therefore viewed from the perspective of an even broader horizon. To plumb the full depth of that well of thinking which was Wittgenstein's later philosophy as we find it in the *Nachlaß*, this even broader horizon of vision must be carefully explored, for it not only sheds further light on some of the themes examined in this study, but also opens up a host of further themes fundamental to his later *Denkweise*. Such, however, is the stuff of another volume.

Notes

In all detailed references to, and citations of specific editions of, Wittgenstein's 'works' published in book form, the work in question is identified by title only or an abbreviation of the same, as specified in square brackets following the individual entries under 'Wittgenstein' in the Bibliography. Where specific editions are cited, they are those identified in the Bibliography.

For all other published material, repeated references cite name of author and the title of the book or article in question, shortened where convenient. Full details can be found on first references in the Notes, or, most conveniently, in the Bibliography.

To facilitate cross references to quotations in the text (labelled 'q.' + number of the identifying notes), notes are numbered in a single sequence throughout the book. However, to assist location, the notes below are grouped by chapter. All 'q.' references relate to the present study. In addition, there are numerous cross-references by chapter, page (p.), note (n.), or a combination of these. They are easily recognizable by context and the absence of accompanying source details. Virtually all 'n.' references are cross-references.

Chapter 1 Some Preliminary Issues

1 G. H. von Wright, "Special Supplement: the Wittgenstein Papers", *Philosophical Review* vol. 78 (Oct. 1969), pp. 483–503. This paper has since been republished with some revisions in G. H. von Wright, *Wittgenstein* (Oxford: Basil Blackwell, 1982). References in the present work are to the 1969 article, except of course in the cases where the information has been substantially revised.

2 This use of the term "Blaues Buch" can be definitively corroborated by collating the references to "Blaues Buch" in MS 165, p. 44 (and MS 180a, pp. 20 and 31) with the corresponding passages in MS 124.

3 I am grateful to Professor G. H. von Wright for having brought this typescript to my attention. This and other additions to the *Nachlaß* since 1969 have been catalogued in von Wright's revision of "The Wittgenstein Papers" (see n. 1).

4 *PI* §133, para. 3, was first written in autumn 1931 (MS 112, p. 95); while *PI* §133, para. 4, was originally written in MS 152, entry date 23 Feb. 1938.

5 *PI*, p. x.
6 MS 168, p. 7. Cf. the original entry in MS 137, p. 243, and the version published in *CV*, p. 76.
7 *Tractatus*, p. 4.
8 G. E. Moore, "Wittgenstein's Lectures in 1930–33", *Mind*, vol. 64 (Jan. 1955), p. 26.
9 MS 155, pp. 72–3.
10 Ibid., pp. 73–4.
11 Ibid., p. 79.
12 Ibid., p. 83.
13 Ibid., p. 58. (Originally written in English.)
14 MS 119, approximate entry date 3 Oct. 1937.
15 MS 159, pp. 69–70. Presumably Wittgenstein is referring here to the lost notebook MS 142 which was the basis for one of the typescripts (TS 220) for which he was writing this preface. See G. H. von Wright, "The Origin and Composition of Wittgenstein's *Investigations*", in *Wittgenstein: sources and perspectives*, ed. C. Luckhardt (Hassocks, Sussex: Harvester Press, 1979), p. 148. As previously stated, TS 220 is virtually identical to §§1–189 of what has been published as *Philosophical Investigations*.
16 There is some evidence, however, suggesting that the materials in Wittgenstein's *Nachlaß* are already the result of a sorting-process, for it has been reported that in 1950 Wittgenstein sorted out and burned a significant amount of material. See *N*, Editor's Preface, p. v. See also von Wright, "The Origin and Composition of Wittgenstein's *Investigations*", p. 141.
17 MS 110, p. 23.
18 Ibid., p. 95.
19 Republished 1977 with an introduction by A. Hübner and Werner and Elisabeth Leinfellner (*WV*).
20 *RPP*, vols I and II.
21 MS 130, p. 1.
22 MS 135, p. 1.
23 Ibid., p. 74. Published in *CV*, p. 65.
24 MS 137, p. 135.
25 Ibid., p. 281. Published in *CV*, p. 78.
26 *PI*, p. x.
27 MS 128, p. 49.
28 See the published (1945) Preface to *Philosophical Investigations*, pp. ix–x, and Wittgenstein's first (1938) draft of this in MS 159, p. 72. From such remarks it appears that Wittgenstein may not have thought very highly of the lecture notes and/or copies of the so-called 'Blue and Brown Books' which were being circulated at the time.
29 MS 132, p. 197. Published in *CV*, p. 53.
30 MS 136, p. 162. Published in *CV*, p. 66.
31 MS 110, p. 69.
32 MS 112, p. 99.
33 *PG*, pp. 487–8.
34 This version (published in 1974) of the editor's note, although dated

Notes

"London–1969", includes several alterations not found in the original editor's note published in 1969. Cf. *S*, vol. 4: *Philosophische Grammatik*, pp. 487–500. We shall take the '1974' version as Rhees' most current effort.

35 L. Wittgenstein, "Ursache und Wirkung: intuitives Erfassen", *Philosophia*, vol. 6, nos 3–4 (Sept.–Dec. 1976), p. 391.

36 If a different point *has* been made, though it is not clear that a wholly different point has been made, then it most likely would be because Wittgenstein has dramatically revised the remark, and not because it now appears in the context of *Zettel* instead of MS 119.

37 *PG*, p. 106.

38 See *Zettel*, Editor's Preface, p. v.

39 For example, Rush Rhees' unhappy use of ellipses in his compilation of remarks for appendix B of "Ursache und Wirkung" (pp. 435–8), and the editorial liberties taken in assembling the 'book' which we now know as *Philosophical Grammar*. The latter case will subsequently be dealt with in relation to the significance of the 'Big Typescript' (TS 213).

40 MS 136, pp. 5–7. And cf. *RPP*, vol. I, §63.

41 Examples of works stressing some of the possible continental influences on Wittgenstein are S. Toulmin and A. Janik, *Wittgenstein's Vienna* (New York: Simon and Schuster, 1973); and N. Gier, *Wittgenstein and Phenomenology* (Albany, NY: State University of New York Press, 1981).

42 MS 162b, pp. 121–2. Published in *CV*, p. 36.

43 MS 135, p. 12. Written in July 1947. Consistent with this notebook entry, earlier that year Wittgenstein had confided to G. H. von Wright that, "in order to *live* and to *work*, I have to allow no import of foreign goods (i.e., philosophical ones) into my mind" (see Wittgenstein's letter of 21 Feb. 1947, published in the *Cambridge Review*, 28 Feb. 1983, p. 57). Wittgenstein had indicated this to von Wright as an explanation of why he would not read a book von Wright had published and would not attend lectures von Wright was giving at the time. Wittgenstein's comments, of course, do not constitute a negative reflection on von Wright's work (the following year, after resigning his professorship at Cambridge, Wittgenstein wrote von Wright a letter of reference recommending him as his successor – von Wright was duly appointed); rather Wittgenstein's comments were simply an expression of his general reluctance to do much reading in philosophy. As he similarly admitted to von Wright later that year, "I read hardly anything. ... Real reading is always bad for me" (see Wittgenstein's letter of 22 Dec. 1947, ibid., p. 58).

44 I shall be dealing with this case in a future volume on Wittgenstein's notion of a 'mythology in language'.

45 MS 113, p. 101. It seems that Wittgenstein may have been introduced to Groag by Paul Engelmann during Wittgenstein's brief period of military training in Olmütz (Moravia) in 1916; see P. Engelmann, *Letters from Ludwig Wittgenstein*, ed. B. F. McGuinness, tr. L. Furtmüller (Oxford: Basil Blackwell, 1967), p. 65. Engelmann mentions a Mr Groag who apparently went on to become a "successful barrister" later in his life. Presumably this is the same Groag referred to by Wittgenstein as a 'secondary-school teacher'. It is not clear

whether Groag's technique for teaching 'grammar' was communicated to Wittgenstein through conversations or whether Wittgenstein directly observed Groag teaching in secondary school. Nor is it clear whether this took place during Wittgenstein's stay in Olmütz or whether Wittgenstein perhaps renewed contact with Groag after the war, during the 'lost decade', in which Wittgenstein himself was involved as a schoolmaster in the educational system for a few years. (In 1920 Wittgenstein mentions Groag in a letter to Engelmann; ibid., p. 25.) Wittgenstein's relationship with Groag seems to have been strong enough for him to have entrusted his manuscripts to Groag when he (Wittgenstein) went off to war (see ibid., p. 6), and thus it is likely that Wittgenstein *did* renew contact with Groag during the 'lost decade'. The latter circumstance would be consistent with the fact that it is only in connection with the notion of 'grammar' as we find it in Wittgenstein's writings *after* the 'lost decade' that there is anything resembling a "method of putting forward a number of examples in a grammatical investigation //beginning a linguistic reflection with a group of examples" (see chapter 4 for a discussion of Wittgenstein's post-1930 notion of 'grammar').

46 MS 126, p. 126. Published in *CV*, p. 43.
47 MS 175, pp. 128–9. Published in *OC*, §387.
48 *PI*, Preface, p. ix^e.
49 G. Hallett, *A Companion to Wittgenstein's "Philosophical Investigations"* (Ithaca, NY: Cornell University Press, 1977), p. 44. By "apparent disorderliness" Hallett surely means 'evident disorderliness' rather than 'disorderliness only in appearance but not in fact', for he goes on to explain why Wittgenstein's later writing is in fact disorderly.
50 Ibid., p. 45.
51 Ibid. There is an important sense in which Wittgenstein in his later philosophy did not consider language to be 'uniform' (see chapters 2 and 5 for a discussion of this); however, this does not necessarily imply that language is disorderly, and it certainly does not imply that in principle one cannot write about language in a "unified, coherent manner".
52 It is much easier to provide evidence that Wittgenstein made such claims about his method, than it is to explain what he meant by them. See chapters 4 and 6 of the present study.
53 J. Rochester, "*Philosophy as Therapy: an examination of Wittgenstein's philosophical method*" (University of Toronto, PhD dissertation, 1978), p. 16. Ms. Rochester's thesis has been cited only as an illustration of what I have called the 'conspiracy theory'. The view expressed by Rochester is also shared by some better-known scholars. For example, J. F. M. Hunter (who supervised Rochester's dissertation) has expressed similar sympathies by contending that Wittgenstein "contrived his most forthright statements in such a way as to conceal the point he wished to make" and that Wittgenstein's philosophical practice was "systematically [to] avoid expressing his views"; see J. F. M. Hunter, *Understanding Wittgenstein* (Edinburgh: Edinburgh University Press, 1985), p. viii.
54 Rochester, "Philosophy as Therapy", Ibid., p. 17.
55 Ibid., p. 18.

56 Ibid., pp. 20 and 22.
57 Ibid., p. 20.
58 Ibid.
59 T. Binkley, *Wittgenstein's Language* (The Hague: Martinus Nijhoff, 1973), p. 49.
60 Ibid., p. 50.
61 Ibid., p. 169.
62 Ibid., p. 168.
63 Ibid., p. 191.
64 Ibid., p. 198.
65 MS 113, p. 64. Reproduced in the "Philosophy" chapter of TS 213, p. 421.
66 MS 146, p. 93. The 'book' to which Wittgenstein refers is probably either TS 213 or a revision of TS 213 that he was working on at the time.
67 *PI*, Preface, p. ix^e.
68 MS 118, entry date 12 Sept. 1937.
69 *PI*, Preface, p. ix (my translation).
70 MS 118, entry date 15 Sept. 1937. G. P. Baker and P. M. S. Hacker in *Wittgenstein: understanding and meaning* (Chicago: University of Chicago Press, 1980), p. 23, have claimed that what Wittgenstein was despairing about was his inability to compose adequately the continuation (TS 221) of part I of the pre-war version of the *Investigations*. This claim is in error. TS 221 was an arrangement of remarks on the philosophy of mathematics drawn primarily from three manuscripts: MSS 117, 118 (from which the above quote was taken) and 119. These manuscripts were not attempts to write a book, but diaries in which a considerable amount of the material had nothing at all to do with the philosophy of mathematics. When Wittgenstein wrote the above quoted passage of 15 Sept. 1937, most of this diary material (MSS 117–19) had not even been written. Therefore, it makes no sense to suggest that Wittgenstein was despairing about "wasting unspeakable effort on putting into order" the remarks for TS 221. He cannot have been wasting time "putting into order" remarks which had not even been written. It should be noted that Baker and Hacker do not explicitly *quote* the pertinent remarks of 12 and 15 Sept., but rather paraphrase those remarks. The paraphrasing tends to render the anachronism in their claim virtually undetectable to a reader not intimately familiar with Wittgenstein's *Nachlaß*. In the forthcoming section, we shall find that in 1937 Wittgenstein was not at all preoccupied with the philosophy of mathematics.
71 An early remark (1931) in MS 112, p. 226, suggests that Wittgenstein did think it would be beneficial if his writing should have this effect: "I ought to be no more than a mirror, in which my reader can see his own thinking with all its deformities so that, helped in this way, he can put it right." Published in *CV*, p. 18.
72 MS 118, entry date 16 Sept. 1937.
73 Ibid., entry date 14 Sept. 1937.
74 MS 119, p. 65, entry date 3 Oct. 1937.
75 Ibid., p. 108. (Written in English.)
76 *CV* p. 59. The probable source is MS 134, pp. 107–8.
77 MS 137, p. 212. Published in *CV*, p. 76.

78 MS 159, pp. 68–9. A similar point is made in a typescript of the Preface to the pre-war version of *Philosophical Investigations*, for which the MS 159 version was no doubt a draft. Cf. TS 225, pp. 1–2.
79 *PI* Preface, p. ix^e.
80 MS 136, pp. 182–3. Published in *CV*, p. 66. In the last year or two of his life Wittgenstein took the trouble neatly to recopy this remark and included it in a collection of remarks on general subjects. Cf. MS 168, p. 12.
81 MS 137, p. 268. Published in *CV*, p. 77.
82 If one goes back and examines the manuscript sources for the *Tractatus*, one will find that, in spite of the formal surface structure and 'order' provided by its decimal numbering system, even this early work was to a certain extent achieved by lifting (verbatim) insights recorded in various notebooks and piecing them together in an ordered sequence.
83 The frustration Wittgenstein felt with his fragmented way of going about things is somewhat humorously expressed in his remark that "I often write my remarks as a housewife gathers old odds and ends – twine, ribbon, bits of cloth, pins – because one could need them sometime. But when one does need them, they aren't to hand." See MS 122, p. 186.
84 MS 136, p. 287.
85 The stylistically conventional qualities of TS 213 do not extend much further than its surface appearance, for much of this work is simply a collection of 'remarks' (from various manuscript sources) which have been pigeonholed under separate headings. In spite of the chapter structure, in TS 213 too there is generally lacking an orderly and cohesive natural progression of thoughts such as would be expected from a more stylistically conventional book.
86 'Main text' here means the *typed* text as opposed to the handwritten notes jotted down in the margins, between the lines, and on the *Rückseiten* (versos) and *Kehrseiten* (inserted leaves).
87 *BBB*, Editor's Preface p. viii. Among the examples Rhees gives are: (1) alleged shifts in Wittgenstein's notion of 'language-games,' and (2) that Wittgenstein "does not find the source of metaphysics in anything specially connected with language . . . [thus] he was not anything like as clear about the character of philosophical puzzlement as he was when he wrote the Investigations" (p. xiii). In forthcoming chapters we shall find that Rhees is wrong on both these counts.
88 This subheading and, for that matter, the title itself are not expressions Wittgenstein used to refer to these texts. Garth Hallett has gone so far as to call the 'Brown Book' a "first draft" of *Philosophical Investigations*. See Hallett, *A Companion to Wittgenstein's "Philosophical Investigations"*, p. 52.
89 Rhees' efforts have left us with the book entitled *Philosophical Grammar*. Only part (157 pages) of *Philosophical Grammar* consists of the projected revision outlined by Wittgenstein in MSS 114, 115 and 140. The other 316 pages consist of a thirty-page table of contents of Rhees' making, and 286 pages of remarks from TS 213 (and other manuscripts) which Rhees chose to include. Among the chapters which Rhees decided not to include is the chapter entitled "Philosophy". More is to be said about *Philosophical Grammar* presently.

90 Wittgenstein numbered MSS 115 and 116 consecutively as "Band XI" and "Band XII". This would seem to suggest that the first 135 pages of MS 116 post-date the 'Brown Book' *Umarbeitung* in MS 115. However, in itself this evidence is not very compelling, since MS 115 was also a conglomerate of 'parts', the first part having been commenced in December 1933 and the second part (the *Umarbeitung*) in August 1936. Wittgenstein would also have had reason to give MSS 115 and 116 consecutive volume numbers merely on the basis that the early passages of MS 116 postdate the *first* part (1933) of MS 115.
91 Von Wright, "The Wittgenstein Papers", p. 495.
92 Ibid., p. 495.
93 Reported by von Wright in "The Origin and Composition of Wittgenstein's *Investigations*", p. 148. In addition to reports that Wittgenstein stayed in Norway, we know from his own notebook entries that he was in Norway during this period. Wittgenstein is not known to have stayed in Norway between 1929 and 1936.
94 The dependency of MS 116 on MS 120 was noted in 1976 by Professor von Wright in a paper made available at a colloquium (Waterloo, Ontario) on the philosophy of Wittgenstein, commemorating the twenty-fifth anniversary of Wittgenstein's death. This paper was subsequently published with some minor changes as "The Origin and Composition of Wittgenstein's *Investigations*" (see pp. 149–50). In addition to MS 120, the first 51 pages of MS 158 (1938) were Wittgenstein's source for many of the remarks between p. 170 and p. 180 of MS 116.
95 Here Kenny refers us to appendix 4B of *Philosophical Grammar*. Appendix 4B up to the ellipsis points on p. 212 was taken from MS 116, pp. 81–2. In his footnote to the appendix (cf. *PG*, p. 211) Rhees gives summer 1936 as the probable date of the manuscript. Thus Rhees, when compiling *Philosophical Grammar*, not only was familiar with the 'revision' of TS 213 in the early pages of MS 116, but also was of the opinion that the latter revision was carried out in 1936, long after the revisions (in MSS 114, 115 and 140) which he chose to publish in *Philosophical Grammar* as the definitive ones. Why Rhees chose to displace TS 213 by *Philosophical Grammar*, when he was aware that there was an even later revision of TS 213 material, is a mystery.
96 Anthony Kenny, "From the Big Typescript to the *Philosophical Grammar*", *Acta Philosophica Fennica*, vol. .28, nos 1–3 (1976), p. 52.
97 Ibid., p. 52.
98 Rhees has dated part I of *Philosophical Grammar* to the years 1933–4. See his editorial note, *PG* p. 487.
99 Von Wright, "The Origin and Composition of Wittgenstein's *Investigations*", p. 149. Von Wright made this same point, though with slightly different wording, in his 1976 version of this paper (cf. n. 94).
100 Ibid.
101 Ibid., p. 148.
102 In all fairness to Rhees, publishing TS 213 would have been an editor's nightmare, owing to the extensive revisions and supplementary remarks Wittgenstein jotted down (at a later date) in the margins, between the lines,

and on the *Rückseiten* and *Kehrseiten*. This, no doubt, helped dissuade Rhees from publishing TS 213, although such a problem does not seem to have dissuaded him from publishing *Philosophical Remarks*. In this case he simply ignored most of the revisions and additions (cf. *PR*, editor's note, pp. 348–9). Perhaps the best option, though admittedly a laborious task, would have been to publish the whole of TS 213, but set off the numerous additional handwritten remarks by presenting them in italics and/or bracketed between the paragraphs of the main text. This would have been (1) a less expensive method, though less desirable from a scholar's stand-point, than the superbly presented *Proto-tractatus* edited by von Wright and others (*PT*); (2) preferable to ignoring the revisions and supplementary remarks as Rhees did for *Philosophical Remarks*; and (3) certainly preferable to the compilation Rhees has published as *Philosophical Grammar*, which has turned out to be a wild-goose chase for a 'definitive revision' of TS 213.

103 The following is a table correlating some of the remarks in the first 135 pages of MS 116 with their origin in MS 119.

MS 116	Origin in MS 119
pp. 51–6	30 Oct. to 2 Nov. 1937
p. 118	5 Nov. 1937
pp. 124–7	10–11 Nov. 1937
p. 130	12 Nov 1937

The correlation, however, does not end here, but rather continues past the so-called end (p. 135) of the first part of MS 116:

MS 116	Origin in MS 119
p. 136	13 Nov. 1937
pp. 138–9	13 Nov. 1937

Shortly thereafter, MS 116 begins drawing remarks from MS 120, which was a continuation of MS 119 and written between 19 November 1937 and 26 April 1938. The first 265 pages of MS 116 are alleged to consist of two parts, because MS 116 apparently stops drawing (and revising) remarks from TS 213 on p. 135 of MS 116. However, the uniformity of Wittgenstein's appeal to MSS 119 and 120 in his drafting of MS 116 spans the alleged gap between pp. 1–135 and pp. 136–265 of MS 116, thus strongly suggesting a temporal continuity in the authorship of the first 265 pages of that manuscript. This supports von Wright's initial (1969) intuition that the first 265 pages of MS 116 stem from the same period (cf. von Wright, "The Wittgenstein Papers", p. 495). It does not, however, support his initial view that that period was 1936.

104 In 1969 von Wright (in "The Wittgenstein Papers", p. 496) described MS 117, pp. 127–48, as follows: "Pages 127–48 are undated but were probably written in the second half of 1938. In this section there are references to a typescript which is evidently item 221 – that is, the typescript of the second half of the prewar version of the *Investigations*." Although von Wright is probably correct in his estimation of the date of MS 117, pp. 127–48, there is no doubt that the typescript to which Wittgenstein refers in these pages in *not* TS 221 but rather TS 213. In MS 117 the references to a typescript fit in with and *follow*

the same order as the passages from TS 213 which Wittgenstein bothered to recopy and/or revise.
105 This procedure is not uncharacteristic of Wittgenstein. Several of his notebooks can be paired in this manner, although in most cases the pairing occurs between a large notebook and a pocket notebook.
106 Von Wright has indicated that Wittgenstein is known to have had a typescript with him in Norway in autumn 1937, but it is not known which typescript it was (see von Wright "The Origin and Composition of Wittgenstein's *Investigations*", p. 144). My findings show that that typescript was TS 213. Further evidence for this is the fact that in MS 157b (Aug. 1936–Dec. 1937), written during his stay in Norway, there are explicit references to page and even paragraph numbers of TS 213 (see, for instance, MS 157b, p. 26). Many of the references are to passages in the "Philosophy" chapter of TS 213, some of which passages, along with other material drafted in MS 157b itself, are to be found in *PI* §§116–31. The latter circumstance is explained by the fact that MS 157b was preparation for TS 220, the pre-war version of the *Investigations*. Thus, clearly Wittgenstein not only had TS 213 with him in Norway in 1937, but he was culling remarks from it for the pre-war *Investigations*, remarks from one of the very chapters Rhees decided to leave out of the revision of TS 213 published as *Philosophical Grammar*.
107 MS 142 (Nov.–Dec. 1936) has been missing for three decades, prior to which it was in the possession of Wittgenstein's sister, Mrs. Margarethe Stonborough, to whom it had been given as a present. The only competent philosopher who seems to have seen this text is Professor von Wright during a visit to Mrs. Stonborough in 1952 (see von Wright, "The Origin and Composition of Wittgenstein's *Investigations*", pp. 141–2). Apparently the manuscript was entitled "Philosophische Untersuchungen", as of course were both the 'Brown Book' *Umarbeitung* and the pre-war version of *Philosophical Investigations*; however, von Wright closely associates MS 142 with the first part of the pre-war version of the *Investigations*. That MS 142 was written before autumn 1937, when Wittgenstein gave up his attempts to write a stylistically conventional book, and yet (to von Wright's recollection) matched closely the beginning of *Philosophical Investigations* (the typescript of which was made after Wittgenstein decided to settle for an "album of remarks") seems to be explained in a draft for the Preface to the 1938 typescript of the *Investigations*. In that draft, having indicated that he had made several (unsuccessful) attempts to compile a more stylistically conventional book out of his remarks, Wittgenstein explained, "The last attempt at a compilation [*Der letzte Versuch der Zusammenfassung*] is the one with which I begin [*beginne*] this publication of my thoughts. It is a fragment [*Fragment*] and perhaps has the merit that it conveys, relatively easily, a conception of my method" (cf. MS 159, pp. 64–70, previously cited). If the "last attempt" at a book to which Wittgenstein is referring is in fact MS 142, this would explain how MS 142 could both have been written prior to his decision to give up trying to write a stylistically conventional book and yet also be incorporated as a dominant part of the beginning of *Philosophical Investigations* (Wittgenstein's "album of remarks").

Baker and Hacker in *Wittgenstein: understanding and meaning* (pp. 25–6), citing the typescript version (TS 225) of the 1938 Preface, claim that by "last attempt" at a more stylistically conventional book Wittgenstein was referring to TS 220 (part I of the pre-war *Investigations*). This might be correct in terms of the philosophical content of TS 220, but it is probably historically inaccurate. In terms of its content TS 220 might *contain* Wittgenstein's "last attempt" at a stylistically conventional book, but that would only be because TS 220, according to von Wright's impressions, was a typescript based on MS 142. TS 220, however, was probably not *itself* that "last attempt", since it was most likely typed after Wittgenstein decided (Sept. 1937) to settle for an "album of remarks" – an album which, according to the 1938 Preface, only *begins* with his "last attempt" at a more stylistically conventional book. I have already demonstrated that the typescript with which Wittgenstein was working during his stay in Norway between August 1936 and December 1937 was still TS 213, not a subsequent typescript.

108 This point seems at least to some extent to have exonerated Rhees. The first 135 pages of MS 116 were not an attempt to rehabilitate TS 213 as such. However, the fact remains that in MS 116 (and MS 117) Wittgenstein undertook an extensive process of selection and revision of TS 213 material several years after the supposedly definitive text presented as *Philosophical Grammar*. Another fact also remains, and that is that two thirds of the material published in *Philosophical Grammar* was included *not* on the basis of instructions in Wittgenstein's own early revisions (MSS 114, 115 and 140) of TS 213, but rather on Rhees' own initiative.

109 Kenny pointed out this oddity in the passage cited as q. 96. My explanation of the oddity, however, does *not* support two of the conclusions which Kenny entertains: (1) "it means that *after* the second revision [MS 140] Wittgenstein came to the conclusion that his book would do better to stick closer to the original text of the typescript"; and (2) "On the other hand, one may wonder whether the dating of the *Grosses Format* [MS 140] by von Wright and Rhees in 1933–34 is correct. May it be that the *Grosses Format* is *later* than the Volume XII [MS 116] revision?"

110 For example, PI §§430, 435, 437, 438 (para. 1), 439 (para. 1), 442–3, 445–6, 448 (paras 3–4), 449, 458–60, 461 (paras 2–3), 465 (para. 1), 466–70, 472–4, 477–84, 493–4, 507, 518, 548–9, 558 (up to dash), 587 and 613. Most of these remarks are in the main text of TS 213 and thus were originally written in manuscripts between 1930 and 1932. A few of the remarks were marginal notes handwritten onto the typescript. I say "at least forty", because I have not attempted an exhaustive cross-referencing of remarks between TS 213 and *Philosophical Investigations*. Cross-referencing these texts has not been a goal of my research. The above cross-references are simply incidental by-products of my work – what I happened to recognize as *Investigations* material while working my way through TS 213. Needless to say, the cross-references offered are sufficient to make my point.

111 Incidentally one could also add to this list several of Wittgenstein's general pronouncements on philosophy published in *Zettel*: for example, §§211 (after dash), 447, 452, 456 and 460).

112 The reader will recall that the "Philosophy" chapter is one of the chapters which Rhees decided to leave out of *Philosophical Grammar*, his 'definitive' revision of TS 213.
113 Von Wright, *Wittgenstein*, p. 130.
114 In his comments about the table von Wright tries to obviate such a misapprehension. Cf. ibid., p. 131, comment 3.
115 Wittgenstein's extensive appeal to his revisions of TS 213, even during the post-war period (c.1945), is evidenced in the explicit and profuse references to these revisions found in a more recent addition to Wittgenstein's *Nachlaß*. Cf. MS 180b, pp. 52–3.
116 Cf. Von Wright, "The Origin and Composition of Wittgenstein's *Investigations*", p. 149.
117 What we have established here by way of dating will be borne out more concretely in subsequent chapters, when the philosophical content of Wittgenstein's writings is examined.
118 For example, see the previously cited account by G. E. Moore of Wittgenstein's 1930–3 lectures (q. 8).
119 Cf. nn. 9, 10, 11 and 12. It was presumably to the early 1930s (if not before) that Wittgenstein alluded when he allegedly told Drury, "my fundamental ideas came to me very early in life". See M. O'C. Drury, "Conversations with Wittgenstein", in *Ludwig Wittgenstein: personal recollections*, ed. Rush Rhees (Oxford: Basil Blackwell, 1981), p. 171.
120 See *PI*, p. x. In this preface Wittgenstein also acknowledged his debt to Piero Sraffa for the ideas in *Philosophical Investigations*, though Wittgenstein gives no indication of *when* Sraffa served as a stimulus to his ideas. This acknowledgement, however, is also in an early draft (1938) of the preface (see MS 159, pp. 74–5) for the pre-war version of the *Investigations*, and even as early as 1931 Wittgenstein cited Sraffa as an influence on his thinking (see MS 154, pp. 30–1; published in *CV* p. 19). These facts, when coupled with the fact that it was in 1927 that Sraffa began (at Keynes' invitation) his lengthy career at Cambridge as a lecturer and don, suggest that Wittgenstein's greatest debt to Sraffa probably stems from the late twenties and/or the early to middle thirties.
121 MS 156a, p. 116. Cf. *CV*, p. 23.
122 MS 129, p. 181. Cf. *CV*, p. 44.
123 MS 130, p. 115.
124 MS 135, p. 140. Cf. *RPP*, vol. I, §1124.

Chapter 2   Metalogic and the Domain of Logic: the shift to ordinary language

125 *PI*, p. x. It has been noted that the published text of the Preface to the *Investigations* is in error and that the beginning of the first paragraph on p. x should read, "Two years ago . . ." alluding to conversations Wittgenstein had with Nicolas Bachtin in 1943. See von Wright, "The Wittgenstein Papers", p. 497, n. 6.
126 See for example H. Leblanc and W. A. Wisdom, *Deductive Logic*, 2nd ed.

(Boston, Mass: Allyn and Bacon, 1976), chapter 3. Carnap has attributed the origin of the term 'metalogic' to the Warsaw logicians (Lukasiewicz and others). See R. Carnap, *The Logical Syntax of Language* (London: Kegan Paul, Trench, Trubner 1937), p. 9. Cf. Carnaps' (presumably borrowed) 1931 definitions of *Metalogik* as "strict formal theories about linguistic forms," and "metalogical propositions" as propositions which speak about "the forms of language" (see Carnap's "Die physikalische Sprache as Universalsprache der Wissenschaft", *Erkenntnis*, vol. II (1932–3), p. 435.

127 See, for example, *PG*, p. 101; and *Zettel* §284.
128 Hans Lenk, *Metalogik und Sprachanalyse* (Freiburg im Breisgau: Rombach, 1973), p. 7.
129 *BBB*, p. xv.
130 See, for example, TS 213, pp. 1, 3, 16, 205, 282, 285 (*Rückseite*), 286 and 412.
131 MS 116, p. 16. The discussion in chapter 1 provides an accurate dating of this manuscript.
132 See TS 213 p. 16; and cf. *PG*, p. 46.
133 MS 110, p. 191 (cf. TS 213, p. 16). The word 'again' (*wieder*) in the last line of the remark is also in the German version of *Zettel* §284. Why Wittgenstein says 'again' is clear when one reads the remark in its original bed of ideas in MS 110, or, for that matter, also TS 213, chapter 1.
134 MS 110, p. 189. This remark was included on the first page of TS 213. Also, another version of this remark, included in MS 114 (II, p. 1), reads, "There is no metalogic. Likewise the word 'to understand', the expression 'to understand a sentence', are not metalogical."
135 MS 114, II, p. 27. This remark is found in the midst of one of Wittgenstein's revisions of TS 213 material and is appended to a remark found on p. 156 of TS 213.
136 See *PG* p. 46. This was written in conjunction with the remark previously cited as *Zettel* §284.
137 TS 213, p. 285 (*Rückseite*). See also TS 213, p. 286, and Wittgenstein's extension of this repudiation in MS 114 (cf. *PG*, p. 101) to apply also to the notion of 'deriving' (*ableiten*) a result (*Resultat*) in arithmetic. It should be noted that *abbilden* could be translated by any number of other English terms, such as 'to portray' or 'to picture'. However, in this context 'to copy' or 'to depict' is perhaps more appropriate, since Wittgenstein uses the verb *kopieren* almost interchangeably in the discussion.

It is also worth noting that the concepts *abbilden* and *Abbildung* are central to Wittgenstein's discussion in *Tractatus* 2.1–3.12 (see also 4.01–4.016 and following). Though for the purposes of the strategy adopted here it is of little help to speculate on the matter, it is quite possible that the view of *abbilden* as metalogical is either implicit in or presupposed by this stretch of text in the *Tractatus*. It is a pity that this thematic connection did not survive the revision and *translation* of TS 213 that we now know as *Philosophical Grammar*.

138 TS 213, p. 283, heading to §64.
139 Ibid., p. 283. Originally written in 1930 in MS 110, pp. 18–19. Cf. MS 114, II, p. 80 (published in *PG*, p. 99).

140 TS 213, p. 2. The first paragraph was originally drafted in 1930-1 in MS 110, pp. 238-9. See Wittgenstein's subsequent versions of this remark in MS 114, II, p. 2 (published in *PG*, pp. 39-40); and MS 116, p. 3.
141 MS 110, p. 239.
142 Ibid., p. 236. It is clear from these last two passages, written in 1930-1, that Wittgenstein was *in the process* of dispelling such 'illusions', and there is no doubt that some of the remarks he makes in his specific attempts to clarify such concepts as *verstehen* became unpalatable to him in later years. Actually it would be quite defensible to claim that during the whole of the last twenty years of his life Wittgenstein was *in the process* of breaking the spell which such illusions held over him. However, it is not my concern in this chapter to give details of what, for him, constituted such illusions, how they were conjured, and how they were to be dispelled. Such matters will be examined in my forthcoming study of Wittgenstein's notion of a "mythology in language". Nor is it my concern here to scrutinize the doctrinal development of Wittgenstein's accounts of such concepts as *verstehen*. Rather, the task of this chapter is to establish *that* Wittgenstein had abandoned his earlier view of 'psychological' concepts as 'metalogical', what such an abandonment consisted in, and how this is tied in with his shift to a concern with ordinary language.
143 Cf. TS 213, p. 16; and MS 110, p. 191.
144 TS 213, pp. 3-4. See also the versions in MS 114, II, p. 4 (cf. *PG*, p. 40); and MS 116, pp. 5-6. Both *PI* §503 and §504 were originally drafted in 1930, in MS 109 (p. 200) and MS 108 (p. 277) respectively. The specific point being made in the above passage will be discussed in chapter 5.

The expression "specific language game" was written by hand in TS 213 as alternative wording; thus it postdates the typescript. As suggested in chapter 1, among the myths propagated by Rhees in his Introduction to *The Blue and Brown Books* (*BBB*) is the view that Wittgenstein's 'later' thinking emerged during the 'Blue and Brown Books period'. One of the by-products of this myth has been the view, most recently championed by Baker and Hacker, that "the notion of a language-game is introduced only [first] in the *Blue Book*" (*Wittgenstein: understanding and meaning*, p. 89). In chapters 3 and 4, where I examine the notion of 'language game', it will be seen that the latter view is wrong.
145 *Zettel*, part of §287. Cf. the other versions in TS 213 (*Kehrseite* 17-18) and MS 140 (published in *PG*, p. 46). Most of *Zettel* §287 was handwritten on the *Kehrseite* in TS 213 and thus postdates the typescript. However, the first two sentences of *Zettel* §287 do constitute a remark in the typescript proper of TS 213 (p. 18) and stem from MS 110, p. 192. Thus *Zettel* §287 is in fact an elaboration on a remark included in TS 213 but originally dating from 1930-1.
146 MS 111, pp. 4-5.
147 TS 213, p. 224. These remarks were originally drafted in 1930: for example, for the second and third paragraphs of the quotation, see MS 109, pp. 177 and 193. The anecdote about the French politician was a favourite one for Wittgenstein. When he first jotted it down in 1930, he wrote after it, "This is a very important remark, though utter nonsense. It characterizes of course a specific view" (ibid., p. 177). The view characterized is clearly the view that the

concepts 'thinking' and 'thought' are metalogical (although I have yet explicitly to define the term). The reader may recognize the anecdote as part of *PI* §336. It crops up time and again in Wittgenstein's writings (for instance, see also MS 114, II, p. 92, published in *PG*, p. 107; MS 115, p. 283, published in the 'Brown Book', *BBB*, p. 148; MS 117, p. 135, which I have established as a revision, c.1938, of TS 213 material; MS 180a, p. 42; and MS 129, pp. 102–3).

148 TS 213, p. 223. Cf. Wittgenstein's comment on the *Rückseite* of p. 221, which by way of MS 114, II, p. 92, has been published in *PG*, p. 107. This remark is intimately bound up with an issue to be examined in chapter 4: namely, Wittgenstein's rejection of the 'causal theory' of meaning.

149 TS 213, p. 222. (Originally drafted in early 1930; MS 108, p. 278.) In several places in the margins of this section of TS 213 Wittgenstein had indicated that some passages were to be inserted here from another chapter ("Sudden Understanding, etc."). In this other chapter Wittgenstein makes a point similar to the one made above. In that context (TS 213, pp. 155–6, but originally drafted in MS 110, pp. 233–4), immediately before a version of *PI* §502, he wrote,

> For the issue is whether by "the sense [*Bedeutung*] in which one uses a word" one must understand a process that we experience while speaking or hearing the word.
> The source of the mistake seems to be (is) the idea of *thoughts which accompany the sentence*. (Or precede its expression.)

In Wittgenstein's MS 114 (II, p. 26) revision of TS 213, this remark is also followed by a version of *PI* §502, as well as a remark on *meinen* and the previously cited disclaimer (q. 135) that "The proposition 'I mean something . . .' is not metalogical."

It is perhaps worth noting here that in a letter (Cassino, 19 Aug. 1919) replying to Bertrand Russell's queries about the *Tractatus*, Wittgenstein emphatically answered the question "Does a *Gedanke* consist of words?" by saying "No! But of psychical constituents that have the same sort of relation to reality as words. What those constituents are I don't know" (*N*, appendix III, p. 130). Thus the now obvious metalogical import of *Tractatus* 3.1: "In a sentence [*Satz*] a thought finds an expression that can be perceived by the senses." There also is indication that Wittgenstein at some early point in his career considered 'thinking' to be a kind of (inner) speaking, perhaps the sort of process referred to in *PI* p. 211 as "speaking in ideas or images" (*in der Vorstellung sprechen*). In at least two places in his manuscripts of the late 1940s there is reference to such an earlier view. In MS 136, p. 91, he wrote,

> It is incorrect to say – as I once wrote – thinking is a kind of speaking. Can one say it is an operating with signs? I ~~may~~ believe so [*Ich glaube ~~kann~~*]. Yet it is also difficult to say what can be called 'signs', and what cannot. . . . [This remark was crossed out in the text]

And several months earlier he had similarly written,

It isn't true that thinking is a kind of speaking, as I once said. The concept 'thinking' is *categorically* different from the concept 'speaking'. But of course thinking is neither an accompaniment of speaking nor of any other process. [MS 135, p. 154; published in *RPP*, vol. II, §7]

The sort of view Wittgenstein repudiates seems to have been expressed in the notebooks from which he drew remarks for the *Tractatus*:

Now it is becoming clear why I thought that thinking and speaking [*Sprechen*] were the same. That is to say, thinking is a kind of language. For a thought is of course *also* a logical picture of the proposition, and consequently it likewise is a sort of proposition. [*N*, p. 82; cited in an editor's note in *RPP*, vol. II, p. 3]

In all likelihood Wittgenstein was so fond of the 'French politician' anecdote (see q. and n. 147) precisely because it at least in part reflected some of his own earlier misconceptions – though with the amusing refraction that the French politician claims that it is the *French* language (word order) that best corresponds to the 'order of thinking', the order of the inner speaking in images or ideas.

150 See the various versions of this suggestion in TS 213, p. 6; MS 114, II, p. 6; MS 140, p. 3 (cf. *PG*, p. 41); and MS 116, p. 8. Wittgenstein seems to allow for similar cases with respect to the concept 'thinking' (MS 116, pp. 103–4; cf. *PI* §332).

151 At least in the early 1930s Wittgenstein tried to separate out the sorts of cases which primarily interested him. Near the beginning of MS 110 (p. 56), the manuscript from which he drew many of the remarks for [the] chapter of TS 213 entitled "Understanding", he wrote,

If I say "All understanding corresponds to an exposition [*Erklärung*] and there is no understanding that cannot be expounded", then by 'understanding' I mean understanding-in-one-way [*das So-verstehen*] (as opposed to understanding differently). – But I don't mean understanding in general (as opposed to not-understanding; that is to say, not grasping as a sentence).

Here Wittgenstein seems to be suggesting that his account of the concept 'understanding' is not directed at the cases where one might speak of understanding or grasping an utterance as a sentence in a familiar language – as opposed to just hearing an unfamiliar foreign language (cf. q. 150).

152 MS 114, II, p. 4; cf. *PG*, p. 41.

153 TS 213 p. 2. Originally drafted in early 1930 in MS 108, p. 277 (see also MS 116, p. 2). The last sentence was written by hand in the typescript (cf. *PG*, p. 41). It is important to note that Wittgenstein uses the term *Meinung* here and not *Bedeutung* or *meinen*. The plurality of terms in German allows Wittgenstein to claim that 'meaning' (*Meinung*) qua psychological phenomenon falls out of consideration, and yet not fall prey to the view that meaning (whether in the

sense of *meinen* or in that of *Bedeutung*) is a metalogical concept. His suggestion in the above passage that "Language must speak for itself" is perhaps put somewhat more lucidly in a later manuscript when he emphatically advises, "Let the use speak!" (MS 119, entry date 31 Oct. 1937). Wittgenstein's notion of a 'system' will be discussed in chapters 4 and 5.

154 MS 116, p. 2. This remark is very similar to one already identified from TS 213 (see n. 134) and may very well be a revision of it. The TS 213 version, instead of occurring immediately after the remarks cited in q. 153, occurs one page before them.

155 Presumably Wittgenstein was making a similar claim in the context of his rejection of the view that 'depicting' is metalogical when he asserted that "The description of the psychological must be something which can itself be used as a symbol." See the passage cited in q. 139.

156 MS 137, p. 120. This remark was entered between what have since been published as §§656 and 657 of *RPP*, vol. II.

157 MS 137, p. 133. Entered between what have been published as §§694 and 695 of *RPP* vol. II

158 MS 137, p. 208. First drafted in MS 167, p. 45; and since published in *LW* §256.

159 Another good way of exposing Wittgenstein's shift to ordinary language would be by carefully examining his notion of 'grammar'. This subject is not examined in the present chapter, but enters the discussion at several junctures in subsequent chapters. See, for example, the discussion of 'grammar' in connection with (1) Wittgenstein's earlier views of 'logic' and 'ideal language' (chapter 3); and (2) his distinction between conceptual (logical) and empirical matters, and his later view of grammar as *descriptive* of (the rules of) language games (chapters 4 and 6).

160 Perhaps this is as good an occasion as any to comment on the issue of Wittgenstein's remarks on 'mathematics'. Although such remarks are fairly plentiful in some of Wittgenstein's notebooks, they will not be given any special attention in the present study. The reason for this is quite straightforward. Wittgenstein's overall *Denkweise* in his remarks on mathematics is no different from his *Denkweise* in any other philosophical context. Thus a focus on his remarks on mathematics, though it may be helpful, is not *essential* to an understanding of his later approach to philosophy. I have the evidence to demonstrate, though I shall not be presenting such evidence in this work, that virtually every major methodological theme examined in the present study also crops up in an analogous form in the context of Wittgenstein's remarks on mathematics. When a passage is cited which seems to be a remark on mathematics, *that* it is a remark on mathematics will invariably be incidental to rather than essential to the general point I wish to make about Wittgenstein's approach to philosophy (see for example n. 137, in which reference is made to an instance where the notion of 'metalogic' crops up in the context of a remark on mathematics). Wittgenstein in his remarks on mathematics is concerned not so much with mathematical problems as such as with conceptual problems having to do with the 'language' of mathematicians. As Wittgenstein put it in a parenthetical remark he entered in one of his notebooks (MS 113, p. 216, *c*.1931–2), "Philosophy doesn't

investigate the calculi of mathematics, but rather just what the mathematician says about these calculi." Thus the overall philosophical problematic in the context of remarks on mathematics is no different from, for instance, that in the context of remarks on 'psychology'. Wittgenstein himself suggests as much in what has been published as the last paragraph of *Philosophical Investigations*: "An investigation is possible in connexion with mathematics which is entirely analogous to our investigation of psychology. It is just as little a *mathematical* investigation as the other is a psychological one." (Cf. Wittgenstein's draft of this remark in MS 138, p. 23).

161 See TS 213, pp. 417–18; and MS 110, pp. 188–9. Incidentally, in MS 110 and TS 213 the expression quoted ("leading problem of mathematical logic") is attributed to Frank Ramsey. The reference to Ramsey is also in the pre-war version of the *Investigations* (see TS 220, §101). Wittgenstein did not delete the reference to Ramsey until his 1943 revision of TS 220 (see TS 239, §134).

162 See also Wittgenstein's MS 114 (II, pp. 108–10) revision of this section, published in *PG*, pp. 121–2.

163 MS 110, pp. 230–1. The above translation (with the exception of para. 4) adheres to Anscombe's translation of *PI* §120. Thus, for the most part, where the above translation differs from Anscombe's translation of *PI* §120, it should be assumed that the German wording in MS 110 was different. In para. 4, my translation of the expression "Äußerliches... sagen (vorbringen)" as "say (adduce) obvious things..." is in keeping with a point that Wittgenstein makes about his philosophy: it is by pointing out what we tend to overlook – namely, the obvious and apparently 'trivial' things about our everyday use of expressions – that philosophical confusions are eliminated. In the "Philosophy" chapter of TS 213, for instance, as part of a continuation of the last sentence of what is now *PI* §116, he wrote, "What we do is to bring words back from their metaphysical to their everyday use.... And so it seems for the solution of all philosophical difficulties. Our answers must, if they are correct, be ordinary and trivial." (See the original 1930–1 version in MS 110, p. 34. The remark is also in the pre-war version of the *Investigations* [TS 220, p. 89] and in its 1943 revision [TS 239 §126].) And in a similar vein in 1930–1 Wittgenstein remarked, "One never looks deep enough for the philosophically significant things; that is to say, one never descends deep enough into the trivial (most trivial)" (MS 110, p. 140). Aside from these reasons for translating "Äußerliches... sagen" as "saying obvious things...", it has never quite been clear to me what Anscombe means by "exterior facts" (as opposed to 'interior facts'?) about language.

164 It is true of course that Wittgenstein himself says such things: see, for example, *PI* §§109, 124 and 126, and MS 140, p. 23 (published in *PG*, p. 66). In subsequent chapters (especially chapter 6) I shall be examining in more depth just what Wittgenstein meant by such claims. In the present chapter I shall be dealing with the 'explanation/description' distinction only in the context of the apparent contradiction that has arisen, and only as a means of shedding light on Wittgenstein's notion of metalogic as it relates to his shift to ordinary language.

165 Baker and Hacker, *Wittgenstein: Understanding and Meaning*, p. 528.

166 MS 114, II, p. 110 (cf. *PG*, p. 122). This is a revision of the remark as it appeared in TS 213, p. 72. The TS 213 version is identical (in this respect) to the one cited from MS 110.
167 Wittgenstein's final version was probably first drafted in the missing MS 142 (1936), which served as the basis for the pre-war version of the *Investigations*. The pre-war version (1937–8) of this passage (TS 220, p. 90, §112) is the same as the published one.
168 MS 110, p. 229. Cf. TS 213, p. 154.
169 MS 110, p. 230. Cf. TS 213, p. 154.
170 MS 110, pp. 233–4. Cf. TS 213, p. 155, where the remark is followed by a version of *PI* §502. I have already cited the TS 213 version and noted that it is directly linked via MS 114 to one of Wittgenstein's repudiations of metalogic (see n. 149).
171 MS 110, p. 290. First drafted in MS 153a, pp. 98–9.
172 TS 213, p. 488. This passage is also to be found in *PR*, p. 84, and thus stems from 1929–30.
173 MS 107, p. 205. This is identical to the version published in *PR*, p. 51, except that in the latter text one finds the term 'necessary' (*nötig*) in place of the word 'possible' (*möglich*) in the second sentence. It is not clear whether this variance is due to a revision or an error in transcription. It should be pointed out that the second to fifth paragraphs of *PR* p. 51 are all from MS 107, pp. 205–6 – and that the apparent contradiction between paras 2 and 5 in the English version is due primarily to the Hargreaves and White translation of the passages. The paragraph cited above is the second in *PR* p. 51. The paragraph which seems to contradict this remark is translated, "A recognition of what is essential and what inessential in our language if it is to represent, a recognition of which parts of our language are wheels turning idly, amounts to [*hinauskommen*] the construction of a phenomenological language." There are a couple of questionable parts to this translation, but the most puzzling expression is the term "amounts to". This makes it sound as if Wittgenstein had not after all abandoned his quest for a phenomenological (or primary) language, but rather considered himself *to be constructing* a 'phenomenological' language by separating the essential from the inessential in our ordinary one. However, Wittgenstein has just finished telling us that he no longer considers phenomenological language possible, suggesting that *instead* one should separate what is essential from what is inessential in *our own*. This apparent contradiction can be resolved if one translates the verb *hinauskommen* in the sense of 'leads to the same results as'. Thus Wittgenstein is claiming that separating the essential from the inessential, recognizing which parts of our language are wheels turning idly, results in or accomplishes what he previously had wanted to accomplish *by means of* the construction of a 'phenomenological' language – presumably the elimination of philosophical confusion stemming from our ordinary language (cf. n. 227 and chapter 3). My own translation of *hinauskommen* (which incidentally is synonymous with the verb *hinausläufen*) is corroborated by a revised version of this remark that was included in TS 213:

Die Untersuchung der Regeln des Gebrauchs unserer Sprache, die Erkenntnis dieser Regeln und übersichtliche Darstellung, läuft auf das hinaus, d.h. leistet dasselbe, was man oft durch die Konstruktion einer phänomenologischen Sprache leisten //erzielen// will

which translates as

> The investigation of the rules of the use of our language, the recognition of these rules and perspicuous presentation [of them], leads to, i.e. accomplishes the same as, what one often wants to accomplish //achieve// by means of the construction of a phenomenological language.

This shift for Wittgenstein, in effect, transformed his earlier 'phenomonological' efforts into a form of strictly conceptual, i.e. grammatical, enterprise (whose domain is ordinary language). It is presumably for this reason that Wittgenstein entitled §94 of TS 213 "Phenomenology is Grammar" (the paragraph cited above is the first remark in that section). As previously indicated, Wittgenstein's notion of 'grammar' will be examined in subsequent chapters.

174 MS 107, p. 176. Similarly, several years later (1938: MS 160, pp. 43–4), Wittgenstein again explicitly referred back to his early attitude toward ordinary language. In the context of a discussion of the possibility of speaking about objects (for example, a tree) in purely phenomenal terms (*von Erscheinungen reden*), though the term 'phenomenological language' was not used, he wrote,

> As I first expressed myself, it seemed as though ordinary forms of expression wouldn't really accomplish what we wanted of them. As if they were an (old) form of historical rubbish. (A form of outmoded furniture.) Something outmoded, baroque, that would be replaced by something direct, modern.

175 See, for example, MS 107, pp. 3–5 (included in *PR*, p. 103); TS 213, p. 467 (included in *PR*, p. 267); and *PR*, p. 273. With respect to the English translation of the last passage (p. 273), it should be noted that the expression "theory in *pure* phenomenology" is a mistranslation, and should read, "*pure* phenomenological colour-theory." Even very late in his life Wittgenstein tended to use the adjective *phänomenologische* in the sense of 'phenomenal' (as in '*phenomenal*ism') – see for instance his remark in MS 135, p. 90 (autumn 1947), which has been published in *RPP*, vol. I, §1070. In the English translation of the latter remark (§1070) Anscombe (assuming of course that it is not a misprint) uses the English term 'phenome*na*logical' rather than 'phenomenological' as the translation of the German word *phänomenologische*. I shall not be adopting this form of translation, if for no other reason than that few would notice the difference in spelling, and even fewer would have any penetrating grasp of what significant philosophical difference might be

involved (going by the secondary literature in the area, this applies as well to many of those who parade about under the banner of 'phenomenology'). Henceforth, I shall usually be referring to Wittgenstein's earlier goal of a *phänomenologische Sprache* as the goal of a 'phenomenal language'. When I use the latter expression as part of a translation, the German adjective will also be provided in brackets so that those who are interested can examine for themselves whether Wittgenstein is using the adjective *phänomenologische* in a more sophisticated philosophical sense.

Very rarely does Wittgenstein ever even flirt with the noun *Phänomenologie* (see n. 173; *PR*, pp. 53 and 88; MS 172, p. 1, published in *RC*, p. 15; and MS 173, p. 151, published in *RC*, p. 49), and he wisely shied away from it. Around the books housing the thoughts of any original thinker there are invariably cesspools of misunderstanding in the secondary literature. Having abandoned his earlier goal of a 'phenomenal language', had Wittgenstein sensed any affinity between his restriction of philosophy to a purely 'grammatical' (i.e. conceptual) examination of (ordinary) language, and, for example, (accounts of?) Edmund Husserl's strict early notion of 'phenomenology' as a purely 'eidetic' enterprise, he certainly was intelligent enough to realize that the adoption of a label ('phenomenology') of such (by then) common coinage would soil both his own and Husserl's thoughts. Nevertheless, even Wittgenstein's rare use of the words *phänomenologische* and *Phänomenologie* has led to a considerable amount of misguided scholarship. See, for example, the wild speculation in Nicholas Gier's *Wittgenstein and Phenomenology*, which manages to contribute simultaneously to no fewer than four pools of secondary literature (Wittgensteinian, Heideggerian, Merleau-Pontian and Husserlian).

It is telling that Rudolf Carnap, during his 'phenomenalist' phase of the 1920s when he was so influenced by his reading of Wittgenstein's *Tractatus*, also was on occasion inclined to speak loosely of the 'experiential' as the 'phenomenological' (*phänomenologische*) and to refer, for instance, to the construction of values from specific experiences (analogous to the construction of physical objects out of 'perceptual experiences') as a 'phenomenology of values' (*Wertphänomenologie*) involving the carrying out of a 'phenomenological analysis' (*phänomenologische Analyse*). See R. Carnap, *Der logische Aufbau der Welt* (Berlin-Schlachtensee: Weltkreis-Verlag, 1928), pp. 81 and 204; cf. the English translation in Carnap, *The Logical Structure of the World* (Berkeley, Calif.: University of California Press, 1967), pp. 96 and 233. Carnap explicitly acknowledged the phenomenalist basis of his early logical positivism or 'logical empiricism,' as he preferred to call it, in his "Intellectual Autobiography" published in *The Philosophy of Rudolf Carnap*, ed. P. A. Schilpp (LaSalle, Ill.: Open Court, 1963), p. 20. Cf. also Carnap's reply to Goodman (ibid., p. 944). It is also telling that in 1931, roughly during the period of the debate with Neurath – see Neurath's "Protokollsätze" in *Erkenntnis*, vol. III (1932–3), pp. 204–14 – in which Carnap was apparently persuaded that he could 'reconstruct ships while floating on the ocean' (an allusion to his shift away from phenomenalism to 'physicalism'; cf. his "Intellectual Autobiography", p. 38), Carnap (as Wittgenstein earlier) was even inclined to refer to the hypothesized (see my discussion in n. 220) phenomenal basis of his *Konstitutionssystem* as a 'primary language' (*erste Sprache*) or a 'phenomenal language' (*phänomenale Sprache*) (see Carnap, "Die physikalische Sprache as Universalsprache der Wissenschaft", p. 438). There will be further discussion of the general views of the members of the 'Vienna Circle' in chapter 6.

176 TS 213, p. 491. First drafted in MS 113, p. 246 (1932). Much of the "Idealism" chapter was originally drafted during the period 1929–31; thus one finds a snippet of the "critique of the word 'sense-datum'" cropping up in *PR*, pp. 270–1 (cf. TS 213, pp. 488–9). The broken line under the word 'language' in the above quotation is found in both the MS 113 and TS 213 versions. Since this is a device Wittgenstein used to indicate that he was not sure about the appropriateness of a word or phrase, the suggestion here is that he now felt it was improper even to use the word 'language' with reference to what he once envisaged as 'primary' or 'phenomenological'/'phenomenal' language. The sporadic discussion of the distinction between 'primary' and 'secondary' signs that one finds surfacing in Wittgenstein's published 'works' is, of course, speaking to this whole issue of a primary or phenomenal language. In 1931 Wittgenstein more explicitly asserted with respect to the notion of a 'primary sign' what he merely intimates above by use of a broken line under the word 'language'. Carrying on a bit of conversation with himself in one of his pocket notebooks (MS 153a, pp. 273–4) he wrote, "The primary signs as you meant them were actually not signs at all. – Though they were in relation to [*verhalten sich*] signs; like a man's portrait to his name (as my portrait to my name)."

When Wittgenstein took up writing philosophy again in 1929–30, having abandoned his earlier metalogical view of psychological concepts and thus abandoned his earlier notion of consciousness or *das Primäre*, it was his view that, *if* there is any sense at all to be made of the distinction between 'primary' and 'secondary' signs (language), it would not be that of a distinction between ordinary language and some sort of *absolutely* basic phenomenal one, but rather would be a relative distinction *within* ordinary language – a distinction made within and thus relative to a 'language game.' Thus we find Wittgenstein asserting later in the same pocket notebook (MS 153a, pp. 332–3, subsequently included in TS 213, §13, "Primary and Secondary Signs"),

> And I can speak of primary and secondary signs – in *a* [*einem*] specific game, or a specific language. – In the catalogue of pastel samples I can call these the primary signs and the numbers the secondary ones. What should one say though in a case such as that of written and spoken letters? Here, which are the primary and which the secondary signs?

In a similar vein several years later (1938) he wrote,

> One says, sense-data are more primary than physical objects – but that after all means that the our (means of) notation 'physical object'

must should after all in the final analysis [*am Schluß*] refer to [*sich beziehen auf*, be based on] sense-data. Therefore surely only one *notation* can be primary and one secondary. And why should one not call what has proved to be simple [*einzig*] the primary? Otherwise, why talk at all here of primary and secondary? A misunderstanding lies at the root of that. If one says a 'physical object' is only a logical construction erected out of sense-data, then what one has constructed is after all only a language game [*Sprachspiel*]. [MS 121, pp. 98–9]

This matter will be discussed again in the broader context of chapter 5: "Wittgensteinian Relativism and the Dynamic View of Language".

It is worth noting in this connection that in his MS 116 (1937) revision of TS 213, as an explanation of what he had in mind in the *Tractatus* by a 'complete analysis' of a proposition, Wittgenstein indicated that he used to think that "one could and should [*könnte und sollte*] use visual impressions, etc. to define the concept say of a chair [*Sessel*] sphere and thus exhibit once and for all the connections between the concepts, the source of all misunderstandings, etc." (MS 116, pp. 80–1; cf. *PG*, p. 211). He went on to suggest that his earlier view was based on a false conception of language, and that ultimately the analysability or definability of one concept in terms of another, as *definiendum* and 'elemental' or 'atomic' *definiens* (for example, defining 'chair' in terms of 'visual impressions'), only makes sense in the context of a 'language game'. What is ultimately fundamental or primary here is not a hypothesized psychic substratum or a system of signs which seem to express 'elemental' or 'atomic' 'ideas' or 'thoughts', but rather the conventions and rules of use which in *some* cases, under some situations, *might* prescribe the relation of one concept to another as that of 'primary' to 'secondary'. Wittgenstein's notion of a 'language game' will be examined in forthcoming chapters.

In the light of this whole discussion, Wittgenstein's apparently innocuous admonition in *PI* §656 (MS 116, p. 291) that we should "Look on the language game as *das Primäre!*" explodes with a force that utterly devastates the metalogical foundations of his 'earlier' *explanations* of language. Wittgenstein's sporadic remarks on primary and secondary signs in his manuscripts during the thirties are, of course, not an extension or persuance of his earlier so-called 'atomism', but rather an epitaph for it.

177 MS 146, pp. 26–7 (published in *PG*, p. 169, by way of MS 115; also published as *PI* §436). Furthermore, there is some indication that the 'requirement' of which Wittgenstein speaks in *PI* §107 was phenomenal language, for directly after what is clearly a draft of part of *PI* §107 he wrote in quotation marks '*Phänomenologische Spr.*':

> The longer (closer) we examine real [*wirkliche*] language, though, the sharper becomes the conflict between the requirement and truth (actual [*tatsächliche*] language). Preserving the requirement becomes something empty [*Leerem*, vacuous, idle] //the requirement seems more and more as something empty// //If we want to preserve it, then it becomes something empty.//
> 'Phenomenal lang.' [MS 157b, p. 21]

178 MS 152, p. 91. Since Wittgenstein is referring back to an earlier view here, it should perhaps be pointed out that in the *Tractatus* he is concerned with *Sachverhalte* not as extant situations in the world, but rather primarily as possible situations (cf. *Tractatus* 2.201 and 2.22). (He makes a similar move with respect to the notion of an 'object', *Gegenstand*.) In the *Tractatus*, *Sachverhalt* is distinguished in that it is 'thinkable' (*denkbar*) – this taken in what appears to be a metalogical sense to mean "we can picture it to ourselves"(see *Tractatus* 3.001).

While we are on the subject of Wittgenstein's early notion of the relation between language (propositions/words) and the world, it is worth noting that in the early thirties he also repudiated the view that "correspondence with reality" is a metalogical expression. In late 1931 or early 1932 he remarked, "If the expression 'correspondence with reality' is used //is to be allowed//, then, not as a metalogical expression, but rather as part of a calculus, as part of ordinary language . . ." (MS 113, p. 98; also included in TS 213, p. 205, in the "Nature of Language" chapter), while in his MS 115 revision of TS 213 he put it thus: "The expression 'correspondence with reality' (for us) doesn't belong to metalogic, but rather to the ~~ordinary~~ practical use of our ~~ordinary~~ language (MS 115, p. 85). Any attempt to go back and reread the *Tractatus* in the light of the findings of the present study will have to contend with the possibility that also the notion of 'correspondence' in the *Tractatus* might have been intended in a *metalogical* sense – as part of a metalogical *explanation* of language.

179 MS 152, p. 92.
180 TS 213, p. 71. Cf. the revision in MS 114, II, pp. 108–9 (published in *PG*, p. 121), where the remarks first take on the order in which they later appear in *PI* §108.
181 MS 107, pp. 239–40. Published in *PR*, p. 61, along with the two snippets later included as part of *PI* §108.
182 MS 157a, p. 120. Published virtually unchanged in *PI* §93, para. 1.
183 MS 157a, p. 122 – after which Wittgenstein jotted down both the second paragraph of *PI* §93 and also *PI* §94.
184 MS 110, p. 221. Cf. *PI* §108, para. 3.
185 MS 109, pp. 212–13.
186 MS 110, pp. 221–2. Paras 5–7 were also included in TS 213, pp. 71–2. By way of the MS 114 (II, p. 109) revision of TS 213, a version of the fifth paragraph found its way into *PG*, p. 121.

In TS 213, p. 67, Wittgenstein very succinctly stated what was the overall consequence of his repudiation of his earlier attempts to discover a general, abstract conception of language (propositions, words): "But if then the general concept of language, so to speak, dissipates, doesn't philosophy dissipate as well? No, for its [philosophy's] task is not to produce a new (ideal) language, but rather to clarify the one at hand." In his MS 114 revision the last part of this latter remark even more clearly asserted, "but rather to clarify the use [*Sprachgebrauch*] of our language – the existing one" (MS 114, II, pp. 105–6; published in *PG*, p. 115).

187 See *Tractatus* 3.325.
188 MS 157b, pp. 10–12 (the fourth paragraph from the bottom is Wittgenstein's

first draft of *PI* §102). In the same notebook, right after the above remarks, Wittgenstein drafted his first versions of *PI* §§91–2. Especially in *PI* §92, there is a similar, though less explicit, linkage of the (metalogical) notion of 'something lying beneath the surface' and the inclination to give a general conception of the nature (essence) of propositions and language.

The parenthetical reference to Sraffa is to Piero Sraffa, whose critical comments Wittgenstein acknowledged (in the Preface to the *Investigations*) as the "stimulus for the most consequential ideas of this book" (*PI*, p. x). In the above passage Wittgenstein seems to acknowledge Sraffa specifically as having been instrumental in getting him to abandon his earlier strict, general conception of language (propositions, signs).

189 For example: on the notion of 'family' see chapters 3 and 5; on the notions of 'homogeneity' and '*must*' see chapter 3; on the notion of the 'pneumatic' see chapter 4; and on the word 'real' (*eigentliche*, authentic) see chapter 3. The notion of 'grammatical illusions' and the emphasis on 'examples' will be discussed in another volume. Wittgenstein was not a systematic thinker. We can only assemble bit by bit the jumbled pieces of the puzzle that is his later *Denkweise*.

190 This perhaps suggests yet another sense in which Wittgenstein considered the propositions of the *Tractatus* to be 'nonsensical' (*Tractatus* 6.54). Not only are the statements of formal logic devoid of empirical content, but his speculations in the *Tractatus* about the *metalogical* underpinnings of language fell beyond or outside the proper concerns of logic.

Chapter 3 Language Games: the heuristic role of the 'ideal'

191 Rush Rhees, Editor's Preface to *BBB*, p. xvi.
192 As cited by Rhees in *S*, vol. 5, p. 11 (cf. the 1958 preface in *BBB*, p. viii). As found in MS 115, p. 292, the full remark reads, "This whole 'attempt at a revision' from page 118 to here is *worthless*" (the revision began on p. 118 and ended on p. 292). This 'revision' was published under the title *Eine philosophische Betrachtung*, rather than 'The Brown Book'. Neither of these titles was Wittgenstein's title for this material. In 1931 Wittgenstein did entertain the idea of using the title "Eine philosophische Betrachtung" (see MS 110, p. 214), but he probably had TS 213 in mind. As Rhees notes in his 1969 Preface, Wittgenstein actually entitled this material "Philosophische Untersuchungen" (see MS 115, p. 118). This revision extends up to roughly p. 154 of the published English version of the 'Brown Book' (in *BBB*).
193 *S*, vol. 5, pp. 11–12.
194 Ibid., p. 12.
195 For example *PI* §§156–78 comes virtually verbatim from MS 115, pp. 172–218. See also n. 198.
196 *S*, vol. 5, pp. 12–13.
197 Ibid., p. 13. (immediately following what has been cited above as q. 196).
198 For instance, 'Brown Book' (in *BBB*) language game no. 1 is in *PI* §§2 and 7

(and cf. §§19–20); 'Brown Book' game no. 62 is in *PI* §151; 'Brown Book' game no. 67 is in *PI* §157.
199 This letter has since been published in *LRKM*, p. 169.
200 To my knowledge, only once in his notebooks does Wittgenstein ever mention a possible methodological difficulty related to his use of hypothetical language games. On 28 May 1941 he scribbled in a notebook (MS 123, p. 80), "One must describe the language game with an already employed language. The problem at the beginning of my book." Here the 'book' to which Wittgenstein refers is probably the pre-war version of the *Investigations* (TS 220, *c*.1937–8), the opening sections of which (1–22) are virtually identical to the beginning of the published post-war version. However, since the language game of 'builders' is one of the first introduced in the *Investigations* and it also appears at the beginning of the 'Brown Book', the 'problem' Wittgenstein mentions might very well be taken to apply to the 'beginning' of *both* works. Actually in at least part of his parenthetical note to language game no. 1 in the 'Brown Book', Wittgenstein seems to be dealing with the sort of 'problem' mentioned above (see *BBB*, pp. 77–8; cf. *PI* §19; and also cf. MS 136, p. 105, part of which has been published in *RPP*, vol. II, §§203–4). In that the difficulty Wittgenstein explicitly mentions in 1941 can be taken to apply to the hypothetical language game introduced in both the 'Brown Book' and the *Investigations*, though, it cannot be the sort of dramatic methodological deficiency that Rhees suggests separates these two works.
201 MS 135, p. 187 (17 Dec. 1947).
202 Ibid., p. 187. This remark as well as much of its original context has been published in *RPP*, vol. II, §51 and the surrounding sections. See also *Zettel* §82.
203 This latter example is suggested by Wittgenstein. See MS 135, p. 187, published in *RPP*, vol. II, §50; and *Zettel* §81.
204 MS 135, p. 187.
205 Ibid., p. 1 (also cited in q. 22).
206 For example, he hints that if one carefully examines the sense of the expressions we use which suggest a *duration* of 'knowing', 'understanding' or the like (for instance, we say such things as 'I have known the answer for a long time'), one finds that, whereas with 'hearing' one can be distracted or fall asleep and stop hearing, one does not fall asleep or get distracted and thereby stop knowing – and the reason for this is not that 'knowing' was uninterrupted or that men are just naturally so dexterous that they can sleep and know at the same time, but rather that what we mean by 'knowing' (or 'understanding') is not a 'state of consciousness' and it makes no sense to speak of our knowledge being interrupted by our sleep (see MS 135, pp. 181–2, published in *RPP*, vol. II, §45).

In another remark in this stretch of text he acknowledges that we do (learn to) use such apparently similar expressions as 'I know that now' and 'I hear that now', but he exclaims, "my God!, how different the occasions, the applications, everything!" (MS 135, pp. 189–90, published in *RPP*, vol. II, §55). A bit of exploration might show that Wittgenstein's position is further buttressed by the latter claim also. For instance, one says, 'I hear a buzzing sound now', indicating that one is *at this moment* having an auditory impression, but if one says 'I know the city well now', one is hardly referring to a mental state (a mental impression of the city?) – rather one is perhaps indicating that one can get about the city without difficulty 'now' (where 'now' does not mean *just* at this moment). A good indication that there is a significant logical distinction involved is the fact that it makes sense to say, '*Now* I am hearing the sound', but it makes no sense to say, '*Now* I am knowing....'

There is much that one would have to contend with in order to *assess* Wittgenstein's point about 'knowing' – but this is not the aim here. For present purposes it suffices to focus on those remarks which shed light on Wittgenstein's *use* of 'hypothetical' language games, regardless of whether or not he *succeeds* in accomplishing what he wishes to accomplish. It is for this reason that remarks which (for Wittgenstein) might not be philosophically very convincing in themselves can nevertheless be methodologically very enlightening from the perspective of the present study.

207 MS 133, p. 17. This was one of a few remarks written between what have since been published as *RPP*, vol. I, §§586 and 587.
208 MS 131, p. 51. Undated, but the probable date of this remark is 1945, since four pages later Wittgenstein wrote down the following sentence recognizable as the opening of his 1945 Preface to *Philosophical Investigations*: "The thoughts which I publish in what follows are the precipitate of philosophical investigations which have occupied me for the last sixteen years" cf. *PI*, p. ix.
209 MS 137, p. 156. Published in *CV*, p. 74.
210 MS 137, p. 17. The question marks in parentheses are Wittgenstein's.
211 MS 162b, p. 138. Published in *CV*, p. 37.
212 MS 133, pp. 19–20. Published in both *Zettel* §295 and *RPP*, vol. I, §588. This language game was originally drafted just a little over a page after Wittgenstein's previously cited remark (q. 207) that "The investigation of language in philosophy is a describing and comparing of concepts, with the help also of concepts set up (constructed) *ad hoc*."
213 For instance, *PI*, §151ff, some of which material appears also in the 'Brown Book', *BBB*, pp. 112–13. See also Wittgenstein's MS 115 (pp. 182–4) revision of the 'Brown Book', published in *S*, vol. 5, pp. 163–4.
214 TS 220, p. 92 (§§114–15). The first three of these remarks were originally drafted in 1933–4 as part of Wittgenstein's revision of §58 of TS 213, entitled,

Strict Grammatical Game Rules and Vague Language Use.
Normative Logic.
In What Way Do We Talk about Ideal Cases, an Ideal Language? ("Logic for a Vacuum")

Thus one finds versions of these remarks on the *Rückseiten* of TS 213, pp. 255–7, and in MS 115, pp. 50–1. I shall be examining much of TS 213 §58 in an attempt to clarify the shift in Wittgenstein's thinking concerning the proper role of the 'ideal'.

The last two remarks in the above quotation seem to have been drafted in 1936-7 in connection with the pre-war version of the *Investigations*, the penultimate paragraph probably having first been drafted in 1936 in the missing MS 142 (one finds an elliptical revision of it in MS 157b, p. 34, from 1937), and the last paragraph having been drafted in MS 152, p. 87 (1936). Versions of all of the above remarks have found their way into publications of Wittgenstein's material: see *PI* §133 (para. 1), *Zettel* §440, *PI* §130, and *PI* §133 (para. 2) respectively.

'Nicod', incidentally, refers to Jean Nicod, a French philosopher and student of Russell's, who died of consumption in 1924. See Bertrand Russell, *The Autobiography of Bertrand Russell* (London: George Allen and Unwin, 1975), p. 327.

215 MS115, p. 129. Cf. 'Brown Book', *BBB*, p. 83.
216 See TS 213, pp. 251-3. This example (concerning the name 'Moses') was first drafted in 1931 in MS 112, pp. 186-8. Wittgenstein's 1933-4 revision (MS 115, pp. 43-5) of the example was later published as *PI* §79 (cf. also MS 152, pp. 77-8).

In addition to the 'Moses' example, in several places in the manuscripts and typescripts of the 1930s other terms are presented which also seem to serve as illustrations that in using our language we are not always playing an exact game according to fixed and precise rules – or, as Wittgenstein sometimes puts it, our concepts do not always have 'sharp boundaries'. See, for example, Wittgenstein's discussion of the terms 'plant' and 'form of an Easter egg', both of which are dealt with in the same section (58) of TS 213 in which we find the 'Moses' example (TS 213, p. 248ff; but drafted in 1931 in MS 111, p. 88ff, and MS 155, p. 8ff). See also TS 213, *Kehrseite* 68-9 and p. 69 (cf. *PG*, p. 117); and MS 152, p. 89. One could perhaps interpret Wittgenstein as dealing with a similar issue in TS 213, §34 (cf. *PG*, pp. 236-40) where he discusses the concepts 'approximately' (*ungefähr*) and 'heap of sand' (*Sandhaufen*). For the most part these other examples were not carried over into the manuscripts and typescripts of the 1940s, though there is a faint trace of them here and there. *PI* §70, for instance, is a revision of a snippet of the discussion of the term 'plant' in TS 213, pp. 248-9; and there is a slight echo of the *ungefähr* example in *PI* §§71 and 88 (these latter remarks, incidentally, are cross-referenced in the pre-war version of the *Investigations*, and the second paragraph of *PI* §88 was first drafted in connection with his discussion of the 'ideal' in TS 213 (see the *Rückseiten* of pp. 255 and 256). Also as late as 1948 (MS 137, p. 106) one finds an echo of the 'heap of sand' example (published in *RPP*, vol. II, §622; and *Zettel* §392).

217 TS 213, p. 253. First drafted in 1931 in MS 112, pp. 188-9. Wittgenstein's much revised 1933-4 version (MS 115, p. 46) of this remark was later published as *PI* §81.
218 See pp. 62-3 of the previous chapter. In his manuscripts Wittgenstein occasionally makes reference to the "game of truth-functions" (see for example, MS 118, entry dated 23 Sept. 1937, published in *RFM*, part I, appendix I, §2). It is worth noting that what we found in the preceding chapter to be the connection between Wittgenstein's Tractarian quest for *generality* (for example the

'general form of a proposition') and his early metalogical explanations of language turns up again in the context of his rejection of the role that the 'ideal' played in his early philosophy and his attempts (by means of an examination of such concepts as 'plant', 'Moses' and 'game') to rid us of the temptation to assume that when we use language we must be operating a calculus according to precise rules (we must be playing one precise game). Thus compare the account on pp. 63–5 of chapter 2 with, for example Wittgenstein's suggestions in the last paragraph of *PI* §81, and the 'Blue Book', BBB, p. 18. Significantly, in both the TS 220 and TS 239 (1943) versions of the *Investigations*, included in the parenthetical remark in the last paragraph of §81, is a reference to the *Tractatus*.

219 TS 213, p. 254. First drafted in 1931 in MS 112, pp. 190–1. Part of this remark was later included in *PI* §83. The importance of Wittgenstein's new attitude towards rules of language is underscored by the fact that he repeated the above point in several places in his manuscripts. For instance, in MS 112, roughly forty pages after the above remark, he again stressed, "We investigate (our) language *in terms of its rules*. If we find no rules anywhere, then *that* is the result (outcome)." See MS 112, p. 232, first drafted in a small pocket notebook (MS 153b, p. 42) presumably earlier that same year (1931).

220 TS 213, pp. 258–9. First drafted in 1931 in MS 111, p. 118. The parenthetical reference to the *Tractatus* was added in his MS 115 (p. 56) revision of TS 213. See the more detailed discussion of this Tractarian 'symptom' in n. 228 below.

The suggestion in the above passage that Russell also held such a view is perhaps an allusion to Russell's early (1914) essay "The Relation of Sense-data to Physics", published in B. Russell, *Mysticism and Logic and Other Essays* (London: George Allen and Unwin, 1959), where Russell refers to the goal of analysing objects in terms of sense-data as "an ideal to be approached as nearly as possible, but to be reached, if at all, only after a long preliminary labour of which as yet we can only see the very beginning" (see ibid., p. 157). Recall in this connection that there is indication that Wittgenstein also seems to have envisaged the ideal calculus as involving some sort of primary or 'phenomenal' language (see chapter 2, nn. 175–6 and pp. 56–7).

Also worthy of note in this connection is the fact that around the time of the brief period during which Wittgenstein had encounters with the members of the Vienna Circle (in the late 1920s, not long before he returned to philosophy), Otto Neurath in his review of Carnap's book *Der logische Aufbau der Welt* also speaks of an *ideale Sprache*. See Neurath's review in *Der Kampf*, vol. 21 (1928), p. 625 (cf. also Neurath's "Protokollsätze", p. 204). In 1928 Neurath used this expression in quotation marks, but Carnap himself does not use it in his book to refer to his *Logistik*. Carnap's *Konstitutionssystem*, of course, having been based on the work of Russell and the early Wittgenstein, also strove for a fundamental (phenomenal) 'basis' in terms of elementary propositions and *Grundgegenstande* (cf. n. 176 and the discussion of Carnap in chapter 6). Interestingly, the sort of Tractarian symptom of which Wittgenstein speaks above (q. 220) also seems to turn up in Carnap when the latter in reference to the phenomenal basis, to which he was also variously inclined to refer as the 'experiential language' (*Erlebnissprache*), 'phenomenal language' (*phänomenale Sprache*), the 'protocol language' (*Protokollsprache*) and the 'primary language' (*erste Sprache*) (cf. the discussion of Carnap in n. 175), indicated that "at the present stage of inquiry the question of the precise characterization of this language (thus of the precise specification of its words, propositional forms and rules) cannot be answered" (see Carnap, "Die physikalische Sprache als Universalsprache der Wissenschaft", p. 438).

221 MS 157a, p. 108.
222 Ibid., pp. 105–7. This remark was preceded by drafts of parts of *PI* §97. Note that in *PI* §97 reference is made to a passage (5.5563) in the *Tractatus* mentioned above (p. 77). In *Tractatus* 5.5563, by suggesting that the propositions of ordinary language are in "perfect logical order", i.e. analysable in terms of elementary propositions, Wittgenstein was in effect claiming that the 'ideal' order is concrete – applicable to, to be found in (by way of 'logical analysis') reality.

In the margin next to the last paragraph quoted above, Wittgenstein had written "not yet clear". As one might suspect from the similarity in wording, a few paragraphs later Wittgenstein drafted a version of what has since been published as *PI* §101.

223 MS 157a, p. 110.
224 Ibid., pp. 117–18.
225 Ibid., p. 112. Cf. *Zettel* §444 (para. 2). *Zettel* §444, incidentally, was very roughly drafted in this same notebook (see MS 157b, p. 20) in the context of a discussion of his previous mistaken view of the role of the ideal, and also is to be found in the pre-war version of the *Investigations* in a lengthy section (see TS 220, §92) that included what we now know as *PI* §§102 and 103.
226 MS 157a, pp. 114–16. Much of the above passage is readily recognizable as a formulation of ideas that later turn up in *Philosophical Investigations*. The third paragraph, for instance, is obviously a draft of the first part of *PI* §103. The precise wording of the second part of *PI* §103, where again the 'glasses' metaphor is used, was written that same year in MS 157b (p. 18). Also see *PI* §114, where Wittgenstein seems to be making a point very similar to the one made above.

Given the above-cited (from MS 157a) explicit critique of his Tractarian views, it is understandable that Wittgenstein should subsequently have remarked that "The edifice of your pride has to be dismantled. And that is terribly hard work." See MS 157a, p. 116 (published in *CV*, p. 26).
227 MS 157a, pp. 132–6. In order that the reader should recognize some of the above remarks as material later included in *Philosophical Investigations*, Anscombe's 'free' translations have been used – with the obvious exception of the last paragraph (cf. *PI* §108, para. 1). The "real need" Wittgenstein mentions is presumably the need to eliminate philosophical confusions stemming from ordinary language, from our forms of expression (cf. n. 173). Most of the fourth and last paragraphs in the above passage are included in *PI* §108 (para. 1).

Much of the first paragraph cited above is recognizable as part of *PI* §100. The other part of *PI* §100 was drafted in this same notebook and also is concerned with the notion of the 'ideal': "But I want to say: we misunderstand the role of the ideal in our language. That is to say: we too should call it a game, only we are dazzled by the ideal and therefore fail to see the actual use of the word 'game' clearly." Incidentally, in the pre-war version of the *Investigations*, the 'πd' analogy was included at the end of what we now know as *PI* §100 (see TS 220, p. 73).

228 MS 157b, pp. 30–2 (1937). Such remarks in MS 157b are clearly a continuation of the discussion from MS 157a concerning the role of the 'ideal' in his new *Denkweise*.

The first paragraph of the cited passage has been published in *CV*, p. 26; and is obviously a draft of *PI* §131. In the pre-war typescript of the *Investigations* the word *Vorbild* (model) was substituted for the word *Ideal* (see TS 220, p. 85). In the above translation an attempt has been made to adhere to Anscombe's version. See *CV*, p. 27, for a publication of the second and third paragraphs of the above passage.

Although, as previously indicated, it is not the concern of this study to speculate in any detail about the Tractarian views that Wittgenstein identifies as examples of the dogmatic role of the 'ideal' in his early philosophy, it is perhaps worth citing from the pre-war version of the *Investigations* some of the passages in which Wittgenstein himself goes into detail concerning some of the specific Tractarian views that, as it were, dogmatically presented an 'ideal' calculus as expressing the 'essence' of language (words, sentences) but to the neglect of the grammar of ordinary expressions. The following is the pre-war version (TS 220, pp. 85–7) of *PI* §131 as it appeared succeeded by a lengthy critique of his 'ideal' Tractarian notion of a 'proposition' and its 'analysability' (in a later – 1944 – redrafting of this critique Wittgenstein cites *Tractatus* 4.22, 3.21, 3.22, 3.14, 2.03, 2.0272 and 2.01 as the passages he is criticizing; see MS 127, pp. 75–9):

> For we can avoid inadequacy [*Ungerechtigkeit*] or emptiness in our assertions only by presenting the model as what it is, as an object of comparison [*Vergleichsobjekte*] – as, so to speak, a measuring-rod; not as a preconceived idea to which reality *must* correspond. (I am thinking of Spengler's way of thinking.) Herein, of course, lies the dogmatism into which our philosophy can so easily fall.
>
> It is true: a unit of measure is well chosen if it expresses in whole numbers many of the lengths we want to measure with it. But dogmatism asserts that every length *must* be an even [*ganzes*, whole] multiple of our unit of measure.
>
> §108. I had formerly said (in the *Tractatus*) the 'elementary proposition' is a concatenation [*Verkettung*] of names. Then names correspond to objects and the proposition corresponds to a complex of them. The proposition "The bottle stands to the right of the glass", if it is true, corresponds to the complex consisting of the bottle, the glass and the relation right–left (or however one wants to label it). – The ungrammatical [*Sprachwidrige*, incorrect] use of the words 'object' and 'complex'!! A housing complex surely '*consists*' of the houses, and not of

them and their relative locations [*gegenseitigen Lagen*]! And if I say I see three objects on the table, then I surely don't mean: the glass, the bottle and their spatial relation.

One can speak intelligibly to others of *combinations of colours with shapes* (perhaps the colours red and blue with the shapes square and circle) just as of combinations of different shapes or bodies. And this is the root of my false [*schiefen*] expression: the fact [*Tatsache*] is a complex of objects. To say that a red circle 'consists of' redness [*Röte*] and circular form, is a complex of these constituents, is a misuse of these words, and misleading. (Related to: the confusion of colour and pigment.) The fact that this circle is red, '*consists*' of nothing at all. (Frege objected to my expression in that he said, "the part is surely less than the whole".)

§109. But I search, frantically search, for one system, for a *uniformity* [*Einheit*] of all propositions. – And then I become the prisoner of the specific forms of expression of my language, caught in the net [*Netze*, network] of language. – For if instead of "The bottle is blue" we say, "The bottle has the property blueness," and instead of "The bottle stands to the right of the glass", "The bottle stands to the glass in the relation of rightness," and so forth, then it can of course yield the impression that every proposition is a concatenation of names. Then all words with, as it were, *material* meaning seem here strewn [*verstreut*] in a network [*Netz*] of pure logical relations. – And further: all words in a proposition correspond to objects: then 'Paul' signifies *that*, '*ate*' signifies *that*, 'three' *that*, and 'apple' *that*. – This *picture* held us captive. And we could not get outside it, for it lay in our language and language seemed to repeat it to us inexorably [cf. *PI* §114]. In order to escape the spell of the forms of expression, we would have to plough through language.

§110. "Every proposition says: This is how things are...." Here is such a form which can seduce us. (I was seduced.)

Caution should be exercised in how one takes the specific illustrations Wittgenstein offers in the above passages. A proposition such as "The bottle stands to the right of the glass" is not an example of a Tractarian 'elementary proposition', nor is the word 'house' an example of a (simple) name (thus a house is not an example of an 'object' in the Tractarian sense). There is a fairly straightforward reason why Wittgenstein's illustrations are not genuine examples of 'elementary propositions' and their purely 'simple' constituents; and that is, as we noted elsewhere (see pp. 56–9 and n. 176; cf. also both q. and n. 220) Wittgenstein in the *Tractatus* assumed the possibility of a purely simple, ideal (perhaps 'phenomenal') language in terms of which the meaningful 'propositions' of our everyday language could be completely 'analysed', but he never managed actually to construct such a language. Thus in a critique of certain aspects of the *Tractatus* his illustrations must of necessity be, as it were, parodies (couched in our ordinary, rough expressions) of that sublime language envisaged in the *Tractatus* when he spoke of 'elementary propositions' and 'names' (and their 'objects').

It is no coincidence that part of the above critique of his own Tractarian notion of 'objects' and 'elementary propositions', having been drafted in the very early thirties, was included along with his critique of the Augustinian view of language in the section (7) of TS 213 entitled "The Concept of Meaning Comes from a Primitive (Philosophical) View of Language" (compare para. 2 of §108 in the above-cited passage from TS 220 with the remark in TS 213, p. 27 (published via MS 114 in *PG*, p. 58, para. 2)). The Augustinian view of language that Wittgenstein mentions near the beginning of the 'Brown Book', *Philosophical Investigations* and TS 213, and his hypothetical 'builders' language game concocted to illustrate the Augustinian view (see 'Brown Book', *BBB*, p. 77; *PI* §2; and TS 213, p. 25, originally drafted in 1931 in MS 111, pp. 16-17) are of interest precisely because they parody Wittgenstein's own Tractarian view; because they present a "picture of the essence of language" in which "the individual words in language name objects – sentences are combinations of such names" (*PI* §1). That such parodies should be taken as significantly resembling but not identical to the 'essence' of language envisaged in the *Tractatus* is pointed out quite clearly in a remark he made in his 1936 revision of the 'Brown Book'. Having presented the Augustinian view of language and a few variations on the 'builders' language game, Wittgenstein wrote,

> With philosophers the opinion emerges that words such as 'there', 'here', 'now', 'this' are the *real* [*eigentlichen*] proper names, but not the words we would ordinarily call proper names. The latter are proper names only in an inexact or rough sense. Think of Russell's notion of the 'individual', or my 'objects' and their 'names' (*Tractatus*); these objects were supposed to be the primary constituents [*Grundbestandteile*] of reality; something about which one couldn't assert it exists or doesn't exist. (*Theaetetus*.) It seems not easy to say what these elements of reality are. I thought it was the task of further logical analysis to discover them. We, on the other hand, have introduced in (4) [(3) of the English version] proper names as designating things, objects in the ordinary sense of the words. [MS 115, p. 125, published in *S*, vol. 5, p. 121; cf. 'Brown Book', *BBB*, p. 81, and also Wittgenstein's reference to the *Theaetetus* in *PI* §§46 and 48. For an illustration of the sort of Russellian view to which Wittgenstein alludes, see Russell's 1918 lectures on logical atomism in B. Russell, *Logic and Knowledge* (London: George Allen and Unwin, 1956), esp. p. 201. Note Russell's reference to 'sense-data' in this connection (ibid., p. 202) and recall my discussion of the notion of 'primary language' in chapter 2, p. 56ff and nn. 176 and 220. Cf. also Carnap's use of the word 'object' in *Der logische Aufbau der Welt*.]

In spite of the fact that Wittgenstein, for want of concrete examples, had to work with illustrations which were parodies of his ideal Tractarian notion of 'elementary propositions' (and their corresponding 'complexes') and 'names' (and their 'objects'), the critical points that he makes, by way of his discussion of such parodistic examples as the Augustinian view of the essence of language or the previously-cited sentence "The bottle stands to the right of the glass", can be taken as levelled, albeit somewhat indirectly, at his own Tractarian views. Thus with respect to the lengthy passage previously cited, in spite of the parodistic character of Wittgenstein's illustrations, we can take his points about the ungrammatical use of the words 'object' and 'complex' as a critique of some of the specific ways in which his 'ideal' Tractarian conception of language led to inadequacies.

An incidental bonus of the above-cited pre-war critique of the *Tractatus* ('incidental' because it is not directly relevant to the concerns of the present chapter) is that one can glean from the critique some information about the *Tractatus* that helps to resolve a controversy which has arisen in the interpretation of the Tractarian notion of 'objects'. Since Wittgenstein never gives us concrete examples of 'elementary propositions' and 'names', the issue might be put as follows. If '$f(a)$' symbolized a true elementary proposition, say of the sort 'a has the property f,' would the elementary proposition symbolized be a concatenation of two 'names' 'f' and 'a' and thus would the constituents of the corresponding 'complex' be the '*objects*' named 'f' and 'a'? Similarly, in terms of a two-place predicate, if 'aRb' symbolized a true elementary proposition of the sort 'a stands to b in the relation R', would the elementary proposition symbolized be a concatenation of *three* names, 'a', 'b' and 'R' and thus would the constituents of the corresponding 'complex' be the '*objects*' names 'a', 'b' and 'R'? There are those who have contended that Wittgenstein did *not* consider properties or relations to be 'objects' (in his Tractarian sense). Among the proponents of this view is Anscombe, who, although she acknowledges that in his pre-*Tractatus* notebooks Wittgenstein explicitly asserted "Relations and properties, etc. are *objects* too" (N, p. 61) states that "On my view, he no longer holds this in the *Tractatus*." See G. E. M. Anscombe, *An Introduction to Wittgenstein's "Tractatus"* (London: Hutchinson, 1963), p. 109, n. 1. Another proponent of this view is I. Copi, in "Objects, Properties, and Relations in the *Tractatus*", *Mind*, vol. 67 (1958), especially pp. 155–6 and 160ff. On the other hand, there are those such as Stenius who take Wittgenstein as including 'logical predicates' under the Tractarian rubric 'names' and thus viewing properties and relations as 'objects' in the Tractarian sense (though Stenius stresses that there are different 'categories' of 'names' and thus 'objects'). See Erik Stenius, *Wittgenstein's "Tractatus"* (Oxford: Basil Blackwell, 1960), pp. 63, 129 and 136.

It is, however, quite clear from Wittgenstein's previously cited pre-war comments that, in spite of the parodistic character of his illustrations, his criticism of the *Tractatus* is obviously aimed precisely at the 'ungrammatical' (Tractarian) treatment of relations and properties as 'objects', and correlatively the treatment of relational terms and property terms as among the 'names' concatenated in 'elementary propositions'. The Anscombe–Copi account of the *Tractatus* on this issue is therefore wrong; whereas at least in spirit Stenius' exegesis seems closer to what Wittgenstein had in mind (Stenius, understandably, does not deal with 'names' in the ideal Tractarian sense, and he speaks of 'elementary propositions' only in a 'relative sense', see Stenius, *Wittgenstein's "Tractatus"*, pp. 125–6).

'Name,' 'object' and 'proposition' are, of course, among those words Wittgenstein lists in *PI* §116 as used by philosophers but in need of being brought "back from their metaphysical to their everyday use". Going by his (above-cited) criticism of the *Tractatus*, there is no doubt whatsoever that he counted his own Tractarian use of the words 'name', 'object' and 'proposition' as prime examples of such words being used in a metaphysical way. As early as 1930 (the second paragraph of *PI* §116 was first drafted in MS 110, p. 34) Wittgenstein identified it as his task to bring words back from their metaphysical to their everyday use. It was in 1937 (MS 157b), just before the pre-war typescript of the *Investigations* was prepared, that he thought of including his statement of this task along with a reference to some of the words used (or rather abused) by philosophers (especially himself). In MS 157b, pp. 28–9, in allusion to his 'ideal' Tractarian notion of a 'name', he noted, "With 'ideal name' and source of the ideal belongs the remark that we bring back to their ordinary use words which the philosopher uses in a metaphysical way. See typescript." Wittgenstein's reference to a 'typescript' is probably to TS 213 (p. 412) where, in the "Philosophy" chapter, we find the same statement of the task published as *PI* §116, para. 2. A couple of pages later in MS 157b (pp. 32–3) we find Wittgenstein's first draft of *PI* §116, para. 1. For a discussion of Wittgenstein's notion of 'metaphysics' see chapter 6.

229 TS 213, pp. 259–60. In the typescript, after the second paragraph of the above passage, Wittgenstein had written by hand, "this paragraph was copied wrong by the typist". Thus the passage has been cited as it was originally drafted (1931) in MS 111, p. 119. The MS 111 version has been published in *CV*, p. 14. See also Wittgenstein's MS 115 (pp. 56–7) revision of TS 213.

It is noteworthy that the term 'prototype' (*Urbild*) is used in *Tractatus* 5.5351 to refer to such (ideal) notions as a 'proposition' and 'thing' (or 'object' in the Tractarian sense). As we have already found, Wittgenstein came to view the role played by such 'prototypes' or 'ideals' in the *Tractatus* to have been an improper, dogmatic one.

230 MS 154, pp. 30–1, published in *CV*, p. 19. As G. H. von Wright first suggested in "Wittgenstein in Relation to his Times", in *Wittgenstein and his Impact on Contemporary Thought: Proceedings of the Second International Wittgenstein Symposium* (Vienna: Hölder-Pichler-Tempsky, 1978), p. 77, the thinkers Wittgenstein mentions may have been listed in the chronological order in which they influenced him – in which case it would be significant that Spengler's name occurs near the end of the list, next to Sraffa's (Sraffa also having been a major influence on Wittgenstein by the early 1930s; see n. 188).

Although it is of primary interest to us *what* Wittgenstein got from Spengler, and not so much *how* he got it, it is perhaps worth noting some of the points Spengler makes in his Introduction to *Decline of the West* – points which, given Wittgenstein's creative imagination, might very well have inspired him to rethink the role that an 'ideal' played in his own *Denkweise*. Much of Spengler's Introduction to *Decline of the West* is concerned with a rejection of the tendency to write history in terms of a preconceived (Western) formula or schema ("ancient–medieval–modern") of simple linear progress. Spengler objects that this schema, which historians have claimed is the pure "inner form of history" (*innere Form der Geschichte*), is just an "unproved intellectual construct" (*ungeprüfter geistiger Besitz*), an "illusion" which has entirely dominated our historical thinking. See O. Spengler, *Decline of the West* (London: George Allen and Unwin, 1926), p. 16. He suggests that humanity (human history) does not have a uniform essence (e.g. one linear, progressive structure), but rather is a multiplicity analogous to a "family (*Gattung*) of butterflies or orchids" (ibid., p. 21). (Incidentally, Wittgenstein's earliest – 1929 – introduction of the notion of a "family" in his discussion of language employs the German term *Wortgattungen* rather than *Familien*. See MS 107, p. 210; and the discussion of 'Wittgensteinian relativism' in chapter 5.) Spengler considered the notion of one linear (progressive) world history as merely an "abstraction", personal (Western) "ideals" imposed on a multiform reality, claiming,

> But conjure away this phantom, break the magic circle, and at once there emerges an astonishing wealth of *actual* forms – the Living with all its immense fullness, depth and movement – hitherto veiled by a catchword, a drydust scheme, personal 'ideals' [*persönliche 'Ideal'*]. I see, in place of that empty picture [*Bild*] of one linear world-history [*Weltgeschichte*] which can only be kept up by shutting one's eyes to the overwhelming multitude of the facts, the drama of a multiplicity [*Vielzahl*] of mighty cultures, each springing with primitive strength from the soil of a mother-region to which it remains firmly bound throughout its whole life-cycle; each stamping its material, its mankind, in *its own* form [*ihre eigne Form*] each having *its own* idea, *its own* passions, *its own* life, will and feeling, *its own* death. [Spengler, *Decline of the West*, p. 21. For a few terms, I have adapted the Atkinson translation so that it more literally corresponds to the original German; see Spengler, *Der Untergang des Abendlandes*, vol. I (Munich: Oskar Beck, 1923), p. 28]

Rather than view world history as 'one linear progression', Spengler viewed it, as it were, as a multiplicity of organisms (cultural epochs) each with its own "rhythm, form and duration", but which can be grouped into kinds. He proposed that to understand any one given cultural epoch or cultural "life-cycle" (in particular Spengler was concerned with getting clear about the *direction* of West European/American culture) one should employ a method of "analogy" (*Analogie*) or "comparisons" (*Vergleichen*); that is, a comparison of the cultural "life-cycle" under consideration with another cultural epoch to which it bears a resemblance. (See the German version of Spengler, *Des Untergang der Abendlandes*, second section of the Introduction. The Atkinson translation renders both *Analogie* and *Vergleich*, which Spengler used interchangeably, as 'analogy'. *Vergleich* is, of course, the term Wittgenstein uses in his expression *Vergleichsobjekt*; see q. 214). The Roman is the cultural epoch

Spengler compared with that of West European/American culture: "*Rome...will always give us, working as we must by analogies [Vergleiche], the key to understanding our own future*" (*Decline of the West*, p. 26; in the German edition, p. 36). It is now common knowledge, and in any event quite obvious from the title of his work, what dramatic conclusion Spengler reached by way of the latter comparison.

Although my account of the shift in Wittgenstein's thinking concerning the role of the 'ideal' ("ideal language, ideal case") has not been predicated on a description of Spengler's thinking (Wittgenstein's references to Spengler having only served the purpose of helping us to *date* that shift that took place in Wittgenstein's own thinking), given the above themes from Spengler's Introduction to *Decline of the West* it is not difficult to get a rough idea of *how* a creative mind such as Wittgenstein's, even if he did not read much beyond the introduction, might have found Spengler's strategies in thinking (*Gedankenbewegungen*; see q. 230) suggestive and perhaps indirectly applicable to his (Wittgenstein's) own concerns with language. Spengler rejects the dogmatic role that an 'ideal' (the formula of 'linear progress') played in his field; Wittgenstein recognized that in the *Tractatus* an 'ideal' (*not* the *same* 'ideal') played an analogously dogmatic role in his own thinking about language. Spengler viewed his subject matter as a *multiplicity* of cultural epochs that might be grouped as kinds or families within (and perhaps between) which there are similarities; analogously Wittgenstein came to recognize language not as a uniformity but as a *multiplicity* within which there may be "family resemblances". Spengler used an epoch (the Roman) as an object of comparison to come to an understanding of our present (West European/American) epoch; analogously Wittgenstein uses language games (of the hypothetical, exact variety) as objects of comparison to shed light on the facts (cf. *PI* §130) of our language (our extant 'language games', see the next chapter). It is therefore perhaps no coincidence that Spengler was on occasion inclined to refer to his method as a 'physiognomic' method (see *Decline of the West*, esp. vol. I, chapters 3 and 4, §XII); and Wittgenstein himself in his own sphere of linguistic concerns sometimes speaks of the 'physiognomy' of a concept (see *PI* §§235 and 568 and Wittgenstein's remarks in the "Philosophy" chapter of TS 213, p. 410; cf. also my discussion in chapter 4, p. 129ff. of Wittgenstein's use of 'spatial' metaphors.)

Such rough analogies between Spengler's and Wittgenstein's *Denkweisen* would hold regardless of the obviously different subject matters with which they were concerned (cultural epochs and language, respectively); and regardless of whether or not Wittgenstein agreed with the substance of Spengler's conclusions about West European/American culture, i.e. whether Wittgenstein agreed that our present culture is in a phase of decline or whether he felt that Spengler may have confused 'prototype' (the object of comparison: the Roman epoch) and 'object' (West European/American culture) and thus dogmatically conferred on the 'object' features which are true only of the 'object of comparison'.

To jump from Wittgenstein's suggestion that there may be an affinity between his own new *Denkweise* and some of Spengler's strategies to an assumption that whatever is characteristic of Spengler's thinking (including its cultural subject matter) must also apply to Wittgenstein's *Denkweise* would simply be wrong-headed. Putting it in terms of the general methodological problematic under consideration in this chapter, such a jump would involve the dogmatic imposition of the features of a model (Spengler's thinking) onto the object (Wittgenstein's thinking) being viewed in its light. This is the trap Nicholas Gier falls into in his book *Wittgenstein and Phenomenology* when commenting (pp. 60–4 and 95–7) on Spengler's relation to Wittgenstein. In Gier's work we find such erroneous, and at best utterly misleading, suggestions as the following:

> Both *PI* §121 and §131 were originally written in direct reference to Spengler's thought. In an unpublished manuscript he writes, "I am thinking of Spenglers' method" [see n. 228], which was a comparative morphology of cultures. This method, according to W. H. Dray, is "an inquiry into the typical form of their life, their rhythms, and possibly their laws" [Ibid., p. 61]

and

> Wittgenstein's general goal is similar to Spengler's morphology of cultures; to get clear, i.e. to have a synoptic view, of the basic structures of experience itself. [Ibid., p. 63]

Gier does not devote a single paragraph to a careful examination of the specific context of Wittgenstein's references to Spengler. Had he done so, he would have found nothing at all to suggest that Wittgenstein borrowed from Spengler a methodological concern with the "life ... rhythms and ... laws" of *cultures* (whether comparatively or otherwise) and the goal of "a synoptic view of the basic structures of experience itself".

231 It is noteworthy that *PI* §132, which contains an explicit repudiation of the task of reforming language, was originally drafted on the *Rückseiten* of the section (58) of TS 213 in which Wittgenstein explains in what way he deals with "ideal cases" (see TS 213, *Rückseiten* of pp. 256 and 257). Recall that the first paragraph of *PI* §133, where there is a similar repudiation, was also initially drafted in this connection (on the *Rückseite* of p. 257; see n. 214).

232 TS 213, pp. 260 and 262 (apparently due to an error in pagination, there is no p. 261 in TS 213).

233 The notion of 'analysis' in Wittgenstein's writings from the early 1930s on (except, of course, when he is alluding to a view to which he does not subscribe) should *not* be taken in a Tractarian sense. We have already seen some evidence that in his new *Denkweise* Wittgenstein rejected his Tractarian notion of 'logical analysis', among the tasks of which it was to discover the 'real propositions' (elementary propositions) and the 'real words' ('names' *qua* Tractarian 'simple signs'). See, for example, the (second) passage cited (in n. 228) from Wittgenstein's 1936 revision of the 'Brown Book'. In that same notebook (MS 115, pp. 174–5, published in *S*, vol. 5, p. 158) Wittgenstein also

wrote a draft of what is now *PI* §39, at the end of which, in obvious reference to his Tractarian notion of 'simple signs' and 'logical analysis', he remarked,

> the word 'Excalibur' must disappear when the sense is analysed and its place be taken by words which name simples. It will be reasonable to call these words the real [*eigentlichen*] names. – This reasoning rests on various errors: (a) that a word must 'correspond' to an object, whereby it has meaning, the confusion of the meaning with the bearer of a name; (b) a false conception of the philosophical or logical analysis of a proposition, as if it were analogous to chemical or physical analysis; (c) a false view of 'logical exactness', ignorance of the concept of 'family'.

In the manuscripts of the very early 1930s one already finds Wittgenstein explicitly rejecting his Tractarian notion of 'logical analysis'. For example in his section (28) on 'elementary propositions' in TS 213 (originally drafted in *1931* in MS 112, p. 267, published in *PG* p. 210) he wrote,

> The idea of constructing elementary propositions (e.g. as Carnap has tried to do) rests on a false notion of logical analysis. It is not the task of that analysis to discover a *theory* of elementary propositions, like discovering the principles of mechanics.
>
> My notion in the *Tractatus* was wrong: (1) because I wasn't clear about the sense of the words "a logical product is *hidden* in a sentence" (and suchlike); (2) because I too thought that logical analysis had to bring to light hidden things [*verborgene Dinge*] (as chemical and physical analysis does).

Clearly, already by the early 1930s Wittgenstein had rejected his Tractarian notion of 'logical analysis'. From the early 1930s on, he still, on occasion, uses the term 'analysis' in commenting on what he is doing (see, for example, *PI* §383; MS 132, p. 19, (published in *RPP*, vol. I, §413); and MS 130, p. 52), but it is devoid of the Tractarian connotations. Thus, when we find Wittgenstein in TS 213 suggesting that logic should be concerned not with an 'ideal language' but rather with our *own* and with the 'analysis' of propositions *as they are*, to take the term 'analysis' in a Tractarian sense would fly in the face of what he is trying to say – for one of the overriding tasks and concerns of the Tractarian notion of 'analysis' was precisely to discover an 'ideal language' as constituted by 'propositions' and 'names' in the 'atomistic' Tractarian sense (though it seems Wittgenstein never accomplished this task).

234 *PG*, p. 77 (MS 140, pp. 33–4). See the German in *S*, vol. 4, p. 77. The above translation differs from Kenny's in the first sentence, and the punctuation of Kenny's translation differs somewhat from the German (for instance, he leaves out the quotation marks in the second paragraph).
235 'Blue Book', *BBB*, p. 28.
236 As cited by Hallett in *A Companion to Wittgenstein's "Philosophical Investigations"*, p. 52. See 'Blue Book', *BBB*, p. 17.
237 Hallett, *A Companion to Wittgenstein's "Philosophical Investigations"*, p. 52.

238 'Brown Book', *BBB*, p. 81.
239 MS 115, p. 81. This is a revision of TS 213, p. 202. The remark was originally drafted in late 1931 or early 1932 in MS 113, p. 89. In his preface to *The Blue and Brown Books* Rhees cites a version of this remark and vaguely attributes it to "one of Wittgenstein's notebooks . . . which he must have written at the beginning of 1934" (*BBB*, p. x). Curiously though, the precise wording of the passage Rhees cites is *not* that of the MS 115 version, but rather the remark as it appears in annotated form in TS 213 (c.1932). (For the *un*annotated TS 213 version, see q. 240.)

Commenting on the above passage, Rhees writes,

> I think that would be a good description of the method in the first part of the *Brown Book*. But it also points to the big difference between the *Brown Book* and the *Investigations*.
> . . . The language games there (in the *Investigations*) are not stages in the exposition of a more complicated language, any more than they are in the *Brown Book*; less so, if anything. But they are stages in a discussion leading up to the 'big question' of what language is (in par. 65). [*BBB*, Preface, pp. x–xi]

It is odd that Rhees should say that the passage "points to the big difference between the *Brown Book* and the *Investigations*", since the methodological point Wittgenstein makes about the heuristic role of language games is precisely the sort of point he also makes in *PI* §130 (see q. 214). And, even if Rhees is correct in saying (though I do not think he is) that in the *Investigations* language games are "stages in a discussion leading up to the 'big question' of what language is (in par. 65)", it is not at all clear that this is a *methodological* difference between Wittgenstein's use of language games in the 'Brown Book' and his use of them in the *Investigations* – if for no other reason than that one is left not knowing what in the world to make of the language games one finds in the *Investigations after* §65. Rhees does, however, correctly seem to suggest that in neither the 'Brown Book' nor the *Investigations* is Wittgenstein constructing a more complicated language out of simpler ones.

240 TS 213, p. 202. This is the remark as it appears in TS 213 *without* Wittgenstein's handwritten annotations. As such it is identical to the original version in MS 113, p. 89 (1931–2).
241 Baker and Hacker, *Wittgenstein: understanding and meaning*, pp. 89 and 95.
242 MS 152, p. 45.
243 TS 213, p. 201. First drafted in late 1931 or early 1932 in MS 113, p. 88. In his MS 115 (pp. 80–1) revision of TS 213, the above language game is introduced after rough drafts of parts of what we now know as *PI* §§1 and 5.
244 TS 213, pp. 202–3. The question marks around the last clause of the first paragraph are Wittgenstein's. These remarks were first drafted in late 1931 or early 1932 in MS 113, pp. 90–2. See also Wittgenstein's MS 115 (pp. 81–3) revision of this material.

Another problem that Wittgenstein addresses by means of the 'light–dark' language game is the philosophical notion of "correspondence with reality".

It is in the context of this further discussion that Wittgenstein offered the previously cited (see n. 178) conclusion that

> If the expression "correspondence with reality is used //is to be allowed//, then, not as a metalogical expression, but rather as part of a calculus, as part of ordinary language. One can perhaps say, in the language game 'Light!–Dark!' the expression "correspondence with reality" doesn't occur.

Chapter 4   Language Games: the logical *versus* the magical views of signs

245 See, for example, J. Bogen, *Wittgenstein's Philosophy of Language* (London: Routledge and Kegan Paul, 1972), pp. 171 and 180ff.
246 Baker and Hacker, *Wittgenstein: understanding and meaning*, pp. 89–93.
247 *PI*, §559. Originally drafted in MS 147 (1934), p. 20. See also the MS 115 (p. 67) version. It is noteworthy that in MS 147 Wittgenstein's use of the term 'calculus' in his characterization of language appears alongside a characterization of language in terms of the 'game' idiom. *PI* §559, as it was originally drafted, was immediately preceded by a remark in which he speaks of the meaning of a word in terms of "the game that is played with the word" (see MS 147, p. 20). It will be demonstrated presently that such a juxtaposition of the 'game' and 'calculus' idioms was typical of Wittgenstein's writings during the 1930s and indicative of the interchangeability of these idioms.
248 *PI*, p. 14.
249 MS 130, p. 214.
250 TS 213, p. 155 (alteration by hand). The content of this passage will be discussed later in the present chapter and again in the next.
251 MS 156b, p. 26.
252 MS 140, p. 18. Included in *PG*, p. 62.
253 MS 116, pp. 65–6. This passage is a reworking of remarks from TS 213, §20 (pp. 81–2), the section entitled "The Sense of a Sentence is no *Soul*." Cf. also Wittgenstein's 1933–4 revision of TS 213 in MS 114, II, p. 125. Parts of the above passage have also found their way into *Zettel* §247 and *PI* §511.
254 MS 156b, pp. 27–8.
255 TS 213, p. 198. Incidentally, Wittgenstein makes a cross-reference to this part of TS 213 in MS 156b (p. 34), a few pages after the passage previously cited in q. 254.
256 TS 213, p. 40. First drafted in 1931 in MS 153a (p. 138) and MS 111 (p. 111). In his revision of TS 213 one finds Wittgenstein making virtually the same sort of point by way of the 'calculus' idiom:

> A name has meaning, a proposition has sense in the calculus to which it belongs. The calculus is as it were autonomous. – Language must speak for itself.
> I might say: the only thing that is of interest to me is the content of a proposition and the content of a proposition is something internal to it.

A proposition has its content as part of a calculus. [MS 140, pp. 19-20; published in *PG*, p. 63]

The notion of 'autonomy' will be discussed in another context in the next chapter.

257 MS 111, p. 17. See also TS 213, p. 26; and MS 114, II, pp. 36-7 (published in *PG* p. 57).

258 TS 213, p. 260. This remark is from §58 of TS 213, the section in which Wittgenstein tries to explain the way in which he is concerned with ideal cases, ideal languages, in his philosophy. (Several passages from this section were examined in the preceding chapter.) The remark was first drafted in 1931 (MS 109, p. 19). Cf. also the draft in TS 213, p. 259 (*Rückseite*), where the word 'calculus' has replaced the word 'game'.

259 *BBB*, p. 81. A good illustration of the fact that Wittgenstein in his post-1930 writings used the term 'system' (system of communication), like 'language game' and 'calculus', to refer to both 'ideal' (hypothetical) and extant loci of linguistic practice is this remark from 1933-4: "Language is after all languages. And in addition such [languages] as I invent by analogy with existing ones. Languages are systems" (MS 146, p. 67; this remark found its way via MS 115 into *PG*, p. 170).

Baker and Hacker have suggested that Wittgenstein's "abandonment" of the calculus conception took some years after his return to philosophy in 1929-30, but that "His abandonment of the *Satzsystem* conception, on the other hand, was rapid" (*Wittgenstein: understanding and meaning*, p. 92). However, in a remark written in the final years of his life (MS 137, p. 215, from 1948-9) Wittgenstein uses the term 'system' not only positively, but also in such a way as to link it fundamentally to his concern with describing the 'use of words': "What am I aiming at here? Just this, that the description of a use of a word [*Wortgebrauchs*] is the description of a system, or of systems. – Though I have no definition for what a system is." So much for 'rapid abandonment'! In addition to what follows in the present chapter, Wittgenstein's post-1930 conception of a 'system' will again be discussed in chapter 5.

In my opinion Wittgenstein's admission in the latter passage that he does not have a precise definition for the term 'system' holds also for the terms 'calculus' and 'language game'. The reason for this is that he tended to use these terms somewhat loosely in order to characterize generally the way in which he was dealing with language, his general approach to language, rather than as an attempt to give a 'precise definition' of some sort of 'essense' of language. It is not his concern to offer a proclamation about the nature or essence of 'calculi', 'systems' or 'language games' – to do so would involve him in the sort of Tractarian attempts to discover 'uniformities' and 'general conceptions' (for instance, the 'general form of a proposition' and a 'sensational definition of number') that he had rejected in his turn to a concern with ordinary language in its multiplicity (see my discussion in chapter 2, pp. 61-3). Wittgenstein makes such a point quite explicitly as early as 1931, when he explains,

Philosophy is concerned with calculi in the same sense in which it is concerned with thoughts (or with propositions or languages). Were it actually concerned with the concept of a calculus, thus with the concept of the calculus of all calculi, then there would be a metaphilosophy. And that there is not. (One might represent all that we have to say in such a way that this appears as a guiding principle.) [MS 111, p. 110; also in TS 213, p. 67; and MS 114, II, pp. 105-6, published in *PG*, p. 116]

260 *BBB*, p. 25. Recall here the previously cited self-critical remark Wittgenstein made in 1930-1: "In logic we (indeed) seem to have to do with '*all propositions*'. But we only construct a calculus and leave use to its own devices" (see chapter 2, q. 186 and my discussion on pp. 62-3). There also "we" referred to 'we logicians' and in particular Wittgenstein himself in the *Tractatus*. It was the Tractatus 'calculus' that was in a sense abandoned. Wittgenstein's post-1930 conception of a 'calculus' (of a non-ideal or non-hypothetical variety), rather than 'leaving the use to its own devices', was, quite to the contrary, an attempt to stress the use of our everyday expressions.

261 See 'Blue Book', *BBB*, p. 28 (cited in q. 235).

262 TS 213, pp. 40-1. Most of these remarks were drafted in 1930-1: see for example MS 109, pp. 89-90; MS 110, pp. 157-9; and MS 113, p. 50. Wittgenstein's MS 114 revision of some of these and related remarks from this stretch of TS 213 found its way into *Philosophical Grammar* (see *PG*, pp. 70-1 and surrounding passages). Cf. also his later MS 116 (p. 38ff) revision of this material.

263 TS 213, p. 38. It is noteworthy that Zettel §66 is one of the remarks included in this section of TS 213 (p. 38) and thus should be taken in the light of Wittgenstein's overall critique of the 'causal theory' of meaning: "Psychological – trivial – discussions about expectation, association etc. always pass over what is really noteworthy and it is noticeable that they talk around, without touching, the *punctum saliens*." Zettel §66 was first drafted in MS 107 (1929) and was also included in TS 211 (published in *PR*, §31). Cf. MS 107, p. 235 (cited in q. 317).

264 For example, I shall go on to discuss some of the distinctly Humean aspects of the accounts of language given by Bertrand Russell and William James. There will be no discussion of Locke in the present chapter. For a pertinent illustration of his views, however, see Locke's "$\Sigma\eta\mu\epsilon\iota\omega\tau\iota\kappa\acute{\eta}$" ('Semiotics') in *An Essay Concerning Human Understanding* (Oxford: Clarendon Press, 1924), esp. book III, chapters I and II; and book IV, chapter XXI.

265 S. Kripke, "Naming and Necessity", in *Semantics of Natural Language*, ed. D. Davidson and G. Harmon (Dordrecht: Reidel, 1972), pp. 253-355. Kripke's 'causal' account (what there is of it) is not identifiable in any obvious way with what we shall find to be the specific views against which Wittgenstein was reacting. However, Kripke's own sketchy view (or "picture", as he prefers to call it), which is little more than speculation about the causal (and

thus contingent) history of the transmission of the nominal terminology that we use, is not particularly novel and has its precursors not only in one of Strawson's footnotes (see ibid., pp. 298–300) but also historically in the empiricist tradition within which the specific thinkers Wittgenstein was reacting to are also situated. Actually the seeds for a Kripkian 'causal' account of names are to be found in one of the key texts Wittgenstein had in fact read and was reacting to – see the causal account of 'indirect reference' in C. K. Ogden and I. A. Richards, *The Meaning of Meaning: a study of the influence of language upon thought and of the science of symbolism* (London: Kegan Paul, 1923), p. 15; thus it is quite possible that Wittgenstein would have taken exception to a 'causal account' of the Kripkian variety also, at least in so far as Kripke's view has any pretentions to being a philosophical (as opposed to psychological or historical) account of 'names'. For a critique of Kripke's account of naming, see J. V. Canfield's "Names and Causes", in *Philosophical Studies*, vol. 35 (1979), pp. 71–80.
266 See preceding note for publication details.
267 Published in *Mind*, vol. 29 (Oct. 1920), pp. 385–414.
268 B. Russell, "On Propositions: what they are and how they mean", *Proceedings of the Aristotelian Society*, 1919, supplementary vol. II.
269 B. Russell, *The Analysis of Mind* (London: George Allen and Unwin, 1921). See especially chapter X.
270 Ogden and Richards, *The Meaning of Meaning*, pp. 151–2.
271 These points of philosophical contact with members of the English philosophical community (as well as Wittgenstein's contacts with members of the so-called 'Vienna Circle') during the 'lost decade' have been noted by G. H. von Wright in "A Biographical Sketch", in *Ludwig Wittgenstein: the man and his philosophy*, ed. K. T. Fann (Atlantic Highlands, NJ: Humanities Press, 1967), p. 21. For documentation, see the Keynes – Wittgenstein – Ramsey correspondence in *LRKM*, pp. 114–21.

It seems that Wittgenstein also met Russell at Innsbruck in August 1922 (mentioned by Wittgenstein in his letter of 4 Aug. 1922 to C. K. Ogden; see *LO*, p. 58). However, the latter meeting has been characterized as the occasion of the "rupture" of their friendship – see G. H. von Wright, Introduction to *LRKM*, p. 2; and K. Wuchterl and A. Hübner, *Ludwig Wittgenstein im Selbstzeugnissen und Bilddokumenten* (Reinbeck bei Hamburg: Rowohlt, 1979), p. 139. Thus though it was clearly an occasion of contact with a philosopher, it may not have been an occasion of philosophical contact. (Presumably there was a fair amount of discussion of Russell's recent (1920–1) experiences in China and Russia, there having been sparked in Wittgenstein around this time an interest in making a trip to Russia (see Wittgenstein's letter to Engelmann of 14 Sept. 1922, published in Engelmann, *Letters from Ludwig Wittgenstein*, pp. 51–2). If, however, the meeting between Russell and Wittgenstein in August 1922, a meeting about which Russell did not have favourable recollections, did involve even a limited philosophical exchange (and it may have, since Russell describes Wittgenstein as having been "at the height of his mystic ardour"; see Russell, *Autobiography*, p. 322), it seems likely that Russell might have conveyed to Wittgenstein during their

stay in Innsbruck some of the central views (or perhaps a copy of the book) he had published the year before (*The Analysis of Mind*, 1921).
272 Russell, *Autobiography*, p. 354.
273 Ogden and Richards, *The Meaning of Meaning*, appendix A, pp. 395–7.
274 Cited by von Wright in *LO*, p. 4.
275 Ibid., p. 69. Wittgenstein, then, was well-aware of Ogden's and Russell's work during the 'lost decade', and no doubt also was aware that they perceived their views as an improvement on his own Tractarian views – this awareness at least (and probably *not* only) by way of Ogden's critical remarks in *The Meaning of Meaning* (see n. 273). It should come as no surprise, therefore, that in early 1930, shortly after taking up writing philosophy again (the *Tractatus* having been accepted as a PhD thesis several months earlier; see von Wright, "A Biographical Sketch", p. 22), when required to show Russell some written work so that Russell could send a report to the Council of Trinity College recommending that Wittgenstein be awarded a grant enabling him to pursue his research on the 'foundations of mathematics' (see Moore's letter to Russell of 9 Mar. 1930, published in Russell, *Autobiography*, p. 435), Wittgenstein, although it seems he felt he had "nothing written which it would be worth while to let you see: all that he has written is at present in too confused a state" (in Moore's letter of 13 Mar. 1930, ibid., p. 436), nevertheless presented Russell with an assortment of remarks he had written during his first year back (since published as *Philosophical Remarks*) and displayed prominently near the beginning of this assortment not remarks on the 'philosophy of mathematics', but remarks trying to distance the *Tractatus* 'picture theory' from the views of Russell, Ogden and Richards and generally critical of their specific treatment of such concepts as 'intention', 'expectation' and 'desire' (see *PR*, pp. 63ff). This very early critique of Ogden and Russell's views was drafted in MS 107 (1929–30) soon after Wittgenstein's return to philosophy. Note that the 'picture conception' still appears to be part of Wittgenstein's terminological (and perhaps doctrinal) baggage in this early manuscripts, but recall also that in the following year (1931, MSS 153a and 111) Wittgenstein explicitly noted that his expression 'the proposition is a picture' was "a false [*schiefer*: distorted] expression which pushed a certain analogy too far" (previously cited in chapter 3, p. 87).
276 *LO*, p. 84. A month earlier Ramsey himself had published a review of *The Meaning of Meaning*; see *Mind*, vol. 33 (Jan. 1924), pp. 108–9.

The apparent contradiction between Russell's declaration to Ramsey that *The Meaning of Meaning* is "unimportant" and his previous encouraging pronouncement to Ogden that the "causal treatment of meaning does give the solution" (see q. 274), can be explained in any number of ways: First, Russell, having now read the book, may have felt that Ogden and Richards had not contributed anything further to his own insights published earlier in *The Analysis of Mind*. Second, the above remark (recounted by Ramsey) may simply have been the confession of a backscratcher, since in addition to his encouraging letter to Ogden (see q. 274) Russell wrote a favourable review of Ogden's book before February 1924. The review in a "political weekly" to which Ramsey alluded is probably the review Russell published in the 21 Apr.

1923 issue of *The Nation and Athenæum* (Vol 33, pp. 87-8), in which Russell assessed Ogden's works as "undoubtedly important". Third, Ramsey and/or Ogden (see q. 275), being aware of Wittgenstein's low regard for Ogden's work, may have conveyed this to Russell, and thus Russell perhaps called it "unimportant" to avoid a clash with Wittgenstein. Fourth, Russell may simply have changed his opinion of the significance of the causal account – after all, continuity of philosophical outlook certainly was not a distinguishing feature of Russell's philosophical career. However, if he did change his opinion of Ogden's work, it seems he changed it back again a few years later when in a second review of the book (in *The Dial*, Aug. 1926, pp. 114–21) Russell once more appraised the book as "one of considerable importance". In any event, an explanation of Russell's apparently conflicting statements is irrelevant to the point made above concerning Wittgenstein's knowledge of (and curiosity about) Ogden's and Russell's views during the 'lost decade'.

277 Russell's views in *The Analysis of Mind*, for example, drew quite heavily from both American and continental authors of the period, especially William James, John Watson (who read Russell's manuscript prior to its publication; see *The Analysis of Mind*, p. 6) and Richard Wolfgang Semon (from whose works *Die Mneme* and *Die mnemischen Empfindungen* Russell exptrapolated his concept of "mnemic causation"). Thus, in attacking Russell's or Ogden's (and, as we shall see, also James') views, Wittgenstein was in effect struggling against a more broadly based and pervasive intellectual trend of the period. In chapter 6 I shall be examining what *Wittgenstein* considered to be the general characteristics and scope of the broader intellectual trend against which he was struggling.

278 Wittgenstein also wrote much on topics on the philosophy of mathematics during this very early period – a subject area which, not incidentally, was one of Frank Ramsey's main areas of interest. Wittgenstein has informed us that he had "innumerable conversations" with Ramsey during the last two years (1928–9) of Ramsey's life (see *PI*, p. x). See my comment on Wittgenstein's work in the philosophy of mathematics in n. 160.

279 MS 109, p. 210. See also n. 275.
280 MS 110, p. 94.
281 Russell, *Autobiography*, p. 136.
282 Ibid.,p. 395. The "influence of physics" to which Russell refers is the impact that Einstein's theory of relativity (as conveyed by J. E. Littlewood and A. S. Eddington) had on his thinking; see Russell's recollections of the year 1919, ibid., p. 328 (cf. Littlewood's letter, ibid., p. 342), and Russell's Preface to *The Analysis of Mind*, p. 5. For a good indication of what at the time was taken to be the philosophical implication of Einstein's theories, see the paper Eddington presented to the International Congress of Philosophy in 1920 and published as "The Philosophical Aspects of the Theory of Relativity" in *Mind*, vol. 29 (Oct. 1929), in which he acknowledged that the upshot of the theory of relativity is that "Time and Space and *Things* sink to mere shadows" (p. 419). See also Eddington's paper "The Meaning of Matter and the Laws of Nature According to the Theory of Relativity", in *Mind*, vol. 29 (Apr. 1920),

pp. 145–58; and his book *Space, Time and Gravitation* (cited by Russell in *The Analysis of Mind*, p. 5). It is perhaps worth noting that Moritz Schlick also perceived an affinity between Einstein's relativity theory and a Humean phenomenalism, though Schlick was perhaps being a bit excessive when in 1922 he declared,

> On a historical view also, we see the kinship between relativity theory and empiricism, for Einstein was directly influenced by Hume and Mach, those outstanding empiricists, whose philosophy we gladly and aptly designate by the name of *positivism*, since it sees the task of all scientific knowledge in describing the positively given in its relationships. At the time of Einstein's discovery of the special theory of relativity, he was actually occupied in studying Hume, and it is well-known that the claim of the general theory, that in physics *all* motions must be viewed as purely relative, had already been most emphatically insisted on by Mach on epistemological grounds. ["The theory of Relativity in Philosophy" (1922), in *Philosophical Papers*, vol. I (Dordrecht: Reidel, 1979), p. 347]

Mach, of course, was also a phenomenalist. Wittgenstein's reaction to the positivism of Schlick and the other members of the 'Vienna Circle' will be discussed in chapter 6.

283 See Russell's letter to Gilbert Murray, published in Russell, *Autobiography*, p. 493. The so-called "neutral monism" of *The Analysis of Mind*, the view that "the 'stuff' of the world is neither mental nor material, but a 'neutral stuff', out of which both are constructed" (which view Russell credited to William James and the American 'new realists'; see *The Analysis of Mind*, p. 6), is, at least in Russell's hands (and as he was well aware), little more than an embellished Humean phenomenalism. The 'neutral stuff' out of which 'mind' and 'matter' are allegedly composed (cf. ibid., p. 10) seems to have been for Russell the 'stuff' of experience itself, though he maintained a 'dualism' of causal laws (see especially ibid., p. 137 and chapter XV) and, unlike James, shied away from using the word 'experience' as the name of the 'neutral stuff' (ibid., p. 82). For instance, his "main thesis" about mind was that "all psychic phenomena are built up out of sensations and images alone" (ibid., p. 279), he having previously explained to us that what he means by an 'image' is approximately what Berkeley and Hume meant by an 'idea' (ibid., p. 214) and that what he means by 'sensations' is roughly what Hume meant by 'impressions' (ibid., pp. 154–5; cf. also Russell, "On propositions", pp. 22–3, and *An Inquiry into Meaning and Truth* [New York: W. W. Norton, 1940], pp. 239–40) – though Russell seems to have disagreed with Hume as to exactly what criterion should be used to distinguish images from sensations (see *The Analysis of Mind*, p. 145ff). This "true metaphysics", as Russell was wont to call his "neutral monism" (ibid., p. 287), was indeed, as he admits, the standpoint of a "Berkeley, without his God" (see q. 282) or of a Hume.

284 Russell, *Autobiography*, p. 433. Cf. also q. 274.
285 Russell, *The Analysis of Mind*, p. 200. This stretch of text was reproduced

virtually verbatim from his earlier (1919) paper "On Propositions" (cf. p. 21 and the surrounding passages).
286 Russell, *The Analysis of Mind*, p. 201. Also in "On propositions", p. 21.
287 Russell, *The Analysis of Mind*, p. 202. Also in "On propositions", p. 22.
288 Russell, *The Analysis of Mind*, p. 198.
289 Russell, "On Propositions", p. 30; and cf. p. 39.
290 See Russell, *The Analysis of Mind*, pp. 80, 154–5; and "On propositions", pp. 22–3. Cf. also n. 283.
291 Russell, *The Analysis of Mind*, p. 78.
292 Russell's inclination to play psychologist was in keeping with his general tendency during this period to emulate the methods of empirical science. During the "Meaning of 'Meaning'" symposium, for example, he asserted,

> I believe that there is one method of acquiring knowledge, the method of science; and that all specially 'philosophical' methods serve only the purpose of concealing ignorance. ... Now meaning is an observable property of observable entities, and must be amenable to scientific treatment. My object has been to endeavour to construct a theory of meaning after the model of scientific theories, not on the lines of traditional philosophy. [Russell's comments in the "Meaning of 'Meaning'" symposium, *Mind*, vol. 29 (Oct. 1920), p. 401]

Such emulation of science was not solely Russell's pastime, nor was it restricted to Anglo-American philosophy during this period – as is obvious from the philosophical tenets and general sympathies of the 'Vienna Circle'. For an account of the emergence of Wittgenstein's post-1930 view of such philosophical trends, see chapter 6.
293 Russell, *The Analysis of Mind*, p. 86. There is also a version of this law in James, but under its more common rubric 'the law of association'. See W. James, *Principles of Psychology* (New York: Henry Holt, 1890), vol. II, pp. 561–3; and my discussion of the subject in chapter 6.
294 To convert this view into a purely 'behaviourist' view one would need only to restrict what is to count as the 'meaning' or effect ('complex reaction B') – dropping, for instance, all mentalistic talk of 'images' as effects and substituting instead purely 'behavioural' reactions, whether in neurophysiological terms (for instance, Semon's "engram" [see R. Semon, *Die Mneme als erhaltende Prinzip im Wechsel des organischen Geschehens* (Leipzig: Willhelm Engelmann, 1908), esp. part I, chapter 2] or the alteration of other physical 'states') or in gross behavioural terms (for example, the 'actions' elicited by the stimulus situation). The extent to which Russell was in agreement with such a purely behaviourist reduction varied from one stage to the next over his protean philosophical career. In 1919 he considered a behaviourist reduction to be untenable, and strongly opposed Watson on the matter (see Russell's "On Propositions", pp. 9–11). In 1921 he was more conciliatory toward Watson, acknowledging that, although 'images' seem undeniable, words "could, theoretically, be explained without introducing images" – at least in those cases where the processes involved have through

habit become "telescoped" (*The Analysis of Mind*, p. 206, and cf. pp. 201-2). Then gradually Russell seems to have wedded himself to a more purely behaviourist standpoint. By 1926, for example, in a review of Ogden and Richards' *The Meaning of Meaning*, one finds Russell praising Watson's recently published book *Behaviorism* (1924) as "massively impressive" (B. Russell, "The Meaning of Meaning", *The Dial*, Aug. 1926, p. 121), avowing that "'images' should not be introduced in explaining 'meaning'" (ibid., p. 117), and giving a purely Watsonian reading to the law of "mnemic causation":

> People used to speak of 'association of *ideas*', but now-a-days association is rather between bodily movements. The essential phenomenon is what Dr. Watson calls a 'learned reaction'. Two stimuli A and B occur together, and B causes a bodily movement C. Later on, A may cause C, though it previously had no tendency to do so. All words are 'learned reactions' in this sense. There is no need to postulate a 'mental' intermediary between the stimulus and the reaction. [Ibid., p. 116]

In this paper Russell even goes so far as to suggest the following as an illustration of the applicability to 'meaning' of such a Watsonian reading of the law of "mnemic causation":

> The 'meaning' of heard words is explained in a closely similar way. A word and an object having been frequently experienced together, the word, when spoken in your hearing, tends to produce certain of the effects which the object would produce. The effects which it thus tends to acquire are those called 'mnemic', which are more or less peculiar to living matter. They are those which are subject to the law of association, i.e. that they tend to be produced by any stimulus frequently associated with the stimulus which originally produced them. A car coming may cause you to jump aside, or, failing that, may break your bones; the words "car coming" may cause you to jump aside, but cannot break your bones.... [Ibid., p. 120]

The suggestion here is that the 'meaning' of the linguistic stimulus (words) "car coming" is 'jumping aside' – though presumably among children in some remote corners of our world the meaning (behavioural effect) of "car coming" is 'waving one's hand' or 'throwing stones', depending of course on the 'mnemic' history of the natives.

The marriage of Russell's fundamentally Humean inclinations with the conceptual apparatus of Watsonian behaviourism was a typically unsettled one. He never quite managed to remain faithful to the conceptual apparatus of behaviourism, even in his later book *An Inquiry into Meaning and Truth* (1940) where this apparatus is most prominent. (Recall Russell's confession that the latter book was "Hume plus modern logic"; see n. 283.) If one carefully examines Russell's views in this text, one finds strong evidence that here also Russell was indeed still engaged in his earlier Humean indulgences, albeit under the conceptual cover of a Watsonian behaviourism. For example,

Russell's view in the early 1920s that the 'meaning' of a "word-proposition" is an "image-proposition" seems, at least on the surface, to have been abandoned in *An Inquiry into Meaning and Truth* in favour of a thoroughgoing Watsonian behavourist account. In the latter work he acknowledges the possibility of the 'image theory' but suggests that it is "in certain respects repellent" (Russell, *An Inquiry*, p. 230). Consequently, in place of the notion of an "image-proposition" Russell now simply speaks of the "significance"/meaning of a sentence ("word-proposition") in terms of the Watsonian expression "implicit behavior": "A sentence is significant to the hearer when it promotes this kind of implicit behavior, and to the speaker when it is promoted by it" (ibid., p. 237). Russell, however, does not use the term "implicit behavior" as Watson used it – see J. Watson, *Behavior: an Introduction to Comparative Psychology* (New York: Henry Holt, 1914), pp. 16–20, and cf. Russell's comments in "On Propositions", p. 9 – but rather as Kaplan and Copilowish used the term. Yet, if one looks carefully, one finds that Kaplan and Copilowish, at least as Russell interprets them (see *An Inquiry*, p. 231), do not, as Watson did, exclude 'images' from their definition of "implicit behavior" but quite to the contrary seem to *include* them. Thus one finds Russell slipping 'images' right back into his account, and defining the significance/meaning of sentences in terms of "psychological and physiological occurrences of certain sorts – complex images, expectations, etc. Such occurrences are 'expressed' by sentences" (ibid., p. 237).

However, the problem of the conceptual miscegenation of Russell's Humean inclinations and a Watsonian behaviourism, and the related issue of just how behaviouristically (as opposed to mentalistically) one ought to take Russell's 'causal theory' (or for that matter Ogden's, since there is a similar ambiguity in *The Meaning of Meaning*), are problems for Russell scholars, and not problems from the perspective of the present chapter and its concerns. First of all, the main texts Russell published *during* the 'lost decade' and in terms of which this chapter attempts to grasp the emergence of Wittgenstein's (post-1930) 'calculus/game/system' conception were "On Propositions" (1919), his contributions to the "Meaning of 'Meaning'" symposium (*Mind*, 1920) and his book *The Analysis of Mind* (1921), all of which texts Wittgenstein was at least aware of even if he had not read them (Ogden and Richards mention these sources extensively in *The Meaning of Meaning*, and we know Wittgenstein had a copy of this book during the 'lost decade'). In these texts of Russell's, though, in spite of his conciliatory posture towards Watson in *The Analysis of Mind*, the presentation of the 'causal theory' is almost exclusively couched in Humean, mentalistic terminology. It is for this reason that the account of Russell's 'causal theory' given in the present chapter is primarily 'mentalistic' in emphasis.

Secondly, however one *ought* to interpret Russell's 'causal theory', it suffices here to note that there is the possibility of a more purely behaviouristic reading (as opposed to a mentalistic, Humean one). What is important for us is how *Wittgenstein* read Russell (and Ogden). If *Wittgenstein* was reacting to the 'causal theory' primarily in its 'mentalistic' incarnation, then this will come out in the course of further examination of Wittgenstein's work.

It should perhaps be pointed out at this juncture that, although, as will be seen, it is more often than not a mentalistic reading of the 'causal theory' which bears the brunt of Wittgenstein's criticism, there are strong indications that he was reacting to 'causal theories of language' in general, including those of a behaviourist inclination. For instance, his previously cited remark in TS 213 (see q. 262) that "to the causal theory of meaning one can simply answer, that if someone received a push and fell, we don't *call* the fall the meaning of the push" lends itself to a very general reading. The fact that the 'push–fall' stimulus–response relation is not a 'conditioned' or 'mnemic' causal relation would suggest that Wittgenstein was making the very broad claim that, whatever the 'effect' of a word, whether unconditioned (for instance, we might discover some incantation that *causes* our enemies to suffer severe bouts of sneezing or perhaps some more sinister affliction) or conditioned (whatever sort of conditioned response, be it a 'neurological reaction', a 'mental image' or a gross 'behavioural reaction'), we would not *call* the effect the meaning of the word. And this, of course, is neither a denial that words might have such effects, nor a denial of the 'law of mnemic causation' *per se*. Rather, it simply is an attempt on Wittgenstein's part to point out that such effects and the laws which govern them are not what we mean by 'meaning'.

295 Russell, *The Analysis of Mind*, p. 231.
296 As cited by Russell in "On Propositions", p. 30 (also in *The Analysis of Mind*, p. 252). Cf. James, *Principles*, vol. II, p. 283. The italics are James'. As one might expect, James considered Hume's account of 'belief' to be "essentially correct" (see ibid., p. 295). It is worth pointing out that the above passage cited by Russell from James is also cited (and endorsed) by Ogden in *The Meaning of Meaning*, p. 402.
297 Russell, "On Propositions", pp. 20–30. See also *The Analysis of Mind*, p. 250; and cf. *An Inquiry*, pp. 261–2. It seems that the unguents used in Russell's (second) 'idealistic bath' may have been a bit more exotic than those of the original Humean version. Hume defined 'belief' in terms of the 'liveliness', 'intensity' and 'steadiness' of ideas – see D. Hume, *Enquiries Concerning the Human Understanding and Concerning the Principles of Morals*, 2nd edn (Oxford: Clarendon Press, 1927) §V, part 2) – rather than (as Russell) in terms of a feeling *apart* from the idea (image) itself. There is, however, some ambiguity in Hume, he having also spoken of 'belief' in terms of an idea being "attended with a feeling" (ibid., p. 48). See Russell's dispute with James over this exotic matter of unguents, in "On Propositions" (pp. 33–5) and *The Analysis of Mind* (pp. 248–50).

Incidentally, Russell's term "propositional attitude" is probably an adaptation of James' terms "psychic attitude" (see James, *Principles*, vol. II, p. 287).
298 Russell, *The Analysis of Mind*, p. 252.
299 Russell, "On Propositions", p. 32. Cf. *The Analysis of Mind*, pp. 250–1. During this period Russell also speaks of a "disbelief-feeling" or a 'not-feeling' (see ibid., p. 250; and "On Propositions", pp. 39–40).
300 Russell, *An Inquiry*, p. 79.
301 Ibid., p. 115.
302 Ibid., p. 23.

303 Ibid., pp. 264-5 (see also p. 263).
304 Ibid., p. 264.
305 Ibid., p. 368.
306 James, *Principles*, vol. I, p. 245. This passage was reproduced by James verbatim from his earlier publication "On Some Omissions of Introspective Psychology", *Mind*, vol. 9 (Jan. 1884), p. 5.
307 See, for example, John Lyons, *Semantics*, vol. I (Cambridge: Cambridge University Press, 1977), pp. 95-9. Russell's lack of recognition on this score is no doubt due to his burdensome philosophical terminology and the circuitous nature of his treatment; but perhaps also, and not least importantly, due to the fact that Ogden and Richards accompanied their 'causal theory' with a convenient and easily rememberable diagram (see n. 308 and p. 119). Such are, occasionally, the ingredients for historical recognition.
308 Ogden and Richards, *The Meaning of Meaning*, p. 14.
309 Ibid., p. 14. Cf. the summary on p. 382, in which Ogden and Richards simply refer to 'thoughts' or 'references' as "mental processes". Also notice that in the summary the phrase "whenever any statement is made, or understood" has become "when any statement is made, or interpreted". Ogden and Richards mean the same thing by 'to understand' and 'to interpret' (see their definition of 'interpretation' in q. 313).
310 B. Russell, "The Meaning of Meaning", *The Dial*, Aug. 1926, p. 119.
311 Ogden and Richards, *The Meaning of Meaning*, p. 200.
312 Ibid., p. 200. For the barbarism "that *symbolized in* the speaker" [my italics] one should presumably read 'that *which occurred in* the speaker'.
313 Ibid., p. 384. See also my comment in n. 309.
314 Ibid., p. 167.
315 Ibid., pp. 145-6.
316 Ibid., pp. 151-2. It should be noted that perhaps more easily than with Russell's theory (see n. 294) one can if one wishes give Ogden and Richards' causal theory a behaviouristic reading. See, for example, John Lyons' suggestion in *Semantics*, vol. I, p. 98.
317 MS 107, p. 235 (cf. n. 263). 'Psychologism' is, generally speaking, the reduction of a logical matter to a psychological one. The term has tended to be used pejoratively as a designation of a form of error.
318 TS 213, pp. 81-2. First drafted in 1931-2 in MS 113, p. 82. Cf. Wittgenstein's 1933-4 revision of TS 213 in MS 114, II, p. 125 (published in *PG*, pp. 130-1). Recall that in his MS 116 revision (see q. 253) of material from this section of TS 213, Wittgenstein terminologically shifted from the phrase "use in the calculus" to the phrase "use in the language game".

What Wittgenstein might have been up to with remarks such as the first of the above paragraphs will be dealt with further in the next chapter. Notice however, for the time being, that what he asserts about the "sense of a sentence" is roughly the same thing he asserts about the "meaning of a word" in *PI* §560. (The parallel sentence in *PI* §560, which is cited by Wittgenstein in quotation marks – "The meaning of a word is what is explained by the explanation of the meaning" – is evidently a self-quotation; see also TS 213,

§9.) Notice also that in the context of *PI* §560 (see *PI* §559) Wittgenstein again claims that meaning/sense is not something hidden but rather is to be understood in terms of the role or function of the words/sentences in the 'calculus'. *PI* §559 is, of course, one of the passages that has been previously cited (see q. 247 and the discussion which follows above on p. 122ff).

319 TS 213, p. 42. First drafted in 1930-1 in MS 110, pp. 117-18. Cf. the versions of this remark in the MS 114 revision (published in *PG*, p. 58) and in the MS 116 revision (to be cited in q. 323). In the above translation I have not translated the three German words *nicht*, *Tisch* and *grün* into their English equivalents ('not', 'table', 'green'), because the visual and phonetic similarity of the German words would be lost, and thus the point being made would be diluted. Not translating these words in effect provides an illustration of how in a foreign language words can look and sound so similar that one might be inclined to think that what really differentiates between them is the feeling that should accompany them. In his MS 116 (1937) version (see q. 323) of the remark, Wittgenstein's choice of words (*nicht*, *mich*, *sieht*) is perhaps an even better illustration of this.

320 MS 114, II, p. 39. Published in *PG*, p. 58.

321 MS 114, II, p. 39. This remark had been crossed out in MS 114 and thus was not included in *PG*.

322 TS 213, p. 29. Wittgenstein's intention to place these remarks in proximity with each other was carried out in his 1933-4 revision of TS 213 (see MS 114, II, pp. 49-51, published in *PG*, pp. 58-9).

323 MS 116, p. 40. One finds a similar clash in a supplementary annotation Wittgenstein appended in TS 213:

> What are we to understand by the 'meaning' [*Bedeutung*] of a word? A characteristic feeling that accompanies the asserting (hearing) of the word? (The and-feeling, if-feeling of James.) Or are we to use the word 'meaning' completely differently; and, for example, say two words have the same meaning when the same grammatical rules apply to both of them? We can take it as we want, but must recognize that these are two completely different forms of use [*Gebrauchsweisen*] (meanings) of the word 'meaning'. (One could perhaps also speak of a specific feeling which the chess-player experiences while moving the king.) [TS 213, *Kehrseite* 33-4]

On this same page of TS 213 one also finds Wittgenstein's first draft of *PI* §560. Cf. n. 318.

324 TS 213, p. 58. First drafted in 1930 in MS 109 (p. 129). Cf. also Wittgenstein's later revision of this remark in MS 114, II, p. 58 (published in *PG*, p. 87); and MS 116, pp. 47 and 260.

Wittgenstein was quite fond of this 'transaction ledger' or 'account books' analogy, and used it often in his manuscripts. For instance, in TS 213, p. 526, he remarked,

> I always want to show that in logic everything which is 'business' [this word was written in English] must be said in the grammar.

As perhaps the transactions of a business must be able to be read off from the account books. Such that one, pointing to the account books, must be able to say: Here! here everything must appear; and what doesn't appear here, is of no concern. For in the end everything of importance must take place here.

325 MS 116, p. 260.
326 TS 213, p. 414. Part of the heading of §89.
327 MS 116, p. 47. First drafted in TS 213, *Kehrseite* 57–8. Cf. also MS 114, II, p. 59 (published in *PG*, p. 87).
328 TS 213, p. 82.
329 MS 110, p. 176.
330 Ibid., p. 135.
331 Ibid., pp. 126–7.
332 MS 130, p. 192. The 'descriptive' nature of 'grammatical remarks' will again be discussed in chapter 6.

A very important aspect of Wittgenstein's post-1930 view of 'grammar' is his distinction between 'surface' and 'depth' grammar. This distinction, however, can only be properly grasped in the context of issues outside the scope of the present volume. In the present chapter Wittgenstein's post-1930 notion of 'grammar' is being considered only in the respect in which it sheds light on the emergence of his post-1930 'calculus/game/system' conception of language.

333 In the *Tractatus* Wittgenstein's concept of 'logical grammar' or 'logical syntax', as he also called it, seems to have been a formal one (see *Tractatus* 3.325, in which context he refers us to the logical notations of Frege and Russell; cf. n. 187 and the discussion in chapter 2, especially pp. 61–3), and thus, when he uses spatial metaphors in the *Tractatus* – for instance, when he speaks of 'logical place' and 'logical space', his comments, to the extent that they lend themselves to interpretation, lend themselves more readily to a formal interpretation (see, for example, *Tractatus* 3.4–3.42 and 4.463). Quite clearly, however, the seeds for his later use of such metaphors were present in the *Tractatus* even though they were spawned there in the ether of his abstract and formal logical concerns.
334 MS 110, p. 126.
335 MS 137, p. 9. Published in *RPP*, vol. II, §421. See the surrounding remarks in the manuscript, where Wittgenstein also speaks of the 'colour system', the 'physiognomy' of concepts and 'language games' in this connection. Some of the latter remarks found their way into *RPP* §§422ff, and *Zettel* §§354ff.

Although it is hazardous to put very much faith in the characterizations of Wittgenstein's thinking given by some of his contemporaries (this due perhaps more to the obscurity of Wittgenstein's thinking and the fact that he did not publish his work than to any deficiency on the part of his contemporaries), every now and then one can detect from within the garbled reports of his contemporaries the echoes of Wittgenstein's own thoughts. One such report, cited here not for its *accuracy* but rather for the fact that in it one can detect an *echo* of Wittgenstein's own pronouncements in the

Nachlaß involving 'spatial metaphors' (see the above discussion), is Bertrand Russell's report of 8 May 1930 to the Council of Trinity College concerning Wittgenstein's work. After having spent five days discussing Wittgenstein's recent work with him, during which period Wittgenstein "explained his ideas" to Russell, Russell included in his report the following impression of "at least a part of the ideas which are *new* [my italics] since the time of the *Tractatus*":

> According to Wittgenstein, when anything is the case there are certain other things that might have been the case in regard, so to speak, to that particular region of fact. Suppose, for example, a certain patch of wall is blue; it might have been red, or green or &c. To say that it is any of these colours is false, but not meaningless. On the other hand, to say that it is loud, or shrill, or to apply to it any other adjective appropriate to a sound, would be to talk nonsense. There is thus a collection of possibilities of a certain kind which is concerned in any fact. Such a collection of possibilities Wittgenstein calls a 'space'. Thus there is a 'space' of colours, and a 'space' of sounds. There are various relations among colours which constitute the geometry of that 'space'. All this is, in one sense, independent of experience: that is to say, we need the kind of experience through which we know what 'green' is, but not the kind through which we know that a certain patch of wall is green. Wittgenstein uses the word 'grammar' to cover what corresponds in language to the existence of these various 'spaces'. Wherever a word denoting a region in a certain 'space' occurs, the word denoting another region in that 'space' can be substituted without producing nonsense, but a word denoting any region belonging to any other 'space' cannot be substituted without bad grammar, i.e. nonsense. [Russell, *Autobiography*, p. 439]

336 MS 137, p. 125. This remark was written between what have since been published as *RPP*, vol. II, §§667 and 668.

337 MS 130, pp. 71–2. Published in *RPP*, vol. I, §46. The above translation is Anscombe's. *Begriffsbildung* can be translated as Anscombe does in the above quotation as 'the structure of concepts', or, as she differently translated the term in the *Investigations*, 'the formation of concepts', or even perhaps as 'conceptual forms'. The term Wittgenstein used in 1930 (see q. 279) was the German word *Struktur*. That this terminological difference is inconsequential is obvious from the next quotation (q. 338), which dates from the same late period as q. 337 and does use the specific expression *Struktur*. See the discussion following q. 337.

Incidentally, in the version of q. 337 which was published in the *Investigations* (*PI*, p. 230) Wittgenstein cites the "invention of fictitious natural history for his own purposes" as an important feature distinguishing his own approach from that of natural science. Here he is, of course, referring to his employment of *hypothetical* language games (see chapter 3, pp. 72ff, and n. 339). Wittgenstein's concern to distinguish between his own 'logical' investigations and the 'empirical sciences' will be discussed in chapter 6.

338 MS 134, pp. 114–15. These were among the remarks between what have since been published as *RPP*, vol. I, §§917 and 918.
339 MS 140, p. 28. Published in *PG*, p. 71. Notice Wittgenstein's use of the 'system' and 'calculus' idioms in the context from which this remark was drawn.

For an illustration of how Wittgenstein might try to enlist the services of *hypothetical* language games in order to clarify the 'use' of such concepts, i.e. the grammar or 'structure of the language game' with the word 'knowing' as opposed to concepts of 'experience' and 'states of consciousness', see the discussion in chapter 3 (pp. 70–2 and n. 206).

340 See (*perhaps*) *PI* §345. It has become very fashionable among philosophers of language in North America to employ symbolic logic to disclose so-called 'logical structure' ('grammar') and thus uncover the so-called underlying 'ontological commitments' of our language. The dangers of such an appeal are that one runs the risk of falling prey to an analogous (not the same) sort of dogmatism and fascination with an 'ideal' of exactness and order (to the 'neglect of the actual use or grammar of our expression'; see chapter 3, pp. 81–2, and chapter 2, pp. 61–3) as befell Wittgenstein during his philosophical adolescence – and thus do violence to that very language (that fine "web"; see *PI* §§106–7) the so-called hidden 'ontological commitments' of which some contemporary philosophers of language claim to be uncovering. (The history of *philosophy* as well can 'repeat itself inexorably'.)

341 MS 140, pp. 15–16. This has been included in *PG*, pp. 59–60. Cf. also MS 114, II, p. 179. For more on his statement that "the place of a word in grammar is its meaning" see TS 213, pp. 30–1 (where, incidentally, he stresses that it is not 'ideas' or 'images' (*Vorstellungen*) that fix the 'place' of a word in 'grammatical space'), and see also the above discussion (pp. 129–32) of Wittgenstein's use of 'spatial metaphors'.

As with his use of 'spatial metaphors', Wittgenstein's reference to 'rules' of language (as in the above passage, his comparison of language with a 'game' or 'calculus' according to rules) should be taken in the light of his emphasis on 'grammar' as the 'ledger of our actual linguistic transactions' and his 'calculus/game/system' conception of language as 'loci of extant linguistic practice'. One finds Wittgenstein speaking of 'grammatical rules' throughout his later writings. In the early thirties, in, for instance, the context of a discussion of the meaning of a sentence, one finds him claiming (MS 146, pp. 28–9), "In order therefore to say what it [the sentence] expresses we describe the system to which it belongs: the grammatical rules of use, different examples, describe its systematic surroundings [*Umgebung* – see my discussion of this in chapter 5]."

But even as late as 1946–7 Wittgenstein can still be found speaking of the 'grammar' of expressions in terms of 'rules' and suggesting that asking about the grammar of an expression is to ask "about (the) rules, about those which govern the use of the expression" (see MS 133, p. 160, drafted between the remarks since published as *RPP*, vol. I, §§751 and 752). His post-1930 notion of 'grammatical rules', however, should be taken in the sense of 'statements about the sorts of moves that can and cannot be made within a given language game, calculus or system of communication'. The conception of 'rules' in his later writings should *not*, as was demonstrated in chapter 3, be taken as an allusion to: "a kind of ideal order. An ideal rule-governed grammar" (see q. 222) or a "complete list of rules for the use of a word" (see q. 214). As Wittgenstein indicated in MS 178b (date unknown), in his efforts to eliminate philosophical troubles he compares language with a "calculus according to rules", but there is the danger of the "mistake" of alleging that "language is through and through just a calculus according to rules and I could completely describe it as such" (see MS 178b, p. 5; and see my discussion in chapter 3, pp. 76–8).

342 MS 121, pp. 35–6.
343 *BBB*, pp. 41–2. Cf. also p. 65, where the concept of a 'calculus' is again introduced in clear opposition to the 'psychological' view of signs. Incidentally, most of the 'Blue Book' from the calculus remark at the bottom of p. 65 onward is to be found in rough form in MS 147, pp. 66–82 (1934). Mrs. A. Lazerowitz (née Ambrose, one of the students who took down the 'dictation' of the 'Blue Book') has reassured me in private correspondence that Wittgenstein did not read from a manuscript when dictating that 'Blue Book'. However, given that it is highly unlikely that he would bother writing down (and in some instances translating) these remarks *after* the dictation had been made, it seems probable that the MS 147 material was an attempt to collect his thoughts (perhaps in haste and inadvertently switching back and forth between German and English) *prior* to giving his lecture – a draft to which (as was his custom) he did not appeal during his session with his students. Professor von Wright has brought to my attention a letter (published in the *Cambridge Review*, 28 Feb. 1983, p. 56) he received from Wittgenstein several years (9 Mar. 1939) after the 'Blue Book' dictation, and in which Wittgenstein quite explicitly indicated that he was not able to 'prepare his lectures in writing and then read them off in front of the class', but rather was inclined to 'think things out afresh while talking'. This would explain why the correspondence between MS 147 (pp. 66–82) and the 'Blue Book' (*BBB*, pp. 65ff) is only a rough one (if indeed the MS 147 material was an earlier draft).

Other passages in MS 147 where Wittgenstein uses the term 'calculus' in a positive way were later included in *Philosophical Investigations*. For example, *PI* §565 (and the whole stretch comprising §§563–7) was drafted in MS 147, pp. 24–8 (cf. MS 115, pp. 68–70), and as previously noted (see n. 247) *PI* §559 was drafted in MS 147, p. 20.

344 *BBB*, p. 42.
345 TS 213, pp. 160–1. First drafted in 1930–1 in MS 110, p. 102.
346 MS 116, p. 105.
347 TS 213, p. 168. First drafted in 1931 in MS 112, p. 221. By way of MS 114, part of this passage has been published in *PG*, p. 55.
348 TS 213, p. 154. Drafted in MS 110, pp. 229–30. The MS 110 version has been previously cited in qq. 168 and 169. For a discussion of these passages and Wittgenstein's early notion of *das Primäre*, see chapter 2, pp. 53–9 and n. 176.

Actually, there is even some question as to whether the term *Bedeutungskörper* was not also used by Wittgenstein with reference to some of his own earlier views. Although the term was clearly on occasion used by him to refer to an aspect of the psychological views of James or Russell (see my discussion on pp. 122-4), it is not a term really used by James, Russell or, for that matter, Ogden and Richards. The fact is that the word seems to have been a term of Wittgenstein's own contrivance. Of course there would be nothing odd about his having coined the term, were it not for the curious circumstance that when he first coined the term *Bedeutungskörper*, in his annotations to TS 213, §39 (p. 166; cf. his revisions in MS 114, II, pp. 32-3 and MS 116, p. 108) the term was introduced as a terminological variant for *Wortkörper* ('word bodies') and in the context of a criticism of his *own* earlier views about 'meaning' and 'grammar' (some of the context has been cited in qq. 345 and 346). At one point in this section of TS 213 (p. 169; drafted in 1931 in MS 112, p. 222) he even seems to cite what he "formerly [*seinerzeit*] wrote about '*Wortkörper*'" as a "clear expression [*klare Ausdruck*]" of a discussed error, though it is neither clear to which 'former writings' he is referring, nor is it clear that what he had written about *Wortkörper* was his own view rather than merely an illustration drawn from someone else's work.

349 It was presumably in critical opposition to his own earlier conception of 'grammar' that Wittgenstein, in the "Philosophy" chapter of TS 213 (p. 412) and in the context of an emphasis on the investigation of grammar as being 'fundamental', parenthetically cautioned, "The word 'fundamental', if it is at all meaningful, also cannot indicate anything metalogical or philosophical." This remark was first drafted in MS 110, p. 194. See my discussion of 'metalogic' in chapter 2.

Chapter 5 Wittgensteinian Relativism and the Dynamic View of Language

350 MS 108, p. 270.
351 MS 109, p. 58. Much further on in this same notebook Wittgenstein made another remark similar to that cited in my preceding quotation from MS 108, though in a wholly different context, when he once again suggested that "The tactic [or strategy] in thinking [*Denkbewegung*, cf. q. 230] which is necessary here is again the sort of tactic of relativity theory. – When I say: Language just works like this . . ." (MS 109, p. 199).
352 TS 213, pp. 355-6. The paragraph in which Wittgenstein likens his views to 'relativity theory' was first drafted in 1929-30 (MS 108, p. 271).
353 MS 108, p. 277. The first of these paragraphs was reproduced innumerable times in Wittgenstein's manuscripts and typescripts. See, for example, TS 213, p. 4; MS 114, II, p. 4 (published in *PG*, p. 40); MS 116, p. 6; and *PI* §504. The TS 213 version has been previously cited in q. 144. Cf. also *Zettel* §3 and q. 356.
354 Previously cited as part of q. 144.
355 Much later in his life Wittgenstein seems to have made a similar point in *Zettel* §432 about the linguistically 'relative' character of the order "Bring something red." The parallel here comes out a bit more clearly if one reads

this remark in the context in which it was originally drafted in 1948 (MS 136, p. 260) immediately following what we now know as *Zettel* §421. See *RPP*, vol. II, §§312–13, where the linkage between these two remarks has not been broken by Geach's ordering of remarks for *Zettel* (cf. my comments in chapter 1, p. 12).

356 TS 213, p. 7; and *PI* §507. First drafted in MS 110, p. 98 (1930–1). See also Wittgenstein's revisions of TS 213 in MS 114, II, pp. 6–7 (published in *PG*, p. 41); and MS 116, p. 10. Cf. *Zettel* §3 for a point made in this connection similar to that previously discussed with respect to q. 353.

357 MS 108, p. 271.

358 TS 213, p. 88. Cf. Wittgenstein's MS 114 (II, p. 128) revision of TS 213; the MS 116 (p. 67) revision; and *PI* §430.

359 MS 114, II, pp. 128–9 (published in *PG*, p. 133, and *PI* §433).

360 Wittgenstein would also want to deny in this connection that 'there in the use life is breathed into a sign' in the sense that when using the sign a whole system of language, a whole system of rules for the use of the sign, is present to our minds. See, for example, Wittgenstein's chess-analogy remark re-cited above on p. 142 (cf. n. 250 and cf. also Wittgenstein's chess-analogy remarks in MS 114, II, p. 26, published in *PG*, pp. 50–1). The locus of linguistic practice as it were delimits a sphere of licit and illicit moves, but these need not be present to our minds as we employ a sign. Wittgenstein makes a similar point in MS 145, where, in clarifying the sense in which "It is the system [or 'game'] that gives the sentence life" (see MS 145, pp. 78ff) or, as he also put it, makes it a 'thought' rather than meaningless marks (see my discussion of his use of the term 'thought', on p. 154ff.), he wrote,

> That doesn't mean that it is while we are uttering [*aussprechen*; in MS 114 *gebrauchen*, 'using'] the sentence that the system of language makes it into a thought for us, because the system isn't present then and there isn't any need for anything to make the sentence alive for us, since the question of being alive doesn't at all arise (occur). If on the other hand we asked, "Why doesn't a sentence strike us as isolated and dead when we (namely) talk about (reflect on) it, its sense, the thoughts, etc.?", then the initial answer is "Because we understand its sense". . . . [MS 145, p. 79; cf. the version published via MS 114 in *PG*, p. 153]

For Wittgenstein, 'to understand' a sign is to be master of the calculus or system to which it belongs; that is to say, it is a matter of *being able to* carry on in accordance with the 'rules' of the game (system/calculus), like being able to multiply or play chess. But this neither entails that the rules are all present to our mind as we make a move, nor even that we can readily give a clear formulation of the 'rules' of the system or game. Indeed, the latter task might not by any means come easily – thus the difficulty of the philosophical task of clearly describing the grammar of a sign, the role of the sign in the system or game constitutive of its meaning. As Wittgenstein at one point admitted in the course of an investigation of the concept 'reading' in his MS 115 *Umarbeitung* of the 'Brown Book', "The use of the word 'reading' in the ordinary circumstances [*Umständen*] of our life is of course extremely familiar to us. (Though it would be *exceptionally* difficult to describe these circumstances even in rough outline)" (published in *S*, vol. 5, p. 172). Or, as he phrased this point in the version of this remark that was later included in *PI* §156, "The use of this word in the ordinary circumstances [*Umständen*] of our life is of course extremely familiar to us. But the role the word plays in our life, and therewith the language game in which we employ it, would be difficult to describe even in rough outline. . . ." Notice that in the latter version the difficulty of describing the *Umständen* has been more explicitly unpacked in terms of the difficulty of describing the "language game in which we employ [the sign]". The sort of difficulty involved here was more generally phrased with respect to expressions involving psychological concepts in the following remark from 1946:

> We of course know [*kennen*] all the language games in which psychological descriptions are used, nothing could be more familiar. But in our description always infiltrate sentences of whose use we don't have a clear surview [*übersehen*, as in *PI* §122], although we *are master of* [*beherrschen*] them. //although we are master of them in the praxis of language.// //though of course we are also master of them.// [MS 130, p. 219]

Similarly, but more specifically, a couple of years later (1947–8) he wrote about the concept of fear (*Furcht*):

> I now want to say that humans [*Menschen*, people] who employ such a concept would *not* have to be able to describe its use. And were they to try, it is possible that they would give a quite inadequate description. (Like most people, if they tried to describe the use of paper money correctly.) [MS 136, pp. 75–6; published in *RPP*, vol. II, §167]

And again, later in the same notebook, he analogously explained,

> I teach someone a word is used in such and such a way in very particular circumstances [*Umständen*]. Must I be able to describe these circumstances? That is to say, must I be in a position to give a description if it were perhaps requested? If I have learned to carry out a particular activity in a particular room (putting the room in order, say) and am master of [*beherrsche*] this technique, it does not follow that I must be ready to describe the arrangement of the room; even if I should at once notice, and could also describe, any alternation in it. [MS 136, p. 271; part of this remark has been published in *RPP*, vol. II, §331, and *Zettel* §119]

Wittgenstein also once gave a very interesting, if convoluted, concrete example of such a point specifically with respect to the psychological verb 'to understand':

One is inclined to think that understanding a sentence must consist in something at least *similar* to having a picture of the 'fact the sentence refers to' before one's mind. What is true in this is that there is a connection between the capability to produce such a picture and understanding. But the idea that understanding means producing such a picture or something similar is just wrong. When we philosophize we are constantly bound to give an account of our tehnique of the usage of words and this technique we know in the sense that we master it and we don't know it in the sense that we have the very greatest difficulty in surveying and describing it. Thus we are inclined to look for an *activity* when we are to give an account of the meaning of a verb and if some (an) activity is closely connected with it we tend to think that the verb stands for this activity. The use of the word understanding however is such that it is very misleading to say it refers to an activity. The technique of use of the verb 'understanding' is most similar to the technique of use of the verb 'to be able to'. In particular in such cases as 'to be able to play chess'. [MS 166, pp. 56–60; drafted in English]

This illustration is especially pertinent (if convoluted – the remark turns in upon itself) because the overall problem is being illustrated with particular regard to that very concept ('understanding') a clear surview of whose grammar or use is needed in order to deal with the problem. To understand a sign is not having before one's mind the whole system of rules, the whole language game constitutive of the meaning of a sign, and this especially applies to the sign 'to understand'. To prove his overall point Wittgenstein tries to describe, to remind us of, that very sign ('understanding') of which we are master yet of whose grammar (use in the *Umständen* of the language game) we seem not to have a clear surview and for which grammar we seem not to have a ready description. To show that 'understanding a sign' is *not* a matter of 'having before one's mind a mental image' (an image which might be taken to constitute the 'life' of the sign), Wittgenstein tries to point out, remind us of (cf. n. 376, and *PI* §127), as he put it elsewhere, "The analogous grammar of: 'to be able to', 'to be master of a technique', 'to know' and 'to understand'" (MS 130, p. 51, dating from 1946). He maintained this view from the very early 1930s on, and even devoted a section to it in TS 213 (see n. 370).

361 TS 213, p. 88. The second paragraph was a handwritten annotation. Cf. the MS 114 (II, p. 128) version (published in *PG*, p. 132), the MS 116 (p. 68) revision, and *PI* §452. Of interest is the fact that in the MS 116 version of the remark, which later found its way into *Zettel* (§56), the psychological interpretation that is being rejected seems to be linked to Tractarian themes:

My idea is always: if someone could see the expectation he would necessarily be seeing what is being expected. (But in such a way that it doesn't further require a method of projection, a method of comparison, in order to pass from what he sees to the fact that is expected.)
But that is the case: if you see the expression of expectation you see 'what is expected'. [Cf. q. 361]

The requirement of a 'projection method' in order for a sentence to be, as it were, laid against reality is a readily recognizable Tractarian theme, a theme which is displayed in full psychologistic flower in the following passages from the *Tractatus* (3.1–3.11):

> In a proposition a thought finds an expression that can be perceived by the senses.
>
> We use the perceptible sign of a proposition (spoken or written, etc.) as a projection of a possible situation.
>
> The method of projection is to think of the sense of the proposition.

See also my remarks about *Tractatus* 3.1 in the context of a discussion of Wittgenstein's repudiation of 'metalogic' (in n. 149).

362 TS 213, p. 90. First drafted in 1931 in MS 153a, p. 143, and MS 111, p. 112–13. Cf. also the MS 114 (II, p. 129; see q. 363) and MS 116 (p. 69) versions of this remark.

363 MS 114, II, p. 129 (published in *PG*, p. 133). Recall in this connection Wittgenstein's previously cited (q. 343) advice to his students:

> I have been trying in all this to remove the temptation to think that there '*must* be' what is called a mental process of thinking, hoping, wishing, believing, etc., independent of the process of expressing a thought, a hope, a wish, etc. And I want to give you the following rule of thumb: If you are puzzled about the nature of thought, belief, knowledge, and the like, substitute for the thought the expression of the thought, etc. The difficulty which lies in this substitution, and at the same time the whole point of it, is this: the expression of belief, thought, etc. is just a sentence; – and the sentence has sense only as a member of a system of language; as one expression within a calculus.

364 In work in progress, tentatively titled "How to Look on Words as Instruments", J. F. M. Hunter is attempting to demonstrate the performative or 'quasi-performative' character of psychological verbs in general. The above discussion, of Wittgenstein's suggestions in *Zettel* §65 concerning the meaning of the verb 'to expect', would not seem to be inconsistent with Hunter's position.

365 TS 213, p. 373. See also Wittgenstein's versions of this suggestion in MS 114, II, pp. 139–40 (published in *PG*, p. 139); and *PI* §444.

366 MS 114, II, p. 143. Published in *PG* p. 143. Wittgenstein also makes a similar sort of remark about the linguistically relative character of the concept 'intending' in his MS 145 (pp. 55–6) drafts for his MS 114 revision of TS 213:

> If I want to describe (the process of) intention, I feel first and foremost that it can do what it is supposed to only by containing an extremely faithful picture (an extremely faithful shadow) of what it intends. But, further, that that too does not go far enough, because a picture, whatever it may be, can be variously interpreted. – When one

has the picture in view alone by itself it is suddenly dead, and it is as if something had been taken away which had given it life before (as if one still had to intend with it).... And it is correct to say the intention is no phenomenon in so far as an intention, if by it should be meant something about my exact system of expression and not likewise something about merely a specific feeling, is not *a* phenomenon so much as a meaningful sentence that is rather a move *of a game*. A chess move is to that extent also no phenomenon, for the chess game itself can't be present in it. A sentence is something only in a language and also an intention is only something in a language.

"*In language* everything is determined [*kommt zum Austrag*]."

The first few lines of this remark made their way via MS 114 into *PG*, p. 148, and into *Zettel* §236.

367 TS 213, p. 379. The last line was a handwritten annotation.
368 MS 114, II, p. 152. Published in *PG*, pp. 161-2. The reader will perhaps recognize the second of these paragraphs as *Zettel* §55. Recall in this connection the discussion of *Zettel* §56 in n. 361. Cf. also *PI* §429.
369 TS 213, p. 189. See also MS 114, II, p. 75 (published in *PG*, p. 97). Significantly, in his MS 114 revision of TS 213 Wittgenstein quite clearly indicates that the connection he is concerned with is that between *words* and things, and that not as a psychological but rather as a linguistic connection, i.e. one which is to be understood in terms of a linguistic 'calculus' rather than in terms of a psychological mechanism (see MS 114, II, p. 77, published in *PG*, p. 97). The 'harmony between thoughts and reality' remark was first drafted in MS 109, p. 31 (1930), where, incidentally, Wittgenstein uses the expression "(pre-established) harmony". Cf. also the TS 213 (p. 189) version of the 'harmony' remark. In a similar annotated remark on p. 370 of TS 213 Wittgenstein refers to the harmony as in fact corresponding to a "rule of our form of expression (form of our language)".
370 First drafted in 1931 (MS 153a, p. 206; and then MS 111, pp. 182-3), this passage was intended as an insert on the bottom of p. 190 of TS 213. It was to be transferred from p. 143 of TS 213, from the section (35) headed,

To understand a word = To be able to use it.
To understand a language: to be master of [*beherrschen*] a calculus.
[cf. n. 360]

Cf. Wittgenstein's suggestion in *PI* §150. See also his MS 140 (p. 19) version of part of the above-cited passage (published in *PG*, p. 63), where the remark is preceded by the linguistically relativistic claim that: "A name has meaning, a proposition has sense in the calculus to which it belongs. The calculus is as it were autonomous. – Language must speak for itself."
371 MS 109, p. 40.
372 Ibid., p. 58. Part of this passage was previously cited in q. 351.
373 Ibid., p. 60. This was included in the chapter of TS 213 (p. 371) from which another of Wittgenstein's 'relativity theory' remarks has already been cited

(see q. 352). Cf. also the version of this remark in Wittgenstein's draft of material for his MS 114 revision of TS 213 in MS 145 (p. 46), later published via MS 114 in *PG*, p. 140.
374 MS 145, p. 65. Later published (via MS 114) in *PG*, p. 149.
375 MS 145, pp. 73–4. Later published (via MS 114) in *PG*, p. 151.
376 MS 156b, pp. 12–13 (cf. q. 342). These remarks are from a small pocket notebook in which Wittgenstein drafted passages for his MS 114 revision of TS 213. By his reference in the above passage to "agreements about language" Wittgenstein should not be taken to be suggesting that 'grammar' is a matter of *coming* to a 'consensus' (*agreement*) which then determines, stipulates or fixes the rules of use of our expressions. Quite to the contrary, it is the loci of linguistic practice which 'determine' the rules in that the loci of linguistic practice involve uniformities of activity which are describable *in terms of* rules. 'Grammar' is a description of these loci, and to the extent that it involves 'agreements' it is more an agreement over which moves *are* and which *are not* made in the various loci of linguistic practice than a prescriptive determination or setting of rules. This is why in the above passage Wittgenstein calls 'grammar' a "gathering of recollections about rules". In another manuscript he can be read as making a similar point where in the context of a discussion of "How is the use of a rule fixed?" he answers that if this question means

> How does it come about that we use them (in agreement) like this and not otherwise? Then through training, drill and the forms of our life [*die Formen unsres Lebens*].
> It is a matter not of a consensus of opinion but rather of forms of life [*Lebensformen*]. [MS 160, p. 51; cf. *PI* §241]

See also my comments about 'rules' in n. 360.
377 MS 110, p. 71. Similarly, but more generally, Wittgenstein claimed earlier in this same notebook that "Language works relatively, not absolutely" (ibid., p. 1).
378 Ibid., p. 70. As one might suspect, several of the remarks from this stretch (for instance, the remark having to do with the question of 'how an order anticipates its execution') were included in the chapter of TS 213 (for instance, p. 377) from which the previously cited (q. 352) 'relativity theory' remark was drawn. In his MS 114 (II, pp. 149–50, published in *PG*, p. 161) revision of this TS 213 material Wittgenstein simply made the outright suggestion that, "When I think in language, there aren't meanings going through my mind in addition to the verbal expressions; the language is itself the vehicle of thought" (drafted as an annotation in TS 213, *Rückseite* of p. 382). Clearly, the psychological view of signs is being attacked here.
379 MS 110, pp. 72–3.
380 In the stretch of text from which the above relativity remark (q. 377) was cited, one finds Wittgenstein illustrating his point with respect to the concept of 'wishing', and making such linguistically relativistic claims as

> An expression must be part of a form of expression [*Ausdrucksweise*].
> The expression of the wish contains the wish and is not a translation of the wish or somehow co-ordinated with it.
> That is to say: the wish itself is articulate.
> The expression of the wish is not a subsequent announcement of the wish which is already imprinted there in miniature beforehand. [MS 110, p. 73]

These remarks are clearly a very early (1930–1) formulation of the sort of point cited previously from MS 145 (cf. qq. 374 and 375) – namely, the claim that 'the expression of a wish is the wish', and the system of language is determinative of its sense, not the presence of some peculiar spirit.

381 MS 110, p. 74. Included in TS 213, p. 226.
382 TS 213, p. 212. See also the versions in MS 114, II, p. 89 (published in *PG*, p. 104) and *PI* §435.
383 TS 213, pp. 213–14. Cf. MS 114, II, p. 89 (published in *PG*, p. 104).
384 TS 213, p. 226. Cf. the version in MS 114, II, p. 95 (published in *PG*, p. 108).
385 TS 213, p. 220, Cf. the MS 114 (II, p. 90) version published in *PG*, p. 106. Versions of this and a succeeding remark from TS 213 were also later included in *Zettel* §§605–6.
386 TS 213, p. 221. First drafted in 1930 in MS 110, p. 3. Cf. the MS 114 (II, p. 90) revision of TS 213 published in *PG*, p. 106.
387 MS 146, pp. 26–7. Previously cited in q. 177 (cf. my discussion of this remark in the context of the issues dealt with in chapter 2, p. 57). The MS 115 version of the remark was included in *PG*, p. 169. Note that in *PI* §436 the remark immediately follows the passage cited above in q. 382.
388 MS 114, II, p. 91. Published in *PG*, p. 107. The last of the above paragraphs was drafted in TS 213 on the *Rückseite* of p. 221. Cf. TS 213, p. 223 (previously cited in q. 148); and qq. 140 and 146. Part of the above passage later found its way into *Zettel* §143, where, incidentally, the remark appears followed by a suggestion that one might just as well be able to account for the signification of signs were there no such thing as psychological accompaniments (impressions) along with the signs – in which case "The sign is alive only in the system" (see *Zettel* §146). It is noteworthy that in MS 114 the passage cited above was immediately followed by a version of Wittgenstein's "French politician" anecdote (see my q. 147 and my comments in n. 149).
389 TS 213, p. 211. Cf. also the versions in the MS 114 (II, p. 88, published in *PG*, p. 104) and MS 117 (1937–8; p. 127) revisions of TS 213.
390 TS 213, pp. 211–12. Cf. Wittgenstein's revisions of this remark in MS 114 (II, pp. 88–9, published in *PG*, p. 104); and in MS 117 (p. 128).
391 MS 114, II, p. 89. Published in *PG*, p. 104.
392 MS 117, pp. 127–9. In another manuscript written during roughly this same period (1937–8), Wittgenstein seems to make the sort of point that he does above, only in terms of the 'language game' idiom, when he similarly advises,

> It will become clear to you about the uselessness of the <u>common view</u> of meaning, sense and truth. (More about this later)

Don't think (so much) about the images which accompany the word, sentence, but rather about its use in the language game. Don't ask whether this sentence 'can be thought' and try to decide it through introspection.... [MS 160, p. 54]

Similarly, the emphasis (in the last paragraph of q. 392) on the 'life surrounding (*umgeben*) an expression' as in fact the mechanism or 'calculus' (see q. 391) we need to understand in order to clarify the meaning of an expression is also distinctly echoed in a general point Wittgenstein made in the early 1940s about the meaning of the expression 'to follow a rule':

> What we in a complicated surrounding [*Umgebung*] call 'to follow a rule', we would surely not call it that if it stood there in isolation.
> Language [i.e. a verbal or written sign] I might say is based on a *way* of life [*Lebenweise*].
> In order to describe the phenomenon of language one must describe a practice [*Praxis*], not an isolated event, of *whichever kind* it is.
> This is a very difficult insight. [MS 164, pp. 98–9, published in *S*, vol. 6, pp. 335–6]

The *Umgebung*, the *Praxis*, of which Wittgenstein speaks is of course the locus of linguistic practice (language game, calculus, system of communication) constitutive of the 'life' (meaning) of a given expression. As Wittgenstein put the point later in this same manuscript: "Only in a praxis can a word have meaning. //Only in the praxis of language//" (MS 164, p. 124; cf. also his remarks on 'linguistic system' (*Sprachsystem*) and 'agreement of activity [or life, *Leben*]' in MS 164, pp. 162–4).

393 See Wittgenstein's annotations in TS 213, p. 209, and on the facing page (the *Rückseite* of p. 208). Cf. also his MS 115 (pp. 87–8) revision of TS 213 and MS 152, pp. 47–8. Recall that qq. 389 and 390 were from TS 213, pp. 211–12.

394 MS 165, pp. 110–11. The second of the above paragraphs was later included in *PI* §206. For the various subsequent draftings of the remarks that went into *PI* §206 see also MS 124, pp. 208, 278; MS 180a, pp. 4–6; and MS 129, pp. 29–30, 89.

It is worth noting that the question raised by Wittgenstein in the second paragraph of *PI* §206 – namely, 'What circumstances (*Umständen*) would be required in order to be able to attribute to a foreign people (a foreign language) language games similar to our own (for instance, "ordering")?' is a question also raised in the general stretch of MS 165 in which the above passage was drafted. In MS 165 (pp. 97–8), Wittgenstein suggested that

> If an explorer came to a land in which was spoken a language wholly unknown to him, he could learn to understand it only through the connection with the rest of the life of the inhabitants. What we call, for example, 'instructing', or "ordering", 'questioning', 'answering', 'describing', and so on, are all linked with wholly specific human

actions [*Handlungen*]; and an order is only distinguishable as an order by the circumstances [*Umständen*] which (accompany it) precede or follow it.

The *Umständen* referred to here are of course not psychological accompaniments (of which we observe nothing anyway, whether with respect to a foreign people or to each other), but rather those *Umständen* essential to the loci of linguistic practice, the language games, constitutive of the meaning of the signs. See for instance my previous discussion (on pp. 151-3) of *Umständen* in connection with *Zettel* §65 (see also my discussion in n. 360). Recall that 'ordering' and 'describing' are on the list of language games published in *PI* §23. In the TS 213 (*Rückseite* of p. 208; cf. also MS 115, p. 87) draft of the *PI* §23 list, 'questioning' and 'answering' were also included as examples of language games.

395 MS 133, p. 54 (1946-7). Cf. the version published via TS 229 in *RPP*, vol. I, §630.

396 There is also a strong indication in Wittgenstein's 1936 *Umarbeitung* of the so-called 'Brown Book' that one of his primary objectives for introducing some of the hypothetical language games at the beginning of that work was to draw a contrast between the multiplicity of possble language games and his own earlier simplistic Tractarian view of language (see q. 215).

397 MS 109, p. 140 (cf. p. 164). Also in this stretch of the manuscript Wittgenstein discusses the meaning of the word 'now', which the reader will recall is one of the candidates logicians had come up with as an example of a real 'name' or simple sign (see the passage cited in n. 228 from Wittgenstein's MS 115 *Umarbeitung* of the 'Brown Book'). A discussion of the meaning of the word 'now' ('here', 'this' [cf. n. 228 and *PI* §§38 and 45], and so on) is the same sort of context of discussion in which Wittgenstein first drafted what we know as *PI* §39 (see MS 115, pp. 173-5, published in *S*, vol. 5, pp. 156-8). In this latter context, consistent with his 'linguistically relative' approach to what constitutes the life of a sign, one finds him stressing that the function of the allegedly simple name 'now' is "entirely different from that of a specification of time [*Zeitangaben*].... This can easily be seen if you look at which role the word plays in the usage [*Gebrauch*] of language, I mean in the whole praxis of language [*ganzen Praxis der Sprache*]...." In the English 'Brown Book' version (of which the above is a revision), instead of the phrase "the whole praxis of language" Wittgenstein had simply written "the *whole language game*" (see *BBB*, p. 108).

398 MS 115, pp. 173-5. Published in *S*, vol. 5, p. 158. Part of this passage has been previously cited in n. 233 in my discussion of Wittgenstein's notion of 'analysis'.

399 MS 153a, p. 149. Included also in MS 111, p. 115.

400 TS 213, p. 13. First drafted in 1931 in MS 112, pp. 182-4. Cf. also MS 145, pp. 80-1; and Wittgenstein's MS 114 (II) revision of TS 213 (published in *PG*, p. 152, but note that Kenny's unfortunate translation of the terms *Spiel* and *systematischen Spiel* voids Wittgenstein's allusion there to his 'calculus/game/system' conception of language).

The 'arrow' illustration Wittgenstein gives in the above passage, and in particular the psychological view of the signification of signs that is being rejected in this connection, also turns up in *PI* §454:

> "Everything is already there in...." How does it come about that this arrow → *points*? Doesn't it seem to carry in it something besides itself? – "No, not the dead line on paper; only the psychical thing, the meaning, can do that." – That is both true and false. The arrow points only in the application [*Anwendung*, use] that a living being makes of it.
>
> This pointing is *not* a hocus-pocus which can be performed only by the soul.

It is not coincidental that in the *Investigations* this passage appears in the context of some of the linguistically relativistic remarks (for instance, *PI* §§452 and 453) that have already been discussed in the present chapter (see pp. 148–50). In *PI* §454 there is both a repudiation of a psychological view of the signification of signs and an indication of Wittgenstein's own linguistically relativistic alternative view. His view, however, is not at all clearly spelled out in the remark, he having only suggested that the 'life' of the sign (the arrow) is not a psychic thing accompanying it but that it is 'alive' (i.e. *points*) only in the *use* (cf. *PI* §§431–2, cited on p. 148). 'Use' here (as elsewhere, see my discussion on pp. 148–50) should be taken as a reference to the function or role ('place') of the sign (in this case the arrow) in the grammatical system or locus of linguistic practice to which it belongs. The linguistically relativistic import of this is perhaps most clearly evidenced in one of Wittgenstein's earliest introductions of the 'arrow' illustrations in TS 213, in the section headed, "A proposition is a sign in a system of signs. It is one combination of signs among a number of possible ones, and as opposed to other possible ones. As it were one position of a pointer [*Zeigerstellung*] as opposed to other possible ones" (TS 213, p. 93; via MS 114 this heading was later included as a remark in *PG*, p. 131). To show that a pointer, an arrow, is a meaningful sign (for example, *points* in a direction) only within, that is to say *relative to*, a grammatical system to which it belongs, Wittgenstein goes on to illustrate how it is that *what* an arrow signifies (for instance, if it is used as an 'order' or 'instruction' to do something, *what* it is that an arrow orders one to do) is relative to the grammatical rules for its application, relative to its role or function within a system (calculus, language game), and there might be any number of grammatical systems relative to each of which the arrow would have a different 'life', a different signification:

> ↑ in contrast to ↗ is a different sign from ↑ in contrast to ↓
>
> "Go in this way ↑ not in this way ↗" only makes sense if it is the direction that is essential to the arrow here and not perhaps just the length....
>
> "Go in the direction in which the arrow points."
> "Go as many metres in the second as the arrow is centimetres long."
> "Take as many paces as I draw arrows."

"Draw a copy of this arrow."
[In MS 114, p. 125 also: "Come at the time shown by this arrow considered as the hour hand of a clock."]
The same arrow can stand for each of these orders. [TS 213, pp. 93–4 (in the typescript Wittgenstein had forgotten to enter the directional arrows in the second paragraph); originally drafted in MS 110, pp. 76 and 134; cf. also MS 114, II, p. 126, published in PG, p. 131]

Whether the sign '→' signifies 'go in the direction from the tail to the point,' or 'Proceed *two* meters' or 'Proceed *one* pace', or 'Come at three o'clock' (as in '⊙') is relative to the 'rules' for the application of the sign in the language game or grammatical system to which it belongs. And the 'rules' of the game, the grammatical system, *need not* be present before our mind as we employ the sign (see my discussion in nn. 360 and 376).

401 BBB, p. 4. See also Wittgenstein's similar suggestion in MS 145, p. 55 (published via MS 114 in PG, pp. 147–8). Compare the discussion which follows q. 401 with the parallel linguistically relativistic illustration discussed in n. 400.
402 Ibid., p. 5.
403 Ibid., p. 4.
404 Ibid., p. 5.
405 TS 213, p. 168. This was drawn from MS 112, pp. 220–1, but the main critique of simples prior to the parenthetical interjection was drafted in 1930 in MS 153a, pp. 307–8. This critique can be taken as levelled at both the Russellian version (see the Russell reference accompanying the passage cited in n. 228 from Wittgenstein's revision of the 'Brown Book') and Wittgenstein's own early views (see my discussion in chapter 4, pp. 135–7 of what Wittgenstein goes on to say in his parenthetical interjection in the above passage [see q. 347]).
406 MS 153a, p. 310. Cf. also Wittgenstein's suggestion in Zettel §24 that it is only within a language game that pointing *qua* sign can determine (*regeln*) the application of a sentence.
407 MS 112, p. 199. Part of this passage was later included in §8 of his chapter on *Bedeutung* in TS 213 (p. 32), headed "Meaning, the place of the word in grammatical space [*Raum*]".
408 As annotated in TS 213, pp. 167–8. First drafted in 1930–1 in MS 110, p. 116. Cf. Wittgenstein's MS 114 version, published in PG, p. 55 – where, incidentally, the translator has failed to convert into its English equivalent ('T') one of the truth values (in German 'W' for *wahr*) in the truth table for negation.
409 MS 110, p. 116.
410 Ibid., p. 127. Part of this has been previously cited in q. 331.
411 Gier, *Wittgenstein and Phenomenology*, p. 27.
412 Ibid., p. 28.
413 Ibid., p. 27. Unfortunately, Gier is by no means alone in offering such a sweeping interpretation of Wittgenstein's notion of 'forms of life'. For example, Hugh Petrie in "Science and Metaphysics: a Wittgensteinian

interpretation", in *Essays on Wittgenstein*, ed. E. D. Klemke (Urbana: University of Illinois Press, 1971), gives such no less stupefying examples of forms of life as "scientism" and "humanism" (p. 153). Incredibly, Petrie offers these as examples on "a narrower view" of forms of life; his real sympathies are that the supposition of more than one possible form of life is "a serious epistemological question" (p. 152; i.e. epistemologically seriously questionable) and that we are "probably trained into only one" (p. 155). As an interpretation of Wittgenstein, this is absurd. Given some of Wittgenstein's *own* examples of forms of life (see, for example, q. 394 or q. 395), what would Petrie's suggestion mean? That we can *only* give orders, *only* give greetings, or *only* report/describe colours?

414 Gier, *Wittgenstein and Phenomenology*, p. 32. Gier refers us in this context to Wittgenstein's early mention in *Philosophical Remarks* (*PR*, pp. 51–2) of what was once his goal of a 'phenomenological' or 'primary' language. For an antidote to Gier's hallucinations about the import of the latter passages see my discussion of the subject in chapter 2, pp. 56–9 and nn. 173–7.

415 J. F. M. Hunter, "'Forms of Life' in Wittgenstein's *Philosophical Investigations*", *American Philosophical Quarterly*, vol. 5, no. 4 (Oct. 1968), pp. 233–43.

416 Ibid., p. 239.

417 Ibid., p. 235.

418 Ibid., p. 236.

419 Ibid., p. 237.

420 Hunter is especially good on this in his discussion of the use of the word 'hope' as an 'expression of hope' (see ibid., p. 240). Here also, however, his remarks are primarily in a negative vein: he denies that an expression of hope is a report about psychological accompaniments, but he does not explain what an 'expression of hope' *does* if not report about psychological accompaniments.

421 This failure, incidentally, leads to some of the not infrequent exegetical errors in Hunter's account of specific passages. Among the exegetical mistakes made are his accounts of *PI* §206 and p. 226 (see Hunter, "'Forms of Life' in Wittgenstein's *Philosophical Investigations*", pp. 242 and 241 respectively). Now examine qq. 394 and 395, and my discussion on pp. 164–5. It should perhaps be noted that Hunter tries to hedge his bets by (rightly) indicating that his 'organic account' is not necessarily inconsistent with a 'language game account' (ibid., p. 241).

422 N. Malcolm, "Wittgenstein's *Philosophical Investigations*", *Philosophical Review*, vol. LXIII (1954), p. 550. Malcolm's parenthetical numerical references are to sections of *PI*. The page reference in the last line of the above passage is an error which was subsequently corrected to read "p. 224"; see, for example, in *Wittgenstein, the "Philosophical Investigations": a collection of critical essays*, ed. G. Pitcher (New York: Doubleday, 1966), p. 92.

This 'game interpretation' of the notion of 'forms of life', incidentally, is rejected by Gier in *Wittgenstein and Phenomenology*, p. 22, on the grounds that

> Malcolm must be wrong in maintaining that "forms of life [are] embodied in language-games". It is the language game and its related

intentions, emotions, etc. that are embedded in the human situations, customs, and institutions of forms of life. This passage from MS 119 secures our claim: "It is characteristic of our language that it is built on fixed forms of life, regular ways of behaving" (119, p. 148). We must conclude that interpretation A [Malcolm's] is incorrect, and that we reach bedrock in forms of life that are basic human activities, not just linguistic ones.

Gier's argument basically is that 'forms of life' are not language games because they (forms of life) consist of more than just linguistic signs or utterances – the assumption being that what Wittgenstein means by a 'language game' is just linguistic (verbal or written) signs. Gier's citation from MS 119, however, is misleading. In its context in MS 119, the remark cited by Gier reads as follows:

> I want to say: it is characteristic of our language that it is built on stable [*fester*] forms of life, regular ways of acting.
> Its [language's] function is *above all* determined by the activity whose accompaniment it is. [MS 119, p. 148, published in Wittgenstein, "Ursache und Wirkung: intuitives Erfassen", p. 405]

What Wittgenstein means by 'language' in the above passage is the verbal or written utterances or signs – but this is *not* solely what he means by 'language game', for indeed he explains in remarks in MS 119 immediately prior and after the above passage that the language game is *itself* the *activity* which is fundamentally determinative of the *function* of the verbal and written signs:

> The origin and primitive form of the language game is a reaction; only from this could the complicated forms be built. [Ibid.]

> The fundamental form of the game must be one in which there is activity. [Ibid.]

> What is essential to the language game is a practical procedure [*praktische Methode*] (a way of acting) – not contemplation [*Spekulation*], not mere talk [*Geschwätz*]. [Ibid.]

Yet one does not even have to search out the MS 119 context of the remark Gier has cited in order to uncover his sleight-of-hand. Wittgenstein in *PI* §7 explicitly characterized the notion of a 'language game' in the context of a discussion of the hypothetical 'builders' language or language game, and indicated that he uses the term 'language game' in a fairly loose way to refer to: "the whole: language and the activities with which it is interwoven". Or, as he more broadly stressed in 1946 in a list of topics he wished to elaborate upon, "The importance of language games. Language is an instrument [*Instrument*] in the language game" (MS 130, p. 27; see also my discussion in n. 427). Thus by 'language game' is meant not only a specific utterance (for example, 'Brick' in the case of language game no. 2), but also more generally the *Umständen* of the locus of linguistic *practice* in which it (the utterance) is embedded. The fact that the remark in *PI* §7 was made with reference to a hypothetical language game in no way restricts its applicability to hypothetical cases – it applies just as well to *extant* language games or loci of linguistic practice. Hence not only is Gier's interpretation of 'forms of life' too broad (see my earlier criticism above), but his interpretation of the notion of a 'language game' is too narrow. His argument against an identification of language games and forms of life must therefore be rejected on the grounds that it is predicated on Gier's gross misconstrual of both Wittgenstein's notion of 'forms of life' and his notion of 'language games'.

423 N. Malcolm, *Ludwig Wittgenstein, a Memoir* (London: Oxford University Press, 1958), p. 72. P. Sherry has rightly taken issue with Malcolm on this. See P. Sherry, "Is Religion a 'Form of Life'?", *American Philosophical Quarterly*, vol. 9 (1972), pp. 159–67.

424 N. Malcolm, "Anselm's Ontological Argument", *Philosophical Review*, vol. 69 (Jan. 1960), p. 62.

425 MS 134, pp. 143–6; part of this has been published in *CV*, p. 61.

426 Carnap, therefore, seems to have been grossly mistaken in his interpretation of Wittgenstein's averse reaction to Schlick's views on religion. Wittgenstein's reaction did not stem from a 'strong inner conflict between his emotional life and his intellectual thinking', or any "love for metaphysics or metaphysical theology" (see Carnap's "Intellectual Autobiography", pp. 26–7). Rather, Wittgenstein's reaction and generally the repugnance (ibid., p. 26) he exhibited in relation to the views and 'scientific' attitude of Schlick, Carnap and some of the other members of the 'Vienna Circle' were an indication that he (Wittgenstein) was in the process of abandoning, or perhaps already had abandoned, his own earlier narrow-minded identification of meaningful statements with the empirical propositions of natural science (see the discussion above, and also the discussion in chapter 6) – an identification naïvely and wholeheartedly embraced by the 'Vienna Circle' during its early years.

427 There is another rare illustration where Wittgenstein seems to exhibit a sort of tolerance for religious (or perhaps quasi-religious) language. In the midst of a lengthy and typical attempt to describe the grammar of several psychological verbs (such as 'to think') Wittgenstein imagines someone raising the issue of the meaningfulness of the concept 'soul' or 'spirit', and in response he offers the following interesting exchange with the hypothetical interlocutor:

> Then is it erroneous to speak of man's soul [*Seele*] or of his spirit [*Geist*]? *So little so* that it is wholly understandable if I say, "My soul is tired, not just my mind." But don't you at least say that everything that can be expressed by means of the word 'soul' can also be expressed somehow by means of words for the corporeal? I do not say that. But even if it were so – what would it amount to? For the words, and also what we point to in explaining them, are nothing but instruments

[*Instrumente*], and everything depends on their use [*Gebrauch*]. [MS 133, p. 11, published in *RPP*, vol. I, §586]

Wittgenstein does not give us here a description of the grammar or the use, the meaning, of the word 'soul' in the expression "My soul is tired, not just my mind", but it would not be excessively daring to suggest that the account he would probably be inclined to give would not be the sort of account that would send shivers of ecstasy up the spine of a spiritualist. He does, however, and this is what is illuminating for present purposes, indicate how one should proceed in order to give an account of the meaning of such an expression. He is not denying the meaningfulness of talk about the 'soul' or 'spirit' (quite to the contrary, he affirms it), nor is he trying to reduce any such talk to talk about physical bodies – he is simply interested in describing the grammar of such concepts, whatever that grammar is, and thus he takes the linguistically relativistic tack of viewing words as instruments and stressing that everything depends on their use. During roughly this same period (*c*.1946-7) but with respect to 'names of sensations', Wittgenstein more explicitly and emphatically explained what he means by such a recommendation: "Perceive the word – the name of the sensation – as an instrument [*Instrument*]! That is to say, always ask yourself how this thing is used (employed). . . ." (MS 131, p. 206, dating from 1946). And by this Wittgenstein means 'how the word is used *in the language game*', as is clear from the following broad point he noted earlier that year (1946) as a topic he wished to elaborate upon: "The importance of language games. Language is an instrument [*Instrument*] in the language game" (MS 130, p. 27; previously cited in n. 422). Thus the suggestion that we should look at a word (*whatever* the word, whether the word 'soul', the name of a sensation, or something else) as an instrument, is tantamount to a recommendation that we ask what is the function or use of the word (the 'instrument') *in the language game* (or games) in which it is embedded. Just as with Wittgenstein's handling of the expression "It was God's will", therefore, his handling of the term 'soul' would also not involve a vague and vacuous appeal to '*the* religious form of life,' but rather a concrete examination of the specific language games constitutive of the meaning or 'life' of the particular signs in question.

Incidentally, Wittgenstein's familiar parallel emphasis in *PI* §360 that we ought to "Look at the word 'to think' as an instrument [*Instrument*]!", should similarly be understood in terms of the linguistic 'relativism' of his later *Denkweise* and especially as this relativism is grounded in his post-1930 'calculus/game/system' conception of language. Hence, it should come as no surprise that, as early as 1929-30 on the page immediately preceding his previously cited remark that "A step is necessary which is analogous to that of relativity theory" (see q. 350), one finds Wittgenstein's earliest rough formulation of the sort of advice he gives in *PI* §360: "One could say: Thinking (thought) is an instrument [*Instrument*] of acting [*Handeln*]" (MS 108, p. 269). Significantly, on this same page of MS 108 (p. 269; later included in TS 213, p. 22 and MS 116, p. 26) Wittgenstein also first introduced his related and virtually interchangeable metaphor of 'tool/toolbox of language' (*Werkzeuge/*

Werkzeugkastern der Sprache). Cf. *PI* §§11 and 23, where the latter metaphor is used in connection with his list of language games or forms of life (see also *PI* §§16, 17 and 53; and the 'Blue Book', *BBB* pp. 67-8). Caution should be exercised when interpreting Wittgenstein's comparison of words with instruments, since he is sometimes prone to use this comparison to point out disanalogies (see, for example q. 400, and perhaps also MS 135, p. 162, which has been published in *RPP*, vol. II, §14).

428 If one had to take a guess as to the historical source of inspiration of Wittgenstein's later (post-1930) emphasis on a *multiplicity* of forms of life or loci of linguistic practice (language games) constitutive of the meaning/life of signs, as opposed to the (Tractarian) emphasis on an 'ideal' notion of the analysability of propositions in terms of a scheme of absolutely simple names (a view of language as consisting, as it were, of a single precise *game*; see my discussion in chapter 3), as good a guess as any would be Oswald Spengler. (See my comments on Spengler in n. 230, with an eye to Spengler's emphasis on a *multiplicity* of *forms* of life rather than an abstract 'ideal' structure of cultural history.) Spengler, of course, did *not* use such notions with respect to the *subjects* of Wittgenstein's concern. As previously indicated, Wittgenstein's debt to Spengler should be understood simply as a matter of Wittgenstein *adapting* Spengler's general "strategies in thinking" (*Gedankenbewegungen*; see q. 230) and perhaps some of his suggestive terminology to his (Wittgenstein's) own very *different* domain of philosophical concerns. It was the nature of Wittgenstein's particular genius that he could stumble onto a general strategy or notion, as with Spengler or 'relativity theory' (see n. 351), and so nurture it in the fertile soil of his own creative imagination that the specific characteristics of that general strategy or notion, as it manifests itself in the mature fruits of his *own* philosophical labours, bear so little concrete resemblance to the specific features of the *source* of inspiration that, if it is worth speaking at all of parallels between Wittgenstein's own thinking or conceptions and the thinking of those who 'influenced' him, one can do so only by way of general analogies or, as G. H. von Wright has suggested to me (using a Spenglerian expression), by "morphological comparisons" (see my introductory comments on pp. 13-14 and my discussion of Spengler in n. 230). One such notion (and strategy) that Wittgenstein got from Spengler, but *radically* transformed in the creative soil of his own imagination and the domain of his own philosophical concerns, was the previously discussed (chapter 3; n. 230) conception of a *Vergleichsobjekt*. Another (I believe, and it is irrelevant to the concerns of the present work to try to give extensive argumentation in support of this belief) is Spengler's emphasis on a *multiplicity* of (cultural) forms, forms of life – and here again it cannot be overemphasized that Wittgenstein *radically* transformed this general conception and *radically* adapted it to the sphere of his own linguistic concerns with the problem of signification or meaning.

A third and intimately related notion for which one could perhaps identify Spengler as a source of inspiration is the notion of 'family' (and 'family resemblance'). The latter is fairly obviously intimately related to an emphasis on a *multiplicity* of forms of life, in that, once one has rejected any absolute 'ideal' (for Spengler an ideal schema of the structure of history; for Wittgenstein an 'ideal' conception of the nature of the structure of propositions and their analysability in terms of supposed *simple* names), the only recourse one has for speaking of similarity or 'commonality' (there is no longer the presupposition of an 'essence') with respect to the *multitude* of actual forms (for Spengler the various cultural epochs; for Wittgenstein the various loci of linguistic practice), is by way of the possible grouping of the sundry members of this multitude into 'families' within (and perhaps between) which there are similarities, 'family resemblances' (and *differences*!). Recall that Wittgenstein himself first used the term 'family resemblance' in reference to Spengler's thinking (see q. 229). Recall also my discussion in n. 230, where it was pointed out that the probable specific terminological source of inspiration for Wittgenstein's notion of 'family' was the analogy Spengler drew in his Introduction to *Decline of the West* between the *multiplicity* of cultural epochs and a "family [*Gattung*] of butterflies or orchids". This sort of Spenglerian emphasis on a multiplicity of forms and the consequent notion of a 'family' within which there are similarities and differences was first *radically* adapted by Wittgenstein to the domain of *his own* philosophical concerns in 1929 almost immediately upon his return to philosophy. As might be expected, his first, and (granted) somewhat rudimentary, adaptation of the notion of a *Gattung* was as a means for criticizing a too simplistic conception of the nature of language – and in particular with respect to substantives:

> If it is charged that language can express everything by means of substantives, adjectives and verbs, then we must say that it is then in any case necessary to differentiate between wholly different kinds [*Arten*] of substantives (etc.), for different grammatical rules apply for them. This becomes apparent in that they do not permit of substitution for one another. Thereby it is evident that their substantive character is only a superficiality [Äußerlichkeit] and that we are actually dealing with wholly diverse families of words [*Wortgattungen*]. The word-family [*Wortgattung*] is (first/now) determined by *all* grammatical rules which apply to a word. And thus viewed our language has a countless number [*Unmenge*] of different kinds of words [*Wortarten*]. [MS 107, p. 210. Cf. *PR*, p. 118]

Recall here Wittgenstein's indication that one of the fundamental errors on which rested the reasoning behind his Tractarian postulation of an 'ideal' language of 'simple names' was the "ignorance of the concept of family" (see q. 398). And along with the realization that 'language is a family or families' (see q. 188), a *multiplicity* of grammars, a multitude of heterogeneous functions in the loci of linguistic practice or forms of life constitutive of the meaning of signs, came the recognition that he had made the mistake (in the *Tractatus*) of simplistically looking for the use of a sign "as though it were an object [whether mental or otherwise] *co-existing* with the sign ... looking for a 'thing corresponding to a substantive'" (see q. 402).

Wittgenstein's subsequent introduction and use of the expression *Familien* (with respect to language) rather than *Gattungen* would of course have been necessitated by the fact that the Spenglerian notion of a *Gattung*, when applied to language (viz. *Wortgattungen*) could (as von Wright has rightly pointed out to me) be taken as merely a reference to common 'parts of speech' – whereas what Wittgenstein found useful about Spengler's notion of a 'family', and indeed his whole purpose for adopting it, was that, quite to the contrary, it provided a means for viewing language as involving a countless *multiplicity* of 'grammars' that exist *within* such superficial categories as the standard parts of speech.

Chapter 6 Metaphysics and Wittgenstein's Struggle against the Intellectual Current of Our Times

429 MS 109, pp. 204–7. Except for the first paragraph and the end of the third, this has been cited as translated in *CV*, pp. 6–7. The 300 pages of MS 109 were written between 11 August 1930 and 3 February 1931. A few pages later (pp. 211–12) in this manuscript, and *still* in the context of drafts of remarks for TS 213 (cf., for example, p. 210 of MS 109 and p. 433 of TS 213), Wittgenstein wrote another in some respects similar draft of this foreword. The latter draft oddly enough was published by Rhees as a foreword to *Philosophical Remarks* – the assortment of remarks (drawn from the very early MSS 105–8) Wittgenstein gave to Russell in March 1930 so that Russell could write a letter of recommendation for him to the Council of Trinity College; remarks to which Wittgenstein apparently had referred as being in a 'confused state' (see n. 275). The potpourri of remarks Wittgenstein had given to Russell and which Rhees published as *Philosophical Remarks*, however, is most certainly *not* the anticipated 'book' of which Wittgenstein speaks in the forewords drafted in MS 109. The closest Wittgenstein came to a 'book' in the early thirties was TS 213.

The issues to be examined in the present chapter are related to some of the questions raised by Professor von Wright in his opening address to the second international Wittgenstein symposium held at Kirchberg am Wechsel, Austria, in 1977. The address ("Wittgenstein in Relation to his Times") has been published in the proceedings of the symposium, *Wittgenstein and his Impact on Contemporary Thought*, pp. 73–8.

430 Moore, "Wittgenstein's Lectures in 1930–33", p. 26.
431 MS 126, p. 126 (1942). Previously cited in q. 46. Recall my comments in n. 160 on Wittgenstein's writings in the philosophy of mathematics.
432 MS 134, pp. 146–7. Published in *CV*, p. 62. Very interesting (but dangerous) reading in connection with Wittgenstein's opposition to a 'scientific way of thinking' (for instance, as this applies to the study of history) is Oswald Spengler's *Decline of the West*, vol. I, chapters III and IV. There is a distinct possibility that there was no single greater positive influence on Wittgenstein's post-1930 *Denkweise* than Oswald Spengler (and also no single greater danger of misconstruing the influence of another thinker on Wittgenstein's later philosophy). A demonstration of this, however, is not the concern of the present work (see my comments on Spengler in nn. 230 and 428).

433 MS 133, p. 90. Published in *CV*, p. 56.
434 MS 124, p. 228.
435 Russell, "On Propositions", pp. 27–8.
436 Russell, comments in the "Meaning of Meaning" symposium, *Mind*, 29 (Oct. 1920), p. 400. It is a manifestation of the very current against which Wittgenstein was struggling that *Mind* (full original title, *Mind: a quarterly review of psychology and philosophy*), one of the most prominent forums of *philosophical* debate in this century, was ambiguously considered a review of *psychology* and philosophy, and that it was not until January 1974, under the editorship of D. W. Hamlyn, that the title of this bastion of philosophical debate was changed to *Mind: a quarterly review of philosophy*. But, alas, this change did not come about because philosophers had ceased confusing empirical issues and philosophical ones, ceased indulging in pretentious pseudo-scientific speculation on matters of 'psychology' (see the discussion above, and my comments on Russell, Ogden and James in chapter 4). Rather, the change of title was necessitated by the fact that *psychology*, in its efforts to establish itself as a genuine empirical discipline, had disassociated itself from philosophy.
437 B. Russell, "On Scientific Method in Philosophy", in *Mysticism and Logic and Other Essays* (London: George Allen and Unwin, 1959), p. 113, and cf. pp. 98, 107 and 124. Not unexpectedly, as has been found to be the case with several other matters (cf. my comments on qq. 296 and 306 in chapter 4 pp. 117–18), Russell seems to have obtained some of his inspiration on the issue of the adoption of a scientific method in philosophy from William James (see Russell's reference to James, ibid., p. 100).
438 B. Russell, *The Scientific Outlook* (London: George Allen and Unwin, 1931), p. 149.
439 Ogden and Richards, *The Meaning of Meaning*, p. 384. Cf. q. 272 and my discussion of Ogden in chapter 4, p. 119ff.
440 James, *The Principles of Psychology*, vol. I, pp. v–vii. See also my comments about the journal *Mind* in n. 436.
441 MS 165, pp. 150–1.
442 Ogden and Richards, *The Meaning of Meaning*, p. 137.
443 See David Hartley, *Observations on Man, his Frame, his Duty, and his Expectations* (Gainesville, Fla: Scholar's Facsimiles and Reprints, 1966), p. 65, quoted in James, *Principles*, vol. I, p. 561. For Hartley's application of this law specifically as an explanation of the meaning of signs, see Hartley, *Observations*, part I, chapter III, §1, esp. p. 271.
444 Alexander Bain, *The Senses and the Intellect* (London: Longmans, Green, 1868), p. 327, quoted in James, *Principles*, vol. I, p. 561. On the same page, James offers his own version of the law of association, calling it the "law of mental association by contiguity".
445 James, *Principles*, vol. I, pp. 556–7. In a note to this remark James allows for the possibility that a name might be uttered so rapidly in a sentence that "no substantive image may have time to arise" (ibid., p. 557). He does not specify whether, according to his view, in such a case the name would be 'meaningless'.

446 W. James, "The Association of Ideas", *Popular Science Monthly*, vol. XVI (Mar. 1880), pp. 577–93.
447 James, *Principles*, vol. I, p. 557. Cf. Bertrand Russell's not unrelated illustration offered in the context of a discussion of his notion of analysis in *An Inquiry*, p. 422. The notion of analysis is discussed later in this chapter.
448 James, *Principles*, vol. I, p. 557. See also James' venerating (cf. ibid., vol. II, p. 51) references to some of Galton's other 'scientific' findings, in his chapter "The Stream of Thought" (ibid., vol. I, pp. 254, 265 and 266). Wittgenstein had most definitely read such passages, because they immediately precede the "Mr Ballard" illustration which Wittgenstein himself cites from James in *PI* §342 (first drafted in MS 165, pp. 195–6; see also his references to the same illustration in MS 116, p. 203; and MS 136, p. 116 (the latter published in *Zettel* §109, and *RPP*, vol. II, §214)). The "Mr Ballard" illustration was cited by James as evidence that there is 'thought without language'. The overall point of James' chapter "The Stream of Thought", however, was, as he put it,

> Now what I contend for, and accumulate examples to show, is that 'tendencies' are not only descriptions from without, but that they are among the *objects* of the stream which is thus aware of them from within, and must be described as in very large measure constituted of *feelings* of *tendency*, often so vague that we are unable to name them at all. It is, in short, the re-instatement of the vague to its proper place in our mental life which I am so anxious to press on the attention. Mr Galton and Prof. Huxley have, as we shall see in Chapter XVIII, made one step in advance in exploding the ridiculous theory of Hume and Berkeley that we can have no images but of perfectly definite things. Another is made in the overthrow of the equally ridiculous notion that, whilst simple objective qualities are revealed to our knowledge in subjective feelings, relations are not. But these reforms are not half sweeping and radical enough. What must be admitted is that the definite images of traditional psychology form but the very smallest part of our minds as they actually live.... Every definite image in the mind is steeped and dyed in the free water that flows round it. With it goes the sense of its relations, near and remote, the dying echo of whence it came to us, the dawning sense of whither it is to lead. The significance, the value, of the image is all in this halo of penumbra that surrounds and escorts it, – or rather that is fused into one with it and has become bone of its bone and flesh of its flesh; leaving it, it is true, an image of the same *thing* it was before, but making it an image of that thing newly taken and freshly understood. [James, *Principles*, vol. I, pp. 254–5; cf. Wittgenstein's critical comments about this in MS 130, p. 291, published in *RPP*, vol. I, §219]

It is ironic that in this chapter (James, *Principles*, vol. I, p. 264), where incidentally James presented his teratoid conception of "the fringe", he viciously derides the "lunatic" and "nonsensical" writings of Hegel (surely a case of the pot calling the kettle black!); see also his "On Some Omissions of Introspective Psychology", *Mind*, vol. 9 (Jan. 1884).

The refutation of Hume and the "re-instatement of the vague to its proper place in our mental life" was undertaken by James in his chapter (XVIII) entitled "Imagination". There he contended that "the slightest introspective glance will show to anyone the falsity of this [Hume's] opinion" (*Principles*, vol. II, p. 46) and that quite to the contrary "a blurred picture is just as much a single mental fact as a sharp picture is" and "Our ideas or images of past sensible experiences may then be distinct and adequate or dim, blurred, and incomplete" (ibid., p. 49). James here obviously is not challenging or refuting mentalistic, associationist accounts *per se*, but merely quibbling over the nature of the associationist furniture found in the 'mind' – it being his contention that the 'mind' is furnished in a far more complicated (and 'flowing'), if at times untidy ('vague'), manner than Hume has suggested. James credits the discovery of the existence of blurred and indistinct mental states or "'blended' images", as he, alluding to Galton (cf. q. 452), referred to them earlier in his career (see "On Some Omissions", p. 4), to the 'scientific' findings of Galton and others (James also cites for instance such scientific 'advances' as the work on *Seelenblindheit* ['mental blindness']; see *Principles*, vol. II, p. 58ff, and my comments in n. 477). There is perhaps no better stretch of material in James than his "Imagination" chapter as an illustration of what might have led Wittgenstein to charge that James' 'scientific' psychological speculations had not at all extricated him from the "cobwebs of metaphysics in which he is caught. He cannot yet walk, or fly at all he only wriggles" (see q. 441 and my discussion of 'metaphysics' later in the present chapter).
449 Francis Galton, *Inquiries into Human Faculty and its Development* (London: J. M. Dent,1907), p. 140.
450 Ibid., p. 137.
451 Ibid., p. 138.
452 Ibid., pp. 136–7. Most of this passage was quoted by James in his note on p. 557 of *Principles*, vol. I.
453 James, *Principles*, vol. I, pp. 557–8. James refers us here to Wundt's *Grundzüge der Physiologischen Psychologie*, vol. II (Leipzig: Wilhelm Engelmann, 1887); see especially pp. 312–14 of the latter work.
454 J. M. Cattell, "The Time It Takes to See and Name Objects", *Mind*, 11 (Jan. 1886), p. 64. Virtually all of this was quoted by James in *Principles*, vol. I, pp. 558–9.
455 Cattell, "The Time It Takes to See and Name Objects", p. 63. James had not cited this passage, and thus it is doubtful that Wittgenstein was aware of it.
456 MS 110, p. 76.
457 MS 153a, p. 145; and MS 111, p. 113. This was included in TS 213, p. 215. Cf. also his MS 114 (II, pp. 89–91) revision of TS 213 (published in *PG*, p. 105).
458 MS 155, p. 75. Written in English.
459 Ibid., p. 80. Written in English.
460 Ibid., p. 130. Also in MS 112, p. 146; and TS 213, p. 432. The version cited above is that in TS 213.
461 MS 146, p. 96 – MS 147, p. 1. Cf. also the version in MS 115, p. 61 (published in *S*, vol. 6, pp. 102–3, and *Zettel* §314).

462 "Brown Book", *BBB*, p. 125. Cf. also the 1936 *Umarbeitung* in MS 115, p. 205 (published in *S*, vol. 5, p. 179).
463 *S*, vol. 6, p. 205. This exclamation was made in the midst of remarks on the philosophy of mathematics (recall my comments in n. 160).
464 MS 162b, p. 88.
465 MS 130, p. 35.
466 MS 133, p. 24.
467 Ibid., p. 125.
468 *PI*, §109. Drafted in 1936 in MS 152, pp. 93–4. At several junctures the above translation diverges from the one in *PI*.
469 *PI* §126. Parts of this passsage were drafted in MS 110, pp. 90 and 217; and all of the passage is to be found in the "Philosophy" chapter of TS 213, pp. 418 and 419.
470 MS 111, p. 111. The TS 213 version has been previously cited in chapter 4 (n. 256). Also appearing here (MS 111, pp. 112–13) in the context of Wittgenstein's emphasis that he is "not in the domain of explanations" is his first draft of the passage cited in q. 362, where he stresses that "what is essential to the sign is the system to which it belongs" – thus reiterating part of the point made in the above passage.
471 MS 114, II, pp. 89–91. Published in *PG*, pp. 104–5. See my discussion of this in the context of the preceding chapter (p. 161ff).
472 MS 111, p. 177. The first sentence was drafted in MS 153a, p. 197.
473 MS 111, p. 180. First drafted in MS 153a, p. 197. Also subsequently included in TS 213, p. 220; the revision of TS 213 in MS 114 (II, pp. 90–1, published in *PG*, p. 106); and *Zettel* §606 (where the remark is mistranslated – see my comments in chapter 1, p. 11).
474 MS 111, p. 180. First drafted in MS 153a, p. 197.
475 MS 110, pp. 180–9. Also included in TS 213, pp. 417–18; and *PI* §124. Cf. my discussion of q. 232 in chapter 3, p. 86ff. Recall in this connection Wittgenstein's statement near the end of his 1930 draft foreword to the effect that he is not concerned with constructing foundations, but rather only with, so to speak, "having a perspicuous view of the foundations of *possible* [my italics] buildings" (see q. 429). In the above passage (q. 475) this issue seems to be linked with the task of *describing* the actual use of language. That the concern with gaining a perspicuous view of 'possibilities' is to be equated with the concern solely to *describe* the actual use or 'grammar' of language is perhaps most explicitly emphasised in *PI* §90: "We feel as if we had to *penetrate* phenomena: our investigation, however, is directed not towards *phenomena*, but, as one might say, towards the 'possibilities' of phenomena. We remind ourselves, that is to say, of the *kind of statement* that we make about phenomena...."
476 MS 110, p. 87.
477 See MS 130, pp. 235–95; and MS 131, pp. 1–60. These notebooks were written consecutively between May 1946 and September 1946. Much of this material has been published in *RPP*, vol. I, §§173–259. In this stretch of remarks, in addition to numerous explicit references to James (see, for example, MS 130, pp. 236, 259, 291; and MS 131, p. 54), there are several themes readily

identifiable with specific theories and conceptions James presented in his writings. For instance, one of the more recurrent of the many Jamesian themes in this stetch of MSS 130–1 (see MS 130, pp. 240, 241, 248, 250, 257, 263, 265, 267, 270, 284; and MS 131, pp. 7, 17, 23, 29, 34–6, 42 and 50) is the notion of what Wittgenstein calls *Bedeutungsblindheit* ('meaning-blindness'). It seems Wittgenstein got the notion of 'meaning-blindness' from James' associationist, psychological accounts of scientific findings concerning 'aphasia' and related disorders, what James was inclined generally to refer to as 'mental blindness' – this following the terminology (*Seelenblindheit*) used by Wilbrand, among others, whom James cites (see James' chapter "Imagination" in *Principles*, vol. II, p. 58ff, and see also vol. I, p. 48ff; cf. my discussion in n. 448 and also Wittgenstein's criticism of James in MS 137, pp. 87–90, published in *RPP*, vol. II, §571–8, again in the general context of a discussion of the notion of 'meaning-blindness'). A second readily identifiable theme from James is the conception of 'tendency' Wittgenstein criticizes in MS 130, p. 291 (see *RPP*, vol. I, §219). The latter is clearly an allusion to some of James' central comments in his chapter "The Stream of Thought" (see, for instance, the lengthy passage cited in n. 448). For a third example see the discussion above.
478 MS 130, p. 217.
479 See MS 130, p. 219 (previously cited and discussed in n. 360).
480 MS 131, pp. 54–6. Published in *RPP*, vol. I; see §§254–8.
481 James, *Principles*, vol. I, pp. 251–2. In this stretch of the text James also speculated about what he called "inarticulate feelings of familiarity" (p. 252). Cf. Wittgenstein's discussion of this in MS 131, p. 91ff (obviously having again renewed his critique of James after the passage cited in q. 480) – much of this has been published in *RPP*, vol. I, §§292ff; and some of it also appears along with other material in *PI* p. 181ff, where there is included a criticism of James' notion of "if-feeling", "but-feeling", and so on.

Incidentally, it was also here that James suggested that our vocabulary is inadequate. See Wittgenstein's comments in *PI* §610, and cf. James' assertion that "our pyschological vocabulary is wholly inadequate [to name the differences between two states of consciousness]", in *Principles*, vol. I, p. 251. Wittgenstein's comments in *PI* §610 on the inability to describe an aroma or *musical* note or tone (*Töne*) are an allusion to James' speculations about the 'inarticulate feeling' of an odour or a musical tone "so deep into our consciousness that we are fairly shaken by its mysterious emotional power" (*Principles*, vol. I, p. 252; and cf. James' speculations about the experiences of musical 'overtones', ibid., p. 258) – in *PI* §610 Wittgenstein is most definitely *not* offering self-indulgent comments about the profundity or "the power and the glory" of his own philosophical remarks, as J. F. M. Hunter seems to suggest in his concluding remark to his article "'Forms of Life' in Wittgenstein's *Philosophical Investigations*" (p. 243).
482 MS 130, p. 29.
483 Ibid., pp. 35–6.
484 MS 138, p. 37 (published in *PI*, p. 220). See Wittgenstein's critical discussion of James on the preceding pages of MS 138 (pp. 29–37), some of which has been published in *PI*, pp. 218–20.

485 See *Tractatus* 4.112–4.1122; and cf. *N*, appendix I, p. 93.
486 See *Tractatus* 4.1121. First drafted in 1914 (cf. *N*, p. 28).
487 See MS 109, p. 212. Published in *CV*, p. 8.
488 MS 109, pp. 212–13. The second paragraph has been previously cited and discussed in the context of chapter 2; see q. 185.
489 R. Carnap, *The Logical Structure of the World/Pseudoproblems in Philosophy* (Berkeley, Calif.: University of California Press, 1967), p. 325. *Pseudoproblems in Philosophy* was first published in German in 1928.
490 See for example the papers of Otto Neurath ("Wege der wissenschaftliche Weltauffassung") and Hans Hahn ("Die Bedeutung der wissenschaftliche Weltauffassung, inbesondere für Mathematik und Physik") presented at the joint meeting of the Ernst Mach Society (whose members were those of the so-called 'Vienna Circle') and the Society for Empirical Philosophy in Prague in 1929; published in *Erkenntnis* vol. I (1930–1), pp. 96–125. See also Phillip Frank's comments in his opening address (ibid., pp. 93–5) and Neurath's "Historical Remarks" (ibid., pp. 311–14). In his "Historical Remarks" Neurath also refers us to a pamphlet put out by the Ernst Mach Society entitled *Wissenschaftliche Weltauffassung. Der Wiener Kreis* (Vienna: Artur Wolf, 1929). This pamphlet, jointly authored by several members of the circle (principally Carnap, Neurath and Hahn) has since been reprinted in O. Neurath, *Gesammelte philosophische und methodologische Schriften*, vol. I (Vienna: Hölder-Pichler-Tempsky, 1981), pp. 299–336. See my discussion in n. 494. It is no doubt to their 'scientific world-view' that Herbert Feigl was alluding when he later indicated that what stood out in his mind about the 1929 Prague conference was that the participants "all had basically a common orientation" – H. Feigl, "The Wiener Kreis in America", *Perspectives in American History*, vol. II (Cambridge, Mass.: Harvard University Press, 1968), p. 641; cf. also Carnap's references to the 'basic scientific attitude and fundamental orientation' of the Vienna Circle (q. 493).
491 R. Carnap, "Die alte und die neue Logik", *Erkenntnis* vol. I (1930–1), p. 12.
492 Carnap, "Intellectual Autobiography", see pp. 21, 22 and 34.
493 Carnap, *Der logische Aufbau der Welt*, pp. iii–iv. Cf. the English translation in Carnap, *The Logical Structure of the World*, pp. xv–xvi.
494 Carnap, *Der logische Aufbau der Welt*, pp. v–vi. With the exception of the first three sentences of the second paragraph, this passage is cited as translated in *The Logical Structure of the World*, pp. xvii–xviii. Consistent with Carnap's suggestions in the above passage, it seems he considered the "basic attitude" of the Vienna Circle to have manifested itself in art and architecture by way of the ideology of the 'Bauhaus' – he even went so far as to send Herbert Feigl as an "emissary" of the Vienna Circle to Bauhaus Dessau in 1929 (see Feigl, "The Weiner Kreis in America", p. 637).

As suggested above, the direct clash between Carnap's 1928 Preface and Wittgenstein's 1930 draft foreword is unmistakable. In fact it is only after one has read the writings of Carnap and some of the other members of the Vienna Circle from the 1920s and the early 1930s that it becomes clear why Wittgenstein should have been so expansive in the draft foreword when he spoke of his own philosophical writings as not being in sympathy with the scientific spirit of the main current of European and American civilization as it manifests itself even in the industry, architecture, music, fascism and socialism of our time. The apparent expansiveness of Wittgenstein's draft foreword was much less a reflection of a grandiose vision of the scope of his own philosophical task than in part a critical reaction to what some of his own contemporaries espoused as the *wissenschaftliche Weltauffassung* and scientific spirit of the times. Some of the core members of the Vienna Circle embraced with almost adolescent abandon what they perceived to be this scientific spirit of the times; a spirit which they saw as present not only in philosophy by way of their own movement (and its forebearers) but in all facets of European culture; a spirit which they perceived as an instrument for sweeping social change and as the dawning of a new social order. The sweeping nature of the outlook of some of the core members of the Circle is to a certain extent quite evident in Carnap's above-cited 1928 Preface to *Der logische Aufbau der Welt*. On behalf of the members of his circle, he speaks for instance of their philosophical work being "founded" on an "intellectual attitude which presently manifests itself in entirely different walks of life", including artistic movements (for instance, architecture, but cf. Wittgenstein's comments in his 1930 draft foreword (q. 429) on the artistic movements of the era) and "movements which strive for meaningful forms of personal and collective life, of education and of external organization in general [*äußeren Ordnungen im Großen*]". This latter manifestation clearly places the *wissenschaftliche Weltauffassung* of which Carnap speaks within the much broader arena of a thrust toward sweeping political and social change (but cf. Wittgenstein's comments in the draft foreword on the political/social movements of the era).

Even more light is shed on the character of this broader perspective, from which Carnap suggests the members of the Vienna Circle viewed their philosophical work, by a short piece published in August 1929 – this after Carnap's 1928 preface, but still before the drafting of Wittgenstein's foreword in 1930. The work in question (previously cited in n. 490) was entitled *Wissenschaftliche Weltauffassung. Der Wiener Kreis* (*Scientific World-view. The Vienna Circle*) and seems to have been the product of a co-operative effort on the part of several members of the Circle, primarily Neurath, Carnap and Hahn; cf. the editors' suggestions with the English translation of the main text published in O. Neurath, *Empiricism and Sociology*, ed. M. Neurath and R. S. Cohen (Dordrecht: D. Reidel, 1973), p. 318. Apparently there was also some contribution by H. Feigl and F. Waismann (cf. Feigl's claims in "The Wiener Kreis in America", p. 646). The complete German version (since reprinted in Neurath, *Gesammelte Schriften*) included an extensive bibliography and précis of the works of the members of the Vienna Circle, as well as of authors "sympathetic" (*nahestehende*) to the circle (for example, Frank Ramsey; cf. n. 510) and of three "leading representatives [*führende Vertreter*] of the scientific world-view" who allegedly had "most effectively publicized [*am wirkungsvollsten in der Offentlichkeit vertreten*] the scientific world-view" (Einstein, Russell and Wittgenstein; see *Wissenschaftliche Weltauffassung* in Neurath, *Gesammelte Schriften*, vol. 1, p. 332). Even James received honourable mention (ibid., p. 301). Name-dropping of this sort was, unfortunately, a perhaps effective, if tasteless, way of gaining notoriety and recognition for the group as a 'movement'. There is little doubt that Wittgenstein (who was *not* a 'member' of the Circle), however much his *Tractatus* had contributed to the views of these people (and it seems the influence was considerable), would most certainly not have taken to being called a 'leading representative and publicizer of the *wissenschaftliche Weltauffassung* of the Vienna Circle'. Even Moritz Schlick, the founder of the Circle and dedicatee of *Wissenschaftliche Weltauffassung* apparently was "appalled and dismayed by the thought that we were propagandizing our views as a 'system' or 'movement'"; see Feigl's report in "The Wiener Kreis in America", p. 646; cf. also Victor Kraft, *The Vienna Circle: the origin of neo-positivism* (New York: Philosophical Library, 1953), part I, n. 4 and p. 15. It would seem, then, that this 1929 publication, to which A. J. Ayer has alluded with apparently informed and well-chosen words as a "manifesto" brought out in the year (1929) "they, as it were, registered themselves as a philosophical party" – see Ayer's "The Vienna Circle" in *The Revolution in Philosophy* (London: Macmillan, 1956), p. 71, and cf. also his editorial introduction to *Logical Positivism* (London: The Free Press, 1963) p. 4 – was an expression of views most but *not all* of which were shared by the group as a whole. Certainly, however, *all* the views expressed in *Wissenschaftliche Weltauffassung* were shared by Carnap, Neurath and Hahn, who were the principal authors of the piece, and thus the piece can legitimately be taken as a source which sheds further light on the expansive perspective of Carnap's 1928 Preface to *Der logische Aufbau der Welt*, if not necessarily on the movement as a whole. Most of the substantive views expressed in that publication, however, can safely be said to have been shared by all members of the group at the time.

It is of course quite common knowledge that, with respect to the domain of traditional philosophy, Carnap, and in general the Vienna Circle, saw it as the fundamental task of 'logical positivism' or 'logical empiricism' to repudiate, by means of 'logical analysis', much of traditional philosophy and especially theology on the grounds that the metaphysical statements of theology and traditional philosophy are "meaningless, because unverifiable, without [empirical] content" (see *Wissenschaftliche Weltauffassung*, in Neurath, *Gesammelte Schriften*, vol. 1, p. 307). It is even somewhat clear how Carnap might have perceived the spirit of a *wissenschaftliche Weltauffassung* as present in a broad spectrum of fields and performing there a similar "task of purification" (*Reinigungsaufgabe*; ibid., p. 313) – the task of 'cleansing' (*reinigen*, ibid., p. 310) those other disciplines of their metaphysical conceptions by demonstrating that such conceptions "do not satisfy the requirement of reducibility to the given" (ibid., p. 312; "the given", here, to be taken in a phenomenal sense – see my discussion in nn. 175 and 220). What was not at all clear in Carnap's 1928 Preface, but becomes quite clear in the 1929 *Wissenschaftliche Weltauffassung*, is why he expansively viewed logical empiricism and its *wissenschaftliche Weltauffassung* within the context of a movement toward sweeping social and political change of *der äußeren Ordnungen im Großen* (see q. 494). It is on this point that the piece published by Carnap (et al.) in 1929 is so informative. The co-authors of *Wissenschaftliche Weltauffassung* were as expansive as Carnap had been the year before in his 1928 Preface to *Der logische Aufbau der Welt*, but somewhat more explicit in their characterization of the reasons why the scientific world-view espoused by the Vienna Circle was seen (at least by some of the core, and historically most influential, members of the group) as an impetus toward social and political change:

> The representatives of the scientific world-view resolutely stand on the ground of simple human experience [an allusion to the phenomenalist foundations of Carnap's logic; see nn. 175 and 220]. With confidence they apply themselves to the task of clearing out of the way the metaphysical and theological debris of millennia. . . .
>
> The increase in metaphysical and theologizing tendencies which today makes itself felt in many associations and sects, in books and journals, in speeches and university lectures, seems to be based on the fierce social and economic battles of the present: one group of combatants, clinging to what is by-gone in the social sphere, even fosters the traditional, long since outmoded attitudes of metaphysics and theology; while the other group is devoted to modern times and especially in central Europe rejects these attitudes and takes its stand on the ground of empirical science. This development is linked to that of the modern process of production, which is becoming more and more extensively mechanized and leaves less and less room for metaphysical ideas. It is also linked to the disillusionment of broad masses of people with the attitude of those who preach the traditional metaphysical and theological dogmas. Thus it happens that in many countries the masses now much more consciously than ever before reject these dogmas and in connection with their socialistic attitude incline toward a down-to-earth, empiricist view. In former times materialism was the expression of this view; but since then modern empiricism has evolved out of several inadequate modes and acquired a sound form in the *scientific world-view*.
>
> Thus the scientific world-view is close to the life of the present. Certainly it is threatened with hard struggles and hostility. Nevertheless there are many who do not despair but, in view of the present sociological situation, look forward with hope to the course of events to come. Of course not every single adherent of the scientific world-view will be a fighter. Some, glad of solitude, will lead a withdrawn existence on the icy slopes of logic; some may even disdain mingling with the masses and regret the 'trivialized' form that these matters inevitably take on spreading. However, their achievements too will take a place among the historic developments. We witness the spirit of the scientific world-view penetrating in growing measure the forms of personal and public life, in education, upbringing, architecture, and the shaping of economic and social life according to rational principles. *The scientific world-view serves life and life receives it*. [Neurath et al., *Wissenschaftliche Weltauffassung*, in Neurath, *Gesammelte Schriften*, vol. 1, pp. 314–15.

The third of these paragraphs has been cited as translated in Neurath, *Empiricism and Sociology*, pp. 317–18]

Carnap was not very outspoken politically – at least not in his publications. It appears he was, unlike Neurath, not much of a "fighter" on the political front, but rather was of the sort inclined to "lead a withdrawn existence on the icy slopes of logic" (to borrow expressions from the concluding remarks of the above passage). However, with respect to his political views during the 1920s and 1930s, Carnap seems once to have advised, "If you want to find out what my political views were in the twenties and thirties, read Otto Neurath's books and articles of that time; his views were also mine" (cited by Marie Neurath in O. Neurath, *Empiricism and Sociology*, p. xiii). Now, obviously, Carnap's and Neurath's political views *in themselves* are of very little interest for our purposes. What *is* of some interest, however, is that Carnap and Neurath seem to have viewed their *philosophical enterprise* from the perspective of their politics; viewed logical positivism and its *wissenschaftliche Weltauffassung* as an efficacious instrument on the broader social and political stage. Traditional philosophy and theology (in general, 'metaphysics') were opposed as the 'ideological expression' of the old social order, the (bourgeois) idealogy of the "combatants holding fast to traditional social forms". The "masses" (the proletariat) in connection with their 'socialist attitudes' are inclined toward empiricism and the repudiation of the (metaphysical) ideology of the old order. As Neurath quite explicitly put it in his 1928 review of Carnap's *Der logische Aufbau der Welt* and *Scheinprobleme in der Philosophie*,

> Empirical rationalism [i.e. 'logical empiricism' or 'logical positivism'] is on the march. The theoretical struggle against theology and theological philosophy was begun by the thinkers of the enlightenment and the materialists. Their expositions are now no longer useful, the present is adapted to the formulation of antimetaphysics for which empirical rationalism strives. Without reserve it [logical empiricism] firmly opposes the prevailing bourgeois philosophy which devotes itself to ever more theologizing lines of thought [*theologisierenden Denkrichtungen*]!
>
> Only in a few places are there philosophers who, with all of the tools of modern research, struggle for an exact world-view [*Weltbetrachtung*] that has powerfully and decidedly advanced forward to the select domain of Marxism! To the antimetaphysical efforts of an Ernst Mach, an Avenarius, a Poincaré are now joined a Russell (England), a Reichenbach (Berlin), a Moritz Schlick (Vienna) in order to pave the way for an exact world-view. Especially the 'Vienna school' around Moritz Schlick, which just now is coming out with a series of publications, is developing into a centre of exact thinking with a metaphysics-free attitude.
>
> By one of the most rigorous representatives of this tendency, Rudolf Carnap, a lecturer at the University of Vienna, two works are out, of

which one tries wholly systematically and comprehensively to characterize the foundations of an exact knowledge of the world, and the other in a universally intelligible way demonstrates certain philosophical problems as falsely conceived and superfluous....
[O. Neurath, *Der Kampf*, vol. 21 (1928), pp. 624–5]

Neurath went on to give a cursory account of some of the aspects of Carnap's works, noting that the renunciation of theology and metaphysics is "progress in the direction of the Marxist intellectual task" (*einen Fortschritt in der Richtung marxistischer Denkarbeit*; ibid., p. 625) and then expressly pointing out Carnap's stress in his Preface on what Neurath called the "collectivistic character" (*kollektivistischen Charakter*) of his (Carnap's) efforts and attitude – therewith citing the concluding passages of Carnap's Preface (precisely as those passages are cited above in q. 494, with the exception that Neurath for emphasis added a few exclamation marks to the punctuation and took the liberty of deleting a couple of superfluous phrases; see ibid., p. 625). Neurath concluded his review with the following spirited ejaculations:

> The Marxist research-work will sooner or later draw impetus [*Anregungen schöpfen*] from the efforts of empirical rationalism – in particular, valuable support is to be found with certain foundational works – is quite certain, but it is perhaps more essential that there be an *active centre of anti-metaphysical thinking*, whose powerful activity, whose effect on popular education [*Volksbildung*] we can wish for in the interests of universal enlightenment! From here will come to us philosophical friends, supplying tools for further development [*Wieterbau*]!
>
> Anyone who seriously wants to familiarize himself with the most modern questions of philosophy, do not neglect to read Carnap's great work, which to be sure makes itself accessible only with penetrating study, but, as the short Preface shows, is open to popular reformulation. It is to be hoped that Marxist students will not pass up the opportunity to absorb as much as possible of this empirical rationalism during their college years and to make use of it for Marxism! In Vienna, where Schlick and Carnap teach, is now again the occasion for that!
> [Ibid., p. 626]

There is more than a touch of irony in the fact that it is in the perhaps imperturbable (certainly still quite unperturbed) bastion of so-called 'capitalist ideology', the United States of America, that the 'logical empiricism' of the Vienna Circle (with its apparently in part politically motivated anti-metaphysical and anti-theological bent) has thrived so dogmatically during the past half-century – for which circumstance there must of course be some rationalization from the 'left'; see for example M. Cornforth's attack on the movement in *In Defence of Philosophy* (London: Lawrence and Wishart, 1950).

The political perspective from which some of the core members of the Vienna Circle viewed the *wissenschaftliche Weltauffassung* they espoused is similarly reflected in an article Neurath published the following year (1929). Using the same hyperbolic, hortatory style as he employed in his review of Carnap, he wrote in a review of one of Russell's works,

> The socialist proletariat travels over any path which serves the anti-capitalist way of thinking and more penetrating clarity! The Englishman Bertrand Russell has, as few others, done both.... This is the same man who today is esteemed world-wide as the leader of exact philosophy, that world-view which traces out the logico-mathematical structure of objects and their complexes [*Verknüpfungen*]....
>
> The impulse toward intellectual cleanliness [*Sauberkeit*], toward the conquest of all theological vestiges [*Reste*: dregs] in thinking, is usually coupled with the renunciation of traditional views and attitudes in other domains. The Marxist is not surprised when he so remarkably often comes across this revolutionary way of thinking in the philosophical domain among men who also as a rule oppose capitalist and religious [*kirchliche*] tradition. Empiricism, atheism and socialism in our age dwell in utmost proximity to each other. The bourgeois order, in which indeed many spend their existence, organizationally supports religious and metaphysical thinking in general; whereas the proletarian front, which allows the individual religious person his convictions so long as he is a good fighter in the class-struggle [*ein guter Klassenkämpfer*], does nothing organizationally for the consolidation of theological or metaphysical thinking. Anti-metaphysicians invigorate the impact of the proletariat!
>
> Marxism is today indeed the most forceful training for the anti-metaphysical world-view [*Weltanschauung*], even if it has not systematically carried on the logical clarity of empirical rationalism. Others have taken over this task. It is only a matter of time before exact philosophy and Marxism are joined together....
>
> The 'Vienna School of exact philosophy' around Moritz Schlick promotes the new spirit of intellectual cleanliness through years-long joint work. Each one stimulates the others, in this manner all enhance their capacities. At the same time, though, there are also exact philosophers over the whole world who hold out their hands to each other across countries. One of the great stimulators, one who radiates his thinking in all directions, is Bertrand Russell, the hero [*Held*]! How few political reactionaries there are among these exact philosophers! Some of them are Marxists and stand in the worker's movement, almost all are opponents of capitalist and religious authority [*Herrschaft*]. [O. Neurath, "Bertrand Russell, der Sozialist", *Der Kampf*, vol. 22 (1929), pp. 234–5, a review of a German translation (Berlin: Dreimasken–Verlag, 1928) of Russell's *The Prospects of Industrial Civilization* (London: George Allen and Unwin, 1923)]

And in yet another review of one of Russell's works around this same period, Neurath again presents the anti-metaphysical task of the Vienna Circle's *wissenschaftliche Weltauffassung* in a political light:

Marxism is *science*. For the scientific world-view science can only be concerned with controllable states of affairs. If statements are made, then the proponent of this orientation asks, what do they signify empirically. In this manner one can to begin with eliminate the *meaningless* [*sinnleer*] statements of metaphysics. . . . [O. Neurath, "Bertrand Russell, Wissen und Wahn", *Der Kampf*, vol. 24 (1931), p. 187, a review of a German translation (Berlin: Dreimasken-Verlag, 1930) of Russell's *Sceptical Essays* (London: George Allen and Unwin, 1928)]

Now what is one to make of all of this? First of all, as previously indicated, the politics *in itself* is insignificant. What is of philosophical worth in the Circle's contributions to logic and the philosophy of science certainly can be assessed quite independently of the jejune political platitudes of some of the more politically outspoken members of the group – and this regardless of the fact that some of the core members of the group (for instance, Carnap, Neurath, Hahn and P. Frank) seem to have perceived their philosophical activity as intimately linked to their politics. In any event, the political backdrop to the Vienna Circle, a backdrop, incidentally, which was consonant with the dominant political fashions in Vienna during the 1920s and 1930, is not an especially novel revelation – see, for example, Rainer Hegselmanns' Introduction to O. Neurath, *Wissenschaftliche Weltauffassung, Sozialismus und logischer Empiricismus* (Frankfurt am Main: Suhrkamp, 1979), and E. Nemeth's *Otto Neurath und der Wiener Kreis: revolutionäre Wissenschaftlichkeit als politischer Anspruch* (Frankfurt am Main: Campas, 1981).

The political backdrop to the Vienna Circle does, however, provide an insight into part of what seems to have led Wittgenstein to speak so expansively of "the spirit of this civilization, whose expression is the industry, architecture, music, fascism and socialism of our time", a spirit characterized by a scientific "way of thinking" and by the word 'progress' (see q. 429). The *wissenschaftliche Weltauffassung* of the Vienna Circle, or the "new scientism" as Neurath affectionately referred to it in 1935 (see "Le développement du Cercle de Vienne et l'avenir de l'empirisme logique", in translation in Neurath, *Gesammelte Schriften*, vol. 2, esp. pp. 693 and 699), is clearly an instance of the manifestation of the scientific intellectual spirit of the age in the field of philosophy (as well as the other disciplines represented by the group). Moreover, the political proclivities of some of the core members of the Circle provide a straightforward instance of how the scientific intellectual spirit manifested itself in the politics, in this case the socialism, of our time – a politics which Wittgenstein expressly repudiated (along with fascism) in his 1930 draft foreword (q. 429). This explicit repudiation is incontrovertible, *whatever* illusions Wittgenstein may have entertained about a Tolstoian existence in Russia – see the potpourri of ridiculously conflicting reports cited by J. Moran in "Wittgenstein and Russia", *New Left Review*, no. 73 (May–June 1972), pp. 83–96. Also, the notion of 'progress' was certainly a fundamental part of the Circle's outlook, even if 'making progress' was not one of its features (cf. Wittgenstein's comments in q. 429). This aspect is evidenced most obviously in the Vienna Circle's adoption of what F. E.

Manuel, in *The Prophets of Paris* (Cambridge, Mass.: Harvard University Press, 1962), p. 13, has rightly called the "ideology of progress" of the enlightenment thinkers. Auguste Comte was in fact cited by the Circle as one of the positivistic progenitors of their *wissenschaftliche Weltauffassung* (see Neurath et al., *Wissenschaftliche Weltauffassung*, in Neurath, *Gesammelte Schriften*, vol. 1, p. 303). In Comte too there was a conception of history in terms of linear progress culminating in a 'scientific' stage of development which supersedes the 'metaphysical' and 'theological'. (There is of course also in Marxism an 'ideology of progress'.) Noteworthy is the fact that even the particular metaphor of progress ("constructing a building") repudiated by Wittgenstein in the last lines of his draft foreword had been used by Carnap in his characterization of the scientific task of his circle of "collaborators" (*Mitarbeitenden*): "stone will be carefully joined to stone and a sound [*sicherer*, secure] building will be erected at which each following generation can continue to work" (Carnap, *Der logische Aufbau der Welt*, p. v; cf. *The Logical Structure of the World*, p. xvii). It is illuminating to recall at this juncture that it was precisely a Comtean enlightenment conception of Western history in terms of linear 'progress' to which Spengler was reacting in *Decline of the West*, and it is the methodological form of Spengler's reaction that seems to have positively influenced Wittgenstein's own later *Denkweise* (see my discussion in n. 230). Thus it is not at all surprising that Neurath early in 1921 should have been so chafed by Spengler's views – citing and attacking, in fact, some of the very passages and aspects of Spengler's thinking that seem to have later been seized upon and adapted by Wittgenstein for his own philosophical purposes. Contrast Neurath's diatribe "Anti-Spengler", in *Gesammelte Schriften*, vol. 1, pp. 139–96, and cf. also the views of R. von Mises in *Positivism: a study in human understanding* (New York: Dover, 1968), pp. 359–63, with my discussion in n. 230 of Spengler's influence on Wittgenstein's later *Denkweise* – note in particular that Neurath cites (see "Anti-Spengler", p. 148) and seems to have been especially disconcerted by precisely one of the same Spenglerian passages as I have suggested may have served as a source of positive inspiration for Wittgenstein contributing to the emergence of his later *Denkweise*.

There is little doubt that it was indeed at least in part the expansive *wissenschaftliche Weltauffassung* of the Vienna Circle to which Wittgenstein was reacting in his 1930 draft foreword. Exhibited in that foreword is a clear opposition to the sort of expansive views one finds in the concluding passages of both Carnap's 1928 Preface and the 1929 'manifesto' put out by the Circle. Evidently, we have in great measure the Vienna Circle, and particularly its radical core, to thank for *provoking* Wittgenstein to the work we now know as his later philosophy.

The clash between the 'spirit' of Wittgenstein's later philosophy and the *wissenschaftliche Weltauffassung* of the Vienna Circle, however, is of genuine interest only to the extent that it can be shown to manifest itself concretely in *specific* features of Wittgenstein's *Denkweise*. To identify some of the concrete manifestations of this clash of 'spirit' one needs only to search out those aspects of Wittgenstein's Tractarian philosophy which the Vienna

316   *Notes*

Circle embraced as standards for their *wissenschaftliche Weltauffassung*. It was that embrace which in part led Wittgenstein to recognize that he himself, even with respect to the 'logical' aspects of his earlier work, had to a certain extent been caught up in the 'scientific' fashions of the times. And it was precisely the features of his Tractarian philosophy embraced by the Vienna Circle that Wittgenstein came to recognize as instances of a 'scientific way of thinking' and to repudiate, in a process so central to the emergence of his later *Denkweise*. Some of the specific Tractarian features repudiated have already been discussed above in this chapter. But the most striking feature of the *Tractatus* championed by the Vienna Circle as a cornerstone, indeed *the* distinguishing feature, of their *wissenschaftliche Weltauffassung* was the notion of 'logical analysis' (see, for example, Neurath et al., *Wissenschaftliche Weltauffassung*, in Neurath, *Gesammelte Schriften*, vol. 1, pp. 305 and 307). The latter concrete and essential feature of Wittgenstein's Tractarian philosophy came also to be repudiated by him and recognized as an instance of a 'scientific way of thinking'. A discussion of this important specific repudiation is forthcoming in the present chapter, and in relation to that discussion the broader considerations of the present lengthy note simply offer a more general perspective and historical background.

495 Feigl, "The Wiener Kreis in America", p. 639. Interestingly, Feigl tries to rationalize away Wittgenstein's strong averse reaction to him (Feigl) and Carnap as a 'clash of personalities' rather than a difference of philosophical substance (see ibid., pp. 638–9). Cf. also Carnap's rationalization discussed in n. 426.

496 Schlick, in opposition to some of the more vocal (such as Neurath) and historically influential (such as Carnap) members of the Vienna Circle, seems to have taken a more moderate 'logical positivist' line during the mid-1930s. See, for instance, Schlick's disagreements with the more radical elements of the movement in his address to the Eighth World Congress of Philosophy in Prague in 1934 – M. Schlick, "L'école de Vienne et la philosophie traditionnelle", in *Gesammelte Aufsätze 1926-1936* (Vienna: Gerold, 1938), especially pp. 391–5. The moderation one finds in Schlick's writings during the 1930s is most probably due to his encounters with and receptivity to Wittgenstein's later views (see, for example, Schlick's explicit acknowledgement in 1936 in "Meaning and Verification", reprinted ibid., p. 340) – which views already by 1928-9 seem to have dramatically clashed with the spirit of 'logical positivism' (cf. my comments in n. 426 and chapter 5, p. 185ff). Schlick apparently had maintained "close personal relations" with Wittgenstein after the latter had gone to teach at Cambridge in the 1930s (see Ayer, "The Vienna Circle", p. 70). In Schlick's writings during the last few years before his untimely death in 1936 there is a very curious (and at times unhappy) amalgam of the influence of both Wittgenstein's *Tractatus* and Wittgenstein's later philosophical views.

497 MS 155, pp. 129–30. The second of the above paragraphs has been cited in n. 460. The two paragraphs remained paired in MS 112 (pp. 145–6), but were later separated in TS 213: the first paragraph was included in the section (13) entitled "Primary and Secondary Signs" (see TS 213, p. 46), while the

parenthetical methodological dictum was included in the "Philosophy" chapter (see ibid., p. 432). Cf. also Wittgenstein's revision of TS 213 in MS 114, p. 60 (published in *PG*, pp. 88-9) and the later more thorough revision in MS 116 (p. 42ff). Also in the "Philosophy" chapter of TS 213 is, incidentally, the version of the 'description, not explanation' dictum later published in *PI* §126 (cited q. 469).

498 MS 153b, pp. 7-8. Also included in MS 112, p. 231. A similar point was more generally made by Wittgenstein as early as 1930 when he warned, "We must be aware of what *explanation* means. There is a constant danger of wanting to use this word in logic in a sense which is derived from physics" (MS 109, p. 108, later included in the "Philosophy" chapter of TS 213, p. 418).

499 MS 112, p. 267 (1931). Cf. n. 233 for the version included in the "Elementary Propositions" section (28) of TS 213 (pp. 100-1; published in *PG*, p. 210). Recall that Wittgenstein's Tractarian conception of logical analysis was also explicitly repudiated in the *Umarbeitung* of the 'Brown Book' (see q. 398).

500 B. Russell, *Our Knowledge of the External World as a Field for Scientific Method in Philosophy* (London: George Allen and Unwin, 1972), pp. 28 and 40; see also p. 189. Cf. n. 437 above.

501 Ibid., p. 7.

502 See B. Russell, "Address", in *Actes du Congrès International de Philosophie Scientifique, Paris 1935 - I. Philosophie scientifique et empirisme logique*, in *Actualités scientifiques et industrielles*, no. 389 (Paris: Hermann, 1936) pp. 10-11). Many of the European organizers and participants at that conference, upon their immigration to the United States during the 1930s, helped to establish 'scientific philosophy' as among the prevailing gospels in North America.

503 Carnap, *Der logische Aufbau der Welt*, p. 1.

504 B. Russell, "The Relation of Sense-data to Physics", reprinted in *Mysticism and Logic and Other Essays*, pp. 156-7. See ibid., p. 155 for the 'maxim' Carnap cited from Russell (q. 503).

505 Reprinted in Gottlob Frege, "Über Begriff und Gegenstand", *Funktion, Begriff, Bedeutung; fünf logische Studien* (Göttingen: Vandenhoeck and Ruprecht, 1962), p. 67. (Cf. *Tractatus* 3.221.) With only a few changes the above translation is that of P. T. Geach in G. Frege, *Translations from the Philosophical Writings of Gottlob Frege* (Oxford: Basil Blackwell, 1980), pp. 42-3.

506 MS 116, pp. 80-1. Except for the last two sentences, this translation is that found in *PG*, p. 211. Part of this passage has been cited in n. 176, in the context of a discussion of Wittgenstein's notion of a 'phenomenal' or 'primary' language.

507 MS 115, p. 55. First drafted in the margins of TS 213, p. 257.

508 MS 161, p. 113, Also in MS 124, p. 49. Published in *CV*, p. 40.

509 Reported by G. E. Moore in "Wittgenstein's lectures in 1930-33", p. 27. It is, incidentally, a historical irony, but perhaps all too typical of our generations' failure to grasp the spirit of Wittgenstein's later *Denkweise*, that excerpts from Moore's notes on Wittgenstein's 1930-3 lectures should as late as 1981 have been selected for inclusion in a collection entitled *Essential Readings in Logical Positivism*, ed. O. Hanfling (Oxford: Basil Blackwell, 1981).

Presumably it was the editor's assumption that Wittgenstein's lectures during the early 1930s, right after his return to philosophy, must still have been of the Tractarian bent which the Vienna Circle found so congenial to their outlook. Quite to the contrary, however, the spirit of Wittgenstein's *Denkweise* captured in Moore's notes on the 1930-3 lectures was not in keeping with but rather constituted a repudiation of the sort of *wissenschaftliche Weltauffassung* and *wissenschaftliche Denkweise* championed by the positivist movement and epitomized by their conception of 'logical analysis'. It is similarly ironic, but not at all regrettable, that A. J. Ayer felt he could not do justice to a work such as *Philosophical Investigations* by selecting *only parts* of it for inclusion in his anthology of readings in logical positivism (see Ayer's editorial introduction to *Logical Positivism*, p. 28).

510 MS 154, pp. 116-17. Later included in MS 113, p. 123. The identification of Ramsey here as one whose thinking reflected the 'scientific spirit' of the age is quite consistent with several other remarks Wittgenstein made about Ramsey in the *Nachlaß*. Most of Wittgenstein's contact with Ramsey's views seems to have been in the form of "innumerable conversations" he had with him during the last two years prior to Ramsey's death in January 1930. Thus many of the views Ramsey expressed to Wittgenstein in conversation are not to be found in what little we have of Ramsey's mostly posthumously published writings. Nevertheless, worthy of note are several of Wittgenstein's remarks about Ramsey's views – remarks which clearly indicate that Wittgenstein considered Ramsey too to have been caught up in the 'scientific' intellectual fashions of the times. In chapter 3 (q. 217) Wittgenstein was cited as attributing to Ramsey the view that logic is a "normative science". Wittgenstein does not seem to have been very clear about just what Ramsey may have meant in saying that, but he indicated that, if Ramsey meant that logic sets up an 'ideal' to which language only approximates (and thus logic would be prescriptive *vis-à-vis* ordinary language), then he disagreed with Ramsey. Drafted in 1931, that reference to Ramsey, as reworked in 1933-4 (see n. 217), later was included in *PI* §81, along with the explicit retort that "logic does not treat of language – or of thought – in the sense in which a natural science treats of a natural phenomenon".

Apparently along similar lines, in 1936 Wittgenstein wrote, "What happens to the ideality [*Idealität*] of logic in our point of view? For I am of course not making a natural sicence of it. I don't want you to take the ideal in the way, if I am not mistaken, Ramsey had done..." (MS 152, pp. 81-2). Also, in 1941 one finds Wittgenstein remarking, "Ramsey was quite right that (in philosophy) one must be neither 'woolly' nor scholastic. Though I don't believe he saw how that is to be achieved; for the solution is not in being scientific." (MS 163, p. 114). And again, around roughly the same period, he charged "Against Ramsey", "Not empiricism, and yet realism in philosophy, that's what's most difficult. //Realism, but not empiricism//" (MS 164, p. 67, published in *S*, vol. 6, p. 325; cf. MS 129, p. 128). It is obvious, then, that also in his disagreements with Ramsey, though we have no record of Wittgenstein's conversations with him, a bone of contention was the 'scientific spirit' of Ramsey's way of thinking.

An issue perhaps related to the sort of general subject raised in the first two critical references to Ramsey just cited – namely, the subject of whether 'logic' is concerned with an 'ideal' which is to serve a normative or prescriptive role *vis-à-vis* ordinary language – is the issue of the reform of language. Wittgenstein's position on the issue of whether or not our ordinary language is inadequate and in need of reform has already been discussed in chapter 2. There it was seen that, although early in his career he apparently considered ordinary language as a "form of historical rubbish ... that would be replaced by something direct, modern" (see n. 174), in his post-1930 writings he repudiated such a view (see p. 55ff). And in q. 475 in the present chapter Wittgenstein's methodological stance that we should 'leave the grammar as it is' and just *describe* the use of our expressions is a vivid reflection of his post-1930 position on the issue of linguistic reform. For present purposes it is relevant to point out that Wittgenstein came to consider also the inclination to refine language by applying words in new ways as characteristic of a 'scientific way of thinking'. This comes out clearly in one of his remarks written in 1948. In the midst of a discussion of the concept 'seeing', he abruptly advised, "One must just take the concept 'seeing' as one finds it; not want to refine it." He then raised the question, "And why not [refine it]?" – to which he answered, "Because it is not our problem to change it, to introduce (as science does) [a sense] adapted for some purpose or other, but rather to understand it; in order not to produce a false conception of it" (MS 137, p. 29; see also MS 127, pp. 72–3, published in *CV*, p. 44).

511 See nn. 175, 176, 220; and chapter 2, pp. 56–7. Cf. also Wittgenstein's comments in the 'Blue Book' (*BBB*, p. 70), where he suggests that "the introduction of this new phraseology ['phrases describing sense data'] has deluded people into thinking that they had discovered new entities, new elements of the structure of the world, as though to say 'I believe that there are sense data' were similar to saying 'I believe that matter consists of electrons'". (And cf. q. 505, where Frege speaks of the introduction of new names for discovered logical simples.)

512 MS 134, p. 153. Later included in *RPP*, vol. I, §949. Cf. also the truncated version which found its way into *Zettel* §458.

513 A. Ambrose, "The Yellow Book Notes in Relation to *The Blue Book*", *Critica: revista hispanoamericana de filosofia* (Mexico), vol. IX, no. 26 (Aug. 1977), p. 6.

514 'Blue Book', *BBB*, p. 18.

515 Contemporary logicians, who consider what they are doing to be 'metaphysics', should at least be given credit for being more honest, if not more enlightened (see n. 340).

516 'Blue Book', *BBB*, p. 35.

517 Ibid.

518 Ibid., pp. 5–6. These remarks were part of a continued discussion of the general question (ibid., p. 1) "What is the meaning of a word?" Note that on p. 5, prior to the above-cited criticism of the psychological, scientific approach to the question of what constitutes the 'meaning' or 'life' of signs, Wittgenstein had introduced his own 'logical', linguistically relativistic,

answer to this question (see chapters 4 and 5; the particular passage in question has been cited in qq. 402–4).

Wittgenstein, incidentally, did not consider the 'metaphysical' confusion of conceptual and factual matters to be the sole province of 'scientific *philosophers*'. He considered scientists themselves to be often guilty of such confusion. As late as 1947 one finds him, for instance, complaining about the field of psychology in general,

"Thinking is an enigmatic process, of which we are a long way off from complete understanding." [Cf. q. 508.] And now one starts experimenting. Evidently without being aware of *in what* for us the enigma of thinking lies.

And this misunderstanding //lack of understanding// permeates the whole of psychology. It is a conceptual confusion, and thus the feeling of the problematical, plus an experimental method. The experimental method does *something*; its failure to solve the problem is blamed on its still being in its beginnings. It is as if one were to determine what matter and spirit are by chemical experiments. [MS 135, p. 114; part of this passage was crossed out and thus was not included in the version later published in *RPP*, vol. I, §1093]

519 This last sentence obviously trades on Hume's famous concluding remark in his *An Inquiry Concerning Human Understanding*. The saying of course has been the war cry of the positivist movement and empiricist philosophy in general, the war cry of the would-be 'scientific philosophers' of our era (cf., for example, Ayer in *Logical Positivism*, p. 10).
520 MS 121, p. 26.
521 'Blue Book', *BBB*, pp. 27–8.
522 Ibid., p. 27.
523 First drafted in 1936 in MS 152, p. 94, where Wittgenstein, parenthetically noting that he had put it better elsewhere, more simply wrote, "Philosophy is a struggle [*Kampf*] against the fascination [*Faszination*] of language."

Bibliography

Ambrose, A., "The Yellow Book Notes in Relation to *The Blue Book*". *Critica: revista hispanoamericana de filosofia* (Mexico), vol. IX, no. 26 (Aug. 1977), pp. 3–20.
Anscombe, G. E. M., *An Introduction to Wittgenstein's "Tractatus"* (London: Hutchinson, 1963).
Ayer, A. J., (ed.), *Logical Positivism* (London: The Free Press, 1963).
——, "The Vienna Circle", in *The Revolution in Philosophy*, ed. A. J. Ayer (London: Macmillan, 1956), pp. 70–87.
Bain, Alexander, *The Senses and the Intellect* (London: Longmans, Green, 1868).
Baker, G. P., and Hacker, P. M. S., *Wittgenstein: understanding and meaning* (Chicago: University of Chicago Press, 1980).
Binkley, T., *Wittgenstein's Language* (The Hague: Martinus Nijhoff, 1973).
Bogen, J., *Wittgenstein's Philosophy of Language* (London: Routledge and Kegan Paul, 1972).
Canfield, J. V., "Names and Causes", *Philosophical Studies*, vol. 35 (1979), pp. 71–80.
Carnap, R., "Die alte und die neue Logik", *Erkenntnis*, vol. I (1930–1), pp. 12–26.
——, "Intellectual Autobiography", in *The Philosophy of Rudolf Carnap*, ed. P. A. Schilpp (La Salle, Ill.: Open Court, 1963), pp. 1–84.
——, *The Logical Structure of the World*, tr. R. A. George (Berkeley Calif.: University of California Press, 1967).
——, *The Logical Syntax of Language*, tr. Amethe Smeaton (Countess von Zeppelin) (London: Kegan Paul, Trench, Trubner, 1937).
——, *Der logische Aufbau der Welt* (Berlin-Schlachtensee: Weltkreis-Verlag, 1928).
——, "Die physikalische Sprache as Universalsprache der Wissenschaft", *Erkenntnis*, vol. II (1932–3), pp. 432–65.
Cattell, J. M., "The Time It Takes to See and Name Objects", *Mind*, vol. II (Jan. 1886), pp. 63–5.
Copi, I., "Objects, Properties, and Relations in the *Tractatus*", *Mind*, vol. 67 (1958), pp. 145–65.
Cornforth, M., *In Defence of Philosophy* (London: Lawrence and Wishart, 1950).
Drury, M. O'C., "Conversations with Wittgenstein". In *Ludwig Wittgenstein: personal recollections*, ed. Rush Rhees (Oxford: Basil Blackwell, 1981).

Eddington, A. S., "The Meaning of Matter and the Laws of Nature According to the Theory of Relativity" *Mind*, vol. 29 (Apr. 1920), pp. 145–58.
——, "The Philosophical Aspects of the Theory of Relativity", *Mind*, vol. 29 (Oct. 1920), pp. 415–22.
Engelmann, P., *Letters from Ludwig Wittgenstein*, ed. B. F. McGuinness, tr. L. Furtmüller (Oxford: Basil Blackwell, 1967).
Feigl, H., "The Wiener Kreis in America", *Perspectives in American History*, vol. II (Cambridge, Mass.: Harvard University Press, 1968), pp. 630–73.
Frank, Phillip, "Eröffnungsansprache" ('Opening Address' to the meeting of the Ernst Mach Society in Prague in 1929), *Erkenntnis*, vol. I (1930–1), pp. 93–5.
Frege, G., "Über Begriff und Gegenstand", in *Funktion, Begriff, Bedeutung: fünf logische Studien* (Göttingen: Vandenhoeck and Ruprecht, 1962). pp. 66–80.
——, *Translations from the Philosophical Writings of Gottlob Frege*, ed. and tr. P. Geach and M. Black (Oxford: Basil Blackwell, 1980).
Galton, Francis, *Inquiries into Human Faculty and its Development* (London: J. M. Dent, 1907).
Gier, N., *Wittgenstein and Phenomenology* (Albany: State University of New York Press, 1981).
Hahn, Hans, "Die Bedeutung der wissenschaftliche Weltauffassung, inbesondere für Mathematik und Physik", *Erkenntnis* vol. I (1930–1), pp. 96–125.
Hallet, G., *A Companion to Wittgenstein's "Philosophical Investigations"* (Ithaca, NY: Cornell University Press, 1977).
Hanfling, O. (ed.), *Essential Readings in Logical Positivism* (Oxford: Basil Blackwell, 1981).
Hartley, David, *Observations on Man, his Frame, his Duty, and his Expectations* (Gainesville, Fla: Scholar's Facsimiles and Reprints, 1966).
Hegselmann, Rainer, Introduction to O. Neurath, *Wissenschaftliche Weltauffassung, Sozialismus und logischer Empiricismus* (Frankfurt am Main: Suhrkamp, 1979).
Hume, David, *Enquiries Concerning the Human Understanding and Concerning the Principles of Morals* (Oxford: Clarendon Press, 1927).
Hunter, J. F. M., "'Forms of Life' in Wittgenstein's *Philosophical Investigations*", *American Philosophical Quarterly*, vol. 5, no. 4 (Oct. 1968), pp. 233–43. Also in *Essays on Wittgenstein*, ed. E. D. Klemke (Urbana: University of Illinois Press, 1971), pp. 273–97.
——, *Understanding Wittgenstein* (Edinburgh: Edinburgh University Press, 1985).
James, William, "The Association of Ideas", *Popular Science Monthly*, vol. XVI (Mar. 1880) pp. 577–93.
——, *Principles of Psychology*, 2 vols (New York: Henry Holt, 1890).
——, "On Some Omissions of Introspective Psychology", *Mind*, vol. 9 (Jan. 1884), pp. 1–26.
Kenny, Anthony, "From the Big Typescript to the Philosophical Grammar", *Acta Philosophica Fennica*, vol. 28, nos 1–3 (1976).
Kraft, Victor, *The Vienna Circle: the origin of neo-positivism*, tr. Arthur Pap (New York: Philosophical Library, 1953).
Kripke, S., "Naming and Necessity", in *Semantics of Natural Language*, ed. D. Davidson and G. Harmon (Dordrecht: D. Reidel, 1972), pp. 253–355.

Leblanc, H., and Wisdom, W. A., *Deductive Logic*, 2nd edn (Boston, Mass.: Allyn and Bacon, 1976).
Lenk, Hans, *Metalogik und Sprachanalyse* (Freiburg im Breisgau: Rombach, 1973).
Locke, John, *An Essay Concerning Human Understanding* (Oxford: Clarendon Press, 1924).
Lyons, John, *Semantics*, vol. I (Cambridge: Cambridge University Press, 1977).
Malcolm, N., "Anselm's Ontological Argument", *Philosophical Review*, vol. 69 (Jan. 1960), pp. 41-62.
———, Review of *Philosophical Investigations*, *Philosophical Review*, vol. 63 (1954), pp. 530-59.
———, *Ludwig Wittgenstein, a Memoir* (London: Oxford University Press, 1958).
Manuel, F. E., *The Prophets of Paris* (Cambridge, Mass.: Harvard University Press, 1962).
Moore, G. E., "Wittgenstein's Lectures in 1930-33," *Mind*, vol. 64 (Jan. 1955), pp. 1-27.
Moran, J., "Wittgenstein and Russia", *New Left Review*, no. 73 (May-June 1972), pp. 83-96.
Nemeth, E. *Otto Neurath und der Wiener Kreis: revolutionäre Wissenschaftlichkeit als politischer Anspruch* (Frankfurt am Main: Campus, 1981).
Neurath, Otto, "Anti-Spengler", in *Gesammelte philosophische und methodologische Schriften*, vol. 1 (Vienna: Hölder-Pichler-Tempsky, 1981), pp. 139-96.
———, "Le développement du Cercle de Vienne et l'avenir de l'empirisme logique", tr. B. Treschmitzer and H. G. Zilian, in *Gesammelte philosophische und methodologische Schriften*, vol. 2 (Vienna: Hölder-Pichler-Tempsky, 1981), pp. 673-702.
———, *Empiricism and Sociology*, ed. Marie Neurath and R. S. Cohen, tr. P. Foulkes and Marie Neurath (Dordrecht: D. Reidel, 1973).
———, *Gesammelte philosophische und methodologische Schriften*, 2 vols (Vienna: Hölder-Pichler-Tempsky, 1981).
———, "Historische Anmerkungen" (Historical Remarks), *Erkenntnis*, vol. I (1930-1), pp. 311-14.
———, "Protokollsätze", *Erkenntnis*, vol. III (1932-3), pp. 204-14.
———, Review of Carnap, *Der logische Aufbau der Welt*, *Der Kampf*, vol. 21 (1928), pp. 624-5.
———, "Bertrand Russell, der Sozialist", a review of Russell, *The Prospects of Industrial Civilization*, *Der Kampf*, vol. 22 (1929), pp. 234-5.
———, "Bertrand Russell, Wissen und Wahn", a review of Russell, *Sceptical Essays*, *Der Kampf*, vol. 24 (1931), pp. 186-7.
———, "Wege der wissenschaftliche Weltauffassung", *Erkenntnis*, vol. I (1930-1), pp. 106-25.
Neurath, O., et al., *Wissenschaftliche Weltauffassung. Der Wiener Kreis* (Vienna: Artur Wolf, 1929). Reprinted in Neurath, *Gesammelte philosophische und methodologische Schriften*, vol. 1 (Vienna: Hölder-Pichler-Tempsky, 1981), pp. 299-336.
Ogden, C. K., and Richards, I. A., *The Meaning of Meaning: a study of the influence of language upon thought and of the science of symbolism* (London: Kegan Paul, 1923).
Petrie, Hugh, "Science and Metaphysics: a Wittgensteinian interpretation", in

Essays on Wittgenstein, ed. E. D. Klemke (Urbana: University of Illinois Press, 1971), pp. 138-69.

Ramsey, Frank, Review of Ogden and Richards, *The Meaning of Meaning*, *Mind*, vol. 33 (Jan. 1924), pp. 108-9.

Rochester, J., "Philosophy as Therapy: an examination of Wittgenstein's philosophical method" (PhD dissertation, University of Toronto, 1978).

Russell, Bertrand, "Address," *Actes du Congrés International de Philosophie Scientifique, Paris 1935 - I. Philosophie scientifique et empirisme logique*, in *Actualités scientifiques et industrielles*, no. 389 (Paris: Hermann, 1936), pp. 10-11.

——, *The Analysis of Mind* (London: George Allen and Unwin, 1921).

——, *The Autobiography of Bertrand Russell* (London: George Allen and Unwin, 1975).

——, *An Inquiry into Meaning and Truth* (New York: W. W. Norton, 1940).

——, *Logic and Knowledge*, (London: George Allen and Unwin, 1956).

——, "On Propositions: what they are and how they mean", *Proceedings of the Aristotelian Society*, 1919, supplementary vol. II, pp. 1-43.

——, "On Scientific Method in Philosophy", in *Mysticism and Logic and Other Essays*, (London: George Allen and Unwin, 1959), pp. 97-124.

——, *Our Knowledge of the External World as a Field for Scientific Method in Philosophy* (London: George Allen and Unwin, 1972).

——, *The Prospects of Industrial Civilization* (London: George Allen and Unwin, 1923).

——, "The Relation of Sense-data to Physics", In *Mysticism and Logic and Other Essays* (London: George Allen and Unwin, 1959), pp. 145-79.

——, Review of Ogden and Richards, *The Meaning of Meaning*, *The Nation and Athenæum*, vol. 33 (21 Apr. 1923), pp. 87-8.

——, Review of Ogden and Richards, *The Meaning of Meaning*, *The Dial*, (Aug. 1926), pp. 114-21.

——, *The Scientific Outlook* (London: George Allen and Unwin, 1931).

——, *Sceptical Essays* (London: George Allen and Unwin, 1928).

Schlick, Moritz, "L'école de Vienne et la philosophie traditionnelle", in *Gesammelte Aufsätze 1926-1936*, (Vienna: Gerold, 1938), pp. 389-98. Also in Moritz Schlick, *Philosophical Papers*, vol II, ed. H. L. Mulder and B. F. B. van de Velde-Schlick, and tr. Peter Heath (Dordrecht: D. Reidel, 1979), pp. 491-8.

——, "Meaning and Verification", in *Gesammelte Aufsätze 1926-1936* (Vienna: Gerold, 1938), pp. 337-67. Also in Moritz Schlick, *Philosophical Papers*, vol II, ed. H. L. Mulder and B. F. B. van de Velde-Schlick (Dordrecht: D. Reidel, 1979), pp. 456-81.

——, "The Theory of Relativity in Philosophy", in *Philosophical Papers*, vol 1, ed. H. L. Mulder and B. F. B. van de Velde-Schlick, tr. Peter Heath (Dordrecht: D. Reidel, 1979), pp. 343-53.

Semon, R., *Die Mneme als erhaltende Prinzip im Wechsel des organischen Geschehens* (Leipzig: Wilhelm Engelmann, 1908).

Sherry, P., "Is Religion a 'Form of Life'?", *American Philosophical Quarterly*, vol. 9 (1972), pp. 159-67.

Spengler, Oswald, *Der Untergang des Abendlandes*, vol. I (Munich: Oskar Beck, 1923).

——, *Decline of the West*, tr. C. F. Atkinson (London: George Allen and Unwin, 1926).
Stenius, E., *Wittgenstein's "Tractatus"* (Oxford: Basil Blackwell, 1960).
Toulmin, S., and Janik, A., *Wittgenstein's Vienna* (New York: Simon and Schuster, 1973).
Von Mises, R., *Positivism: a study in human understanding*, tr. J. Bernstein and R. G. Newton in collaboration with the author (New York: Dover, 1968).
Von Wright, G. H., "A Biographical Sketch", in *Ludwig Wittgenstein: the man and his philosophy*, ed. K. T. Fann (Atlantic Highlands, NJ: Humanities Press, 1967), pp. 13–29.
——, "The Origin and Composition of Wittgenstein's *Investigations*", in *Wittgenstein: sources and perspectives*, ed. C. Luckhardt (Hassocks, Sussex: Harvester Press, 1979), pp. 138–60.
——, "Special Supplement: the Wittgenstein Papers", *Philosophical Review*, vol. 78 (Oct. 1969), pp. 483–503.
——, *Wittgenstein* (Oxford: Basil Blackwell, 1982).
——, "Wittgenstein in Relation to his Times", In *Wittgenstein and his Impact on Contemporary Thought: Proceedings of the Second International Wittgenstein Symposium*, ed. E. Leinfellner et al. (Vienna: Hölder-Pichler-Tempsky, 1978), pp. 73–8.
Watson, John, *Behavior: an introduction to comparative psychology*, (New York: Henry Holt, 1914).
Wittgenstein, Ludwig, *The Blue and Brown Books*, 2nd edn, ed. with a preface by Rush Rhees, (New York: Harper and Row, 1965). [*BBB*]
——, *Culture and Value*, ed. by G. H. von Wright in collaboration with Heikki Nyman, (Chicago: University of Chicago Press, 1980). [*CV*]
——, *Last Writings*, ed. by G. H. von Wright and Heikki Nyman, tr. C. G. Luckhardt and M. A. E. Aue (Oxford: Basil Blackwell, 1982). [*LW*]
——, *Letters to C. K. Ogden*, ed. with an intro. by G. H. von Wright, (Oxford: Basil Blackwell, 1973). [*LO*]
——, *Letters to Russell, Keynes and Moore*, ed. with an intro. by G. H. von Wright, assisted by B. F. McGuinness (Oxford: Basil Blackwell, 1974). [*LRKM*]
——, "Letters to G. H. von Wright", *Cambridge Review*, 28 Feb. 1983.
——, *Notebooks 1914-16*, ed. G. E. M. Anscombe and G. H. von Wright, tr. G. E. M. Anscombe (Oxford: Basil Blackwell, 1961). [*N*]
——, *On Certainty*, ed. G. E. M. Anscombe and G. H. von Wright, tr. Denis Paul and G. E. M. Anscombe (New York: Harper Torchbooks, 1972). [*OC*]
——, *Philosophical Grammar*, ed. Rush Rhees, tr. Anthony Kenny (Berkeley, Calif.: University of California Press, 1978). [*PG*]
——, *Philosophical Investigations*, 3rd edn, ed. G. E. M. Anscombe and Rush Rhees, tr. G. E. M. Anscombe (New York: Macmillan, 1968). [*PI*]
——, *Philosophical Remarks*, ed. Rush Rhees, tr. R. Hargreaves and R. White (Oxford: Basil Blackwell, 1975). [*PR*]
——, *Proto-tractatus*, ed. G. H. von Wright, B. F. McGuinness and T. Nyberg (Ithaca, NY: Cornell University Press, 1971). [*PT*]
——, *Remarks on Colour*, ed. G. E. M. Anscombe, tr. L. L. McAlister and M. Schattle (Oxford: Basil Blackwell, 1977). [*RC*]

——, *Remarks on the Foundations of Mathematics*, ed. G. H. von Wright, G. E. M. Anscombe and Rush Rhees, tr. G. E. M. Anscombe (Oxford: Basil Blackwell, 1967). [*RFM*]

——, *Remarks on the Philosophy of Psychology*, 2 vols, ed. G. H. von Wright, G. E. M. Anscombe and Heikki Nyman, tr. G. E. M. Anscombe, C. G. Luckhardt and M. A. E. Aue (Oxford: Basil Blackwell, 1980). [*RPP*]

——, *Schriften*, 6 vols (Frankfurt am Main: Suhrkamp, 1960–). [*S*]

——, *Tractatus Logico-Philosophicus*, tr. D. F. Pears and B. F. McGuinness, with an intro. by Bertrand Russell (London: Routledge and Kegan Paul, 1977). [*Tractatus*]

——, "Ursache und Wirkung: intuitives Erfassen", ed. Rush Rhees, tr. Peter Winch, *Philosophia*, vol. 6, nos. 3–4 (Sept.–Dec. 1976).

——, *Wörterbuch für Volksschulen* (Vienna: Hölder-Pichler-Tempsky, 1977). [*WV*]

——, *Zettel*, ed. G. E. M. Anscombe and G. H. von Wright, tr. G. E. M. Anscombe (Berkeley, Calif.: University of California Press, 1970). [*Zettel*]

——, "The Wittgenstein Papers" (Ithaca, NY: Cornell University Microfilms).

Wuchterl, K., and Hübner, A., *Ludwig Wittgenstein im Selbstzeugnissen und Bilddokumenten* (Reinbeck bei Hamburg: Rowohlt, 1979).

Wundt, W., *Grundzüge der physiologischen Psychologie*, vol. II (Leipzig: Wilhelm Engelmann, 1887).

Index

ability, *see* being able to
abstract, 64–6, 130, 200, n. 186, *see also under* calculus; grammar; language
abstraction, 63–4, 79–81, 96, n. 230
accompaniment
  physical, 94, 151, 176
  psychological, 47, 53–5, 57, 94–6, 122, 124–5, 127–8, 135–6, 140–3, 145–6, 148–51, 160, 170, 183–4, 224, n. 149, n. 319, n. 323, n. 388, n. 392, n. 394, n. 400, n. 420
  see also association
activity, 146, 163–5, 180, 183–4, 186–7, 196, n. 360, n. 376, n. 392, n. 422, *see also under* scientific
alienation (Wittgenstein's), 190–1
Ambrose, A., 69, 222, n. 343
amorphous, 46, 55, 83, 139–40
analysis, 110–13, 117, 118, 165–7, 171, 175, 177, 179, 202, 214–21, 223–4, 226, n. 220, n. 233, n. 428, n. 447
  chemical, 168, 177, 216, 223
  complete, 214, 218–20, n. 176, n. 222
  logical, 76–7, 80–1, 86–7, 90, 168–9, 210, 214–15, 219, n. 222, n. 228, n. 233, n. 494, n. 509
analogy
  account books (transaction ledger), 127–30, 132–3, n. 324, n. 341
  chemical, 168, 177, 216, 218, 220–1, 223, n. 233
  chess, 59, 61, 74, 101, 124–5, 129, 136, 159–60, n. 323, n. 360, n. 366
  false, 44, 53–5, 136, 141
  game, 77, 78, 82, 88, 102, 106, 125, 128–9, 133

money, 51, 54, 159–61, n. 360
picture, 54–5, 87, n. 275, *see also* picture theory; sentence, as a picture
therapy, 3, 18, n. 71
tool/instrument, 125, 166, 170, 209, n. 422, n. 427, *see also under* word
  see also under method
Anscombe, G. E. M., 11, 51, 53, 100, n. 163, n. 175, n. 227, n. 228, n. 337
Anselm, St, 184–5
application, 72, 78, *see also under* calculus; signs; use
association(s), 60, 109, 115–16, 121, 124–5, 194, 197–201, 224, n. 263, n. 293, n. 294
associationism, 109, 194, 196–9, n. 444, n. 448, n. 477
atomism, 167, 171, 176, 224, n. 176, n. 228, n. 233, *see also* simples; proposition, atomic
Augustine, 19, 92, 104, 105, 169, 172, n. 228
Ayer, A. J., n. 494, n. 509, n. 519

Bachtin, N., n. 125
Bain, A., 197
Baker, G., 52–3, 91, n. 70, n. 107, n. 144, n. 259
behaviourism, 119, n. 294, n. 316
being able to (can), 44, 70, 132, 170, 207, n. 360, n. 370
believe/belief, 46, 55, 117, 118, 132, 134, 140–1, 147, 151–3, 158, 160–3, 170, 180, 195–7, 202, 205, n. 296, n. 297 *see also under* feeling

Index

Berkeley, G., 114–15, n. 283, n. 448
Binkley, T., 18–19
brain, 159, 163, 176
Breuer, J., 13

calculus, 77, 122, 125–6, 130, 133–6, 139, 142, 145–6, 157, 161–4, 180–1, 205–6, n. 259, n. 341, n. 343, n. 360, n. 370, n. 392
  abstract, 81, 211
  application of a, 79, 136, 219
  exact, 83, 86, 105–7, n. 218
  of logic, 79, 219–20
  model/view of language, 98–9, 101, 104, 105–6, 110–11, 113, 117, 121, 128–9, n. 247, n. 256, n. 259, n. 369, *see also* language, calculus/game/system conception of
  post-1930 notion of, 98–102, 104–5, 108, 122, n. 260, *see also under* language
  role/use in a, 100–1, 103, 122, 125, 128–9, 131, 134, n. 318, n. 400
  term in a (part of a), 155, 205, n. 178, n. 256
  Tractarian notion of, 81, 98–9, 100, 106–8, 135, 219, n. 260
  see also under construct; description; ideal
Canfield, J., n. 265
Carnap, R., 212–13, 216–18, 220–1, 224, n. 126, n. 175, n. 220, n. 228, n. 233, n. 426, n. 490, n. 494, n. 495, n. 496
Cassirer, Ernst, 181
Cattell, J., 198, 200–2
cause, 114, 133, 192, 194, 196–7, 204, 207, 209, *see also under* explanation; meaning; mnemic causation
change in perspective, 60, 77–8, 139, 146–7, 167, 171, 176, 215, *see also under* emergence; *Denkweise*
circumstances, surroundings (*Umständen*, *Ümgebung*), 151–3, 174–5, 177, 180, 188, n. 341, n. 360, n. 392, n. 394, n. 422
clarity, purity, 58–9, 64, 79–80, 213
  complete, 75, 82
  see also philosophy as clarification
colour, 165, n. 335
  samples, 171–7
  words/concepts, 100, 108, 115, 130–1, 171–7, 220

command, *see* orders
complete, *see under* analysis; clarity; grammar; language; rules
complex, *see* simple
complex(es), 172, 176, 223, n. 228, n. 494, *see also* concatenation; simples
complexity, *see* language, complexity of
Comte, A., n. 494
concatenation, 172–3, n. 228
concepts
  geometry of, 130–1, n. 335, *see also* metaphors, spatial
  historical development of, 73
  ordinary, 74
  see also under colour; construct; geometry; ideas; landscape; psychological; structure
conceptual
  distinctions, 70–1, 73, n. 206, *see also under* investigation; philosophy, problems of
  geography, 130–1, *see also* metaphors, spatial
  landscape, 8, 16, *see also* metaphors, spatial
  world (microcosm), 72–3
concrete, 64, 78, 82
confusion, philosophical, 49, 56, 58, 63, 161, 163, 168, n. 173, n. 227, n. 518, *see also* misunderstanding
consciousness, 53, 55–8, 136, 141, 201, 208, n. 176, n. 481, *see also under das Primäre*; state
construct, 191, 217, n. 283, n. 292, n. 475, n. 494
  a calculus, 62, 81, 87, n. 260
  a concept, 71
  a language, 56–7, 61–3, 66, 86–91, 93, 97, 167, n. 173, n. 228, n. 239
  a proposition, 80, 214, 216, n. 233
contextualism, 9–15, n. 36
convention, 171, 204, n. 176
Copi, I., n. 228
correct (symbol, word), 115, 119
correspondence, 80, 94, 115, 147, 156, 167–8, 172, n. 178, n. 228, n. 233, n. 244, *see also* harmony
culture, 180–1, 190–1, 193, n. 230, *see also* spirit of our times

definition, 57, 62–3, 153–4, 165–6, 169, 171, 211, 218–20, n. 176, n. 259

formal, 63, 214
ostensive, 100, 153–4, 176–7, 215, *see also under* gesture; language; pointing
Denkweise (way of thinking), 5–6, 18, 21, 27, 38–9, 40, 42, 65, 69, 74, 79, 82–4, 90–1, 97, 98, 102, 137, 139, 141, 157, 166, 180–1, 183–5, 189, 190–3, 202, 224–6, n. 160, n. 189, n. 228, n. 230, n. 233, n. 427, n. 432, n. 494, n. 509
  shift in Wittgenstein's, 60–1, 63, 66, 69, 76, 78–9, 81–3, 86–7, 90, 97, 138–9, 177, 179, 210, n. 87, n. 142, n. 159, n. 164, n. 230, *see also under* change; emergence
  transitional period in Wittgenstein's, 26–8, 30, 34–5, 37–9, 67–9, 86, 89–92, 96, 98, n. 144
  turning round his, 83, 97
  see also under method; scientific
description, 57, 113, 165, 181, 194, n. 155, n. 394, n. 413
  of a calculus, 104, 136, 142, 205–6
  vs explanation, 16–17, 51–2, 55, 202–9, 215, 223, n. 164, n. 497
  of language, 16–17, 23, 51–2, 55, 71, 78, 80–1, 90, 156, 179–80, 205–6, 209, n. 360
  of language game, 102, 129, 187, 189, 205–6, n. 360, n. 376
  of meaning, 129, 170
  psychological, 150, 152, 154, 158–9
  of a reality, 72, 77–8, 187–8
  of structure, 131
  of a system, 129, 178, 205–6, n. 259
  of use, 133, 154, 178–9, 206, 209, n. 259, n. 360, n. 475, n. 510
  world-description, 72
  see also philosophy as descriptive
discovery, *see under* philosophy; scientific
dogmatism, 61, 80–1, 83–5, 87, 96–7, 106, 214, n. 228, n. 229, n. 230, n. 340
Drury, M., n. 119

Eddington, A., n. 282
effects, *see under* language; signs
elementary, *see under* individuals; propositions; simples
emergence
  of notion of forms of life, 157, 165–7, 179, 183, 189
  of notion of language game, 98–9, 108, n. 87, n. 144

  of post-1930 view of signs/language, 108, 110, 117, 121, 125, 132–3, 136–7, 169, 196, 204, n. 294
  of Wittgenstein's linguistic relativism, 166, 179, 189
  of Wittgenstein's method/approach to philosophy, 3, 6, 26–8, 30, 34–5, 37–9, 40–2, 49, 59, 65, 68–70, 74–5, 82, 84, 92, 97, 109, 114, 137, 166, 192–3, 204, 225, n. 119, n. 120, n. 494
  see also under change; *Denkweise*, transition period in, shift in
emotion(s), 117, 185, 225
empiricism, 109, 114, 195, 212, n. 175, n. 265, n. 282, n. 494, n. 510, n. 519
Engelmann, P., n. 45
error, 159, 162, 168–9, 172, 177, 222, n. 173, n. 175 n. 317, n. 421
  of insufficient specificity, 179–80, 183, 185
  see also mistakes
essence/essential, 44, 46, 55, 56, 80, 115, 159, 206, n. 173, n. 230, n. 259, *see also under* logic; name; proposition; word
ethereal, 45, 47, 58–60, 142, 159, 163, *see also* pneumatic; process; queer
exactness, 82, 121, 168, n. 216, n. 233, n. 340, *see also under* grammar; ideal; language game
exist/existence, 166–8, 172, 212, n. 228
expect/expectation, 46, 117, 139, 141, 144–53, 155–8, 163, 180, 181, 197, 224, n. 263, n. 275, n. 361, *see also under* expression; fulfilment
experience(s), 47–8, 54, 56–7, 118, 119–20, 122, 124, 132, 135–6, 140–1, 152, 159–60, 195–7, 204, 207, n. 149, n. 175, n. 220, n. 230, n. 283, n. 323, n. 335, n. 339, n. 448, n. 481, n. 494
experiment, 199–202, n. 518
explain/explanation, 51–4, 58, 113
  causal, 205, 221–2, 224–5
  of language, 55, 58, 60, 63, 65–6, 71, 143, 194, 196–8, 202, 206, 208–10, 215, 224, n. 176, n. 178, n. 218
  metalogical, 54–5, 58, 60, 63, 65–6, 71, 210, n. 176, n. 178, n. 218
  psychological, 196, 205–10, 221, 224
  see also under description; grammatical; meaning; philosophy; scientific
expression
  of belief, 134, 151

expression (cont.)
  of expectation, 140, 147, 149–53, 155
  form of, 60, 81–2, 187–8, n. 227, n. 228, n. 369, n. 380, *see also* form of representation
  of hope, 134, n. 420
  of an order, 150–1
  symbolic, 54, 63
  of thought, 46, 56, 58, 108, 113, 134, 154, 159, 170, 194, n. 149
  of a wish/desire, 94–5, 134, 155–6, n. 380
  see also philosophy, concerns of

fact(s), 59, 127, 131, 156, 165, 202–4, 220–2, n. 228, n. 335 n. 360, n. 361, *see also under* grammatical; language; mental; psychological
family (family resemblance), 64, 83–4, 90, 168, n. 230, n. 233, n. 428
fascism, 191, n. 494
fate, 186, 188
feeling(s), 109, 117, 127, 160, 165, 197, 208–9, n. 297, n. 299, n. 366, n. 448, n. 481
  belief-feelings, 117, 194–5, n. 297, n. 323
  as the meaning of connectives (if-feeling, or-feeling, and-feeling, but-feeling), 117–18, 123–5, 208, n. 323, n. 481
  as the meaning of words, 123, 127, 138, 194, 224, n. 319, n. 323
  of negation, *see* negation
Feigl, H., 214, n. 490, n. 494, n. 495
'form of life', 139, 146, 157, 163–6, 179–89, 212, 220, n. 376, n. 392, n. 413, n. 427
  cultural-historical interpretation of, 180–1
  language game interpretation of, 183–9, n. 421, n. 422
  multiplicity (diversity) of, 165, 167, 170–1, 176, 179–80, 185, n. 428
  "organic" interpretation of, 182–3, n. 421
form of representation, 64, 73, 83, *see also* expression, form of
formal, 63, 64–6, 130, 181, 210, 214, n. 333
  see also under definition; language; structure
Frank, P., n. 490
Frege, G., 63, 217–18, 220, n. 228, n. 333, n. 511
Freud, S., 13

fulfilment
  of expectation, 146–8, 150, 156
  of an order/command, 147, 157, n. 378
  of a wish, 147, 154, 156
function, 77, 151, 157, 174, 177, 181, 187–8, 214, *see also under* language; language game; logical; proposition; sign; truth-function; use; words

Galton, F., 198–200, 208, n. 448
game
  move of the, 94, 104, 122, 126, 129, 155, 204, *see also* language game, moves in
  see also under analogy; ideal; language game; rules
Geach, P., 12
general conception, 64–5, 76, 81, n. 186, n. 188, n. 259
generality, 61–3, 78, 81, 85, *see also* proposition, general forms of
gesture, 123, 130, 149, 176–7, 215, *see also* definition, ostensive; pointing
Gier, N., 180–1, 185, n. 41, n. 175, n. 413, n. 414, n. 422
goal, aim
  of philosophy, 4, 17–19, 23, 56–8, 74, 131, 169, 191, 214–15, n. 175, n. 220, n. 494
  stylistic, 22
  of Wittgenstein research, 3, n. 110
  see also philosophy, task of
God, 114, 115, 184, 186–9, n. 283
Goodman, N., n. 175
Groag, H., 14, n. 45
grammar 64, 81–2, 93, 96, 108, 113–14, 125–33, 139, 149–50, 154–6, 158, 161–4, 169–70, 178–80, 189, 194, 205–6, 222, 224, n. 45, n. 159, n. 173, n. 324, n. 332, n.335, n. 339, n. 340, n. 341, n. 348, n. 349, n. 360, n. 427, n. 475, n. 510
  abstract, 82, 132
  complete, 135–6
  exact, 82–3
  hypothetical, 82
  logical, n. 333
  as a mechanism, 162
  multifarious, 96
  surface vs depth, n. 332
  see also under ideal
grammatical, 62, 110, 211
  explanations, 153–4

facts, 127
investigation, 14, 108, 126–7, n. 45, n. 173, n. 175
illusion, 64, n. 189
mistakes, 7, n. 228
remarks (sentences/propositions/statements), 129–31
rules, 61, 76, 79, 135–6, n. 323, n. 341, n. 400, n. 428
space, n. 341
system, 149, n. 400

Hacker, P. M. S., 52–3, 91, n. 70, n. 107, n. 144, n. 259
Hahn, H., n. 490, n. 494
Hallett, G., 89, n. 88
harmony, between language or thought and reality 154–6, n. 369, *see also* correspondence
Hartley, D., 197, n. 443
Hegel, G. W. F., n. 448
hidden 64–5, 100, 122–3, 135, 137, 145, 158, 162–3, 204, 206, 216, 224, n. 233, n. 318, n. 340, *see also* language, behind; signs, behind the
hope, 134, 152, 180, 181, *see also under* expression
Hume, D., 109, 114–16, n. 264, n. 282, n. 283, n. 294, n. 296, n. 297 n. 448, n. 519
Hunter, J. F. M., 180, 182–3, n. 53, n. 364, n. 420, n. 421, n. 481
Husserl, E., n. 175
hypotheses, 56, 80, 172, 179, 195, 202–4, 210, 215, 217, 222
hypothetical, 57, 80, 96, 105–7, 172, 203, 217, *see also under* grammar; language games

idea (*Vorstellung*) 53–6, 57, 64, 79, 116, 132, 136, 138, 141, 171, 197, 199–201, 206, n. 149, n. 176, n. 283, n. 294, n. 297, n. 341, n. 448
preconceived (prejudice), 83–4, 203, n. 228
see also concepts; images
ideal 81, 83, 136, 218, n. 220, n. 229, n. 230, n. 340, n. 428, n. 510
calculus, 78–9, 81, 106–7, 135, 214, 219–20, n. 220, n. 228
cases, 76, 81, 84, 86–7, 89–93, 96–7, 105–6, n. 230, n. 231

game, 76, 78, 80–2, 89, 96–7
grammar, 79, 82, 135–7, n. 341
name, 80–1
order, 75–7, 79, n. 222, n. 340, n. 341
role of, 69, 74, 76–88, 90–1, 97, 106, n. 218, n. 225, n. 227, n. 228, n. 230
see also under abstraction; language; language game
idealism, 56–7, 114–15, n. 176, n. 297
illusion, 44, 61–2, n. 141, n. 230, *see also under* grammatical
image-proposition, 115–17, 122, n. 294
image(s) (mental), 54–6, 57, 103, 110, 115–20, 122–3, 153, 171, 176, 198, 200, 206, n. 149, n. 283, n. 294, n. 297, n. 341, n. 360, n. 392, n. 445, n. 448
imagine/imagination, 7, 46, 94, 103, 121–2, 152, 161, 163, 171, 197, *see also* to picture
imagination-image, 115
impression(s), 70–1, 109, 197, 199, 219, n. 176, n. 206, n. 283, n. 388
inadequacies, 75–6, 83–5, 90–1, 95, n. 228
individuals, 172, n. 228
influences, intellectual (on Wittgenstein), 12–13, 40–1, n. 41, n. 43, n. 45, n. 120, n. 428, n. 432, n. 494
inner, n. 230
mechanism, 162
processes, 44, 170
speech, n. 149
instrument, *see under* analogy, words
intention, 43, 46, 53, 65, 141, 169, 208, n. 275, n. 366
interpret/interpretation, 46, 119–20, 122, 135, 169, 176, 195–6, 217, n. 309, n. 366
introspection, 163, n. 392, n. 448
intuition, 46, 55
investigation(s)
conceptual/philosophical, 16, 47, 71–2, 78, 202, 209, 222, n. 160, n. 173, n. 175, n. 475
factual/empirical, 222, n. 337
logical, 66, 114, n. 337
psychological, 114, 127, 196, 210
see also under grammatical; scientific

Jacquard loom, 161–2
James, W., 99, 117, 118, 121, 123–5, 134, 194, 196–9, 200–2, 204–10, 212, 224–5, n. 264, n. 277, n. 283, n. 293,

Index

James, W. (cont.)
  n. 296, n. 297, n. 323, n. 348, n. 436,
  n. 437, n. 444, n. 445, n. 448, n. 477,
  n. 481, n. 494

Kant, I., 181
Kenny, A., 11, 28–9, 31, n. 109, n. 400
Keynes, J. M., 110, n. 120
Kierkegaard, S., 185
knowing, 46, 55, 64, 70–4, 132, 134, 152–3,
  196, n. 206, n. 339, n. 360
Kripke, S., 109, n. 265
Kuhn, T. S., 138

language
  abstract, 62–3
  acting like a drug/potion, 44, 109,
    159–60
  agreements about, 157, n. 376
  as autonomous, 104, 122, 127–8, 154,
    204, n. 256, n. 370
  behind, 45, 54, 56, 138, 145–6, *see also*
    signs, behind the
  calculus/game/system conception of 99,
    110–11, 113–14, 117, 121–2, 124–6,
    129, 131–4, 136–7, 142–3, 145–6, 149,
    156–7, 162–3, 178, 180, 205, 207, 215,
    n. 294, n. 332, n. 341, n. 400, n. 427,
    see also signs, logical view of
  complete, 89
  complexity of, 17, 23–4
  demonstrative use of, 115
  disorderliness of, 16–17, 20
  dynamic view of, 177–9
  effects of, 100, 108, 113–17, 133, 194,
    206, n. 294, *see also under* signs
  essence of (nature of), 66, 79–83, 92, 95,
    106–7, 134, 139, 166, 187, 211–12,
    223–4, n. 188, n. 228, n. 259, n. 428
  facts of/about, 75, 127, 130, 202, 215,
    222, n. 163
  formal, 63, 82–3, 131, n. 126
  foundations of, 206
  functioning of, 95–6
  ideal, 76, 78, 84, 86–91, 96, 215, 218–20,
    223–4, n. 186, n. 220, n. 228, n. 230,
    n. 233, n. 428
  'in order as it is', 17, 77, *see also*
    proposition, is in order
  of ideas (*Vorstellungen*), 56
  logical view of, 126, 138, 162, 200, *see
    also under* signs
  magical view of, *see under* signs
  mentalistic view of, 138
  multiplicity (diversity) of, 76–7, 85, 90,
    165–6, 224, n. 230, n. 259, *see also
    under* language game
  narrative use of, 115
  order in, 79
  ordinary/everyday, 40, 47, 49–51, 54–66,
    77, 79, 81–2, 86–90, 94, 97, 105, 133,
    138–9, 171, 185, 210–11, 214–15, 220,
    222–3, n. 142, n. 159, n. 163, n. 164,
    n. 173, n. 174, n. 175, n. 176, n. 178,
    n. 186, n. 222, n. 227, n. 228, n. 259,
    n. 260, n. 510, *see also under* concepts
  ostensive use of, 115
  as phantasm, 59, 61, 65
  phenomenal ('phenomenological'),
    56–9, 61, 66, 167, 169–70, 214, 218–19,
    n. 173, n. 174, n. 175, n. 176, n. 177,
    n. 220, n. 228, n., 414, n. 506
  primary, 56–8, 66, 167–70, 176, 214–16,
    219–21, 223, n. 173, n. 175, n. 176,
    n. 220, n. 228, n. 414, n. 506
  private (possible candidates for a notion
    of), in Russell, 118, 217; in Frege, 218
  protocol, n. 220
  psychological view of, 121, 125, 137,
    138, 183, 196, 206–7, *see also under*
    meaning; signs
  reality of, 78–81
  reform, refine, regulate, 74–6, 86, 88,
    n. 231, n. 510
  relativity theory of, *see* relativism,
    linguistic
  religious, 185–9, n. 427
  secondary, 56
  simple, primitive, 87, 89–90, 92–3, 128,
    167, 172, 223, n. 228
  speaks for itself, 48, n. 153, n. 256, n. 370
  state view of, 138, 177–9
  sublime, 79, n. 228
  symbolic, 62–3
  system of, 89, 103, 104, 121, 128, 134–5,
    142–4, 149–50, 156, 161, 172, n. 259,
    n. 360, n. 366, n. 380, *see also under*
    grammatical; language, calculus/game/
    system conception of; signs
  uniformity (homogeneity) of, 61–2,
    64–6, 77–8, 81–3, 85, 90, n. 51, n. 228,
    n. 230, n. 259
  see also under calculus; construct;
    description; explanation; harmony;

language game; practice; proposition; relativism; sentence; signs; structure; system; vagueness; words
language game(s), 45, 89–96, 102, 106, 122, 125–6, 130, 139, 144–6, 152–3, 155, 162–6, 169–71, 174–7, 180–1, 183–8, 205–7, 212, n. 176, n. 259, n. 335, n. 360, n. 394, n. 397, n. 422
of builders, 92–6, n. 200, n. 228
exact/precise 75–8, 80, 82, 84, 87, 90–1, 105, 107, n. 216, n. 428; as heuristic device, 74–6, 78, 82, 86, 88, 90–3, 95–7, 107, n. 218, see also rules, precise
extant, 69, 105, 107, n. 230, see also practice, locus of linguistic
hypothetical (constructed, ad hoc), 67–74, 80, 86, 89–91, 96–7, 105–7, 172–7, n. 200, n. 244, n. 396; role (purpose, use, function) of, 70–2, 74–5, 78, 82, 91–3, 95, 177, 199, 206, n. 206, n. 339, see also objects of comparison
ideal, 78, 84, 91, 105
invention of, n. 337
model of language, 98–9, 101, 104, 105, 107, 121, 137, see also language, calculus/game/system conception of
moves in, 108, 129, 132–3, 138, 143, 157, 161, 179, n. 341, n. 366, see also game, move of the
multiplicity of, 164–7, 172, 174, 176–7, 185, n. 396, n. 428 see also under language
role/use/function in a, 103, 124–5, 128–9, 131, 133, 138, 150–1, 178, 182, 209, n. 360, n. 392, n. 400, n. 427
rules of, see under rules
simple, 75, 82, 89–91, 105, n. 239
see also under description; emergence; method
Lenk, H., 41
life, see form of life; signs, life of
Littlewood, J., n. 282
Locke, J., 109, n. 264
logic, logician 40–1, 48–9, 62, 64–5, 71, 76–7, 82–3, 86–8, 105–6, 115, 118, 125, 131–2, 138–9, 166, 210, 220, n. 190, n. 260, n. 294, n. 333, n. 340, n. 397, n. 498, n. 510, n. 515, see also under calculus; philosophy
domain of, 49–50, 59–60, 63, 66, 81, 87

normative, 76–7, see also science, normative
logical/logically, 168, 180, 182, 189, 210–11, 217, 221–2, n. 149, n. 317, see also under analysis; atomism; conceptual distinctions; grammar; investigation; positivism; signs; structure; words
connectives, see under feelings; words, logical
construction, 217, 219, n. 176
essential, 74, 95
form, 210, n. 126
function, 217
order, 77, n. 222
product, 216, n. 233
simple, 218, n. 511
'lost decade', 40–1, 43, 110–15, 118, 120–1, 123–4, 126, 137, 189, 211, 214, n. 45, n. 271, n. 275, n. 276, n. 294
Lukasiewicz, J., n. 126
lying, 128

Mach, E., Ernst Mach Society, n. 282, n. 490, n. 494
Malcolm, N., 180, 183–5, 189, n. 422
Marxism, see socialism
mastery, of a technique, 155, n. 360, n. 370, see also being able to
mathematics, 50, 61, 110, 180, 183, 192, 209, 217, 218, n. 70, n. 160, n. 275, n. 278
meaning
Bedeutung, 48, 51, 53–5, 56, 57, 64, 108–11, 113, 115–16, 118, 120, 123–4, 127–9, 133–7, 138, 141, 143–6, 149–51, 153, 155, 157–9, 161–74, 176–84, 189, 194–7, 202, 204–9, 212, 222, 224–6, n. 149, n. 153, n. 292, n. 294, n. 318, n. 323, n. 341, n. 348, n. 370, n. 378, n. 392, n. 394, n. 427, n. 443, n. 518
causal theory of, 108–20, 126, 133–4, 178, 194–5, 204, 206, 209, 221, 224, n. 148, n. 263, n. 265, n. 276, n. 294, n. 307, n. 316, see also mnemic causation
contextual theory of, 120
criterion of, 145, 212, see also meaningfulness
explanation of (sense) 113, 122, 133, 144, 153, 167, 183, 186–7, 189, 194, 205,

meaning (*cont.*)
  207, 209, 221, 224–5, n. 318, *see also* explanation, causal
  is no soul, 176, *see also under* soul
  meinen 42–9, 53, 59, 94–6, 103, 104, 106, 121–2, 134, 138, 143–5, 169, 170, 202, 210, 224–5, n. 149, n. 153
  psychological view of, 115–18, 125, 142, 148, 170, 183, 200, 206–7, 224, n. 400, n. 518, *see also under* language; signs
meaning-blindness, n. 477
meaning-body (*Bedeutungskörper*), 100, 122–5 n. 348
meaningfulness, 66, 80, 166–8, 171, 177, 179–80, 181, 182, 186–8, 211–12, 214, 220–1, 223, n. 335, n. 360, n. 400, n. 426, n. 427, n. 445, n. 494, *see also* meaning, criterion of
mechanism, *see under* grammar; inner; Jacquard loom; mind; psychological; sentence; thinking
memory, 117, 197, 199
mental
  activity, 135, 159, 182, 196, 201
  entities, 138, 154
  events, 120, 138, 150, 154
  facts, 118, 208, n. 448
  occurrences, 117–18, 122, 144, 182, 195, n. 294
  phenomena, 221
  picture, 46, 54–5, 94–5, n. 360, n. 448
  process, 47, 54, 59, 94–6, 134–5, 138–9, 151, 171, 202, 224, n. 309
  state, 94–6, 138, 150, n. 206
  see also under association; idea; image; impressions; mind; picture; psychological
metalogic/metalogical, 40–50, 54–6, 58–61, 63–6, 71, 95, 134, 136, 138–9, 141–2, 145, 179, 210, 224, n. 126, n. 134, n. 137, n. 142, n. 147, n. 149, n. 153, n. 155, n. 176, n. 188, n. 190, n. 349, *see also under* explanation
metaphor(s)
  glasses, 81
  spatial 129–32, 157–8, 177–8, n. 333, n. 335, n. 341, n. 400, *see also* geography; geometry; grammatical space; physiognomy
metaphysics, 43, 50, 60, 154, 185, 196, 202, 213, 221–6, n. 87, n. 163, n. 228, n. 283, n. 340, n. 426, n. 448, n. 494, n. 515, n. 518, *see also under* question
method/approach
  of analogy, n. 230, n. 259, n. 360, *see also* analogy; objects of comparison
  language game, 67, 71–3, 91–3, 96, n. 200, n. 239 *see also* language game, hypothetical; object of comparison
  new, 5, 30, 34, 38, 40, 91, 192, 212, 220, n. 45, n. 230, n. 335
  philosophical, 3–6, 9, 25–6, 49, 52, 74, 88, 127, 171–2, 180, 190, 195, 202–9, 212, 215, 217–18, n. 45, n. 107, n. 292
  vs style, 15–25, 69
  see also under Denkweise; emergence; scientific
mind, 46, 54–5, 94–5, 101, 108–14, 116–18, 121–3, 127, 136, 142, 144, 150–1, 153, 159, 171, 178, 194, 196–9, 200, 204, 206, 208, 224, n. 283, n. 360, n. 378, n. 400, n. 448
  mechanism of, 225
  model in one's, 73–4, n. 360
  state of, 150, 152, 154, *see also under* state
  see also mental
mistakes, Wittgenstein's confessions/recognition of, 42, 46, 53–5, 60, 64, 66, 68–9, 76–81, 87, 107, 135–6, 141, 168–9, 171–2, 215–16, 219–21, n. 149, n. 176, n. 228, n. 233, n. 275, n. 341, n. 348, n. 360, n. 361, n. 428, *see also* grammatical mistakes
misunderstanding, misconception, 51, 65, 74–5, 82–3, 95, 128, 140, 145, 150, 158, 161, 203, 210, 219, n. 176, *see also* confusion
mnemic causation, 110, 116–17, 119–21, 194–5, 197, n. 277, n. 294
model, 85, n. 228, n. 230, n. 292, *see also under* calculus; language game; mind; prototype
Moore, G. E., 5, 68, 192, 220, n. 275, n. 509
multiplicity, *see under* form of life; language; language game
must, 64–5, 78–80, 83–5, 87, 107, 134–5, n. 228
mystical, n. 271, *see also under* style
mythology, 188, 195, n. 44, n. 142

name(s), naming, 77, 80, 109, 166–77,
    197–8, 201, 208–9, 214, 223–4,
    n. 228, n. 256, n. 265, n. 370, n. 428,
    n. 445
  bearer of a, 166–70, 172, 177, n. 233
  essence of a, 81, n. 228
  'real' (authentic), 87, 167–8, 223, n. 228,
    n. 233, n. 397, see also under 'real'
negation,
  feeling of, 118, 208, n. 299
  sign, 46–7, 178
  truth table for, 178
Neurath, O., n. 175, n. 220, n. 490, n. 494,
    n. 496
neutral monism, 117, n. 283
Nicod, J., 75, 76, 83–4, 90, 111, n. 214
nonsense, 57, 135, 168, 187, n. 147, n. 190,
    n. 335, see also meaningfulness
notebooks (Wittgenstein's)
  destroyed, n. 16
  diary nature of, 6–9, 21, 24, n. 70
  microfilms of, 2
  missing, 33, n. 15, n. 107
  system of reference for, 1–2
'now', n. 228, n. 397

object(s), 79, 116, 171, 198, 219, 223–4,
    n. 176, n. 178, n. 228, n. 494
  of the mind, 54, 169, n. 448
  simple, 166–9, 172, 176, 214, 218, 220,
    n. 220, n. 228, n. 229
object(s) of comparison (Vergleichsobjekte)
    75–6, 78, 83–8, 90–1, 97, 107, n. 228,
    n. 230, see also language games,
    hypothetical; method of analogy
Ogden, C. K. (and Richards, I. A.), 99,
    109–14, 118–22, 126, 131, 134, 194–6,
    199, 202, 204–6, 209–10, 212, 224,
    n. 275, n. 276, n. 296 n. 297, n. 307,
    n. 309, n. 316, n. 348, n. 436
order, see under ideal; language; logic; style
orders, 43, 45, 47, 143–4, 148, 150–1, 155,
    157–8, 164–5, 181, 186–7, n. 378,
    n. 394, n. 413, see also under
    fulfilment; expression
ordinary language (see under language)

perception, 57, 202
perspicuous, 19, 191
phenomenalism, 221, n. 175, n. 282, n. 283,
    n. 494, see also language, phenomenal

phenomenology, 181, n. 173, n. 175, see
    also language, phenomenological
philosophical view/notion/idea, 71, 73,
    94–5, 172, 185, n. 228
philosophy
  and argumentation, 19, 71–2
  as clarification, 52, 58–9, 72, 75, 86, 91,
    93, 113, 131, 145, 150, 170, 185, 191,
    194, 210, 222, 224, n. 186, n. 339,
    n. 392, see also clarity
  concerns of, 63, 222, n. 259, n. 436,
    n. 494; and linguistic expressions, 43,
    50, 55, 61, 82, 122, 139, 143, 149–50,
    183, 211, 222, 226, n. 378
  dead-end in, 57, 121, 159
  as descriptive, 16–17, 23, 51–2, 57, 71–2,
    129, 131, 156, 178–80, 181, 202–9,
    223, n. 282, n. 360, n. 376, n. 392,
    n. 427, see also description
  and discovery, 50, 61–3, 65–6, 81, 117,
    130, 194, 204, 211–12, 214–18, 220–2,
    224, n. 228, n. 233, n. 259, n. 511, see
    also under scientific
  doctrines of, 3–6, 13, 38–9, 140–1, n. 142
  and explanation, 194, 202–10, 215,
    222–5, n. 470, n. 498, see also
    description vs explanation
  leaves everything as it is, 50, 62, 205–6
  and logic, 49, 66
  and poetry, 19
  (conceptual) problems/muddles of, 3–5,
    7, 9, 25, 49, 61–2, 73, 75, 90, 92–5,
    151, 161, 165–6, 179–80, 203–4, 207,
    209–11, 221–2, 225–6, n. 87, n. 160,
    n. 163, n. 200, n. 341, see also
    misunderstanding
  role of examples/cases in, 3, 14, 63, 65,
    79, 96, 177, 219, n. 45, n. 189, n. 228
  and science, 5, 131, chapter 6 passim
    n. 436, n. 510
  talent for, 5, 8, 13–14, 18, 24
  task of, 63, 203, 222–3, 226, n. 186,
    n. 360, n. 494, see also under goal
  theories in, see theory
  and therapy (see under analogy)
  see also under goal; investigation;
    method; questions
physics, 114, 195, 216, 217–18, 224, n. 282,
    n. 498
physiognomy, 130, n. 230, n. 335, see also
    metaphors, spatial

picture, 46, 54–5, 135, 163, n. 228, n. 230, n. 265, n. 360, n. 366
 false, 219
 theory, 80–1, 87, n. 149, n. 176, n. 275, see also sentence, as a picture
 see also under analogy; image; mental
to picture, 144, 151–2, 160–1, n. 137, n. 178, see also imagine
Plato, 172
pneumatic (spiritual, ethereal), 122, 128, 203, 205, see also under processes
pointing, 135, 153, 169, 176–7, n. 406, see also gesture; definition, ostensive
positivism, n. 282, n. 494, n. 519
 logical, 187, 211–14, n. 175, n. 282, n. 494, n. 496, n. 509
possibility, 56–7, 58, 167, 181, 184, n. 475
practice, 69
 locus of linguistic, 97, 130–3, 138, 145–6, 149–50, 153, 157, 162–6, 171, 173–81, 184–5, 205, n. 259, n. 341, n. 360, n. 376, n. 392, n. 394, n. 397, n. 400, n. 422, n. 428, see also language games
das Primäre (the primary), 53, 55, 57–8, 136, 141, n. 176
primary, 167, 171–2, 174, 176, n. 176, n. 228, see also under language
private language, see under language
problem
 empirical, 203
 logical, 49
 mathematical, 50, n. 160
 see also philosophy, problems of
process(es), 46, 56, 94, 139, 163, 205, n. 149
 physical, 151, 176, 195
 pneumatic (spiritual, ethereal), 64–5, 139, 171
 symbolic, 44, 46, 55
 see also under mental; psychological
progress, 191, 193, 199, n. 230, n. 494
projection, method of, 64, n. 361
properties, 59, 61, 135, n. 228, n. 292
proposition, 50, 53, 87, 94, 113, 135, 147–8, 154, 158, 194, 223–4
 atomic, 218
 content of a, 154–5
 elementary, 76–7, 79–81, 166, 171, 210, 214, 216, 218–20, n. 220, n. 222, n. 228, n. 233
 elliptical, 95–6
 empirical, 211–12, n. 426

 essence/nature of a, 64, 79–81, 95, 110, 187, 211, n. 188, n. 228, n. 428
 function of, 91, 93, 95, 187–8
 general form of a, 62–6, 76–8, 80–1, 187, 211–12, 214, 223–4, n. 186, n. 218, n. 259
 is in order, 77, see also language, in order as it is
 meaning/sense of a, 18, 59, 66, 94, 110, 166–7, 171, 177, 210, 212, 214, 220–1, n. 256, n. 361, n. 370
 'real' (authentic), 79–80, 87–8, 223, n. 233
 understanding a, 43, 155, n. 309, n. 370
 see also under construct; image-proposition; scientific; sentence; structure; truth-function; word-proposition
propositional attitudes, 117, n. 297
prototype, 85–6, n. 229, n. 230, see also model
psychological, psychic 54, 135, 206, n. 155, n. 263, n. 317
 activity, 64
 concepts, 12, 43, 46–50, 53–6, 63–6, 95, 134, 138–42, 144, 152, 161, 207, 210, n. 142, n. 176, n. 360, n. 481
 constituents, 134, 170–2, n. 149
 context, 120
 effects, see under signs
 event, 152
 facts, 131
 mechanism/apparatus, 143, 144, 153, 158, 160, 162–4, 205, n. 369
 occurrences, 143, 145, 151, 206
 phenomena, 43–4, 48, 95, 140, 182, 202, n. 153, n. 283, n. 400
 processes, 43–4, 65, 71, 95, 134, 148, 150, 158, 160, 162, 170, 199, 201, 210, 224
 theory, 196–9, 205–7, 209
 verbs, 152–3, 161, 170, 179–80, n. 360, n. 364
 states, 43, 46, 56, 64–5, 71, 73, 95, 134, 140–2, 153, 199, 210
 substratum, 54, 64–5, 96, 134, 171, n. 176
 see also under accompaniment; description; explanation; investigation; meaning; mental; language; reaction; signs

psychologism/psychologistic, 121 198, 200, n. 317, n. 361
psychology, 109, 113, 116, 143, 155, 163, 178, 194, 196–202, 217, n. 160, n. 292, n. 436, n. 448, n. 518
psychometrics, 197–202

queer, 60, 64, *see also* ethereal; pneumatic
questions
  about language, 55, 222, 224
  metaphysical, 224–5
  of philosophy, 51, 63–4, 195, 222
  see also under scientific

Ramsey, F., 38, 110–12, 221, n. 161, n. 276, n. 278, n. 494, n. 510
reaction
  behavioural, 184, n. 294
  physiological, 201, n. 294
  psychological, 48, 119, 122, 195, 201, n. 294
reading, 198, 201, n. 360
'real', 64, *see also under* name; proposition; word
realism, n. 510
reality, 58, 77–8, 81, 83, 85, 88, 117, 147–8, 154–6, 166, 172, 214, n. 149, n. 178, n. 222, n. 228, n. 244, n. 361, *see also under* description; harmony; language; world
reference, 116, 119–20, 197, n. 265, n. 309, n. 360
refine/reform, *see* language, reform
relations, 221, n. 228, n. 448
relativism
  linguistic, 138–47, 149–50, 153–8, 161, 163, 165–7, 169–72, 174, 176–7, 179, 189, 212, 215, n. 176, n. 351, n. 355, n. 366, n. 370, n. 377, n. 380, n. 397, n. 400, n. 427, n. 518
  see also under emergence; language
relativity theory (Einstein), 115, 139–40, 146, 189, n. 282, n. 351, n. 494
religion 184–9, 213, *see also* language, religious
report, 95, 140, 141, 148, 150–3, 158, 162, 165, 170, n. 413, n. 420
Rhees, R., 10–11, 26, 28–9, 31, 38, 42–3, 67–9, n. 34, n. 39, n. 87, n. 89, n. 95, n. 102, n. 106, n. 108, n. 109, n. 144, n. 200, n. 239, n. 429

rules, 59, 61, 64–5, 73, 76, 82, 101, 157, 159, 161, 182
  acting in accordance with, 136, 142, n. 360
  complete list of, 41, 48–9, 74–6, 136, n. 341
  description of, 133
  following, 78, n. 392
  of grammar, *see under* grammatical
  of language, 62, 78, n. 173, n. 219, n. 341, n. 369
  of language games, 77–8, 161, n. 360, n. 400
  precise, fixed, strict –, 76–8, 82–3, 88–9, 106–7, 135, n. 216, n. 218
  system of, 74, 76–8, 107, 160, n. 360
  of use, 76–7, 79, 171, n. 173, n. 176, n. 341, n. 360, n. 376
Russell, B., 63, 75, 76, 79, 83–4, 90, 99, 110–18, 120–4, 134, 145, 169, 172, 189, 194–6, 199, 202, 204–10, 212, 216–21, 224–5, n. 149, n. 214, n. 220, n. 264, n. 271, n. 275, n. 276, n. 277, n. 282, n. 292, n. 296, n. 297, n. 299, n. 307, n. 333, n. 335, n. 348, n. 405, n. 429, n. 436, n. 437, n. 447, n. 494

Schlick, M., n. 282, n. 426, n. 494, n. 496
science, 62, 109, 131, 189, 190–3, 195–7, 199, 210–14, 216–17, 220, 223, n. 292, n. 426, n. 494, n. 510
  normative, 77, n. 510, *see also* logic, normative
  overrating of, 186–7, 212
scientific, 180
  activity, 197
  attitude, 213–14, 220, 222, 225, n. 426, n. 490, n. 494
  discoveries, 198–201, 208, 222, n. 282, n. 448, n. 477
  explanations, 196, 198, 202, 205–6, 222, 224–5
  hypotheses, 210, 222, n. 448
  investigations, 196, 218, 220, 226, n. 292
  knowledge, 193, 195, 209, n. 282
  method, 195–6, 199, 202, 212, 216–17, 220, 223, n. 292, n. 437, n. 518
  philosophy, 195, 216–18, 225, n. 502, n. 518, n. 519
  problem, 203, 222, 225
  questions, 196, 222, 224–5

scientific (cont.)
  research, 197–202
  spirit, 195–6, 202, 204, 209–12, 214–17, 221–2, 225–6, n. 494, n. 510
  statements/propositions, 187, 210, 214
  theories, 210, 222, n. 292
  way of thinking, 5, 191–4, 202–4, 209, 211, 213–16, 219–26, n. 432, n. 494, n. 509, n. 510
  world view (*wissenschaftliche Weltauffasung*), 212–14, 216, n. 490, n. 494, n. 509
Semon, R., 116, 194, n. 277, n. 294
sensation(s), 115–17, 123, 133, 170, 197–8, 209, n. 283, n. 361, n. 427
sense data, 57, 217, n. 176, n. 220, n. 228, n. 511
sentence, 60
  affirmative, 186–8
  as a mechanism, 100
  as a picture, 80, *see also* analogy, picture; picture theory
  sense/meaning of a, 45–6, 48, 55, 58–9, 64, 103, 122, 128, 134, 143, 158, 162–3, 166–8, 224, n. 294, n. 318, n. 341, n. 392
  soul of a, 122, 128, 133, *see also* signs, life of, soul of
  use/employ a, 77, 103, 158, 186–7, n. 318, n. 360
  see also under proposition
signal, 47
signification, 119, 159, 161–3, 165–6, 172, 174, 176–7, 179–81, 183, 185, 189, 194, 196, 204–6, 210, 222, n. 294, n. 388, n. 400, n. 428, *see also* meaning, *Bedeutung*
signs, 44, 47, 55, 64, 111, n. 170
  application of, 48, n. 400
  behind the, 44–6, 55, 58, 60, 64–5, 71, 94, 144, 210, *see also* language, behind
  concatenations of, *see* concatenation
  effects of, 108–10, 127, 178, 204, 206, n. 294
  function of, 43, 48, 60, 149, 151–2, 177–8, 180, n. 397, n. 400, n. 422
  magical view of, 99, 100–1, 108–10, 113–14, 121–3, 126–7, 132–3, 160
  meaning of, *see* meaning, *Bedeutung*
  life of, 135, 145–6, 148–50, 153, 155–63, 165–7, 169, 171–2, 174–9, 181, 184–5, 189, 225, n. 360, n. 388, n. 392, n. 397, n. 400, n. 518
  logical view of, 99, 100–1, 108, 110, 113–14, 121, 125–7, 132–3, 137, 138, 142–3, 145, 156–7, 161, 169–70, 178, 204, 222, n. 518, *see also* language, calculus/game/system conception of, logical view of
  primary, 171, 174, 176–7, 215–16, n. 176, *see also* signs, simple
  propositional, 59, 155
  psychological view of, 99, 110, 113–14, 121–6, 132–4, 143, 145–6, 157, 160–1, 169, 180, 183, 194, 196, 205–6, n. 343, n. 361, n. 378, *see also under* language; meaning
  role of, 129, 151–3, 161, n. 360, n. 400, *see also under* calculus; language game; system; words
  secondary, 171, 174, 215, n. 176
  simple, 80, 168, 171, 176, 179, 214–15, 221, n. 233, n. 397; parody of, 92, 169, 171, n. 228, *see also* signs, primary
  soul of 135, 138, 169–70, *see also under* meaning; sentence
  system of, 56–7, 104, 171–2, 176, n. 400 *see also under* language
  use/employment of, 129, 143, 148, 154–5, 170–2, 176–8, 180, 206, 209, n. 360, n. 428
  see also under language; proposition; sentence; words
simple/complex, 57, 86, 89, 174–7, 217–18, n. 176, n. 239, n. 399, n. 428, *see also under* language games; signs
simples, 80, 166–9, 171–4, 176–7, 215, 218–20, n. 228, n. 233, n. 405, *see also* objects
Skinner, F., 69
socialism, 191, n. 494
soul/spirit, 156, 163, 214, n. 380, n. 400, n. 427, *see also under* meaning; sentence; signs
speech, 47, 118, 140, 143, 182–3, 201, *see also under* accompaniment; inner
Spengler, O., 83–6, 96, 114, 189, n. 228, n. 230, n. 428, n. 432, n. 494
spirit
  of our times, 191, 193–6, 202, 209–16, 221–2, 225–6, *see also under* thinking; scientific

of Wittgenstein's later philosophy, 3–6,
    191, 193, 209, 211, n. 494, n. 509
see also soul
spiritual, *see* ethereal; pneumatic
Sraffa, P., 64, n. 120, n. 188, n. 230
state, 44, 46, 55–6, 139, 150, 197
    of consciousness/mind, 70–2, 132, 144,
        159, 208, n. 206, n. 339, n. 481
    see also under mental; mind;
        psychological
states of affairs (*Sachverhalte*), 58, 146,
    151–2, 165, 167–8, 188, 212, n. 178
Stenius, E., n. 228
Stonborough, Margarete, n. 107
Strawson, P. F., n. 265
structure
    of concepts, 130–2, n. 337
    formal, 132, 181, *see also* metaphors,
        spatial
    of language, 83, 113–14, 126, 131, 166–7,
        194, 206
    of a language game, 132, n. 339
    logical, 65, 135, 213, 216–17, n. 340,
        n. 494
    of a proposition, 76, 78, n. 428
    of the world, 58, n. 511
    see also under description
struggle, 189
    against contemporary intellectual
        fashion, 14, 190–3, 209–10, 221–2, 225
    against language, 18, 226, n. 523
style (Wittgenstein's), 15–25, 38, 89, n. 82,
    n. 85, n. 107
    aphoristic, 3, 9, 11–12, 24
    conspiracy theory of, 16, 17–18, 20–1,
        23, n. 53
    disorderly subject matter view of, 16–17,
        20, 23, n. 49, n. 51
    mystical view of, 16, 18–19, 20, 23
    Wittgenstein's opinion of his own, 8–9,
        18, 20–5, n. 83
    see also under goal
sublime, 58
surview (*Übersicht*), 16, n. 360, n. 475
symbol/symbolic, 44, 47, 111, 119, 129,
    142, 175, 180, n. 155, *see also under*
    correct; expression; language; process
system, 22, 41, 48, 99, 103–4, 129, 149, 161,
    179, 216, n. 341, 360, n. 388, n. 470
    of communication, 89–90, 104–7, 125–6,
        129–30, 139, 145–6, 155, 157, 161–4,
        180–1, 205–6, n. 259, n. 366, n. 392
    role in a, 125, 129, 150–1, 178, n. 360,
        n. 400
    term in a part of a, 104, 108, 121–2, 127,
        129, 131, 133–4, 155, 172, 176–7, 204
    uniform, 89–90, n. 228
    see also under description; grammatical;
        language; rules; signs

teaching, 5, 18, 20, 72, 182
technique, *see* mastery; being able to
tendency, n. 448, n. 477
theology, 185, 188, 222, 225, n. 426, n. 494
theory, 16–17, 19, 23, 194–8, 202–10, 216,
    222, n. 126, n. 233, n. 292, n. 294, *see
    also under* meaning, causal theory of;
    picture; psychological; relativity;
    scientific; style
thinking, thought 46–7, 54–8, 60, 64–6,
    109, 113, 118–20, 122, 134–5, 138–42,
    147–8, 152, 154–60, 161–3, 165–6,
    170–1, 194–6, 199–200, 202–3, 205–6,
    210, 224–5, n. 147, n. 149, n. 150,
    n. 176, n. 178, n. 309, n. 360, n. 361,
    n. 378, n. 392, n. 448, n. 518
    fashions/trends/currents in, 12, 14, 98,
        190–4, 197, n. 277, n. 292, n. 340,
        n. 436, n. 494, n. 510, *see also under*
        struggle
    mechanism of, 158
    strategy/tactic in, 86, n. 230, n. 351,
        n. 428
    see also under expression; harmony;
        scientific; *Denkweise*
this/that, 80, 176, n. 228, n. 397
tools, *see under* analogy; words
Tractatus, 7, 16–17, 40–1, 43, 61–3, 65,
    76–82, 87, 92, 96, 98–9, 106–7,
    110–12, 131, 135, 166–70, 172–3, 179,
    187, 189, 192, 210–12, 214, 216,
    218–20, 223–4, n. 82, n. 137, n. 149,
    n. 175, n. 176, n. 178, n. 190, n. 218,
    n. 220, n. 222, n. 226, n. 228, n. 229,
    n. 230, n. 233, n. 260, n. 275, n. 333,
    n. 335, n. 361, n. 396, n. 428, n. 494,
    n. 509, *see also under* calculus
training, 5, 182, n. 376
tribes, 73, 90
truth, 4–6, 19, 154, 159, 167, 186, 187–8,
    193, 196, n. 392, n. 408
truth-function, 76–7, 81, 118, 219, n. 218

understanding, 42–50, 55, 63–6, 70–2, 104, 106, 115, 121–3, 128, 134–7, 138, 148, 155, 170–2, 176, 182, 198–9, 202, 210, 225, n. 134, n. 151, n. 206, n. 360, n. 370
  medium of, 64–5, 135, 137, *see also under* proposition
uniform, uniformity, *see under* language; system; words
use, 45, 46, 50–2, 54–5, 62, 66, 76, 82, 94–5, 113, 122, 125, 128, 130, 136, 143–4, 149–50, 159, 161, 163, 178, 182–3, 186–7, 194, 206–7, 208–9, 211, 219, 222–4, n. 153, n. 186, n. 260, n. 339, n. 340, n. 400, *see also under* application; description; function; language; language games; rules; sentence; signs; words

vagueness/unclarity, 47, 76, 79, 82, n. 448
Valentin, G., 198
verification, 212, n. 494
Vienna Circle, 211–14, 216, 222, 225, n. 175, n. 220, n. 271, n. 282, n. 292, n. 426, n. 490, n. 494, n. 496, n. 509
von Wright, G. H., 1, 27–31, 35, 37, n. 43, n. 94, n. 103, n. 104, n. 106, n. 109, n. 230, n. 271, n. 275, n. 343, n. 428, n. 429

Watson, J., n. 277, n. 294

wish, 46, 55, 134, 139–41, 144–5, 147–8, 152–6, 158, 160, 161, 170, 180, n. 380
word(s), 48–51, 53–4, 59–60, 64, 102, 116, 118, 148, 200–1
  essence of a, 81, n. 228
  function of, 76, 100, 122–3, 182, n. 318, n. 427
  gap of a, 207–8
  as instruments/tools, 209, n. 364, n. 427, *see also under* analogy
  logical, 117–18, *see also under* feeling
  meaning of, *see* meaning, *Bedeutung*; feelings, as the meaning of words
  order of, 46, n. 149
  'real' (authentic), 79–80, 87, n. 233, *see also* 'real'
  role of, 66, 100, n. 318, n. 360, n. 397
  syncategorimatic, 117, *see also under* feelings; words, logical
  uniformity of, 125, *see also* language, uniformity of
  use/employment of, 54, 74–6, 79, 88, 94 132–3, 135, 169, 182, 186, 208–9, 222, n. 227, n. 259, n. 360, n. 427
  see also under correct; feelings; signs
word-proposition, 115, 117, n. 294
world, 58, 72, 123, 130, 167, 169, 181, 187–8, 211–13, 216–17, 223, n. 178, n. 283, *see also under* conceptual; description; reality; structure
Wundt, W., 198, 200–1, n. 453

056125

DATE DUE

SE 6 '91			

```
B                    56125
3376
.W564      Hilmy, S. Stephen.
H53           The later
1987       Wittgenstein.
```

HIEBERT LIBRARY
Fresno Pacific College - M. B. Seminary
Fresno, Calif. 93702

DEMCO